SCIENCE FICTION AND FANTASY WRITER'S SOURCEBOOK

SECOND EDITION

Edited by

DAVID H. BORCHERDING

WRITER'S DIGEST BOOKS
CINCINNATI, OHIO

Science Fiction & Fantasy Writer's Sourcebook. Copyright © 1996 by Writer's Digest Books. Printed and bound in the United States of America. All rights reserved. No part of this book may be reproduced in any form or by any electronic or mechanical means including information storage and retrieval systems without permission in writing from the publisher, except by a reviewer, who may quote brief passages in a review. Published by Writer's Digest Books, an imprint of F&W Publications, Inc., 1507 Dana Avenue, Cincinnati, Ohio 45207. (800) 289-0963. Second edition.

This hardcover edition of *Science Fiction and Fantasy Writer's Sourcebook* features a "self-jacket" that eliminates the need for a separate dust jacket. It provides sturdy protection for your book while it saves paper, trees and energy.

00   99   98   97   96   5   4   3   2   1

International Standard Serial Number
ISSN 1087-1829
International Standard Book Number
ISBN 0-89879-762-4

Cover Illustration: Bob Eggleton

Attention Booksellers: This directory is published every two years by F&W Publications. Return deadline for this edition is December 31, 1998.

TABLE OF CONTENTS

SECTION III
Markets for Short Fiction
✳ ✳

SECTION IV
Novel Markets
✳ ✳

SECTION V
Finding an Agent
✳ ✳

* * *
From the Editor

The other day, I saw a guy walking his dog and talking on his tiny cellular flip-phone. The dog was doing his usual dog business and this guy was casually chatting away. He could have been talking to Tokyo, for all I know. Quite likely, he owns a notebook computer more powerful than the computers that put men on the moon. He probably surfs the Net, microwaves his food in a few seconds and watches *The X-Files* on his fiberoptic cable TV service. Maybe he jogs in water-cushioned cross-trainers with red flashing lights in the heels.

Ten years ago, that guy could only have been a character in a science fiction novel; now he's just some guy in my neighborhood. It's wild, isn't it? We're *living* yesterday's science fiction. And not only that, we're seeing tomorrow's reality all over the place. Speculative fiction (the vogue term for science fiction and fantasy) has moved into the mainstream not only in bookstores, but on TV and in the movies. Sure, some didn't quite make it (*seaQuest DSV* and *Earth 2*, for example), but others have hit big (like the aforementioned *X-Files*, shows like *Sliders* and the *Star Trek* incarnations). There's even a 24-hour SciFi Channel! Yes, more people are watching—and reading—sf and fantasy than ever before.

That's the good news. The bad news is that a greater number of people are also *writing* science fiction, fantasy and horror than ever before. Editors are flooded with manuscripts. To be a successful speculative fiction writer today, you must be more creative and daring with your stories and more prepared and professional in your marketing.

This sourcebook is designed to help you do just that. Part directory and part how-to, this book is a hybrid of the two kinds of resources Writer's Digest Books has published for years. We begin in the **Craft & Technique** section, where established sf and fantasy authors teach you how to enrich your work with better near future settings, help you create stronger hooks and plots, and show you how to write humor.

In the two **Markets** sections, you'll find interviews with editors at the field's major magazines and publishing houses, telling you just what they look for in a manuscript. Four of those editors give you even more detail in the **Success Stories** section, when they show you exactly what made them buy the works of Raphael Carter, J.V. Jones, Susan R. Matthews and Julie Stevens—complete with excerpts of those works. We've also interviewed four new writers to discover how they made their first sales.

Literary representative Russell Galen of the Scovil, Chichak, Galen Agency tells you how to find a good agent and what that agent can do for you in the **Agents** section. Following that are listings of agents that specialize in representing sf and fantasy authors. And in **Resources**, we list organizations, conferences, contests, online resources and references all geared toward the speculative fiction writer.

In short, we've tried to give you all the tools you need to build your writing career, centering on the most up-to-date information about the markets. No market is completely static, however, and the speculative fiction market is especially dynamic. Therefore, continue to read widely, both in your chosen genre and outside of it. Also keep up on the latest market news by subscribing to trade publications such as *Locus*, *Science Fiction Chronicle*, *Scavenger's Newsletter*, *Gila Queen's Guide to the Markets* and, of course, *Writer's Digest Magazine*. Query publishers before you send your work and ask for guidelines if they offer them. And if you find some information in this book that has changed, help us keep you and other sf and fantasy writers updated by letting us know. Likewise, we also want to hear about your successes. When you sell that first novel or short story, drop us a note. Our address is:

The Marketplace Series
Writer's Digest Books
1507 Dana Avenue
Cincinnati, Ohio 45207
E-mail: Wdigest@aol.com

David H. Borcherdt

Good luck!

SCiENCE FiCTiON &
FANTASY TRENDS

Doors to Other Worlds:
Trends in Science Fiction
and Fantasy

PETER HECK

Market research (i.e. reading widely within your chosen genre) keeps you from wasting your time and annoying editors by adding to the bulk of unsuitable submissions that clog the slush pile at every publishing house. You should be aware right off the bat that it's only one step in the process, and it requires knowing what you're looking at if your conclusions are going to be worth anything. Let me start by giving you my impression of recent trends in science fiction and fantasy, after which I'll try to provide enough context to let you become your own expert.

One topic that remains hot is nanotechnology, the growing science of automatic microscopic machinery that can be released into the environment or into the human body to do work (from terraforming to genetic engineering) on a molecular level. A good recent example is Neal Stephenson's *The Diamond Age*, in which nanotech provides the foundation for a recreated Victorian society. Similarly, the exploration of cyberspace—the whole world of computer networks and interactive programs—remains a popular subgenre.

Trends in the use of contemporary social material, which is always volatile, are a bit harder to characterize. Several writers have gotten good mileage out of sensational tabloid material, as in the anthology *Alien Pregnant by Elvis*, edited by Esther Friesner, or John Kessel's novel *Good News from Outer Space*—not to mention passing allusions to "the Church of Elvis" and similar bits of business in writers from Connie Willis to Jack Womack. "Political correctness" has become an almost obligatory target for satirists of all stripes. The more serious issue of child abuse has also figured in novels ranging from Steven C. Gould's

Jumper to several titles by Piers Anthony—many of them quite explicitly aimed at younger readers.

Several recent books by established sf writers have been published and marketed to appeal to the thriller audience. *Ill Wind* by Kevin Anderson and Doug Beason postulates a genetically-altered microbe that devours the world's petroleum supplies; *Oaths and Miracles* by Nancy Kress asks what could happen if organized crime got hold of *really* advanced science. While either book could be published as straight sf, both appeal to a wider audience by adopting a setting in the near future, populated by ordinary people in a recognizable world. This sort of near-future hard sf is by no means easy to write well, but in the hands of writers of the caliber of Kress or Anderson and Beason, it can be very exciting—and reach a large audience.

Unfortunately, knowing these trends gives you very little advantage over any regular reader of the genre. The contents of this month's *Analog* or *Asimov's* tell you what their editors were buying a year or more ago; the books in your local chain or specialty store reflect what came across their editors' desks as long as two years ago—or even longer, if they're the third volumes of trilogies. That's an eternity in the publishing world, where entire book lines can rise and fall, and half the editors in the field change jobs in the course of a couple of years. What you, as an aspiring professional, need to know is what the editors are buying *now*.

You can find some of the answers by reading market reports in such news magazines as *Science Fiction Chronicle* and *Locus*, or the more detailed *Gila Queen's Guide to Markets* and *Scavenger's Newsletter*. Members of SFWA (Science Fiction and Fantasy Writers of America) get the *SFWA Bulletin*, which publishes market reports as well as useful information on the business; nonmembers can subscribe to the *Bulletin* directly. Computer bulletin boards and websites have become important channels of news, too. You can find market reports, data on response times, and professional advice on Genie, Compuserve, or in the various author pages at http://www.greyware.com. A number of editors are active on these boards, as well the writers.

But trend-following is the equivalent of trying to pick the winners of tomorrow's horseraces from past performances: sure things are few and far between. Rather than trying to dope out the current trends in sf and fantasy, you want to write a story that will seem fresh and exciting a year or two from now. In a sense, you have to be your own trend-starter—choose some new development in technology or society and imagine what it'll look like in 50 years.

The best sf and fantasy writers often bring their readers a perspective beyond the narrow windows on reality provided by TV news shows and slick magazines. You can read the off-beat magazines of culture and opinion (*Wired*, for example); peek into the latest issues of *Science News* (or more specialized journals, if you have the background to understand them) for a glimpse of the current frontiers of science and technology. Or for fantasy, look beyond the popular writers of today into the deeper source material of myth and legend. Here again, the computer nets can be a gold mine of information. Find something that interests you, and ask yourself, "If this is happening now, what happens next?" Figure it out and write your story!

Mapping the Territory

Now for a bit of context. As science fiction and fantasy have grown and expanded over the years, they have spawned several distinct subgenres. While there is probably a greater degree of overlap between the readers of Jerry Pournelle and Ursula K. Le Guin than (for example) between fans of Elmore Leonard and P.D. James, only the most naive writer would expect to appeal equally to both groups. Knowing where to send a finished story is often a question of being able to identify exactly what it is you've written, and finding out who's buying it. Market reports often use such terms as "hard sf," "high fantasy," or "space opera." The best way to understand these terms is to look at their origins.

Commercial science fiction as we know it today grew out of the "pulp" magazines of the 1920s. The pulps were printed on cheap paper, with lurid covers and non-stop action plots aimed at an adventure-seeking reader. Many of the authors of that era took as their model the wildly successful Barsoom novels of Edgar Rice Burroughs. The popularity of the pulp magazines was reflected in early media treatments such as the *Buck Rogers* comic strips and movie serials.

The visceral kick of *Buck Rogers* (and other action heroes from Flash Gordon and Captain Video to Luke Skywalker) remains a large part of the appeal of sf. Most science fiction readers become fans at a young age, when swashbuckling adventure and clever gadgetry appeal most strongly; "the Golden Age of Science Fiction is 12 to 14" is an oft-repeated quip. While many readers outgrow that stage of uncritical admiration, the emotional rush of a good action story remains powerful. Nowadays, this sort of adventure-oriented sf is frequently called space opera, and its popularity has never really faded.

Space opera puts the emphasis on sweeping action, larger-than-life characters, and good-guys/bad-guys plotting, but in the hands of a more ambitious author, space opera can take on remarkable depth and resonance; see Samuel R. Delany's *Nova* for a striking example. Well-written space opera may have the widest intrinsic appeal of any of the subgenres of sf. Its action orientation gives it a strong potential for film and TV adaptations—the *Star Wars* trilogy, perhaps the most successful film series of all time, is uncompromisingly space opera. Almost every publisher is a potential market for science fiction that captures the raw energy of classic space opera—especially when written for audiences who don't want to stop thinking just because they're supposed to be having fun.

The Power of Myth

In many ways, the pedigree of fantasy goes back even further than that of science fiction. Greek myths and medieval romances, not to mention all the tales and lore of non-Western cultures, are the lifeblood of the fantastic impulse. A much-acclaimed recent series has been the Fairy Tale anthologies compiled by Terri Windling and Ellen Datlow, featuring modern reworkings of material from the Brothers Grimm, Hans Christian Anderson and other such sources. Similarly, there have been several recent reworkings of the Germanic legend of Siegfried, familiar to opera fans as the source material of Wagner's Ring cycle. And it seems that every few years, a new re-examination of Arthurian legend— an important subgenre that includes everything from *The Once and Future King* to *Mists of Avalon*—makes the bestseller lists.

Fantasy as an identifiable commercial genre is really a phenomenon of the last three decades. J.R.R. Tolkien's great *Lord of the Rings* is the model for "high fantasy." Here, the emphasis is on the fates of entire races and nations, threatened by a world-encompassing evil—much in the way that Tolkien's generation saw the threat of Nazi Germany. The cast of characters is typically large and varied and we see the action from multiple viewpoints. Magic and magical races (elves, dwarves, goblins, etc.) play important roles, as well.

There are fewer professional short fiction markets for fantasy than for sf; for whatever reason, fantasy readers appear to prefer their stories in book-length doses. Besides the magazines whose names make clear their fantasy orientation, many of the science fiction magazines will publish stories that are clearly fantasy. But the real surge in the popularity of fantasy has been at book length—not to mention multi-book series. And this applies especially to high fantasy.

High Fantasy

High fantasy probably has the greatest potential for widespread popular success of any current genre of sf/fantasy: Terry Brooks (*The Sword of Shannara*), David Eddings (*The Belgariad*) and Robert Jordan (*The Wheel of Time*) are just three authors who have scored enormous successes with work in this vein. Recent examples include J.V. Jones's series beginning with *The Baker's Boy*, and Robin Hobb's series beginning with *Apprentice Assassin*. Every publisher in the business recognizes the appeal of this genre. At the same time, the competition is fierce: publishers' slush piles are loaded with the work of novice authors all convinced that they are the next Terry Brooks.

Game-Related Fantasy

A somewhat specialized offshoot of high fantasy is game-related fantasy, best known from TSR (the publishers of *Dungeons and Dragons*). Again, the emphasis is often on a large cast of characters, world-shaking events, and a well-realized magical world. Whether original works set in the world of popular role-playing games, or works that follow the general pattern of a gaming campaign, gaming fantasy often aims at a slightly younger reader. Margaret Weis and Tracy Hickman began as game designers at TSR, but their Dragons series made them into bestselling fantasy writers. A familiarity with role-playing games, and especially with the somewhat exotic *Dungeons and Dragons* system of myth and magic, is an asset for an author interested in this subgenre, though an ability to write good plot and dialogue is a far greater asset. TSR has also been more open than many publishers to new talent; several fine writers—notably R.A. Salvatore and Christie Golden—got their starts writing game-related fantasy.

Heroic Fantasy

Heroic fantasy—best exemplified in the Conan the Barbarian series begun by Robert E. Howard and continued by a variety of talents—is less popular today than in its heyday. In a sense, this style is the fantasy equivalent of military science fiction. Elizabeth Moon's very popular Deed of Paksenarion, which follows the career of a woman soldier in a realistically-drawn fantasy universe, shows that the genre's potential is far from limited. And as Michael Moorcock's Elric series (long-running and widely admired) demonstrates, the genre has plenty of potential for style and subtlety. As with military sf, Baen is one of the leading publishers of current heroic fantasy.

Contemporary Fantasy

Contemporary fantasy—often featuring elves or other traditional magical creatures in the everyday modern world—can be popular as well. Writers from Emma Bull (*War for the Oaks*) to Mercedes Lackey (*The SERRAted Edge*) have portrayed the elves working in the modern world as rock musicians or stock-car racers, dressing in modern clothes and speaking modern slang. Also characteristic is editor Terri Windling's "elf-punk" series set in Bordertown, where the young discontents of the human and faerie worlds mingle. A different angle is that of the Elfquest series (originally a graphic novel), in which the elvish characters display characteristically modern personalities and attitudes. While the great trend for this particular sub-genre was a few years ago, there is evidently still some demand for it, especially when aimed at teen readers.

Historical Fantasy

Historical fantasy has been a growth market in recent years, almost simultaneous with the decline in straight historical fiction—and with the rise of "alternate history" in science fiction. The setting can be almost any era in which the belief in magic was strong; one writes a well-detailed historical novel in which the magic is a key ingredient. Recent examples have included Judith Tarr's novels set in ancient Egypt, Susan Schwartz's *Silk Road and Shadow*, and a spate of interesting novels set at various points in English history, from the early Renaissance (Margaret Ball's *No Earthly Sunne*) through the Romantic period (Tim Powers's *The Anubis Gates*). Fantastic alternate history is also a possibility—perhaps the most popular recent series in this mode is Orson Scott Card's Alvin

Maker, set in an alternate America where magic works, and featuring cameos of such historical figures as William Blake and Daniel Webster. A sound knowledge of history is a clear prerequisite for this subgenre, whose readers are quick to catch anachronisms.

The Broadening SF Genre

As the original science fiction audience grew up, the more mature readers tired of the limitations of the pulp magazines and of stylistic conventions that assumed a juvenile readership. Much of the loosening of commercial sf's adventure-story straitjacket took place in the pages of *Astounding* magazine in the early 1940s. Editor John W. Campbell urged his writers to think more rigorously about the ideas behind the stories, and to attempt a realistic extrapolation of what the future might be like. At its peak, *Astounding* published many of the milestones of modern sf: Isaac Asimov's Robot and Foundation stories, Robert A. Heinlein's Future History stories, and such seminal writers as Theodore Sturgeon, A.E. van Vogt, and L. Sprague de Camp—all well worth reading (or re-reading) by aspiring sf writers.

Campbell's emphasis on extrapolation from real science eventually led to what is nowadays known as hard science fiction, which its fans often describe in terms of "putting the science back into science fiction." The prototypes of hard sf include the worldbuilding novels of Hal Clement (e.g. *Mission of Gravity*) and the near-future, near-space stories of Arthur C. Clarke and Robert A. Heinlein. Perhaps the most admired writer of modern hard sf is Larry Niven, especially in *Ringworld* and the Known Space series.

Writing hard sf requires a solid grounding in the sciences (especially astronomy and physics) as well as an ability to extrapolate believable hardware and social institutions from current theory. Not that Niven or Robert L. Forward won't resort to "rubber science" or fudge an explanation, when faced with a plot problem that flies in the face of current knowledge; but they know they're fudging, and they know the real science well enough to make the explanation plausible. The scientific background is sometimes more important than the characters— although well-drawn aliens are the high points of many hard sf novels. *Analog* magazine (the direct descendent of Campbell's *Astounding*) remains a major focus for hard sf at shorter lengths; but almost every book and magazine editor in the field, when asked what they would like more of, will put good hard sf very close to the top of the list.

Mixing Science and Fantasy

"Science fantasy" sounds paradoxical at first, but it may be the least ambiguous term for a blend of traditional fantasy elements—dragons, witches, magic in general—with a pseudo-scientific rationalization (genetic engineering, mutations, higher dimensions, etc.). The Force in *Star Wars* is another example of a fantastic element inserted in a high-tech science fictional world. One could think of science fantasy as a variant of space opera. Many publishers seem to think of science fantasy as written by women for women, as evidenced by the enormous popularity of Marion Zimmer Bradley, Anne McCaffrey, Mercedes Lackey, Julian May, and many others. That is probably an oversimplification; for one thing, many of the writers just mentioned have strong followings among male readers. And male authors from Heinlein and De Camp to Christopher Stasheff have effectively introduced magical elements into science fictional settings.

Science fantasy is an extremely flexible subgenre; it can accommodate humor, adventure, romance, or social commentary with equal ease. It is often the most character-driven of sf genres, perhaps another reason why women readers find it more congenial than gadget-oriented hard sf. Del Rey and DAW have been among the most active publishers of science fantasy novels over the years, with Baen and Ace not far behind. But none of the major publishers is likely to turn up its nose at a well-written novel that appeals to the numerous fans of Pern or Darkover. Indeed, the first Pern stories were published in *Analog* by that champion of hard-nosed science, John W. Campbell himself.

Social Values

A less easily defined category is social science fiction, which is less interested in hardware and science than in how people react to their environments. Elements of this approach have always been present in utopian novels and satires. But social satire got a major boost with the publication of Orwell's *1984*, as well as the arrival on the scene of a number of writers whose interests didn't quite parallel Campbell's at *Astounding*. During the '50s, many of these writers found a niche at *Galaxy* magazine. Fred Pohl and C.M. Kornbluth were major influences with their series of novels beginning with *The Space Merchants*, satirizing the conformist consumer culture of the '50s. More recently, the social elements have often included anthropology, folklore, and (especially since the '60s) feminist issues. Ursula K. Le Guin may be the leading modern writer of social sf, especially in such novels as *The Left Hand of Darkness* and *The Dispossessed*.

A common variation is dystopian sf, not so much a genre as a set of attitudes. Many of the classics of the field adopt the approach of portraying an oppressive future society, often ending by overthrowing it in a revolution or by sending the protagonists off to found a new society of their own. Dystopian satire is also a common mode for mainstream writers who decide to take on thought-provoking issues, for example Margaret Atwood in *The Handmaid's Tale*. In the hands of a writer with a well-honed comic vision (such as James Morrow or Connie Willis), dystopian satire can often be hilarious; handled with less skill, it runs the risk of being merely depressing. The "cardboard oppressive society" is one of the problems editors frequently cite in rejection letters; a conscientious writer will make the effort to make even a negative society credible.

Because it is often the best way to point a finger at abuses in society, or disturbing trends, social sf attracts many writers who might otherwise never consider writing science fiction. As a result, the publishers' slush piles are full of half-baked satires and depressing dystopias. More than almost any other subgenre, serious social sf demands excellent writing skills from its practitioners. Strong world-building, good characterization, a compelling narrative voice, the ability to raise thought-provoking questions, and (where applicable) a sense of humor are the best ways to give your manuscript an edge over the others on the editor's desk.

Future Conflict

Stories about future war are as old as science fiction itself, but military sf as an independent subgenre probably got its start in the late 1950s with Heinlein's *Starship Troopers*, a controversial look at the career of a young soldier in a war against aliens. Military sf has become an important part of the market over the last 15 to 20 years; current favorites include David Drake, Jerry Pournelle, Joel Rosenberg, and S.M. Stirling. The genre is by no means confined to male writers, as witness the efforts of Janet Morris, Elizabeth Moon and S.N. Lewitt.

While many authors of military sf can write about combat from personal experience, a respectable number came to the field through wargaming, and others through an academic background in military history. Still, the genre requires at least a solid layman's knowledge of military organization, traditions, tactics, the history of warfare—and the ability to extrapolate these principles convincingly into a future setting. Tactics that worked with Athenian triremes aren't necessarily possible for spaceships in free fall.

Baen Books has published many of the best examples of the genre; but Ace, Roc, and Tor have been active publishers of military sf over the years, and most publishers would undoubtedly be open to well-written fiction with a military theme. Also, Jerry Pournelle's anthologies are often open to new writers, and the packager Bill Fawcett frequently includes new talent in his anthologies with military themes.

Cyberpunk

The hottest new genre of the '80s was cyberpunk: William Gibson's *Neuromancer* and the film *Blade Runner* may be the most familiar examples of this style. Bruce Sterling, Pat Cadigan, and Lewis Shiner are other writers often associated with cyberpunk, a word most of them dislike (although no widely accepted substitute exists). *Omni* magazine was originally the prime outlet for cyberpunk; nowadays, it is equally likely to find a home in *Asimov's*. The rhetoric of cyberpunk owes a great deal to the hard-boiled detective fiction of the '40s, as does its focus on tough outsiders in a corrupt high-tech society, making their way by their wits (and without regard to legal niceties). The setting is usually a decaying near-future world in which advanced computer applications (virtual reality, direct neural connection to the Net, etc.) have produced major changes in society as we know it.

While many observers feel that cyberpunk has lost its initial momentum, there is plenty of evidence of a continuing market for books like Neal Stephenson's *Snow Crash* and Wilhelmina Baird's *Crashcourse*, which have the look and feel of classic cyberpunk. Bantam, Ace, and Tor have been important outlets for cyberpunk recently, but even game-oriented publishers like TSR have found room on their lists for a few books featuring near-future lowlife characters in a computer-heavy environment. Conversely, Baen and Del Rey—and for short fiction, *Analog*—would appear to be the least likely markets for writing in this vein.

Cross-Fertilization

More and more editors these days seem willing to take chances with work that crosses genre boundaries. Science fiction readers are frequently also mystery fans, and books that combine a science fiction setting with a mystery plot are more and more common. These range from more or less straight-forward detective stories with a future setting to uncompromising sf stories that have solving a mystery as a key plot element. (There have even been sf "sequels" to Sherlock Holmes!) Practically all the standard subgenres of mystery can work as sf, but the police procedural set in the future seems especially effective and popular. Asimov's *The Caves of Steel*, Bester's *The Demolished Man*, and Phillip K. Dick's *Do Androids Dream of Electric Sheep?* (which was the basis for *Blade Runner*) are three classic sf cop stories, while Lynn S. Hightower's *Alien Blues* is an excellent recent example.

The biggest problem facing a writer planning a science fiction mystery is keeping the two halves of the story in balance. The future setting has to be credible and consistent for the story to work as sf, and the criminal investigation has to be logical and convincing for the story to work as a mystery. If the key to solving the crime lies in some esoteric future gadget or some strange characteristic of the environment, that has to be made clear to the reader at an early stage—preferably without tipping off the fact that it's a clue. Likewise, a straight transplant of the '40s-style hard-boiled dick into the 23rd century is hard to justify without making it clear why such an anachronistic type has survived—or why society has changed so little. In short, the story has to meet the requirements of two very demanding fields; not easy, but satisfying when it works.

Similarly, there is some genre-blending between sf and romance. Anne McCaffrey has had considerable success with such books as *The Rowan*, set in a distant future and focusing on the emotional life of its protagonist, a powerful young woman with highly developed psi powers. DAW Books has been especially good at finding writers (Melanie Rawn, Kate Elliot) who can combine romance plots with strong sf materials—although it might be just as accurate to describe their books as a romantic strain of science fantasy. Again, as with the mystery/sf blend, the most successful novels are those that do justice to both halves of the hybrid, rather than setting a conventional romance in a sketchy future scenario. In the romance field itself, one of the classic science fictional premises has become the basis of a popular subgenre, the time travel historical romance. In these novels, time travel is used primarily as a means for getting a modern woman into a suitable past era where she can meet her ideal man, as in *A Knight in Shining Armor*, by the very popular romance author Jude Deveraux. A few science fiction writers have been successful in breaking into the time travel romance field, often under pseudonyms.

The Young Adult Market

As noted above, sf fans are fond of quoting the aphorism that "the Golden Age of Science Fiction is 12 to 14." Not surprisingly, the market for books that appeal to a younger readership has always been strong in sf. Many of the giants of the field have written explicitly for young readers: Heinlein's "juveniles," such as *Have Spacesuit, Will Travel*; Asimov's "Lucky Starr" series; and the great bulk of Andre Norton's work were the main reading fare of many of today's fans (and writers) in their teen years. And even now, many "adult" publishers find that books originally published as "YA" can be successfully remarketed to a general audience. Even Pocket Books has begun a series of *Star Trek: The Next Generation* spinoff novels featuring the characters of that popular show as teenagers.

As a rule, short novels with youthful characters in central roles are best suited for the YA market, but other than that, there are very few restrictions. Jane Yolen, who has written for both audiences, has noted that there is often a greater freedom of subject and treatment for authors working for the YA market than among many "adult" publishers. The one great sin for writers attempting to break into this area is underestimating the readership—there is no quicker way to get a rejection slip from a YA publisher than "writing down" to the audience. Strong work that can be expected to appeal to a YA audience can go to most of the "adult" publishers as well as to the large number of YA markets— Athenaeum, Scholastic, Jane Yolen Books, etc. (See the specific listings for others.)

The Best Genre Is Your Own

While some authors will set out deliberately to write a space opera or a quest fantasy, some of the best writing in the field stubbornly defies easy categorization, as a look at a few lists of recent award finalists will suggest; how does one describe Michael Swanwick's *Iron Dragon's Daughter* or John Varley's *Steel Beach* in subgenre terms? Dan Simmons seems to be making a career of writing big, ambitious novels (notably the Hyperion books) that fit no clear-cut category. And Ursula K. Le Guin moves with no apparent effort from sf to fantasy to mainstream, all without losing her distinctive voice. There is clearly an audience for imaginative fiction that does not derive from pulp traditions or take sf fandom as its primary audience. Aldous Huxley and George Orwell were probably only vaguely aware of the commercial sf market when they wrote *Brave New World* and *1984*.

Even today, *The New Yorker* will publish an occasional story that might just as easily have appeared in *F&SF* or *Asimov's*. And a fair amount of work that clearly qualifies as science fiction of some sort appears without that designation on the cover, especially if published by one of the mainstream publishers who do not target the genre readership. P.D. James's futuristic dystopia *The Children of Men* is one recent example. Kurt Vonnegut began as a genre sf writer (with *The Sirens of Titan*), and a good bit of his writing still draws on sf themes and techniques. While it seems snobbish to refer to this non-genre work as "literary sf," there is probably no other widely-accepted term for it. The essential point is, there are plenty of potential outlets for writers willing to leave behind the friendly confines of the commercial sf/fantasy fields.

Trends come and go, as do popular subgenres (and terms for them); I've barely skimmed the surface here. But this quick survey of the broad (and ever-changing) sf/fantasy field should give you enough notion of the lay of the land to arrive at your own conclusion as to where your work is most likely to receive a positive response, preferably in the form of a check! Good luck marketing your writing in this fascinating field.

PETER HECK is the writer and editor of *Hailing Frequencies*, the sf/fantasy newsletter of Waldenbooks. He is a former editor at Ace Books, and has worked as a freelance editor and copywriter for sf fantasy publishers including Avon, Baen, Bantam, Ace, and Tor. He has written book reviews for *Asimov's*, *Newsday*, and *Kirkus*. His Mark Twain, Detective mystery novels (*Death on the Mississippi*, *A Connecticut Yankee in Criminal Court*) are published by Berkley.

Craft &

Technique

Creating and Using Near Future Settings

MAUREEN F. MCHUGH

Much of what I do for my settings relates to how I handle exposition. Settings are expository in nature. Most of the techniques I describe for settings can be used to convey background information of lots of different types.

There's an immediate problem with near future settings, and it is one that I haven't any clue how to avoid—they date. No matter how good you are, you're going to assume some things that aren't going to be. All those sf books from the '50s continued to think of computers as huge mainframe systems and never foresaw the personal computer. What do you do if the Soviet Union collapses and you've referred to it in your book or story? Many writers are facing that particular dilemma and I don't have much answer for it except to make your setting so convincing that people are willing to suspend disbelief. In other words, they think that the future setting is *so* realistic and *so* cool that they don't care if it is inconsistent with reality.

Near future settings should feel real. They have to feel possible in a way a far future setting isn't necessarily expected to. And they should be cool, too, because what is the point of writing science fiction if it doesn't have fun future stuff?

There are a number of ways to make your setting real, and a number of ways to make it cool.

Making It Cool

People are always talking about Sense of Wonder and how we all read sf in our adolescence for that joy. I always try to put something unexpected and fun in my settings. I try to make it something that people can do.

Readers seem to give the setting the benefit of the doubt if it lets them other 14-year-old at a party who is about to be offered drugs. But her town is a city underwater, so the experience has to be strange, and yet the reader has to be able to relate to it. So I used airplane glue and grafitti as my starting points.

> . . . David had his arm around my waist and I was as drunk as I have ever been. We walked to an exchange and took it to the bottom level, way under ground. We walked till we came to a place where there weren't any people around. The wall was smooth and shiny with sealer. I put my hand against it, felt how cold it was. One of the guys took out a cutter and started burning the sealer. He'd burn a line and then one of the others would lean forward and inhale the sense.

Create your setting by having your character experience it. A few words of what your character sees and thinks while he's delivering his briefcase of contraband nanites can go a long way in setting the scene. When I go somewhere I make some basic assumptions about where I am—like, will my car still be here if I forget to lock the doors? My characters make some basic assumptions, too, and sometimes those assumptions are different than what the reader would expect. Show them to me.

Significant details do something else, too; they make the reader trust you. A significant detail should be so right, so true and so unexpected that it fools the reader into thinking "this must be true because who would ever have thought of that?" Getting the details is an art and it takes practice.

There are a couple of useful tricks for creating a detail and a setting. Don't establish a setting purely through the use of visual and auditory images. Television works entirely in those two senses and television is hard to compete with. One way writing can seem more vivid is that it can evoke texture and taste and smell, and balance and orientation and all of those other senses—the famous five and the not-so-famous ones— that television can only suggest.

Writing also allows the reader to fill in things. Over-describing is a big, big temptation. There is something called the Two Color rule that I use as a broad rule of thumb. If I describe a guy and I tell you he's 6'2" tall, black, has dreadlocks and is wearing a shirt in Marley colors of red, green and gold, a long face that indicates that somewhere in his ancestry some of his great-grandparents were probably Caribbean Indians and his nose is aquiline and his eyes are cold, he's wearing kahki cutoffs that haven't seen a washing machine in far too long and he gives off that oily, incense, body-odor scent of someone who oils his dreadlocks rather than washing his hair, I've overwhelmed the reader.

In the story "The Queen of Marincite," I want to describe the protagonist's boyfriend. He's a drug dealer and bad news.

> . . . Macandal was dark, like me, and he wore his hair in long tight, wine-colored braids. Always, it was his mark. He wore red lenses, too and nobody looked like Macandal. He was a real maroon, real wild. People turned to look at him after he passed by, because they were scared, right?

In a paragraph, about two colors is enough. About two of anything is enough, at least if that anything is a detail that I want the reader to retain. If it is a real socko image it is going to swamp everything else in the story anyway. If it isn't a pretty powerful description, then why do I want it? So Macandal has wine-colored braids and red eyes—only one color, one image associated with him. I don't say what he's wearing. I know he's wearing a sweater and wetsuit tights like divers wear but I don't expect or care if my reader does. My reader may picture him in blue jeans. What's important is that my reader pictures him.

Be careful about explaining things. I've never explained my television to anyone, although I've told a child how to turn it on. People don't explain the things in their lives, they just use them. People don't usually tell the history of their town or their country unless there are some unusual circumstances—tourists hanging around or it is a history lesson or something. But I don't go driving into town thinking about how amazing are the social changes brought about by the microchip. I just go to McDonald's and feel vague irritation that kids today don't have to learn to count change because the register does it for them. I certainly don't admire the microchip in my bread machine, I just use the thing. If I want someone to see how different things are, I have my characters live in a world where those things are different. I have the character get his coffee out of a vending machine, get on the train, whip the seal off the lid and then sit and wait for the coffee to heat itself up. Does he care that there are little nanites activated by removing the seal? No, what he cares about is his commute.

There are a couple of things people always notice when they go abroad. One is the stuff that is weird that no one ever told them about. For me, it was the fact that in China, drivers still turn off their engines and coast downhill, thinking that it will save gas. I try to create some of those unexpected details in my fiction. After all, science fiction is sort of like going abroad without having to worry about dysentery.

The other thing I notice is the unexpected similarity, like geraniums in Russia. I never thought much about geraniums in Russia, but they kind of surprised me when I saw them. They seemed so . . . familiar. Unexpectedly so. Sometimes the unexpectedly familiar can be as jolting as the unfamiliar.

Researching Your Setting

I have a confession to make: I don't build my world before I start writing in it. Sometimes I have a general idea of the place, but most of the time I just make it up as it fits the story. Not everyone does it this way. Some people know enormous amounts of material about their setting. I don't think there is a right way or a wrong way, but I would suggest always being ready to make things up or twist things around on the spot.

Research is tricky. Research can give some of those significant details and it can give ideas for the familiar and the unfamiliar. Research is important, unavoidable, and can lead to a deadly sin. Just because I really like all the neat stuff I'm learning doesn't mean that the reader will like learning it. And when I've found it out I want to use it so bad. I've done all this work on field systems in medieval Europe (there's the three-field system and the two-field system and in a three-field system they would plant a third of the available common land in spring wheat and a third in whatever grain they planted for their spring planting and they'd leave a third fallow, whereas in a two-field system . . .) and I can just see the village and I know it is a three-field system and I've figured out that it is time to plant winter wheat and I want so bad to say that they're only planting a third of the field—but the guy going out to plant doesn't explain what he already knows to other people who already know it. The reader will never know or care that I knew all this information about agricultural techniques. Use only what is needed. The setting is very rarely the story, and you have to make yourself remember that the information serves the story.

I always try to remind myself that my setting shouldn't make too much sense. People aren't very rational and we do some really stupid things. We have a pretty twisted moral code. It's okay to drive five to ten miles an hour over the speed limit even though it is technically breaking the law—something that it is difficult to explain to a child, by the way. But if you really want to make someone crazy, while you're walking with them, throw a piece of litter on the ground and keep walking. A soft drink bottle, a candy wrapper, a tissue. Watch the result. They will probably be shocked. We've a pretty knee jerk reaction to litter. So why don't we have the same knee jerk reaction to speeding? Culture isn't consistent. Just because we speed doesn't mean we are or aren't a law-abiding society. Don't try to make your culture consistent. In fact, I try to make mine messy.

Of course, it all must feel like one culture. The guys with the khaki shorts and the guys with the Harley t-shirts may be different from each other, but compared to someone from, say, Tokyo, they are instantly identifiable as members of the same larger culture.

I tend to treat settings as a character in my work. I think of them as complicated-like characters but not so complicated that they appear to have a severe personality disorder. Although a setting with a severe personality disorder would probably make an interesting book (maybe a kind of Philip K. Dick setting . . .). Some of my settings are good guys, some are less good. I have some empathy and compassion for all my settings. None of them are straight-out villains, some of them have rough histories and their twisted nature is as much a product of circumstance as anything else.

For very cool effects, startle the reader a bit. Give the reader some astonishingly just right, unexpected visuals. Or cool costumes to wear. Strange places. Funky animals. Life is positively weird, usually weirder than science fiction. I try to steal from experience to make my settings interesting. Driving from Ohio into Indiana one time, there were many places that sold fireworks—because Ohio has slightly stricter laws about the sale of fireworks than Indiana. But in this particular town it seemed like one store out of every five sold fireworks—and something else. Not like fireworks and souvenirs, but like fireworks and auto parts. Fireworks and beer and wine (scary combination). Carry-out grocery and fireworks. Fireworks and doughnuts. It turns out that the town had a law that said no one could open just a fireworks stand. So there were beauty salons that sold fireworks. I haven't used it in a story but it is too good to have been made up. It's the kind of thing that sounds true. And weird. Too weird to be true. I give this detail to you, free for reading this essay. It's yours. Use it in a story.

MAUREEN F. MCHUGH is a Hugo- and Nebula-award-nominated writer of science fiction who has lived in New York City and in Shijiazhuang, China, but whose current exotic locale is a suburb of Ohio, where her house is situated next to a dairy farm. She's at work on a book titled *Mission Child* which will be published by Avon sometime before the end of this century.

❋ ❋ ❋
The Fantasy Series: Tips, Pitfalls . . . and Joys

JOEL ROSENBERG

Why write a fantasy series, anyway?

Well, take a look at some of the bestseller lists and look for the fantasy writers. David Eddings, Raymond Feist, Robert Jordan, Terry Brooks—all series books. Or wander around the science fiction and fantasy section at your nearest chain bookstore. Yes, certainly, there are stand-alone fantasy novels—although at least some of those will turn out to be the first book in a new series—but the field is, and has been, dominated by all sorts of series books for years now, and the trend shows no sign of slowing or stopping. Sell a fantasy novel and the first thing your editor will ask you might well be, "Well? What are you going to do for the second book in the series?"

Thankfully, it's not just a matter of necessity. The fantasy series offers the writer some advantages, as well. Hang in there; we'll get to them.

Terms of Enchantment

Words like *series* and *trilogy* and *sequel* and *prequel* get thrown around, often with reckless abandon. Let's start there, with the word *trilogy*, which gets the most abuse—and not just in marketing, where we read about a fourth book in a trilogy. (There can't be a fourth book in a trilogy, anymore than you can have a third person be part of a couple. When you add a fourth book, it's not a trilogy anymore; it's a tetralogy.)

Generally, a trilogy is understood to mean a three-novel series, in which each of the novels stands by itself, albeit the second and third ones perhaps somewhat shakily, and in which one or more major plot or character element will persist through all three, only to be wrapped up in the final novel.

Think about it—by that standard, the most famous fantasy trilogy of all, J.R.R. Tolkein's *The Lord of the Rings*, isn't a trilogy at all. Not one of the novels in any way stands alone; nothing—no plot complication, no thematic issue, no character's internal problem—is resolved in either of the first two books. There's no dramatic reason why they couldn't have been broken into smaller parts for publication, or, alternately, been published as one huge novel under one cover. (And in fact the latter has happened, at least once. Makes a nice big book.) That's not a trilogy. It's one long book, broken into three non-independent parts. Nothing wrong with that, of course.

For a good example of a real trilogy, take a look at the *Back to the Future* movies. The first one stands alone perfectly well, and even the ending, while inviting a sequel, doesn't really require one. The second, while a lot of fun of itself, really needs the first to set up the situation—and it needs the third movie in the series to pay off. And while I think that those who claim it's merely a 90-minute trailer for the third are off the mark, they're not *way* off the mark. The third movie resolves the plot complications and—and this is important—the thematic problems set up by the first two, and finishes the story. Sure, it would be possible to write another movie, or set of movies, involving some or all of the same characters . . .

But it isn't necessary. The third movie has completed the trilogy; it's done.

That's not a bad model for a fantasy trilogy. That tension between wrapping things up at the end of a novel and keeping a plotline going for more than one novel is important.

In practice, a fantasy series is anything that can be packaged as a fantasy series. It can include a long novel broken into publishable parts, like *The Lord of the Rings*, or a formal trilogy, or a closed-ended series, or, to pick my preferred form, an ongoing series.

What Kind of Series?

The world is divided into two kinds of people: those who divide the world into two kinds of people, and those who don't. While things tend not to be black and white, ongoing series can be divided into two kinds: the single-character-oriented series, and the ensemble series.

Single Character

My friend Steve Brust's Vlad Taltos novels fall clearly into the first kind. Steve follows the adventures of his ongoing assassin protaganist, Vlad

Taltos, through his life and career. The books, all but one told from Vlad's point of view (Steve was showing off), follow him through ongoing and acute problems, some of which he at least addresses in each individual book, and some of which persist through more than one novel. My own D'Shai books—*D'Shai* and *Hour of the Octopus*—fall into the same category, as well.

It's a good form, at least structurally reminiscent of a detective-based mystery. The writer and reader both form an attachment to the protagonist, and can have fun playing with what happens next (or even what happened before; there's no reason not to set, say, the fourth novel in a time between the first and the second). Steve's Vlad—like Robert B. Parker's Spenser, or Raymond Chandler's Philip Marlowe—is the focus of the book. And it's that character—who does change and grow both out of the dramatic necessities of the plot, and because the guy behind the keyboard is growing and changing as a person and a writer—who *is* the series. If Spenser or Marlow or Vlad dies, that series is pretty much over.

I don't think it's a coincidence that many (most?) protagonists of single-character-driven series tend to be smart alecks. If you're going to spend, literally, years at the keyboard writing from a single character's point of view, it's pleasant for both the writer and the reader to have the character blow off steam with a trenchant comment or two, every now and then.

It's a lot freer a form than it sometimes seems, but the limitations are real. The character can grow and change, yes, but he really can't change in a way that has him settling down to a humdrum existence for very long, because humdrum existences won't drive a novel's plot. It's credible to believe that somebody might want to give up having exciting things happen around him, and then have something happen to upset those mundane plans, but you can do that only a limited number of times before both you and the reader say, tiredly, "okay, what's going to bring him out of retirement *now*?"

That aggravates the basic problem with the single-character-driven series: the fact that it *is* a single-character-driven series. Just as in its equivalent TV series, the reader fundamentally doesn't believe that the protagonist is really threatened in the book in his hand. He knows that Parker's Spenser is going to be back for the next book, and so is Steve's Vlad or my Kami Dan'Shir. There may be changes in their lives, but the changes can't affect the parameters of the series. Spenser isn't going to give up the detective business for good to become a house husband for Susan Silverman; Vlad isn't going to give up killing people and settle down as a storekeeper, not for good. My D'Shaian fantasy detective, Kami Dan'Shir, isn't going to stop finding murders to solve and members of the ruling class to blame them on.

Ensemble

The ensemble series is a more flexible form.

I started writing my Guardians of the Flame series more than a dozen years ago. The series followed the adventures of a group of college students thrust into the world of their fantasy role-playing game, watching them grow up and change as the years went by, mainly from the point of view of Karl Cullinane, one-time college dilettante, later warrior and Emperor.

I'm not a cruel guy, honest, but it was starting to get irritating, a few books along. Here I'd been writing about Karl going into dangerous situations for years, and he's always gotten out of them. Oh, he'd blown off a few fingers, and picked up some scars here and there, but Karl wasn't really in danger.

Or was he?

I killed him—dead—at the end of the fourth book in the series, *The Heir Apparent*, and then spent the fifth book, *The Warrior Lives*, having the rest of my cast chase around to see if he really was dead. (He was; he is. Honest.)

Now, if it really was the Karl Cullinane series, that would have been the end of it. But since the series really was about a whole group of people, many of whom could be brought to center stage, I could—and did—continue on with the series from the points of view of other characters. And the reader wouldn't be able to count on any of those characters, either, permanently defying the law of averages.

Think of a soap opera. *Guiding Light* and *Days of Our Lives* aren't about the most prominent character at any given time—they're about the whole bunch of them, and it's entirely possible that the character you've been following over time will change in serious ways, or even die. And he or she can do that without changing the form of the series.

I'm doing it again with my Keepers of the Hidden Ways books, *The Fire Duke* and *The Silver Stone*. While Torrie Thorsen and Ian Silverstein are, at least for now, the main protagonists, my readers and I both know that it's by no means sure that they'll survive. So, now, when I put either of them in a swordfight, the reader's got to wonder not

How *is he going to get out of it this time?*

but rather—

Is *he going to get out of it?*

Which do you think is going to be more of a page turner?

Me too.

Background and History

"As we all know, Melvin, the Invasion of the Small But Remarkable Hairy Things ended the Finster Dynasty, replacing it with—"

Nope. Can't lecture. But you've still got to clue them in, anyway. Freedom from the constraints of the real world—historical, physical, whatever—is one of the twinned virtues and problems in writing fantasy fiction anyway, but it gets even tougher in a fantasy series, simply because you have to keep doing it.

In any fantasy novel, you have to let the reader know important things about the world you're presenting him with, but you have to do it subtly enough that you don't turn it into an obvious—and boring—lecture. In a fantasy series, you have to do that, too; and you have to, to some extent, do it over and over again in each subsequent book in a way that will inform new readers without boring old ones, and then you *also* have to give enough background in what's happened in previous books to bring new readers up to speed.

I'm as devoted a fan of Ed McBain's 87th Precinct series as they come, but every time I hear about how his bald, patient detective, Meyer Meyer got his name, developed his almost inhuman patience, and lost his hair, I cringe; I'm none too fond of hearing how Steve Carella looks vaguely Asian, either, and I've stopped counting how many times Bert Kling has lost girlfriends because they either dump him or they're killed.

Homework assignment: watch a soap opera. If you already watch soap operas, watch one you've never seen before. But don't watch it with a friend who has been following the multiple storylines for years; do it alone. You'll have to pay close attention to have any chance to figure out what's going on. The characters have background that not only do *they* know, but that the experienced viewers do as well, and until you're clued in, you're going to be awfully confused.

If it was a book, you might put it down. And not pick it up again. So might your readers.

That's an ongoing issue, and one you have to keep thinking about. You need to make it possible—ideally, as easy as possible—for new readers to start your series with, say, the third or fourth book, and then go back later and read the earlier ones, and you need to do that without boring your devoted readers.

Some Words About Magic

Magic can mean a lot of different things to different people. For some, it's a metaphor for science, or for art, or for God; for some, it's showmanship that lets the writer do things that he couldn't otherwise make happen; for some, it's a built-in way to solve a plot problem that has to be used with caution.

Fiction—mainstream or fantasy—is about people having problems. Magic is one way to solve those problems, but if unrestrainedly powerful magic can solve all problems, then there is no problem, and no story. If you really can wave your magic wand and make everything fine, then what's your problem? And where's your book? And if this is a series, well, where's the sequel going to come from?

Think about Superman. Double-talk about growing up under a red sun on a high gravity planet aside, Superman's powers are basically magic. And he quickly became too powerful—not only was he able to leap tall buildings in a single bound, outrace a locomotive, but he became able to travel in time, move the Earth, and do all sorts of handy things.

So, enter kryptonite. Now, at least sometimes, he's got a problem to worry about, and a vulnerability to drive some dramatic possibilities. Just as there wouldn't have been a story about Achilles if he didn't have a weak spot on his heel, there wouldn't have been Superman without kryptonite. Otherwise, there's no problem, and without a problem, there's no story.

It probably makes sense, when putting together a magic system for a stand alone fantasy novel, to think clearly about the limitations you want to place on that magic, but for an ongoing fantasy series, it's vital, and you'll only be able to invent a bit of kryptonite here and there.

Back in 1981, when I was writing *The Sleeping Dragon*, the first book of the Guardians of the Flame series, I introduced Ellegon, a somewhat sarcastic telepathic fire-breathing dragon the size of a Greyhound bus.

Ellegon's dialogue is a whole lot of fun to write—I've rarely had a character I've enjoyed writing as much as I do when Ellegon's onstage—but as a plot element, he's a pain in the butt. As a plot element, he's equivalent to an always-on-call helicopter gunship—that fiery breath can do a lot of damage—that doesn't need fuel. As a result, if I want to or need to put my characters into a situation that they can't get out of, I've got to come up with a reason—a good reason—that Ellegon can't simply drop out of the sky, flame any and all of the opposition, and lift them out.

I've introduced dragonbane—a plant whose extract is poisonous to magical metabolisms—but that can only go so far, and plotting around Ellegon's abilities doesn't get easier as the years go by.

In Steve's Vlad books, magical teleportation is commonplace—just like beaming up and down in *Star Trek*, sort of. Which means that nobody can be trapped anywhere, so if Steve wants his hero to be in a situation that he's got to talk or think or fight his way out of . . .

Magic's a terrific tool for telling a story, but it's a sharp one, and if you're going to handle the same magical system for a number of books, you're going to find that it can cut you.

Grow Old With Me

Which is not to say that writing a fantasy series is all problems. There's a particular pleasure that I can only get from returning to a world I've already invested time—more than a decade in some cases—in exploring and developing, and returning to characters I know as well as I can know anybody. Developing a whole universe that's different from our own leads to endless possibilities, some of which you can develop in years to come. Characters can change, and their concerns can be a thoughtful reflection of your concerns as you and your readers change.

Every time I start a new Guardians book, I'm once again dealing with characters that I first created and met as a young man in my 20s, and with whom I've spent numerous hours ever since, watching them develop as circumstances in their lives—and mine!—have changed over the years.

It's good to renew acquaintances with old friends.

I've got a couple waiting at the keyboard for me right now.

JOEL ROSENBERG's latest book is *The Silver Stone*, the second in his Keepers of the Hidden Ways series, from Avon. He lives in Minneapolis, Minnesota, with his wife, his two daughters, his sister, five cats, one dog, and 23 fish.

∗ *∗* *∗*

Take My Wizard . . . Please!
The Serious Business of Writing
Funny Fantasy and Science Fiction

ESTHER M. FRIESNER

A centuries-old story tells that when a great Shakespearean actor lay on his deathbed, someone asked him how he was doing. The world is *still* full of people who insist on asking questions like that, and they need to have objects of middling weight flung at their heads at every possible opportunity or they will keep on doing it. Since the dying actor was too weak to perform the necessary public service of chucking a chamber pot at the busybody in question, he is instead reported to have settled for making the memorable quote: "Dying is easy. Comedy is hard."

(The smart money claims that what the great actor *really* said was, "How am I doing? He wants to know how I'm doing? I'm *dying*, you moron, how do you *think* I'm doing?" But all experienced fiction writers—and most politicians—know better than to let the truth get in the way of a good story.)

The rules for writing effective funny fantasy and science fiction (both fields hereafter to be called collectively Speculative Fiction or SpecFic, in the interests of convenience, efficiency and because catchphrases are *so* cool) are only variations on the rules for writing effective comedy of any stripe. Taking it one step further, some of them are the same rules that apply to writing effective fiction, period. Let's begin with a few useful general guidelines.

Begin With A Character

In "The Rich Boy," F. Scott Fitzgerald wrote: "Begin with an individual, and before you know it you find that you have created a type; begin with a type and you find that you have created—nothing." A quote from the creator of *The Great Gatsby* is not as out of place in an article about funny SpecFic as you might think. Check out his story "The Diamond as Big as the Ritz" sometime. Besides, he's more than right: Always begin with a character.

The best characters are drawn from life. They are also recognizable and comprehendable to the reader. Even in SpecFic, where your characters can be ogres or aliens more often than not, they still need to be *approachable* ogres and aliens, with some vaguely human quality tucked in among all that Otherness.

Have a Little Sympathy

Readers tend to prefer characters who are at least somewhat sympathetic. In the case of villains, *sympathetic* is perhaps the wrong word: *Understandable* is better. *Interesting* is best of all. The bad guy whose sole reason for blowing up the galaxy is *Because that's what bad guys do* won't be around for a sequel. Even Darth Vader needs motivation. It changes him from a cardboard cut-out villain to a three-dimensional character, and three dimensions are far more interesting than two.

Interesting characters make for an interesting story. Whether they're rooting for the good guy to win or eager to see the villain get what's coming to him, readers must care about your characters. A writer's first task is to insure that his audience becomes interested in and involved with the story he has to tell, and the best way to do that is to make it a story about interesting people. Remember, part of your audience is the editor to whom you are trying to sell your story. Lose reader interest, lose sales.

Make the Joke Fit the Character

Unfortunately, one of the worst errors made in writing funny SpecFic is when the writer forgets to think of his characters as living beings and instead turns them into joke machines. Jokes come in many guises, but all kinds of jokes work best when presented by a believable character.

Taking this a step farther, a joke or humorous situation works best when presented by a character whose traits either suit the gag or provide an element of sharp contrast that proves to be humorous, often on multiple levels. For example, when the bumbling apprentice magician has his cauldron blown up yet again it's pretty much what the reader expects of him. As far as comedy goes, an occurence like that only works on the elementary level of slapstick.

However, when the character in question is an expert wizard, preferably one with an inflated self-image, the incident of the backfiring spell works not only as simple slapstick but also on the principle of upsetting audience expectations for the character involved. In addition, since we've already said that the hapless wizard has an unsuitably high opinion of himself, the reader can easily identify him with some real-world stuffed shirt (and don't tell me you can't name at least half a dozen of your own acquaintance!) and get lots of vicarious enjoyment out of seeing the high and mighty taken down a peg or two.

In brief, the more smug, snooty, self-satisfied, and seemingly untouchable your character is, the more satisfying it is to see him get hit in the face with the proverbial cream pie.

Upset the Reader's Expectations

Now let's talk about characters specific to the realm of funny SpecFic. Despite F. Scott Fitzgerald's words of wisdom, sometimes you really do need to begin with a type. To speak about comedic characters in SpecFic, we must first speak about easily recognizable types (stock characters, if you will) found in the *non*-comedic side of the field. These include but are not limited to: the wizard, the witch, the dragon, the unicorn, the elf, the barbarian, the inept apprentice, the robot, the rogue, the scientific genius (mad or sane, with or without beautiful daughter), the alien (friendly or hungry), the swashbuckling hero, the evil galactic overlord, the overlord's toady, the all-purpose sidekick, and so on.

The point is, these are all roles which are *familiar* to the reader of SpecFic, and in this case, familiarity breeds comedy, not contempt. When the reader encounters one of these types, certain expectations click into place: The robot will not understand human emotions; the elf will be beautiful and noble; the galactic overlord will be ruthless, etcetera. The writer of funny SpecFic often operates by taking these reader expectations and setting them on ear.

For this method to work, you must first be absolutely sure that your main characters can be matched to one of the genre's easily identifiable types. You can't make light of a subject with which you are not familiar, nor can your reader appreciate the humor in a situation if he doesn't understand the context. Someone who has never read any Conan the Barbarian stories won't see what's so funny about Terry Pratchett's creation, Cohen the Barbarian. As far as this hypothetical reader knows, *all* barbarian swordsmen are in the dotages, sick and tired of a life of high adventure, and plagued by the usual aches and pains of age. He also won't recognize the pun in the character's name. Cohen the Barbarian is funniest *by comparison* with Conan, so if the reader has no basis for this comparison, the humor won't work. (Luckily, the big, brawny barbarian has become such a standard image in fantasy that most readers are well acquainted with the Conan-type even if they *haven't* ever read an actual Conan story.)

Naturally this does not mean that your characters should be stereotypes. On the contrary, they must be easily recognizable types from the SpecFic lexicon while at the same time having distinct personal traits that make them believable, living people (or beings). What your characters *are* (wizard, robot, vampire) defines them for the purposes of comedy, but *how* they behave and *why* they behave that way makes them real.

Create the Illusion of Reality

You gave a comedic character the illusion of reality by much the same means as you would apply to any fictional character. This is where our earlier advice about drawing characters from life comes in. Apply real-life attributes to your SpecFic type and you will find you have created a living character. For example:

Give him a family and consider their influence on him. Give him a self-image and be ready to explain why he thinks of himself in one way and not another. Imagine his childhood, his upbringing, his environment, his desires, ambitions, fears, loves, hates, and then . . . file it. File it well out of the way, too, or else you'll fall into one of a writer's most common pitfalls, namely: "I know all about this character and what makes him tick, and *now*, by golly, I'm going to put *all* of it into the story *whether it has any bearing on the action or not*, because I didn't do all that background work for nothing!"

Sorry, but no one likes a lecture. There's a word for stories where the author stops the action to make sure the reader realizes how hard he worked: dull. You'll just have to have the personal satisfaction of knowing you did your homework. A character's job is to keep the story moving, not to bog it down. This is especially vital when writing comedy, because timing *is* as important as they say.

Flesh out your characters for your own reference, then only present as much of this information as is necessary for your audience to understand the action. If your reader can imagine your characters going on with their lives after the story ended (not merely "They lived happily ever after") then you've done your job.

Give Them a Place to Go

There's nothing sadder than seeing a bunch of wonderfully fleshed-out, beautifully conceived characters all dressed up with nowhere to go. Writing funny SpecFic isn't the same as writing stand-up comedy: Jokes aren't enough. If you're writing a short story, you might be able to get away with making the whole piece nothing more than a set-up for the punchline, but it had better be mighty short and with a mighty good punchline.

An effective comedic story is more than a series of set-ups, punchlines and rimshots. Few things are less likely to get a laugh than the author who interrupts his story just to tell a joke, particularly if the joke hasn't got much to do with the story itself and especially if the story remains stopped cold in its tracks while the author in effect demands, "Get it? Get it? Wasn't that funny? Amn't I a *scream*?" Well, he's right about the scream part.

Obey the Rules

To write a funny SpecFic story that works, first write a good story according to the usual rules: It should have a beginning, a middle, and an end. The middle and the end should derive logically from the beginning. Remember all of those three-dimensional characters you developed? Their actions ought to remain in keeping with their established personalities, but as in life, these personalities may evolve in the course of the story. If so, you must account for it. When your cowardly squire suddenly becomes a fearless knight, you'd better show the reason why.

You know, sometimes the jokes don't all work. Sometimes you get one bunch of readers who thinks Scene A is hilarious while Scene B goes right over their heads, and sometimes you get a group for whom the reverse holds true. Not all situations are funny to all readers. If your funny stuff doesn't have the solid foundation of an interesting plot underpinning it, you're going to lose your audience's attention. Not good.

So where *do* you get your ideas for SpecFic stories that will both amuse and involve your readers?

Schenectady

All right, I admit that *Schenectady* is the canonical wiseguy reply that most SpecFic writers have been trained to give whenever anyone asks us "Where do you get your ideas?" It's what you call an in-joke, and as such is a very good example of where *not* to shop for story ideas.

In-jokes are by their very definition exclusive. Exclusivity is all right for country clubs but death to comedy. If you present a funny situation to a large audience and only one person laughs while everyone else says, "I don't get it," something is gravely wrong. (It is all right to have one or two in-jokes if they are not intrusive. When Robert Asprin named a bunch of vampires after a group of well-known literary agents, those in the know had an additional giggle, but other readers didn't feel excluded because their enjoyment of the story itself did not depend on them getting this particular jibe.) It can't be said enough: To be accessible and understandable, humor must have some basis in the familiar.

Choose a Recognizable Plot . . .

In the case of funny SpecFic, the familiar includes not only recognizable character types from ordinary SpecFic, but recognizable plots as well. These include but are not limited to: The Quest; The Clash of Cultures; Saving the Universe/Kingdom by Blowing Up Something Bad; Saving the Universe/Kingdom by *Not* Blowing Up Something Good; Coming *That Close* to Blowing Up the Entire Universe/Kingdom (a subset of which is the Sorcerer's Incompetent Apprentice); Discovering that the Underdog is Really the Royal Heir/Wizard/Messianic Figure; and of course Boy Meets Girl/Dragon/Alien/Implanted Computer Chip.

. . . Then Make It Your Own

Once you have chosen a basic plot, you can make it your own. This is not stealing. Disney's animated *Cinderella* is as far removed from the movie *Pretty Woman* as it is from the Brothers Grimm version in which one ugly stepsister chops off her own heel and toes to make her foot fit the glass slipper, but they're all the same story at bottom.

Each of the already mentioned basic plots has been retold so many times that it carries with it certain expectations. Humor relies on the upsetting of audience expectations. (Please be aware that cultural forces are constantly changing our expectations. We used to expect the brawny hero to save the princess, so when the princess saved the brawny hero instead it could be played for laughs. These days, most SpecFic princesses, elf or alien, are usually packing steel, so there went *that* gag.)

Verbal vs. Situational Humor

You have your characters, your basic plot, and some idea of how you are going to retell that basic plot in your own unique way. Now what?

That all depends on *how* you choose to tell your story. Earlier on, we mentioned that jokes come in many guises. By jokes, we mean humor in general and not just "A troll, an elf, and an orc walked into a bar . . ." Before you choose your route, you'd better have an overview of the territory.

There are two main subsets of humor: verbal and situational. In a given piece of comedic writing it is possible for either to exist independently of the other, but you obtain better results by a judiciously balanced combination of the two. A pie-fight and a pun-fest are each funny in their own way, but only in small doses.

Verbal Humor

Verbal humor includes puns, of course. Puns are the black sheep of verbal humor. This is because puns are fairly easy to come up with, and so certain writers tend to over-use them. If you do choose to include puns in your work, strive to avoid the rimshot phenomenon. ("This must be the dragon's cave. I see the mark of his mighty tail in the dirt." "So *that's* what he's been draggin'!" *rimshot* Author grins, says "Get it? Get it?" and bows to audience for being so clever. Audience leaves.) The less obvious a pun is, the better the effect. The deadly "stealth" pun works best. In Terry Pratchett's *Soul Music*, an aspiring rock band in search of leopardskin trousers instead acquires a whole, live leopard, cheap. Why the bargain price? The beast can't hear. Deaf leopard. Def Leppard. This author's "Get it?" sounds in your ear as a whisper, not a shriek. He's made you work for it. You groan, but you really have no one but yourself to blame.

Double entendres are close kin to puns, since they too play with multiple levels of meaning contained in a word or phrase. In this case, the double meaning is sexually suggestive. Laughter is often a nervous reaction—we laugh because we don't know what else we *can* do in a given situation—and in our post-Victorian society the mere mention of sex still makes some people nervous. (This knowledge is a holdover from childhood, when we first discovered that using *those* words usually got one heck of a fun-to-watch reaction out of Mommy.) Sexual and scatalogical words in and of themselves will sometimes get you a laugh just by being there, but it will be a cheap laugh. If that's the effect you want, use them.

Another example of purely verbal humor is proper nouns. Names for characters and places can get an extra giggle from the reader. From my own work, *Majyk By Design*, I've had a number of compliments on my choice of names for the romance writer, Raptura Eglantine (overwrought and flowery enough to suit the reader's preconceived notion of what a romance writer's name *ought* to sound like), and her favorite cover-model Curio (not quite Fabio, but close enough for jazz). Sometimes names are also puns. Legolam the elf in *Bored of the Rings* is both a pun on and a parody of the elf Legolas from Tolkien's *Lord of the Rings*.

Finally, there are jokes, *per se*. It's perfectly all right to *tell* the one about the Martian, the robot, and the chopped liver; just don't stop the story to do it. Only tell those jokes that sound natural coming from a particular character at a specific time in the narrative. No fair cheating by having your characters lead off with the unprovoked remark, "That reminds me of a funny story."

Situational Humor

Situational humor is a broader field. What makes a situation funny? Once more we return to the principle of upsetting reader expectation. We expect certain beings to act in certain ways in certain situations. We don't expect people to act like machines, which is why it's funny when they do. If there's a banana peel in our path, we adjust by picking it up and throwing it away. In comedy, we remain inflexible, keep going, and take a pratfall.

In SpecFic, the inverse applies: We don't expect machines to act like people. We expect the computer/robot/android to process data or, in the case of super-advanced Artificial Intelligences, to try to eliminate imperfect, illogical humankind in favor of a more "perfect" machine-based civilization. In SpecFic comedy, the super-advanced AI exhibits distinctly human behavior, illogical, imperfect, and as downright moody as it can get.

Apart from writing comedy by creating generally humorous situations, there are a few specific methods, including parody, satire, and topical humor. All are interrelated and all have their advantages and disadvantages. It will be up to you as the writer to decide whether the pros outweigh the cons when you decide which and how many of these techniques to use in your work.

Parody upsets reader expectations by *extremely* strict imitation of a specific work of SpecFic. A funny story based on the legend of King Arthur can be set in New York City as easily as in Camelot (as Peter David did in *Knight Life*). A *parody* of the same legend *must* be set in Camelot, with the appropriate costumes, trappings, and even speech patterns, but with the author inserting a series of changes that are close to the original but just different enough to ambush the reader's expectations. (The screenplay of *Monty Python and the Holy Grail* is rich with such examples.) If you are not deeply familiar with the original story in all its aspects, you can't write a parody of it. If the original story itself is too obscure, not enough readers will be familiar enough with it for your parody to work.

If you want to write *satire*, be prepared to write with bite. Satire's purpose is to point out what's wrong with the world—whether it's crooked politicians, the war between the sexes, or yet another Spunky Teenagers Morph 'n' Mutate novel—and through ridicule, to encourage change for the better. (It doesn't always work, but at least you'll know you tried.) To write good satire, be sure that you choose a target that truly bothers you . If you're indifferent to something, you lack the motivation to make fun of it effectively.

Topical humor is the most risky. It involves parodying and/or satirizing a specific subject that is of current interest. If you wish, you can take Rush Limbaugh (please!), transform him into a SpecFic character (the king's personal wizard/advisor) and make fun of him within that context ("And another thing, Sire, it's a well-known fact that the reason your knights can't slay that dragon is because of all these Amazonazi swordswomen taking their jobs away!"). However, things change. Future generations may well ask "Limbaugh? Isn't that some kind of weird dance with a stick?" There goes your audience accessibility, and with it your comedy. Today's topical humor can quickly become tomorrow's in-joke that only a scant audience of history buffs will appreciate. If you want your work to retain its comedic appeal over time, keep topical humor and satire to a minimum. Parody too only endures in value as long as people remain familiar with the subject parodied.

Get Serious

While we're on the subject of writing humor with staying power, remember this: Your story need not be one long laugh-fest. Humor is dead serious stuff. In fact, humor gains depth when it's *about* something more than just making the reader laugh. Food for thought—serious thought—goes down a lot more readily if it's coated with a little laughter. Humor observes, analyzes, and comments on the human condition, which can sometimes be a pretty scary thing to face head-on. Humor helps us cope with some of life's harsher realities through laughter.

There's a very good reason that Death and Afterlife show up in so many funny SpecFic works: We need a handy way of dealing with our fears of mortality. When we laugh, we experience feelings of superiority to the object of our laughter. Humor lends us the conviction that we have a measure of control over beings and situations seemingly beyond our power to influence. Authority figures know this, which is why dictators whose rule most relies on Because I Say So (plus a lot of backup armed thugs) are also the ones who most fear laughter. Death is the ultimate authority figure from whose grim dominion none may escape. Dying is easy.

Fair enough. Where did I put my cream pie?

Award-winning author **ESTHER M. FRIESNER**, best known for funny fantasy and science fiction novels such as *Majyk By Accident* and *The Sherwood Game*, has previously penned (PC'ed, actually) a number of articles about writing humor. However, she also writes on the serious side of the genre, with works such as *The Psalms of Herod* and *Child of the Eagle*. She lives in Connecticut and has a Ph.D. in Spanish from Yale University. This strikes her as pretty funny too.

Finding Your Short Story's True Beginning

DARRELL SCHWEITZER

hoot the sheriff on the first page, is the proverbial western writer's
advice. The science fiction version may involve denting the sheriff's
carapace, but it's pretty much the same. Begin your story at the beginning. That should seem too obvious to merit further discussion.

But it isn't. One of the most common problems I see, as editor and as
teacher, is the story that begins at the wrong place. *The story starts on
page seven*, is a common, devastating criticism; worse if it's only a seven-
page story.

"But I started on page one," the author protests. "See. Right here.
That first sentence."

"No, that's where you started *typing*," I reply. "It took you several
pages to reach the beginning of the story, if you ever got there."

How do you tell? Think of it like this: Remember the comic strip
"Krazy Kat," in which the love-smitten Ignatz Mouse was always hurling
bricks at Krazy Kat to get her attention? Exactly. *Wham!* The story starts
when your character gets hit in the head with a brick.

In other words, the story doesn't start with a long and detailed description of who your character is, a history of the world up to this point or
even what your character does every day. It starts when the protagonist's
life is disrupted. When the routine *changes*. When something extraordinary manifests itself.

Sometimes the incoming brick can be really obvious:

At high noon on May 4, 1999, the sun went out!

That's from Jack Williamson's 1930 *Amazing Stories* serial, "The
Green Girl." You can be certain that as soon as the sun goes out, *nobody*
in the story is able to go on with their lives as before. The story has
begun. The conflict starts rolling.

But many stories seem to start with descriptions of characters' routines, where they live or both. Something static, set up to show how things were at the moment of interruption—what the glass window looked like right before the brick came through.

Here's an example from Ray Bradbury's "Ylla," one of the stories in *The Martian Chronicles*:

> They had a house of crystal pillars on the planet Mars by the edge of an empty sea, and every morning you could see Mrs. K eating the golden fruits that grew from the crystal walls, or cleaning the house with handfuls of magnetic dust which, taking all dirt with it, blew away on the hot wind. Afternoons, when the fossil sea was warm and motionless, and the wine trees stood stiff in the yard, and the little distant Martian bone town was all enclosed, and no one drifted out of their doors, you could see Mr. K himself in his room, reading from a metal book with raised hieroglyphs over which he brushed his hand, as one might play a harp. And from the book, as his fingers stroked, a voice sang, a soft ancient voice, which told tales of when the sea was red steam on the shore and ancient men had carried clouds of metal insects and electric spiders into battle.
>
> Mr. and Mrs. K had lived by the dead sea for 20 years, and their ancestors had lived in the same house, which turned and followed the sun, flower-like, for ten centuries.
>
> Mr. and Mrs. K were not old. They had the fair, brownish skin of the true Martian, the yellow coin eyes, the soft musical voices. Once they had liked painting pictures with chemical fire, swimming in the canals in seasons when the wine trees filled them with green liquors, and talking into the dawn together by the blue phosphorous portraits in the speaking room.
>
> They were not happy now.
>
> This morning Mrs. K stood between the pillars, listening to the desert sands heat, melt into yellow wax, and seemingly run on to the horizon.
>
> Something was going to happen.
>
> She waited.

What's about to happen, the reason this Martian housewife has had her disturbing premonition, is that Earth men are about to land and ruin everything. Before long, the old Mars will be gone, the population dead of disease, the towns in ruins, beer cans floating in the canals.

The opening of "Ylla" seems, at first, rather leisurely for a short story, with considerable description before the first hurled brick. ("Something was going to happen.") But the theme of the story demands this. "Ylla" is about the threatened destruction of paradise. The lives of Mr. and Mrs. K are as changeless as the ancient society in which they live. We are shown the whole Martian experience and mind-set very economically in those first few paragraphs. This opening, in an effect Bradbury uses again and again (compare it to the first page of his novel *Fahrenheit 451*), functions like the overture to a symphony. It introduces the key images, ideas and characters, striking the notes that are to be developed in the course of the story.

Therefore: a static, beautiful Mars. A Martian couple going about their lives. They are threatened with a permanent interruption, and resist. The story actually ends with Mr. K killing the first astronauts who land, and while Mrs. K is comforted, and her bad dreams stop, there is no sense that this is a lasting solution. Mars is doomed, even if the Martians themselves don't know it yet. This story is a farewell snapshot.

A story, then, begins with *change*. The archetypical story opening may be paraphrased like this:

> Routinely, Harold Hero went through the motions of his life, doing what he always did. And then, *one day* . . .

This disruption of routine introduces the most basic sort of conflict. Most of us don't like having our lives changed. We try to get things back to normal. If something intrudes, we struggle against it, even if in the course of the struggle things are irreparably changed. Ultimately Bradbury's Martians cannot return to the way life was before Earth men discovered them. Mr. K, by shooting the first explorers, attempts to achieve a new equilibrium, but he has either guilt or doubt. He conceals what he has done from his wife. He, at least, is no longer innocent.

And, needless to say, in "The Green Girl," the characters must devote their full attention to saving the human race from the imminent extinction implied by that first line.

So, to begin a story, think of the hurled brick: intrusion, disruption, the sudden explosion of conflict that yanks a character out of daily routine, the extraordinary happenstance that is a story worth telling.

The Many Tasks of the Story's Opening

The short story requires extreme efficiency; the first few paragraphs must accomplish many things in addition to the hurling of the first brick. They must introduce the tone of the story, its emotional flavor, from the first note struck. They must present a coherent point of view, through which the events in the story will be perceived. They must provide a setting, possibly a whole new world, and show characters alive within that setting. If there is some extraordinary idea or premise on which the story will turn (as do most science fiction and fantasy stories), some hint of this, too, must come in the first few paragraphs. And all these tasks must be performed *at the same time*. There is no room for lecturing, for setting the stage or filling in the characters' backgrounds before the action starts.

Here's an opening of my own, from a story called "The Outside Man," published in Peter Crowther's anthology, *Narrow Houses* (Little, Brown):

Jeffrey Quilt tells you this. It is a story, all of it, but it is also true. Listen—! Listen—! It's time.

"When you walk with the Outside Man," I said, "you walk forever. You may choose to do so. Indeed, you *must* choose, for he will never compel you, but when you walk with him, when he has given you whatever it is you most desperately desire, you cannot stop walking, and you are always alone."

I paused in my circular pacing, listening to the sounds of the night: the wind in the leaves, crickets, birds. And as I listened, they grew still, one by one.

"What the Hell do you mean, Quilt?" he said. "Cut the amateur theatrics."

I started again, one step, another, another, encircling him where he sat. He turned to follow me with his gaze, the rusty chair creaking. Footsteps and ancient metal; the only sounds now.

"My grandmother told me about the Outside Man for the first time when I was six or seven," I said. "She was really neat, I thought then, like the Gypsy woman in *The Wolf Man*, the one who intones so solemnly about wolfbane and the full moon and your prayers not being much good under the circumstances; only she lived at my house and her secrets were just for me.

"She spoke of *Der Waldganger*, the Walker-in-the-Forest who meets hapless—but never innocent—travelers in the darkness and extracts from them, not their souls, but the *truth*, the sort of truth you're afraid to admit even to yourself. Which is pretty much the same thing as losing your soul, I guess. *Whatever you tell the Outside Man is true*, she used to say with a kind of terrifying finality that thrilled me, back then."

"I don't get it, Quilt," he said, rapping his knuckles on the metal chair arm, for the comfort of the sound.

I continued pacing, around and around. He sat facing forward, turning only slightly as I passed.

"*Der Waldganger*. Grandma was full of stories of the Old Country—haunted castles along the Rhine, headless knights, maidens back from the grave—but she wasn't really German German, just Pennsylvania German, though through her our family went back a long, long ways, and was, at times suitably witchy. My grandmother was the sort of person who never left the house without her copy of John George Hohman's "Powwow" magic book, *Long Lost Friend*. Hohman gives a charm against *Der Waldganger*, or the Outside Man, to use the New World name—"

"Quilt, what has this crap got to do with . . . ? Why have you brought me here?" He stopped rapping his knuckles. I stood still. He seemed to hold his breath, and the woods were utterly, utterly silent, and somehow I could *hear* the plaintive, pained note in his mind. I fancied that his eyes gleamed like those of a frightened animal, but of course they did not.

"I brought you here because it is a suitable setting for a little story I have to tell. Just sit and listen. I must have mentioned my little brother, Stevie—"

"The one who . . . died?"

"The very one. But how did he die? How, really? Only the Outside Man truly knows, and I do, and very soon, you will, too."

"Quilt, please—"

"*Listen.*" I was pacing again, around and around, three times and more; three times three times. "Now Stevie and I were what you'd call rival siblings. In most cases it is the older child who has gotten used to being the center of the familial universe and can never forgive the younger for usurping Mamma's affections. But Stevie had it backwards. He wanted *everything*, and I was in his way; so he existed solely to make my life miserable, spilling milk on my drawings, 'accidentally' knocking ink into my aquarium and poisoning the fish. His answer to anything I did back was 'I'll tell. You wait. I'll tell.'

"Once, when I was 14 or so—that would have made him 9½— I'd had enough, and we were alone in the house for several hours, so I locked him in a closet. I heard him pounding and threatening to tell, then sobbing, then pleading, and finally there was silence, which suited me just fine. But shortly before our parents got home, I had to let him out. He stank. He'd had an accident in his pants. He was red-faced but, for once, very, very quiet.

" 'I'll get you,' was all he said."

Here we have, in the space of 700 words, what might be called the first *movement* of a story, a whole barrage of hurled bricks, which take us deeply into the rather labyrinthine plot of what is only a 3,400-word tale.

Introduction. The narrator, Jeffrey Quilt, presents himself. Point of view is established: Quilt is narrating, in the first person. He is telling how he told a story to an unnamed character, whose own life has clearly been disrupted already. The other character is coming to Quilt under extraordinary, stressful circumstances, for some kind of help or comfort.

This introduction serves as what is commonly called the *hook*, the striking or unusual element that grabs the reader's attention.

(A word of warning: Make sure that your hook is actually an integral part of the story, not just an attention-getting gimmick. A story once came in to *Weird Tales* with the opening line: "Blood spurted!" After several more gory sentences, it became evident that the protagonist had cut himself shaving. This had nothing to do with the actual plot. The author, who probably thought he was being clever, was saying, "Well, now that I have your attention, I'll get around to starting the story now, maybe in a page or two when I feel like it." Not a manuscript we could take seriously.)

Premise. Quilt begins to tell the other man about the Outside Man, an allegedly traditional demon of truth.

Tone. There are already hints of a Faustian bargain, and of lurking menace, as the possibly sinister Quilt paces around in the darkness of the forest, telling this increasingly disquieting tale about a brother who died under mysterious circumstances.

Conflict arises on several levels at once. Quilt is manipulating his listener, who is increasingly irritated and demands an end to the "theatrics." Within the story Quilt is telling, conflict also quickly builds. The brothers hate one another. One day the routine is interrupted: The older brother, Jeffrey, can't stand it anymore and locks Stevie in the closet. This resolves nothing. It is very important not to resolve anything so early in the story. Instead, this action only makes things worse. Stevie vows dire revenge. Presumably Quilt is telling this story—of Stevie's revenge and what he (Jeffrey) did about it—for a reason, to illustrate something about the supernatural Outside Man, and about his listener's own problem, which will be worked out by supernatural means.

The initial disruption of routine occurs in the very first line. Perhaps Jeffrey Quilt takes walks in the woods every night. Perhaps he tells lots of stories. But he is saying, *Listen. This one is different.*

But all of the other elements that the beginning of the story introduces—the listener with the problem, the bargain with the Outside Man, probable fratricide—must tie together by the end. In a short story, there is no room for an extraneous motif. Therefore the opening must introduce *only* what is going to be crucial to the later story. It is, indeed, like an overture.

And if you can't find all these elements in your story's opening? What then?

Flip to the end. Consider the possibility that the brick you hurled at the end, the supposed climax of the story, may actually be the opening barrage of the story you *should* have written.

The Beginning and the End

The question remains: Is my beginning really a beginning?

All too often the amateur story *stops* where the professional one *starts*. This is a particularly common failing in science fiction, although it occurs elsewhere. The story builds up to an idea, presents it, then stops, as if the idea by itself were sufficient to hold the reader's interest.

A typical such effort might go like this: In a future where robot technology has made enormous advances, a man is barraged with advertisements from a firm that makes robotic duplicates of its clients—the very thing for the busy executive who has to be in two places at once, or for the cheating husband. He goes to the showroom and gets a guided tour.

The process is explained to him at length. He is startled and disturbed, and tells the salesman he'll think about it. He goes home to his wife. As he is lying awake beside her in bed, the worst implication sinks in: *How can he tell who's human and who isn't?* Why, his very wife, lying beside him, might be . . . Unable to resist, he gets out a stethoscope, places it very gently against his sleeping spouse—and listens to the mechanical whirring of her heart. The End.

My standard advice to writers who have produced such efforts is this: Write a sequel, in which all the characters know and take for granted what happened in the original story, then throw out the original.

Why? Because the brick wasn't thrown until the end. That supposed ending is really a *beginning*. The story introduces characters, premise, setting, tone and even conflict—but only at the climax. Nothing is resolved, completed or closed off. The hurled brick came when the man discovered that his wife was a robot, and that, by implication, society may be infiltrated with robots masquerading as people.

Now what? How does he cope? Not surprisingly, when Ray Bradbury wrote a story along similar lines ("Marionettes Incorporated"), the plot spun out from that point. He didn't build up to—surprise!—the idea that people might be impersonated by robots on a commercial basis.

Instead, he *started* with it.

One can only repeat the advice from *Alice in Wonderland*. Start at the beginning, go on to the end, then stop.

The essential thing, literally the *first* thing you must figure out, is precisely where the beginning *begins*.

Look for the hurled brick.

DARRELL SCHWEITZER is the editor of *Worlds of Fantasy and Horror* magazine (formerly *Weird Tales*), for which he shared a World Fantasy Award (with George Scithers) in 1992. His novella, "To Become a Sorcerer" was also a finalist that year, but didn't win. (But don't blame it on the novella's opening: It was brilliant.)

Markets for Short Fiction

Marketing Your Short Fiction

A glance at the magazine shelf of your local bookstore may tell you a great deal about the growth of the modern speculative fiction market. Just a few years ago, the only magazines you were likely to find there were *Analog Science Fiction and Fact*, *Isaac Asimov's Science Fiction Magazine* and perhaps one or two others. Most likely, you had to dig to find them, since they tended to get buried under the copies of *People*, *Time*, *Good Housekeeping*, etc. The digest-sized magazines were especially vulnerable to this, since the front rack of the magazine shelf was for the top-selling titles, not "those little sci-fi things."

Now, however, speculative fiction magazines have grown in number, size and circulation. While still digest-sized, *Analog* and *Asimov's* have found their way to the front rack and are accompanied by large, glossy, colorful magazines like *Realms of Fantasy* and *Science Fiction Age*. A good bookstore might even carry smaller, semi-pro magazines that before you would have only been able to get by subscription or at conventions.

While all this is great news for the genre in general, it also means that more people are writing science fiction and fantasy as well as reading it. Editors are receiving 100-200 manuscripts *per week* in some cases, which means your story has to really stand out on the first page in order to have a chance. Readers and editors are demanding more literary stories, more originality and more accuracy than ever before. And since this type of demand is also impacting the publishers, book editors there are looking at a writer's short-story track record when considering his novel submission.

Sound like a Catch-22? It's not, really, if you know how to market your work effectively. It just takes preparation, professionalism and persistence.

Preparation

Preparation means knowing where to submit before you start sending your work out. More than anything, editors say to know their magazine and know the type of fiction published in it. Submitting something completely inappropriate wastes both the editor's time and your time, and gives you an unnecessary rejection when you might have made a sale elsewhere. The listings in this book will give you an idea of where to start your market research, but nothing replaces actually reading a few issues of the magazine before submitting.

In your preparation, don't fall into the topic trap. Just because there are three dog-based stories in the two issues you've read, doesn't mean you need to write a dog-based story. For one thing, the editor has probably had her fill of dog-based stories and doesn't want anymore. For another, you are trying to find a magazine that fits your work, not a magazine to fit your work to.

In addition to reading magazines, you can research the market in other ways. Trade journals such as *Locus* and *Science Fiction Chronicle* are regular sources of information on new markets, closed markets and more. They'll give you news on conventions, book deals, reviews and other data that will keep you updated on what's happening in your field (see page 451 for a list of **Nonfiction Magazines & Publications of Interest**).

Online bulletin boards, webpages and such are also good ways of keeping up on market news and can be useful networking tools, as well. Many sf and fantasy writers and editors are online, participating in regularly-scheduled chat sessions, answering questions through bulletin boards, maintaining websites for information and reader response and so on. Be professional when using such resources, however. Just because you can't see the person on the other end doesn't mean he'll forgive you for being rude and pushy, and bad manners can quickly give you a bad reputation and hurt your career. Courtesy is key and can go a long way in helping you to get your foot in the publication door (more information on **Online Resources** can be found on page 417).

Conventions are another way of researching the market and meeting professionals. Courtesy and professionalism are even more important in this arena, since you will actually meet with authors, editors and agents face to face. These professionals usually will be on a panel or two, giving you the chance to ask them questions without fear; if they're on a panel, they expect and want questions. They may even be open to your asking them a question or two in the hallway after the panel (see page 430 for a listing of **Conventions**). Many people advise treating a convention like you would a job interview, and that's not a bad idea. While putting on a suit and tie may be a bit much (especially if other fans are dressed as Klingons and barbarians), wearing a nice shirt or blouse and slacks or a skirt will make you stand out from the fans in t-shirts and jeans. And just as you wouldn't barge into a prospective employer's office, also don't barge in on a conversation or a meal or other such private moments. Finally, unless there's a workshop or critique panel at the convention, don't try to get your manuscript read. It's a much better idea to introduce yourself to the person you wish to meet, ask a question or two, have a brief conversation if he or she seems receptive and then move on, perhaps giving a business card as a reminder of your name. This way, you can send them a story when you get home (with a brief cover letter reminding them of the meeting) and stand a better chance of avoiding the slush pile.

Professionalism

Whether meeting editors online, at conventions or through a cover letter, professionalism is important. Since we've already covered online and in-person professionalism, let's look now at how to make your letters and manuscripts look expert.

The first step is making your manuscript readable. Manuscripts should be set in 12 point type, double-spaced with one-inch side, top and bottom margins. They should also be free of errors and handwritten corrections. Single-spaced manuscripts or manuscripts with tiny type are not only a strain on the eyes, but impossible to have typeset. Even if an editor takes the time to read your story and likes it, he won't buy it if it can't be typeset. Generally, such manuscripts don't even get read.

Hand-in-hand with this are the basic rules of grammar, spelling and punctuation. If your manuscript is loaded with errors, the editor will assume you haven't taken the time to learn your craft and will therefore not take the time to read your work. After all, it's not her job to correct your mistakes. If you are not strong on the basics, take a refresher English course and find a critique group to help you out.

When printing your manuscript, make sure the type is dark. Use a fresh ribbon or toner cartridge in your printer. If at all possible, have your manuscript laser-printed. Ink jet printers can give blurry print and dot-matrix printers are even worse. If forced to use an ink jet, buy ink-jet specific paper (available in most computer or office stores) for printing your final draft. If dot-matrix is the only option for you, try making a professional photocopy at a print shop; sometimes they can make a dot-matrix manuscript look better.

For short fiction, a cover letter is optional. If you have nothing of substance to say to the editor beyond "Here's my story," don't bother. If you have published fiction in other legitimate magazines (i.e., not fanzines, newsletters or self-published ventures) or if you have experience in life that relates to the details of the story (i.e., you work at NASA and your story is about a NASA-related subject), a brief mention can be helpful. You should also include an estimated word count.

When using a cover letter, keep it short and professional, always including your address and daytime phone number (they'll most likely be calling you between 9 and 5). You may want to get a quality bond for your letters, or possibly even have some letterhead printed up. Avoid any frills; spaceships or unicorns on your letterhead may look spiffy to you, but in an editor's eyes it marks you as an amateur. Keep in mind that what the editor is really interested in is your story. The quicker he gets to it, the better (see our **Sample Short Story Cover Letter** on page 57).

If you want your manuscript returned to you, include a self-addressed, stamped envelope (SASE) as large as the envelope in which you sent it and with the same amount of postage. If the manuscript is disposable and you only wish a response returned, send a #10 (standard business letter-sized) SASE or a stamped postcard. Without a SASE, you will get no response and, again, you will be branded an amateur.

Persistence

If you can't handle rejection, you're in the wrong business. In writing more than anywhere else, persistence pays. Never stop writing and never stop sending your work out. Doubtless you've heard the common story of the writer who papered her bathroom with rejection slips before she finally made a sale; it's true. You will get rejected but you can't let it get you *de*jected.

The best way to keep your mind off of your story's fate is to finish another story and send it out. Most working writers have three to five stories out at once and continue to write more. When one story comes back, they send it on to the next magazine. You shouldn't send all five stories to one magazine, however, nor should you submit one story simultaneously to five magazines. Some magazines will accept simultaneous submissions, but most don't. If you do simultaneously submit, be sure

ANTHOLOGIES

Anthologies are another high-paying market for short sf and fantasy. For the newer writer, however, it can be difficult to break into anthologies. Most anthologies acquire stories by invitation only—the anthologist contacts the authors and asks them to write a story for the book. Usually, the authors are people the anthologist knows, either from working with them in the past or by meeting them through a convention or online service.

Most often, the new writer must wait for the rare open-submission anthology. Rarely do anthologies advertise for open submissions, due to the nature of the beast more than anything. Most complete their story selection process in less than a year, leaving the anthologist little time to get the word out for open submissions.

If you do hear of an anthology advertising for submissions, make sure the story you submit fits its theme; *Alternate Einsteins* isn't going to want an alternate Pooh story. Next, send at least two disposable copies of your manuscript. Often one anthology will have multiple editors, even though they aren't mentioned in the submission specs. Even if there is only one editor, that editor will still need to send a copy of your manuscript to the publisher once he accepts your story. Remember, the fewer excuses you give an editor to reject your work, the more likely you are to make the sale.

With your multiple copies, include a cover letter that briefly lists your publishing credits. List stories and books you have under contract as well as the ones you've already published. A brief bio on a separate page is also acceptable.

Finally, let your work attract attention with its literary merits rather than its format. Again, take the professional, no-frills approach in formatting your submission and correspondence; don't have spaceships, unicorns and such on your letterhead or manuscript.

Good luck!

Marketing Your Short Fiction

Geoff Sanders
443 Main St.
Norwood OH 45212

December 5, 1997

Margaret Fields
Editor
Outer World Magazine
3474 W. 50th St.
Brookside Park, IL 60633

Dear Ms. Fields:

Enclosed is my short story, "Lan's Soft Landing," for your consideration. It is 2,000 words and would fit well into your "Outer World Voices" short story feature.

As a professional anthropologist, my studies have taken me to South America, the setting for much of this story, and my research into both South American and West African cultures has helped me depict the fictional tribe my protagonist meets in "Lan's Soft Landing."

I look forward to your reply. I've enclosed a SASE for your convenience. Thanks for your consideration.

Sincerely,

Geoff Sanders
(513)555-5555

Encl.: Manuscript
        SASE

Sample Short Story Cover Letter

to let the other editors considering your manuscript know if your story is accepted and no longer available for consideration.

As they say, waiting is the hardest part. We've asked editors to give us their average response time, but keep in mind that it is just that—an average. Give them about three weeks past their reported response time before sending a *polite* follow-up letter. Chances are, they're swamped or behind schedule, and a courteous letter may prompt them to pick up your manuscript.

The Final "P"–Publication

Hopefully, your work will pass muster and be accepted. You may receive in payment a complimentary copy or a nice fat check. Newer writers often feel a publishing credit is payment enough, and publication in non-paying markets can help you gain experience and get your work noticed. So remember: preparation, professionalism and persistence pay!

Primary Short Fiction Markets

L isted in this section are the commercial magazines that publish science fiction and fantasy. Some are devoted entirely to fiction, while others publish one or two stories each issue, but have become known for publishing the best in the field. We've also included some of the promising, professional-looking newcomers in the field.

The markets in this section include detailed interviews with the editors and examine their philosophies and how they approach their work. We asked the editors about the history of their magazines and how they came to work for them. The editors told us a little about their own influences and what authors or books got them interested in science fiction. Knowing this "inside" information can help you determine exactly which editors to target with *your* manuscript.

From there we asked about what they look for in a manuscript, what to avoid and what they'd advise new writers to do. To help you choose which publisher will be most receptive to your work, each interview includes a detailed description of the publication and the type of science fiction and fantasy included within its pages.

Before each interview, we've included brief information on the magazine's date of establishment, circulation, frequency, size and number of pages. This information will help you get a feel for the audience and prestige of the magazine. For example, newer magazines are often the most open to the work of new writers. Slick, glossy magazines with large circulations have more prestige (and more money to spend on manuscripts), but it may be harder for the new writer to break in there.

Next, we've included a list of the subgenres that interest the editor. These will help you identify those magazines most likely to be interested in the type of science fiction stories you write. Read the interview and a few issues of the magazine to get a more complete picture of the kinds of material published in each.

After the profile, you'll find specific information on how to contact the magazine and how to submit your short story. If a magazine is open to simultaneous submissions, we've noted it. If you send a story to several publications and it is purchased by one of them, be sure to inform all the editors who are considering your story that it is no longer available. We've also indicated if electronic submissions are acceptable, but check with the magazine to make sure your disk and program are compatible—and be sure to include a hard copy.

Reporting times are given, but keep in mind these are estimates. Allow an additional three or four weeks before checking on the status of your submission. Include a self-addressed, stamped envelope (SASE) with your submission for a reply or to have your story returned. If you are sending to a magazine published in a country other than your own, include International Reply Coupons (IRCs) instead of stamps. These are available at most main post office locations. In this section you will find magazines published in North America. Many more, smaller North American markets can be found in the **Other Short Fiction Markets** chapter (see page 110) and overseas markets are listed in **Overseas Short Fiction Markets** (see page 205).

For more on how to prepare a manuscript for submission to a magazine, see "Marketing Your Short Fiction," starting on page 52.

ABORIGINAL SCIENCE FICTION

Established: 1986 • Circulation: 12,000 • Frequency: Quarterly • Size: 8½×11

Contact: Charles C. Ryan, Editor

CATEGORIES
Cyberpunk, Hard Science Fiction, Humorous Science Fiction, Military Science Fiction, Sociological Science Fiction, Space Opera

After a two-year hiatus, *Aboriginal Science Fiction* has resumed publication. Charles Ryan, who has acted as editor, publisher, and business manager for the magazine for ten years, has turned the financial reins over to others and is now solely editor. "It's a move that allows me to concentrate on the stories and the magazine," Ryan says.

With ten to twelve stories in every issue, and only four issues a year, a beginning writer needs to have a strong submission to catch Ryan's eye. New writers are still a big part of *Aboriginal*, though, with up to half the spots going to previously unpublished authors.

What Ryan wants in a story is what he's sought all along: "an opening that grabs" and a story that does not waste "space, words, or time."

"I want just the most well-written, gripping science fiction," Ryan says. "I look for good action adventure stories, good space opera, humor, science fantasy, and hard science fiction. I don't publish fantasy, sword and sorcery, horror, or Twilight Zone-type stories." Specifically, Ryan wants stories that "will make unique use of the latest scientific theories and scientific ideas, yet still have lively, convincing characters, an ingenious plot, a powerful well-integrated theme and an imaginative setting. I prefer stories with tight writing and unique characters. If the plot is a road, I need interesting characters to walk along it with the readers."

Ryan is determined to maintain an independent editorial philosophy, despite what he terms "the homogenization of the genre."

"The business aspects of publishing are turning science fiction literature into a product," he says. "I prefer to let my writers reach and challenge." Ryan says he deplores the direction some publishers have been moving. "As science fiction becomes more mainstream, thanks to movies like *Star Wars*, some of its vitality is sapped. One of science fiction's fundamental roles is to challenge accepted beliefs, and this is being restricted as the audience becomes bigger and more conservative."

To fight this, Ryan not only publishes *Aboriginal*, but has also started his own small press book line, First Books. First Books grew out of discussions with aspiring and unconventional writers who had trouble dealing with the larger publishing houses. The press only works with writers well known to Ryan and *Aboriginal*—they do not accept unsolicited manuscripts. To date, First Books has published Kristine Kathryn Rusch's *The White Mists of Power*; *Quad World* by Robert Metzger; *Letters of an Alien Publisher* (a collection of "the pearls of wisdom shelled out by this strange visitor from another planet"); and *Conscience of the Beagle*, by Patricia Anthony.

"While it's unfortunate that most people are only familiar with science fiction movies, some have also begun to write, which can bring more quality fiction," Ryan says. "Diversity outside mainstream science fiction does exist in some of the smaller magazines and presses."

For those unfamiliar with *Aboriginal*, Ryan recommends reading several copies before sending a submission. The concept, after all, is unique; Ryan and his inventive staff created an imaginary alien publisher for the magazine. The alien publisher is an anthropologist, sent to Earth to observe humanity. Though the publisher looks askance at humans, it is fascinated by our literature, sending its favorites back to its home planet to entertain others of its species. Ryan and his cohorts intercept this signal to produce *Aboriginal Science Fiction* for themselves and all the other "aborigines" of Earth.

Although the magazine has undergone some changes, most of Ryan's columnists are still on board. Susan Ellison continues to cover movies, games, and television; Robert Metzger discusses scientific topics in his "What If?" column; and Laurel Lucas still covers the contributors in "Aborigines." The magazine also contains reviews of science fiction, fantasy and horror novels and anthologies, written by Mark Olson and Darrell Schweitzer.

As possibly the only science fiction editor nominated for a Pulitzer Prize (for investigative reporting of hazardous waste dumping outside of Boston), Ryan knows good writing, inside and outside of the genre. He recommends reading such authors as Robert Heinlein, Ray Bradbury, Isaac Asimov, Eric Frank Russell, Hal Clement, Larry Niven, and Robert L. Forward within science fiction and such diverse writers as William Shakespeare and Stephen Hawking outside the field. Other than that, Ryan has only two simple tips for beginning writers: "Write. Submit."

HOW TO CONTACT: Send your complete manuscript with SASE. They report back in two to three months. A sample copy is available for $5.95 plus $1.75 postage and handling and fiction guidelines for a #10 SASE. For reviews of anthologies or novels, send to Mark Olsen, 10 Shawnee Terrace, Framingham MA 01701 or Darrell Schweitzer, 113 Deepdale Rd., Strafford PA 19087.

PAYMENT: Pays $200 and two contributor's copies.

TERMS:: Pays on publication for first North American serial rights and nonexclusive reprint and foreign options.

ADDRESS: P.O. Box 2449, Woburn MA 01888-0849

PHONE: (617)935-9326 ✳

ABSOLUTE MAGNITUDE

Established: 1993 • Circulation: 9,000 • Published: Quarterly • Size: 8½ × 11 • Number of Pages: 96

Warren Lapine, Editor

CATEGORIES
Cyberpunk, Hard Science Fiction, Military Science Fiction, Sociological Science Fiction, Space Opera

"If you're a science fiction writer right now, you have a better chance of publishing than you've ever had since 1955," says Warren Lapine, editor of *Absolute Magnitude* magazine. "The short fiction market is the healthiest it's been since the Golden Age."

Lapine's magazine is evidence of this. In the three years since its inception, *Absolute Magnitude* has grown from a small press "zine" to semi-professional status topped only by the big four: *Asimov's*, *Analog*, *The Magazine of Fantasy & Science Fiction*, and *Science Fiction Age*.

Absolute Magnitude began after Lapine and members of his writers' group looked at some of the current magazines in the field and decided they could produce something better. Initially *Absolute Magnitude* was called *Harsh Mistress*, but "not enough people got the allusion to *The Moon Is a Harsh Mistress* by Heinlein." After receiving a number of "unusual" story submissions and calls in the middle of the night, the name was changed. Then, with extreme determination, persistence and "a few lucky breaks," Lapine was able to establish *Absolute Magnitude* as a premiere forum for science fiction. "We put together an attractive package," he says, including a professional layout, competitive rates for writers and exposure in a full-size, slick-cover, high-circulation magazine. The layout includes such touches as ending each story with a featured spaceship. The spaceships, which are different each issue, are created by Tim Ballou, one of the original members of the writers' group.

This package has attracted some of the brightest stars of science fiction. Recent issues of *Absolute Magnitude* have included stories by Hal Clement, Barry Longyear, and Allen Steele. Upcoming issues will feature Algis Budrys and Harlan Ellison. Artists appearing in *Absolute Magnitude* include Bob Eggleton and Kevin Murphy.

The sub-title of *Absolute Magnitude* is "Science Fiction Adventures," which reflects Lapine's attraction to stories with high drama and lots of action. "I like to see movement in a story," he says. "There should be more to it than just a couple of guys sitting around wondering if the world is right or wrong. If all that's at stake is 'feeling good' then it's not a story for *Absolute Magnitude*." Although he admits that he might occasionally let in a story that breaks those rules, he says that to do that "you've got to be really, really, really good."

"What I really like is the straightforward storytelling style of the Golden Age, but I also like some of the depth and scope of the New Wave." Lapine's view of New Wave predates such subgenres as cyberpunk and includes authors like Michael Moorcock, Samuel R. Delaney and Harlan Ellison. "I'd like to see a melding of the two styles," he says.

Lapine's current favorite authors include Allen Steele, Shariann Lewitt, and Orson Scott Card. Lapine's other favorites include authors he grew up with: Roger Zelazny, Frank Herbert, and Robert Silverberg, and "the classics"—Isaac Asimov, A. E. Van Vogt, and Arthur C. Clarke.

Absolute Magnitude actively seeks out new writers. Lapine says, "I have a newcomer's corner in every issue that is held open for a writer who is not eligible for SFWA." Not eligible for SFWA, the Science Fiction and Fantasy Writers of America, means a writer who has not had three professional short story sales, and has not published a novel.

Lapine finds his new writers in the slush pile, which he reads himself. While *Absolute Magnitude* receives 20 to 50 manuscript submissions a day, Lapine says that 90% of everything he receives "never has a prayer. They ignore my guidelines in some manner. I know what I want and I mean what I say in my guidelines. And people should be aware of that." Lapine also says that about three months after a mainstream science magazine comes out he will receive a deluge of stories based on articles in that magazine. "If *Discover* has an article on Pluto, for example, I can expect to get swamped with stories about Pluto." It might be wise for writers to avoid that trend when submitting to *Absolute Magnitude*.

Lapine attends science fiction conventions and he recommends that "any writer who is serious about making it in science fiction attend any one they can get to." He is quite willing to talk to writers at conventions. "I'm very approachable," he says, "But I don't want to go home with a bunch of manuscripts." He prefers writers mail in their stories.

As for general advice on writing, Lapine says, "Write as often as you can. Send it out. Keep it out. Don't spend a lot of time re-writing the same old stories. Keep writing new stories, so that you're getting better." And, finally, "Know what editors are after, know the market."

HOW TO CONTACT: Send your complete manuscript. Include a SASE. Simultaneous and reprint submissions are acceptable. They report back in one month. A sample copy is available for $5

PAYMENT: Pays 3-5¢/word

TERMS: Buys first serial rights.

ADDRESS: P.O. Box 13, Greenfield, MA 01302

PHONE: (413)772-0725 ✳

ART: JIM BURNS

ANALOG SCIENCE FICTION AND FACT

Penny Press • Established: 1930 • Circulation: 70,000 • Frequency: 11 times/year • Pages: 200 • Size: Digest

Contact: Stanley Schmidt, Editor

CATEGORIES
Cyberpunk, Hard Science Fiction, Humorous Science Fiction, Military Science Fiction, Sociological Science Fiction, Space Opera

---

Recently Published: "Teleabsence," by Michael Burstein; "Mona," by Addie Lacoe; "Paving the Road to Armageddon," by Christopher McKitterick.

Analog is one of the dominating forces in the field of science fiction. This venerable publication was founded in 1930 and has achieved a circulation approaching six figures. It appears 11 times a year, with a double issue in July.

The magazine is digest-sized, resembling a wide paperback book, with an attractive, glossy cover illustration relating to the feature story. The interior, however, emphasizes *Analog*'s focus on the written sf word. It generally consists of close to 200 pages of text, comprising a mixture of novellas, novelettes and short stories, as well as several columns. Editor Schmidt writes a column every month, addressing some topic of interest to sf readers. There is also a monthly "Science Fact" column, written by a variety of scientific experts. "The Alternate View" examines and discusses themes common to sf stories, "Biolog" gives background on one of the issue's contributors, and "The Reference Library," by Tom Easton, reviews a handful of books every month.

The fact that most agents don't deal with short fiction creates a perfect situation for beginning and aspiring writers, says editor Stanley Schmidt. Schmidt is committed to discovering new writers and publishes several every year. The most fascinating part of editing *Analog*, he says, is "the thrill of reading a well-written work by a new author."

The magazine, however, has room for only a tiny percentage of the hundreds of submissions it receives each month. Because the competition is so fierce, good writing alone is not enough, says Schmidt. "Many stories are rejected not because of anything conspicuously wrong, but because they lack anything sufficiently *special*. What we buy must stand out from the crowd. Fresh, thought-provoking ideas are important." He advises authors to familiarize themselves with the magazine without imitating the works within.

Analog is looking for hard science fiction, but Schmidt qualifies his definition of this subgenre of science fiction. To him, hard sf means only that science must be integral to the plot and that the story is plausible. *Analog* will not print fantasy. He shies away from the supertechnical connotation that hard sf often implies. He is definitely not more interested in machines than people—"the science should be smoothly integrated into the story." When asked how *Analog*'s content has changed during his tenure as editor, Schmidt says, "Our subject matter has evolved with new developments in real science. One fact I've been pleased to observe, though it's not a result of deliberate design, is an increase in the number of women writers."

Schmidt has been at the helm of *Analog* for seven years and has been consistently nominated as Best Professional Editor by the Hugo Awards. Of his early interest in sf, he says, "My father recommended several stories when I was about nine; I read them and was hooked. My influences include John W. Campbell, Robert A. Heinlein, Isaac Asimov, A.E. van Vogt, Poul Anderson, Clifford D. Simak and Gordon R. Dickson. Among newer writers, I enjoy Michael F. Flynn, Harry Turtledove and W.R. Thompson."

Schmidt did his undergraduate work at the University of Cincinnati and then received his Ph.D. in physics from Case Western Reserve University in 1969. From then until 1978, he taught physics, astronomy and science fiction at Heidelberg College in Ohio. He left his tenured position because "editing *Analog* sounded like too much fun to pass up."

Schmidt began writing science fiction in 1968. To date, he has written four novels and dozens of short stories. His most recent novel, *Tweedli-oop*, was published in 1986. Schmidt describes the book as "a hard sf tale of an alien marooned on earth with the misfortune to look like something that belongs here." He has also been involved with a dozen or so anthologies, his favorite being *Analog's Golden Anniversary Anthology*, published in 1980. He has also written several articles for *Writer's Digest*, and coedited *Writing Science Fiction and Fantasy*, which appeared in 1991. His latest book is *Aliens and Alien Societies*, a comprehensive guide for writers who want to populate their works and worlds with extraterrestrial life-forms.

On current trends in sf, Schmidt comments, "A disturbing one I've been seeing for some time and would like to see go away is a tendency to treat science fiction and fantasy as if there's no real difference between them. I like both, but they are *not* the same and it's important to know which you're doing."

You can catch Schmidt out and about at various science fiction conventions. He tries to hit three a year, he says, including the WorldCon and others scattered geographically around the country.

HOW TO CONTACT: Send your complete manuscript with SASE. Include a cover letter with "anything that I need to know before reading the story. For example, if it's a rewrite I suggested or that it incorporates copyrighted material, say it. Otherwise, no cover letter is needed." Only query with SASE on serials. Schmidt reports back in one month and does not accept simultaneous submissions. Fiction guidelines are available for SASE, and a sample copy is $3.50. Send books for review to Tom Easton.

PAYMENT: Pays 5-8¢/word.

TERMS: Pays on acceptance for first North American serial rights and nonexclusive foreign rights.

ADDRESS: 1270 Avenue of the Americas, 10th Floor, New York NY 10020

PHONE: (212)782-8564

E-MAIL: 71154.662@compuserve.com (For correspondence only—not submissions.) ✳

 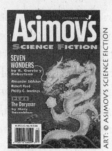

ASÍMOV'S SCÍENCE FÍCTÍON

Penny Press • Circulation: 59,000 • Frequency: 11 times/year • Pages: 175 • Size: Digest

Contact: Gardner Dozois, Editor

CATEGORIES

Cyberpunk, Dark Fantasy, Hard Science Fiction, High Fantasy, Military Science Fiction, Sociological Science Fiction, Space Opera, Traditional Fantasy

Gardner Dozois is a model for hopeful writers of science fiction—he has been writing and publishing for 30 years. In 1966 he was 18 years old and stationed with the army in Fort Dix, New Jersey when he made his first fiction sale. Since then he has published over 30 anthologies and written two novels and three collections of science fiction stories. The editor of *Asimov's Science Fiction*, he is the recipient of six Hugo Awards for Best Professional Editor.

Dozois became the editor of *Asimov's* in 1985, after a seven-year hiatus from working on the magazine. During his absence from *Asimov's*, he began an annual anthology series entitled *The Year's Best Science Fiction*, by St. Martin's Press, which is in its eleventh issue this year. In 1983 and 1984, he received two Nebula Awards for his own short stories. "I guess on the strength of my writing sales and other editorial experience they essentially tapped me to take over the editor's job at *Asimov's* in 1985," he says.

Asimov's Science Fiction is a digest-sized magazine published 13 times a year, but includes 15 issues worth of material—two double-size issues come out in April and November, at about 320 pages each. Standard-size issues run about 175 pages each. *Asimov's* has several features each month, including a Guest Editorial column. The column was formerly written by the magazine's namesake, Isaac Asimov, and has included Geoffrey A. Landis, Pat Cadigan and Michael Swanwick among others. Also, the magazine includes a book review section, illustrations, poetry, and a listing of science fiction conventions in each issue.

The magazine was the recipient of the Locus Award for Best Magazine in 1993, and its writers have won 22 Hugos and 21 Nebula Awards. Its founder, Isaac Asimov, was, according to Dozois, "perhaps one of the most famous science fiction writers of the last half of the twentieth century." Asimov is the author of hundreds of books, among them *Foundation's Edge* and his final novel before his death last year, *Forward the Foundation*. Dozois encourages writers to read the words of legendary science fiction writers and cautions, "If you're not aware of what has gone on, you really put a handicap on yourself."

Dozois has specific advice for beginning writers—be familiar with current works of science fiction. "If you're not familar with science fiction," he says, "you'll spend your time reinventing the wheel instead of progressing." He suggests subscribing to science fiction magazines and reading voraciously. Homework may involve studying a variety of subjects that could spark a science fiction story, including archaeology, history, natural science and astronomy.

Perhaps the most critical piece of advice Dozois can offer is to persevere. "Many people have sort of a fantasy idea of what the writing life is meant to be, but unfortunately the writing life in reality is not a series of gentle encouragements, balms to soothe your ego; it's more often like a series of kicks in the teeth," he advises. But his realistic view is not meant to be discouraging. "Those writers who have the strength of spirit and strength to persevere are to some extent more likely to make it as professional writers," he adds.

Asimov's publishes a broad range of science fiction. It is more likely to publish hard science, sociological science fiction or cyberpunk than high fantasy. But Dozois is diplomatic. "I won't rule it out because if a story is extraordinary enough in quality, then we'll certainly give it serious consideration no matter what subgenre you can pigeonhole it into."

Although *Asimov's* is selective, Dozois is careful not to completely exclude anything, even clichéd stories. "There's the Adam and Eve story or the story where it all turns out to be a computer game or simulation of some sort. I hesitate to say that I'm tired of anything though because it's my experience that as soon as I say I don't want to see a certain kind of story because it's too clichéd, some writer of genius takes it and turns it on its ear, does something worthwhile with it," he says.

Asimov's will review unsolicited manuscripts, although it is more likely that established writers will be published. Dozois and three other readers review all manuscripts, selecting about 10 percent to publish. Dozois sections the manuscripts into a "pro" pile comprised of known writers, a "semipro" pile and the slush pile. "I'm pretty generous with my definition of semipro," he adds. Dozois reads the top two piles, and three other readers review slush pile submissions, passing favored stories to him.

Dozois stands firm that the future of science fiction depends on the steady influx of new writers. "It's the nature of the science fiction business that we're losing people off the top end," he says, because well-known writers become recognized by agents, sign novel contracts, and cease writing short fiction. He has good news for novices—science fiction is in healthy condition, and, in comparison to many literary fields, it is fairly easy to break into.

Dozois offers a trick of the trade that can keep a hopeful writer from going in circles: Avoid weak, passive beginnings. "Grab the reader's interest—the best way to do this is to start with people. If you involve the reader in the characters in the first page or so, then usually they are willing to stick with those characters if they find them interesting. There's no writing rule that doesn't have exceptions to it, but that's a rule that's true more often than not," he says.

As for the future of *Asimov's Science Fiction*, Dozois has a vision—he wants to see it break into new markets. Although *Asimov's* is sold on some newsstands and in chain bookstores, he would like to see it appear in college and military PX stores.

Dozois makes a trip once a week to his New York office, but lives in Pennsylvania, his home for the past 23 years. He is the editor of three recent works from St. Martin's Press: *Modern Classics of Science Fiction*, *Modern Classic Short Novels of Science Fiction*, and *The Year's Best Science Fiction 11th Annual Collection*. His latest work of fiction is entitled *Geodesic Dreams: The Best Short Fiction of Gardner Dozois*, from Ace.

HOW TO CONTACT: Send your complete manuscript with SASE. No simultaneous submissions are accepted. They report back in 1-2 months. Fiction guidelines are available for SASE and a sample copy for $3.50 plus a 9×12 SASE. Send anthologies and books to the book reviewer.

PAYMENT: Pays 6-8¢/word up to 7,500 words, 5¢/word for stories over 12,500 words, and $450 for those in between.

TERMS: Pays on acceptance for first North American serial rights plus specified foreign rights, as explained in the contract. They rarely buy reprints. Sends galleys to author.

ADDRESS: 1270 Avenue of the Americas, 10th Floor, New York NY 10020

E-MAIL: 71154.662@compuserve.com ✳

ART: ALICIA AUSTIN

MARION ZIMMER BRADLEY'S FANTASY MAGAZINE

Circulation: 5,200 • Frequency: Quarterly • Pages: 64 • Size: 8½×11

Contact: Marion Zimmer Bradley, Editor and Publisher

CATEGORIES
High Fantasy, Traditional Fantasy

"Try to stop showing me how beautifully you write and tell me a story," Marion Zimmer Bradley says firmly. "That's the most important advice I ever got." And indeed, given the choice between a story with beautiful prose and one with a good plot, she'll take the good plot. "I have one rejection slip that says 'too much good writing.' Writing is not about beautiful prose; it's about characters."

That's what you'll find between the covers of *Marion Zimmer Bradley's Fantasy Magazine*—good stories with strong characters. Bradley started the magazine eight years ago after *The Mists of Avalon* hit the best-seller list and earned her "quite a bit" of money. "I discovered that I really don't care that much for fur coats or jewels, and I decided the best thing I could do was start a magazine." She likens herself to Melville's whalers who hunted their whale oil fresh at the source and always kept their ships ablaze with its light. "I hunt up the best stories at the source, and that's the fun of having a magazine."

Bradley is probably best known for her popular Darkover series, and for her aforementioned Arthurian novel, *The Mists of Avalon*. Living in California with her pet wolf dog, Signy, she has prospered from a writing career that began in 1952. That was when she published her first short story, "Fantastic Universe," for the pulp magazine *Venture Science Fiction*.

Ask her the secret of her success, and Bradley will tell you. "There really is a magic formula," she says, adding that it was given to her by Jerome Bixby when she was 22. "I never had another serious rejection slip." The formula, simply enough, is to remember that "Joe has his fanny in a bear trap and his adventure is in getting it out," which, she adds, is just another way of restating the old cliché "A likable character goes through hell and high water, overcoming all the machinations of the world, the flesh and the devil to win a worthwhile goal. And I only reject stories if the character is not likable enough, the goal is not worthwhile enough, and the obstacles are not high enough. Or, of course, if I'm overstocked," which is often, considering she receives on the average about 70 manuscripts per week.

When asked what she thinks of newer subgenres of fantasy, such as magic realism or urban fantasy, she replies, "Let's say that I don't use that kind of language in public." Bradley wants only well-plotted fantasy stories for her magazine, preferably without dragons. "It seems everyone in the field wants to write a dragon story, and I'm sure they all send them to me."

Cliché dragon stories and stories in which the reader finds out in the end that the protagonist has been dead all along are two of the types of tales Bradley has seen enough of. If a writer is going to submit a dragon story, it should be something new, like one of Bradley's favorites, "Dragon Three Two Niner," by Peter L. Manly, which she published in the Summer 1989 issue. Or like Charlotte Brisbon's "Virgins Are Best," from the Winter 1993 issue. These are stories that look at dragons in a new, and often humorous, light. The punch line of Brisbon's story, for example, is that virgins are best because they're easier for dragon hatchlings to chew.

Her advice to new writers is as simple and traditional as her publishing philosophy. "I often tell people, stop talking about what you want to write. Put the seat of the pants to the seat of the chair and stay there until you've written something." And then, of course, submit that something, and the next thing, and the thing after that. Remember that one rejection doesn't mean future rejections.

Also, Bradley says to remember that a manuscript is the writer's equivalent of a job interview. Just as you wouldn't go to an interview dressed in jeans and an old T-shirt, don't send the publisher a manuscript that is full of poor grammar and spelling errors. "One thing I absolutely will not tolerate is misspellings. Three misspellings on the first page and you're out. I am not going to have my staff spend their whole time correcting illiterate mistakes."

Although her staff helps her with some of the editing, Bradley reads all the submissions personally. It is her decision whether to accept or reject a manuscript. "I'm one of the few editors out there who enjoys reading slush," she says.

If you submit a clean, proofread, traditional fantasy story, there isn't much need for a cover letter. If you do include one, however, keep it short and to the point. "My absolute pet hate is the writer who tries to tell me the names of all his dogs and children before I've bought anything of his." And writers shouldn't use fancy stationery with hand-drawn stars and planets, Bradley says, "because I'm likely to write back and tell them to grow up a little."

But even such a rejection should not stop a writer from submitting again. "The trouble is, so many people send one manuscript and then I turn it down, and they're never heard of again." The first experience of every writer is rejection, so every writer must develop something like rhinoceros hide. "You have to be simultaneously very sensitive and very thick skinned." One of the most published writers in *Marion Zimmer Bradley's Fantasy Magazine* is Lynne Armstrong-Jones, and even her rejection to acceptance ratio is six to one. Perseverance eventually pays off, as many of the 40 to 50 new writers Bradley publishes each year can tell you.

It may seem like Bradley has a lot of rules, but that should not stop a writer from submitting. Best bets for new writers are shorter stories, because "they're easier to squeeze in" and therefore more likely to be purchased. Bradley absolutely cannot use anything that's longer than 5,500 words.

One look at the magazine and you can see why. The 8½" × 11" publication runs about sixty-four pages, into which Bradley packs as many stories as will fit. Issue #22, for example, had 16 stories, mostly by new or beginning writers; Bradley's editorial and her regular column "Marion Zimmer Bradley Talks to Writers"; a column by Rachel E. Holmen (who shares publishing responsibilities with Bradley); and half a page of letters to the editor. Although it has no interior color artwork, the black-and-white sketches are plentiful and well-done.

HOW TO CONTACT: Send a #10 SASE for guidelines *before* submitting a manuscript. Do not send simultaneous submissions. A sample copy is available for $4.

PAYMENT: Pays 3-10¢/word and 1 contributor's copy.

TERMS: Pays on acceptance for first North American serial rights.

ADDRESS: P.O. Box 249, Berkeley CA 94701

PHONE: (510)644-9222 ✳

Markets

CENTURY

Established: 1994 • Frequency: Bimonthly • Number of pages: 100+

Contact: Robert K.J. Killheffer, Editor

> **CATEGORIES**
> Cyberpunk, Dark Fantasy, Hard Science Fiction, Magic Realism,
> Sociological Science Fiction

"Start with the heart of the story. Don't waste time," says Robert Killheffer, editor of *Century* magazine. *Century* is a newer entry into the science fiction magazine market—its first issue appeared in February of 1995—but it is quickly establishing a reputation as a magazine with a difference.

With such authors as Jonathan Lethem, Avram Davidson and Michael Bishop exemplifying the type of stories published in *Century*, the first-time reader will notice that the fiction is difficult to pigeonhole. The stories are not traditional science fiction and fantasy; they defy such instant classifications as "hard science fiction" or "sword-and-sorcery." Instead, *Century* stories touch on several different areas—or create their own. "We avoid formula fiction," Killheffer says. "We are looking for an extremely broad spectrum of fiction. Don't try to predict what I'll like. I want ambitious work, work from deep inside the writer."

Killheffer established *Century* in part because of his work at *Omni* magazine, where he served as an assistant to Fiction Editor Ellen Datlow. Well-written stories with thoughtful and provocative ideas were crossing his desk, but the stories were not right for *Omni*. Killheffer noticed no other market was picking up these stories and was bemoaning this fact with Meg Hamel—now his co-publisher—when she suggested starting

Century.

Killheffer is currently receiving 250 to 300 manuscript submissions a month, of which only eight or nine can be published. On one hand, this makes for some pretty stiff competition. On the other, however, about half to three-quarters of the stories published are by beginning writers—either first-time writers or writers with few publication credits to their names.

"Our bread and butter is new writers," Killheffer says. And he is willing to work with writers whose stories he likes, often sending his opinions on how to improve the story. "We want to be writer friendly. Our contract is minimal; we pay as much as we can; and we want a good relationship with our writers."

Killheffer reads about one third of the slush pile personally, leaving another two-thirds to his assistant editor. Writers with previous publication credits will get his personal look, as well as any the first reader thinks warrant his attention. "Catch my attention, but don't go overboard with a hook."

Aside from the submissions he receives for *Century*, Killheffer does quite a bit of reading for his freelance work: He writes reviews for *New York Review of Science Fiction*, *Kirkus Reviews* and *Publishers Weekly*, among other magazines.

For a better idea of what kind of stories Killheffer is looking for, the best thing to do is read *Century*. He also suggests reading Harlan Ellison, Avram Davidson, Terry Bisson, Jonathan Lethem and Ursula K. Le Guin. "These writers are producing the type of material I'm looking for," he says. "They're difficult to pin down stylistically or in terms of theme. They can be read but not imitated."

"I want stories that function on a couple of different levels and don't play on a reader's knowledge of standard genre conventions." Killheffer says there are no taboos, as long as the potentially offensive material is necessary to the story, except for material that would not be accessible to a mainstream reader. "Don't rely on a reader's knowledge of old ideas, and their previous treatments. I want fresh ideas."

Aside from the previous mentioned authors, Killheffer advises all writers to read, "voraciously," in and out of the genre. He recommends Gene Wolfe, William Gibson, Kate Wilhelm, and Avram Davidson, to name but a few.

"Remember common sense and courtesy with your submission,"

Kilheffer says. "Editors are on the side of the writer; we want to work with you. A rejection of a story is not a rejection of you as a person. It is only one person's opinion."

HOW TO CONTACT: Send complete manuscript with a SASE. A sample copy is available for $5.95.
PAYMENT: Pays 4-6¢/word.
TERMS: Acquires first world English language and nonexclusive reprint rights.
ADDRESS: P.O. Box 150510, Brooklyn NY 11215-0510
E-MAIL: robkill@aol.com ✳

CRANK!

Broken Mirrors Press • Established: 1993 • Circulation: 2,000 •
Frequency: Quarterly • Pages: 80 • Size: 6 × 9

Contact: Bryan Cholfin, Editor

> **CATEGORIES**
> Hard Science Fiction, Humorous Science Fiction, Nontraditional Fantasy,
> Sociological Science Fiction, Surrealism

"Boredom" was the impetus for *CRANK!*, says Bryan Cholfin. "I wanted to see more exciting original short fiction. The larger sf magazines are too homogenized and aren't adventurous." Cholfin laments this "consistency of tone and lack of unique voices."

Cholfin dryly labels himself a "lit snob" who likes "an interesting prose style which is not flat or dull. The emphasis here is on imagination and literary quality. I am looking for science fiction, fantasy, magical realism and surrealism. I want to be startled by the writer's originality, prose, ideas and intelligence. I want to see big thoughts about weird things. If you can do all that and be funny too, so much the better. I'm probably more open to conceptually and stylistically weird stuff than any other professional genre magazine."

He is very specific on what he does not want. Cholfin likes "way out, surprising fantasy" but "stories about Dum-Dum the Dwarf and his Elf buddies aren't likely to get very far with me." He feels the same way about sword and sorcery tales. He intensely dislikes military sf à la Jerry Pournelle and David Drake, which he terms "war pornography." And no horror, which he terms "too boring for words."

To inject variety into the field of sf magazines, he started his quarterly,

CRANK!, in 1993. At the time of this writing, the sixth issue had recently appeared, and plans were well underway for the seventh issue. He prefers stories from 3,000 to 10,000 words in length, but says, "no story will be rejected solely because of length."

In the first six issues of *CRANK!*, a wide variety of authors have appeared in its pages—A.A. Attanasio, Carol Emshwiller, Robert Deveraux, Karen Joy Fowler, Gene Wolfe, James Blaylock, R.A. Lafferty, Gwyneth Jones, Ursula K. Le Guin (whose novelette "The Matter of Seggri" won the prestigious James Tiptree Jr. Award, and was also nominated for the Hugo and Nebula awards), Jonathan Lethem, Carter Scholz, Brian Aldiss, Michael Blumlein, and Michael Bishop, among others. Editor Cholfin last year won the World Fantasy Award in the Special Non-Professional Category, for his work on Broken Mirrors Press. The magazine now has a circulation of almost 2,000 readers, and is distributed into every major bookstore chain.

CRANK! is 6″×9″ and is 80 pages long. The covers are full color and there is no interior illustration. To attract high-quality submissions, Cholfin pays well: 10 cents per word for original material.

These generous terms attract between 30 and 50 submissions per week. Despite this amount of material and the desire to find breakthrough material, Cholfin says, "I have only bought a couple of stories out of the slush pile. There is simply not enough good stuff." Writers who include SASE will receive a response in less than a month.

Cholfin gets much of his material from authors he has worked with through Broken Mirrors Press, Inc. He founded the company in 1987 to fill a void in the larger publishing world. He publishes books by eccentric authors or brings into print offbeat works by established writers. He has published several books by R.A. Lafferty, including the anthology *Lafferty in Orbit* and the short novel *Sindbad, the Thirteenth Voyage.* Cholfin also recently published *BUNCH!*, the Philip K. Dick award-nominated collection of 32 stories by David R. Bunch. He has also published works by Gene Wolfe and Michael Kandel. Though Cholfin has no plans for more books, a reading of these limited-edition trade paperback or hardcover books should give you an idea of the kind of fiction he likes.

Cholfin has been reading science fiction since the age of ten, and has thousands of books in his personal library. His day job involves typesetting and book production for a legal publisher. He does not write, as he has chosen to devote his free time to his many publishing ventures. You can track him down at ReaderCon or WisCon, or write him at the address below.

HOW TO CONTACT: Send your manuscript in standard format with SASE. Cholfin will respond within a month. A sample copy is available for $5. Payments should be made out to Broken Mirror Press.
PAYMENT: Pays 10¢/word for original material.
ADDRESS: P.O. Box 380473, Cambridge MA 02238
E-MAIL: bmpress@world.std.com
WEBSITE: http://www.world.std.com/~bmpress ※

ART: JILL BAUMAN

THE MAGAZINE OF FANTASY & SCIENCE FICTION

Established: 1949 • Circulation: 52,000 • Frequency: Monthly • Pages: 162 • Size: Digest

Contact: Kristine Kathryn Rusch, Editor

CATEGORIES
Cyberpunk, Dark Fantasy, Hard Science Fiction, High Fantasy, Humorous Science Fiction, Military Science Fiction, Sociological Science Fiction, Space Opera, Traditional Fantasy

Recently Published: "Communion," by Gordon Gross; "Sisterhood of the Skin," by Arinn Dembo; "Acheter," by Jaquelene Hooper.

The *Magazine of Fantasy & Science Fiction* has been a respected voice in the science fiction field since 1949. Although the magazine began by publishing exclusively fantasy, its focus was later broadened to include science fiction. This widening of the magazine's scope has accelerated since Kristine Kathryn Rusch became editor in 1991. She welcomes works from all genres, especially those stories that "fall through the cracks, stories which are related to sf or fantasy but can't be exactly classified as either one."

Her primary criterion is strong characterization. Rusch loves to read about well-imagined, interesting people and to have learned something about humanity after finishing a piece. She cites the hard sf novelette "Remoras," by Robert Reed, published in her magazine in May 1994 as a representative example. It concerns a woman who lives on a space vessel surrounded by people who live off the ship as parasites in space suits. The characters were in no way likeable, she says, but were so fascinating and stunning that she felt as if she'd "been somewhere else, been transported into other people's lives. The stories I print must have this power."

Stories appearing in the *Magazine of Fantasy & Science Fiction* are frequently nominated for Hugos and Nebulas and have won numerous awards. Joe Haldeman's "Graves," a short story about a mysterious corpse in the Vietnam War, won a 1993 World Fantasy Award. The magazine also won two 1991 Nebula Awards. "Ma Qui," by Alan Brennert, won Best Short Story for his tale of the dead's fate during the Vietnam War. And Mike Conner won Best Novelette for "Guide Dog," a story about a human's role as a servant to a blind, insectlike alien. As proof of the magazine's eclecticism, Ed Gorman's "The Face," a horror tale about what soldiers see in a medical tent during the Civil War, won the Golden Spur, an award given to westerns.

The average issue contains from five to seven short stories and one to three novelettes or novellas in its digest-sized, 162-page format. The October and November issues appear as a double issue, with nearly twice the amount of fiction in 242 pages. Several columns also appear in the magazine, including Rusch's editorial comments on science fiction happenings or stories and authors appearing in the issue. Charles de Lint, Rob Killheffer and Michelle West handle book reviews. Janet Asimov and Gregory Benford examine important issues in science, such as a recent column on the history of science on computer networks. Kathi Maio and Harlan Ellison discuss the latest sf releases in film and television.

Beginning writers are encouraged to submit to the *Magazine of Fantasy & Science Fiction*. Some issues contain up to half the pieces written by previously unpublished writers. New writers are always needed to replace those writers snapped up by publishing houses to write full-length works. This continuum within the science fiction field leaves Rusch "always looking to fill empty slots."

She cautions all writers: "Keep up with current science!" She sees more and more stories that have flawed science or speculate about technology that already exists, especially in the area of virtual reality. She follows scientific news with avid interest—"I read *Science, Discovery*, and a good daily newspaper; watch the news and Science Watch on CNN; and listen daily to National Public Radio." She is also a frequent convention goer, attending from eight to ten a year. You can always find her at the WorldCon and the other large conventions.

The knowledge gleaned from these various sources has helped Rusch in her own writing. She states, "I am a writer first," but enjoys her view from both sides of the publishing industry. She received the John W. Campbell Award for best new writer in 1990. She writes in a myriad of genres, including fantasy, science fiction and horror. Of her numerous shorter works, her most outstanding is her Locus Award-winning novella, "The Gallery of His Dreams," which appeared in *Asimov's Science Fiction* in September 1991. Rusch weaves a tale of time travelers who take Mathew B. Brady away from the Civil War era so he can capture future wars on film. She has also published 12 novels, spanning the genres of horror, fantasy and science fiction. One of her most recent is the science-fantasy novel *Traitors*, published by NAL/Roc. It recounts the tale of Emilio Diate, the greatest dancer of his nation. When his family is killed by his own government, he seeks asylum in a neighboring land and conflict ensues. Her latest horror novel, *The Devil's Churn*, will be published by Dell in May, 1996.

Rusch notices a rather disturbing trend in sf: "Writers seem to be afraid to look into the future, to extrapolate trends, unlike ten years ago." She sees more and more stories set in the near future, which are often less daring. "What we need is courage," she states. "Authors need to take risks, to speculate more. I want to see common themes tackled from different angles, with imaginative interpretations of the future."

A positive side effect is that many writers look to the past for inspiration. This has produced "an upsurge in good fantasy," which Rusch certainly welcomes.

HOW TO CONTACT: Send your complete manuscript with a cover letter and SASE. They report in 6-8 weeks. A sample copy is available for $3 and fiction guidelines for SASE.

PAYMENT: Pays 5-7¢/word.

TERMS: They pay on acceptance for North American serial rights and sometimes request foreign rights or an option on anthology rights.

ADDRESS: P.O. Box 420, Lincoln City OR 97367

PHONE: (541)996-8211 ✳

OMNI

General Media • Established: 1978 • Frequency: Monthly

Contact: Ellen Datlow, Fiction Editor

> CATEGORIES
> Hard Science Fiction, Cyberpunk, Sociological Science Fiction,
> Contemporary Fantasy, Technological Horror

Omni is known for its accessible, yet highly polished approach to a whole spectrum of currently popular science topics, including science fiction. From 1978 to 1995, *Omni* was a large, slick, full-color glossy magazine with a circulation of nearly one million. In 1995, however, *Omni* ceased print distribution and became strictly an online publication. "Despite news reports, we are very much in business and publishing a magazine," says Ellen Datlow, *Omni*'s fiction editor.

Although the magazine includes just one or two short stories in each monthly issue, fiction is viewed as an integral component and it has been a part of *Omni*'s mix from the start, she says. Datlow came to the magazine in 1980, just two years after the publication started. With the help of a part-time reader who goes through the slush pile each week, Datlow has sole responsibility for the selection of *Omni*'s fiction, a job she seems to relish. It's also a job she does well, as evidenced by several Nebula and Hugo nominations and awards the magazine has garnered over the years.

Harlan Ellison's story, "The Man Who Rowed Christopher Columbus Ashore," first published in the July 1992 issue of *Omni*, was included in the 1993 *Best American Short Stories*, the first time an *Omni* story has appeared in that prestigious annual anthology. Yet, awards have not been limited to stories from established authors. For example, says Datlow, in 1991, Ted Chiang's first story, "Tower of Babylon," received a Nebula. The story, set in ancient times, is a mystical fantasy about the life of one of the builders of the Tower of Babel. Chiang came to Datlow's attention through a recommendation by Tom Disch, an instructor at the Clarion workshop, a writing workshop designed for science fiction and fantasy writers.

When asked how she would characterize *Omni*'s fiction, Datlow says, "It's sophisticated in style and in content, and we've always prided ourselves on that. In the past a lot of people said science fiction was for children. Well, it's not. I'm not talking about sex, necessarily, but what we publish is mature. Our fiction is meant to be for adults."

Beyond this, "it's a particular combination of language and a use of a theme," she says. Since she's been at this for a while, Datlow says, it's easy to become jaded. She can read through stacks of stories and find nothing that grabs her. "A story must move me. It doesn't happen that often, but a few of the stories I've published have moved me to cry. I'm always looking for a story in which the language draws me into it so that I become totally engrossed."

In addition to science fiction, *Omni* does include some contemporary fantasy and technological horror, although Datlow admits every editor she knows in this field would like to publish more hard science fiction. "It's really difficult to find a good science fiction story based on actual scientific principles. Unfortunately, many of the people who write that kind of story are primarily interested in the idea and are not necessarily good stylists—so it's really a joy when I find someone who can write hard science fiction and who also has very graceful or sharp, expressive writing."

Datlow receives from twenty-five to seventy-five manuscripts each week. She is first reader on solicited material and established writers, taking recommendations on other manuscripts from her reader. Sometimes it's hard to keep up. Although her guidelines say she'll respond in six weeks, writers should be aware, she says, that it all depends on what's going on in her office at the time.

The magazine's guidelines also say Datlow will consider submissions of stories between 2,000 and 10,000 words, but most of what she publishes falls in the 5,000- to 6,000-word range. "We did publish a novella, 'Mefisto in Onyx,' by Harlan Ellison, in October 1993 [which received a 1994 Edgar Award nomination], but this was very unusual. We wanted to do it because it was Ellison, but generally we don't publish things that long." While she's also published longer stories in two parts in the past, this, too, is something she does only on rare occasions. "It's just not fair to the reader," she says.

Before coming to the magazine, Datlow worked as an editorial assistant and assistant editor in mainstream publishing for about five years. This experience has served her well in her numerous anthology projects both in-house for Omni Books and out-of-house for a variety of New York publishers. Omni Books publishes anthologies every few years, Datlow says. The first two anthologies in the Omni Best Science Fiction series featured one-half original (from the magazine's inventory), one-half reprint material, but the most recent edition (number three) includes only one reprint and the rest original material. Another series is called Omni Visions and it features stories reprinted from the magazine.

Datlow is perhaps best known for the anthologies she's edited on a freelance basis. Although Datlow began reading science fiction when she was young, her first love is horror. This interest carries over into her freelance projects. She started doing *The Year's Best Fantasy and Horror* for St. Martin's Press with coeditor Terri Windling in 1988 and has just finished up the seventh volume in the series. The two editors divide the work into separate realms—Windling handles fantasy, Datlow handles horror. The pair have also just completed the second in their series of "fairy tales for adults" for AvoNova, titled *Black Thorn, White Rose*, the sequel to the popular *Snow White, Blood Red* (published first by Morrow).

In addition to these series, Datlow has edited several themed horror, fantasy and science fiction anthologies including two vampire collections, *Blood is not Enough* and *A Whisper of Blood* for Morrow and Berkley and the science fiction anthology, *Alien Sex*, published in 1992 by Dutton/Roc. In early 1996, St. Martin's Press published Datlow's follow-up anthology to *Alien Sex* entitled *Off Limits*.

Datlow finds stories for her anthologies mostly by word of mouth. She's found that she can't hold completely open solicitations because each of her anthologies requires very specific material. It works best for her, she says, when she has the opportunity to limit submissions to those active in the field and to explain in detail exactly what she does and does not want to see. This is not to say her anthologies are completely closed to the work of new writers, but interested writers should look for announcements on bulletin boards, in newsletters and at conferences. If a writer submits a story to Datlow that fits her criteria, she will look at it regardless of the writer's credentials. Writers, she says, just need to be sure to make themselves very aware of an editor's specific needs before submitting.

One way Datlow likes to keep tabs on the field is by attending conventions. "I think it's important to go to conventions. It's the only opportunity to meet some of the writers and let people know what you're looking for. I like to be on panels because you can try to get the audience interested in new things they might not otherwise consider."

It can also be dangerous, Datlow cautions, for a new writer to go to a convention. "You run the risk of possibly offending an editor, if you don't know the etiquette involved. I mean, you don't just go up and hand an editor your manuscript. As a matter of fact, when I've taught courses [she has taught at both Clarion and Clarion West] and whenever I've had the opportunity to speak to new writers, I try to give them a mini-course on author-editor etiquette. I try to give them an idea of what to expect from an editor and what is expected of them."

Editors especially like attending conventions at which the fans in attendance are avid readers of the genre. "Sometimes you can go to a conference and the fans are more into gaming or costuming—very dull for an editor to go to. I like to go to ArmadilloCon in Austin where the fans really read. I go to the New Orleans Fantasy and Science Fiction Festival each year, WorldCon and World Fantasy Convention, and I try to go to the World Horror Conventions as well."

Conventions give Datlow the opportunity, too, to talk to other editors and keep tabs on the field. She cautions writers to be careful about saturation in the market by certain trends. "I think the field is inundated with alternate histories right now. I would discourage anyone from writing alternate histories or famous people stories. Writers seem to be trying to take any piece of history just to redo it. There seems to be a rash of sf novels about Mars and novels/stories on nanotechnology, too. In the 1980s you had cyberpunk and an interest in the computer, but I don't think there's anything comparable now that seems to be exciting writers. Keep in mind that things like virtual reality should just be a tool; they should not be the point of the story."

Science fiction and fantasy writers are very fortunate, Datlow says, because of the great number of professional magazine markets. "It seems science fiction writers have more options than, say, horror writers. Short stories are crucial to the field in that they offer the writer a place to experiment in either style or content. In novels, you just don't have the time. To me short fiction is the most exciting form of science fiction."

HOW TO CONTACT: Send your complete manuscript with SASE. Do not send simultaneous submissions. Datlow will try to report within six weeks.

PAYMENT: Pays $1,250-$2,500 plus three contributor's copies.

TERMS: Pays on acceptance for first North American serial rights with exclusive worldwide English language serial rights and nonexclusive anthology rights.

ADDRESS: 277 Park Ave., 4th Floor, New York NY 10172-0003

WEBSITE: http://www.omnimag.com ✳

PiRATE WRiTiNGS: TALES OF FANTASY, MYSTERY AND SCiENCE FiCTiON

Established: 1992 • Frequency: Quarterly • Size: 8 × 11 • Pages: 72

Contact: Edward J. McFadden, Editor-in-Chief

> **CATEGORIES**
> Contemporary Fantasy, Cyberpunk, Dark Fantasy, Hard Science Fiction, High Fantasy, Humorous Science Fiction, Military Science Fiction, Science Fantasy, Sociological Science Fiction, Space Opera, Splatterpunk, Steampunk, Traditional Fantasy

When you're publishing a 72-page magazine, it doesn't matter whether 100 people see it or 15,000 people see it, the work that goes into it remains the same. It was this revelation that prompted Edward McFadden to take his publication, *Pirate Writings: Tales of Fantasy, Mystery & Science Fiction*, to the next level.

"I'd been doing the magazine for about two years," says McFadden. "And I just thought, 'Hey, if I'm going to do all this work, I might as well have somebody read it.' So, I started paying writers. I started soliciting big names. Naturally, the quality of the editorial material went up. Along with that, we put together a better physical package—paper upgrades, 16 pages of color inside. We really slicked up the product."

And what a difference it's made. In just two years, *Pirate Writings* has gone from a semiannual, 200-copy fanzine to a quarterly, standard-sized magazine whose glossy covers have borne the names of some of fantasy and science fiction's leading luminaries—Allen Steele, Algis Budrys and Roger Zelazny. The publication's readership is now close to 15,000, and it is recognized by critics and readers alike as one of the genre's top semiprozines.

One thing that has always set *Pirate Writings* apart, besides its distinctive title ("I do get people from time to time that think it's about Long

John Silver," laughs McFadden), is its tremendous breadth of content. The subtitle of the magazine says it all: *Tales of Fantasy, Mystery & Science Fiction.* "I've been a subscriber to a bunch of magazines," says McFadden. "At some point in my life, I've subscribed to all the big boys': *Analog, Asimov's, Magazine of Fantasy and Science Fiction, Ellery Queen.* One thing I found was that I never read them all cover to cover—every single story. I think very few people do." This discovery has shaped *Pirate Writings* since its inception. "My big thing has always been: You like fantasy; you like mystery; you like science fiction? I'm going to give you two or three stories in each genre. You don't need five magazine subscriptions. You just need one. I'm going to try to give you a taste for whatever mood you're in. We fit the mood of any reader at any time."

Something else that really hasn't changed since the beginning is McFadden's dedication to publishing new writers in the field." I do solicit the big guys; I do believe in the marquee value of having the big guys in the magazine (and on the cover)," says McFadden. "But on the flipside, I also make a tremendous effort to get the new guys in as well. The majority of the writers I feature are new and up-and-coming writers. I have seven to nine stories each issue—not including poems and short shorts—and out of all those only a couple are real big names. The rest is from relatively new people. I am extremely open to new writers."

Actually, it is in working with these new writers where McFadden gains his greatest satisfaction. "When I contacted Roger Zelazny for my summer 1995 issue," he says, "and we talked on the phone about an Amber story, I knew there was going to be very little editing involved. I mean it was Roger. It was going be great. That story wasn't a credit to me. It was a credit to him. Where I really feel *I* have an effect and what I really enjoy doing is helping these new writers turn something good into something that's great—whether by going through rewrites with them or doing the editing myself."

Despite publishing such a broad range of subject matter, McFadden's editorial policy is fairly simple: Write something that is entertaining to me.

"When it comes to fiction submissions," says McFadden, "I really don't have a lot of hard and fast rules about what a writer can and cannot write about. I don't have any crazy rules that science fiction has to be hard science fiction or that I won't accept time travel stories. I publish speculative fiction, and I am looking for things that are different.

I'm looking for new angles on old themes. However, I am a human being, and I do have personal things that I dislike. When those things come across my desk, obviously I am going to have a bias." So be forewarned, Adam and Eve stories, alien invasions and psychic cats probably won't go very far with McFadden. "I am sick of cats, I don't want to see cats. The cat's a mysterious animal so automatically people think they have to do some funky stuff with it." Also stay away from science fiction or fantasy romances. "I am not a romance-type guy. I dislike romance so much that I put it in my writer's guidelines." And please no monster stories. No vampires. No werewolves.

"There are a lot of great ideas out there that have been done a number of times," says McFadden. "All I ask is that you put a different spin on them. If you're going to write me a fantasy, don't write it about a magic ring, don't write it about a magic sword. Stay away from these overly-clichéd and overdone themes."

But, McFadden adds emphatically, it takes more than just a fresh idea. "You would not believe the stuff that comes across my desk. People have the seed of a good idea, but the writing is just incredibly poor. People don't put enough time in. That's what it really comes down to. People write and they're so enamored with their work that they don't have the ability to edit it. You have to go through and tighten things up. You have to pay attention to the structure of the story. That's what makes a good piece—not just a good idea. A good idea will not get you published. You have to do all the hard work, too."

With a very open submission policy, *Pirate Writings* accumulates more than 400 manuscripts a month. Assisting McFadden with the Herculean task of sifting through the mountain of slush is Associate Editor Tom Piccirilli, a novelist in his own right. With such a tremendous number of submissions—more than 1,000 per issue, one might well wonder, does everyone get a read?

"Absolutely," says McFadden. "All I ask is that you stay within my word limit (2,500-8,000 words), doublespace your manuscript and send a SASE. You do those few basic things and you're going to get an honest look from either me or my associate. And you're going to get a response in an extremely timely manner. However, send me a manuscript without a SASE and it goes in the garbage. Now, am I saying that every manuscript will be read from beginning to end? No, but attention will be paid to your manuscript. We know how hard it is to put your heart into a manuscript, mail it off and get it back in a day without it even getting a look. We have sympathy. That's why we don't operate that way."

HOW TO CONTACT: Unsolicited manuscripts welcome. Send full manuscript. Receives approximately 400 unsolicited manuscripts each month. Preferred word length: 2,500-8,000. Reports on manuscript in 1-2 months. Sometimes comments on rejected manuscripts. Writer's guidelines available for SASE. Sample copy available for $4.95. Subscription cost is $15 for 4 issues; $25 for 8 issues (foreign subscribers add $5).

PAYMENT: Pays 1-5¢/word. Additional copies available at 25% discount. Pays upon publication.

TERMS: Purchases first North American serial rights. Manuscript published 1 year after acceptance.

ADDRESS: P.O. Box 329, Brightwaters NY 11718-0329 ✳

REALMS OF FANTASY

Established: 1994 • Circulation: 44,000 • Frequency: Bimonthly • Size: 8½ × 11

Contact: Shawna McCarthy, Editor

CATEGORIES
Traditional Fantasy, High Fantasy, Dark Fantasy

As a child, Shawna McCarthy read fantasy novels by C. S. Lewis and Edward M. Eager and anything else that fell into the realm of children's fantasy fiction. At the time, there were fewer fantasy novels on the shelves than there are now, so when the fantasy reading ran out, she discovered science fiction. The first sf novel she read was *Podkayne of Mars, Her Life and Times*, by Robert A. Heinlein.

"The book was so cool I found more books by him and other sf stuff that opened up a whole new world to me," says McCarthy, editor of *Realms of Fantasy* magazine. "As a kid I didn't really differentiate between science fiction and fantasy the way people do now. Growing up I thought it was just all magical stuff—it really didn't matter to me whether the magic came from a machine or from a magic amulet."

Today it still doesn't matter to McCarthy whether the magic and wonder of a story fall under the category of fantasy or science fiction. "It's hard to rule anything out," she says. "There are things that I ordinarily think I don't like, such as real hard science fiction about logarithms and the boiling point of mercury, but even that can be done well by a good writer. It can be fascinating. As far as fantasy goes, I'm not all that fond of sword and sorcery and barbarians and standard quest fantasies, but again, those can be done well, too."

McCarthy pulls double duty: she's been editor of *Realms of Fantasy* since the first issue was launched by Sovereign Media in October, 1994, and she's an agent with the Scovil Chichak Galen Literary Agency in New York City. Her first job in publishing was as an editorial assistant for a magazine called *Firehouse*, a four-color, 96-page glossy. There, she found herself "reading science fiction under the desk." From 1978 to 1986 she worked at *Asimov's Science Fiction*, guiding the magazine as editor from 1982 to 1986 and winning a Hugo for her work in 1984. McCarthy then moved on to Bantam Books, acting as senior editor for the Spectra imprint until 1988. "I thought it was great that I could get paid to read science fiction," she says.

At *Realms of Fantasy* McCarthy receives roughly 60 manuscripts a week, too much reading for one person to handle alone. An assistant, Becky McCabe, reads the slush pile after McCarthy has culled the submissions for recognizable names and names of members of the Science Fiction Writers of America. McCabe returns stories to McCarthy that deserve a second look. From the manuscripts that she and her assistant select, McCarthy picks six stories to publish in each issue of the bimonthly magazine.

Stories that stand out for McCarthy typically have an exotic setting. "I've found myself being very interested in stories with settings such as ancient Egypt or the Mayan people or Eastern European gypsies as opposed to just the standard Celtic fairyland with the elves running around. So that will always get my attention, something a bit more ambitious than traipsing across the barren land to save the queen."

Concerning plot, McCarthy leans toward the ones that are fantasy and not science-driven, however, she reiterates that the line between fantasy and science fiction isn't always clear. "The Perseids" is a perfect example of a story the blurs the line between the two sub-genres. Written by Robert Charles Wilson, it was published in *Realms of Fantasy* and nominated in early 1996 for a Nebula Award.

"Readers could very easily argue that this story was a science fiction story because it has to do with what might perhaps be aliens, although, then again, they might not be," McCarthy says. "I decided to look more at the fantasy element than the science fiction element and publish it anyway because it was such a wonderful story."

McCarthy encourages writers to develop fresh story ideas and not fall into the trap of writing on worn-out subjects, such as the "little magic shop that suddenly appears and provides whatever miraculous thing it is the person needs and then can never be found again." Another over-done idea that keeps cropping up is the "basic general quest fantasy where they have to march across the hills to save the creeping darkness from the beautiful land of fairy." Stay away from talking unicorns and chipper little elves, McCarthy advises. "That stuff is old, but I'm not saying it can't be done."

Stories should avoid scenes that depict gratuitous injury to children, the one thing that McCarthy finds unacceptable in any piece of fiction. "It will probably be a really cold day in hell before I'd ever publish anything that has to do with harming a child," McCarthy says. "I don't think I could read past that and say the story has dramatic value beyond that."

Some stories are never read, and not because they don't measure up to McCarthy's criteria of what a story should be. "If the manuscript is not double-spaced, it doesn't get read," McCarthy says. "If words are misspelled, if the punctuation is sloppy, it doesn't get read." Aside from unprofessional manuscript preparation, what irks McCarthy is when authors send manuscripts via certified mail. "I'm forced to stand in line at the post office for half an hour to get their manuscript. That immedi-ately turns me off."

McCarthy does not actively seek new writers since they always find her first. One such writer is Noreen Doyle, who wrote "The Chapter of Bringing a Boat Into Heaven," one of *Realms of Fantasy*'s most popular stories. Another new writer, Judith Berman, made an impression with her celebrated story, "The Year of the Storms."

Writers can expect their stories to be professionally showcased in *Realms of Fantasy*. Like *Science Fiction Age*, which is also published by Sovereign Media, *Realms of Fantasy* is full-size and full-color with re-print cover art. The magazine sells for $3.50. McCarthy says the news-stand distribution is in the neighborhood of 50,000 with subscriptions hovering around 12,000.

Short fiction markets like *Realms of Fantasy* and *Science Fiction Age* are proving grounds for novelists. Unfortunately, says McCarthy, the market for short fiction is shrinking. "*Realms of Fantasy* and *Science Fiction Age* are the only two successful magazine launches in the last 20 years. Traditional magazines are losing their subscription base mainly because Publishers Clearing House decided not to carry them anymore. Few short fiction markets exist in the world as it is and I hate to see more of them go."

New writers of fantasy should still persevere, first by learning the basics. "You have to learn how to spell, punctuate paragraphs, organize, all the stuff in basic composition you thought you didn't need to learn because you were creative," McCarthy says. "The second most important thing is to read widely to learn what's being published and what editors like, since the scattershot technique is not necessarily effective. Read very closely. Find out why you liked or didn't like a story. Were the characters and plot convincing? You have to read very, very academically."

HOW TO CONTACT: Send manuscripts of up to 10,000 words to the address below (include return postage). Editorial guidelines are available for SASE. They report back in 4 to 6 weeks.

PAYMENT: Pays 4-8¢/word.

TERMS: Pays on acceptance for first North American serial rights.

ADDRESS: P.O. Box 527, Rumson NJ 07760 ✳

ART: STEPHEN YOULL

SCIENCE FICTION AGE

Established: 1993 • **Circulation:** 58,000 • **Frequency:** Bimonthly • **Size:** 8½ × 11

Contact: Scott Edelman, Editor

> CATEGORIES
>
> Cyberpunk, Hard Science Fiction, Humorous Science Fiction, Military Science Fiction, Sociological Science Fiction, Space Opera, Traditional Fantasy

Recently Published: "Just a Couple of Extinct Aliens Riding Around in a Limo," by Adam-Troy Castro; "Freaks," by James David Audlin; "Trizark," by Dana Paxton.

"I look for the best writing. When I forget I'm reading for work and it becomes reading for pleasure, I know I've found a good story." It's a simple formula but it seems to work. What Scott Edelman likes, the public likes. He edits *Science Fiction Age*, the publication named most successful new magazine of 1993 by *Locus*. As proof, its circulation stands around 70,000.

The formula works because Edelman has the experience to back it up. He has worked both sides of the field, as writer and editor. He started off twenty-something years ago in the comic industry where he fielded questions for Marvel Comics' "Bullpen Bulletins" (a new release and information section) and worked on *Captain Marvel* and *Master of Kung Fu*. He writes poetry, short stories and novels in the science fiction, fantasy and horror genres. He has even written a few scripts for Hanna Barbera cartoons and television horror anthologies such as *Tales From the Darkside.* One of his short stories was included in the *Best New Horror #4*. Other stories have been published in *Pulphouse* and the *Twilight Zone*, while his poetry has appeared in *Asimov's* and *Analog*. He also reads (when he gets time) the small press publications, attends conventions (like WorldCon where the magazine premiered), and personally reads the 500 or so manuscripts the magazine receives each month. With that much reading, and all the extra work of editing, "I've pretty much put my writing career on hold for the last year and a half," Edelman admits. "But it's worth it to be able to share a new discovery with my readers."

An unpublished writer might be intimidated. The first anniversary issue had cover art by Michael Whelan; original stories by Harlan Ellison, Thomas Monteleone and Barry Malzburg; an essay by Norman Spinrad; and an artist portrait by David Drake. Book reviews were written by David Brin and Allen Steele, to name but two. And the regular contributors to *Science Fiction Age* include Piers Anthony, Ben Bova, Bruce Sterling and Jerry Pournelle. In spite of this impressive lineup of big-name talent, the first story in the first issue was by Adam-Troy Castro who had only small press publications at the time. His story, "The Last Robot," went on to be voted fourth favorite short story of the year by readers of *Locus*.

Edelman stresses it is good writing with a professional voice, not a professional author, that he is looking for. Every issue has big-name authors, but every issue is also open to the first-time writer. There is no formula he's looking for, no character-driven versus plot-driven criterion that makes a story instantly accepted. "I skim the cream off every sub-genre and style," Edelman stresses, so a beginning writer has a good chance of being accepted here with any style as long as it is well done. Competition is stiff, with only six to eight stories being published every two months (the magazine is bimonthly), but fair.

So what should a first-time writer send in? The magazine is an eclectic cover of all science fiction, humorous to hard-core, cyberpunk to space opera. There is even a reserved space for one fantasy story per issue. There is no science fiction subgenre off-limits, but this is not an outlet for straight horror, unless it has a science fiction backdrop. Neither are any subjects taboo, within reason. Blatant hate stories and hard-core sex are discouraged. Stories' lengths run from 1,000 to 18,000 words, though 4,000-7,000 words is standard. If you attempt a short short,

Scott advises to stay away from pun endings and adds, "the subgenre is so difficult that most who attempt it fail."

And though fiction is the place for first-time writers to break in (no unsolicited nonfiction is accepted), *Science Fiction Age* also has professional, literate reviews of books, movies, comics and games; a science roundtable interview with three scientists (including such luminaries as Marvin Minsky), conducted by Edelman, in each issue; and thought-provoking essays on the science fiction field and people in it by contributors such as Jerry Pournelle.

In a field where magazines come and go with an alarming frequency, how does one know even a quality magazine like *Science Fiction Age* will be around? There are no assurances but a comparison by Edelman is very telling: "*Science Fiction Age* is what *Asimov's* would be if it were a full-size, slick glossy." The strong production values and impressive lineup of writers and artists should ensure that the magazine remains a welcome addition to the field for many years.

HOW TO CONTACT: Send your complete manuscript with cover letter, estimated word count and SASE. Edelman will report back in 4-6 weeks. A sample copy is available for $5, and writer's guidelines are available for SASE.

PAYMENT: Pays 10¢/word and 2 contributor's copies.

TERMS:: Pays on acceptance for first North American serial rights.

ADDRESS: P.O. Box 369, Damascus, MD 20872-0369

PHONE: (703)471-1556 ✳

PHOTO: JAY KAY KLEIN

ART: BOB HOBBS

TOMORROW SPECULATIVE FICTION

The Unifont Company • Established: 1993 • Circulation: 5,200 •
Frequency: Bimonthly • Size: 8½ × 11

Contact: Algis Budrys, Editor and Publisher

CATEGORIES
Cyberpunk, Dark Fantasy, Hard Science Fiction, High Fantasy, Horror,
Humorous Science Fiction, Military Science Fiction, Sociological Science
Fiction, Space Opera, Traditional Fantasy

Recently Published: "Doomsday Tours," by Michael Andre Driussi;
"Me and You and a Dog Named," by José de Hokkaido; "Were I You,"
by Mary Catelli.

Tomorrow magazine was started in early 1993 by Pulphouse, Inc., a
well-known and well-respected multigenre publishing operation run by
Dean Wesley Smith. It was an ambitious launch, and when it looked like
the new venture was causing financial strain on the company, the editor,
Algis Budrys, stepped in and bought it with his own money. The transi-
tion from the first issue published by Pulphouse and the second by Budrys's company, the Unifont Company, went smoothly, and when we
spoke, the editor-turned-publisher was putting together the twentieth
bimonthly issue.

When asked how he likes having total control, Budrys says, "It's a
very good feeling in many ways and it's unusual to be both publisher
and editor. I only wish I were younger. At 65 you're supposed to be
winding down, and instead, I'm winding up."

Budrys is not new to publishing or to science fiction. In fact, you could he grew up with the genre, although he detests the term "genre." His first exposure to science fiction came when he was very young through Sunday comic strips like "Buck Rogers," "Flash Gordon" and his favorite, "Brick Bradford and His Time Top." In school he read *Young America*, which featured reprints of science fiction stories, and later he read *Planet Stories* and the popular pulp magazines of the day. By age 12 he was writing stories, and he sold his first one to *Astounding* at age 21.

"When I found *Astounding* magazine, it was all over. I knew then science fiction was actually for adults. After I sold that story, which I actually wrote when I was 17, I've never looked back, and I've been writing and editing ever since," he says.

His first job in publishing was at a small book publisher, Gnome Press, and he went on to hold editorial positions at *Galaxy* magazine, the *Magazine of Fantasy and Science Fiction* and its companion publication, *Venture*. After a stint at the short-lived *Infinity* magazine in the 1950s, Budrys turned to book publishing and held editorial positions at an Illinois publisher, Regency Books and at Playboy Press. He left to try his hand at public relations and advertising for a time before taking a position as operations manager at a specialty magazine publisher, Woodall Publishing, an experience he says has helped him to understand the business side of publishing.

Although he had been writing and editing all the while, Budrys decided to go into freelancing full time in 1975. Until a few years ago, he also served as coordinating judge for the L. Ron Hubbard Writers of the Future Contest (see listing page 446) and edited an anthology of the award winners.

His writing career includes "too many short stories to mention" and eight novels. *Who?* was a near-future thriller published in 1958. *Rogue Moon* was published in 1960 and was considered ahead of its time for its matter-transmission and emphasis on the personal psychology of its hero. *Michaelmas*, about a computer-hacking electronic journalist, was published in 1977. David Pringle, editor of *Interzone* magazine, in his book *Science Fiction: The One Hundred Best Novels*, called *Michaelmas*, a "marvelously detailed and seductive novel." It was 17 years between that well-received book and Budrys's latest novel, *Hard Landing*, which was published in 1993 by Warner Books and was nominated for a Nebula Award.

Because of his experience as both editor and writer, Budrys has great sympathy for new writers in particular, and this carries over into his publishing philosophy. He's proud that *Tomorrow* features the work of many of the newest writers in the field. "I only publish one or two stories per issue by people who have more or less 'made it.' I've got a bunch of good stories in inventory by people like Ursula K. Le Guin and Norman Spinrad, but I like to feature stories by people hardly anyone has heard of because these people don't stand much of a chance [to be published]. There's nobody else publishing these guys in volume and they're very good—as good or better than many of the people selling science fiction, fantasy and horror today."

Budrys says the magazine's subtitle, *Speculative Fiction*, best fits the broad range of material he publishes. The term allows him the flexibility to consider all types of science fiction as well as other types of imaginative work, including fantasy and horror.

"I just sent a bunch of copies of the magazine to the World Fantasy Awards. There are quite a few fantasy stories in my magazine, which strikes me as unusual [considering his background and interests], but I think it's good. Every once in awhile I also publish a horror story. I'd publish more if I got more."

As for science fiction, stories feature a wide variety of currently popular topics from alternative universes to hard science to artificial intelligence. For example, one issue included a story about a deadly game of lacrosse set on future earth, one about alien-human relations, and one about the trial of a "very angry woman" on another world. What seems to tie them together is that each has a strong emphasis on character.

When asked about this, Budrys says "That's probably a component of whether I like a story or not. My own stories are character-driven." Actually, he says, he has only three criteria he uses in judging a story: "It should be well-written, have a consistent story line, and I should like it. I don't really have to know why I like it, but I can tell pretty quickly whether or not I do."

Budrys is open to work of all lengths and the magazine sometimes includes novel excerpts, serials, as well as one or two novellas and novelettes. The magazine also features anywhere from six to ten short stories, with an average length of about 4,000 words.

Although he used to receive 20 to 30 manuscripts a day, Budrys now gets five or six a day after he put out the word that he's been buying very, very selectively. His usual routine is to pick up the mail early each day, read every submission and reply within one or two days, barring his once-a-year vacation.

The editor says he's able to turn around material so quickly because he makes all the publishing decisions himself. "I read all the submissions myself. I consider that to be the most important part of my job. One thing I've learned from being around so long is most stuff editors do doesn't matter very much. What matters is you get a story in and if you read it and like it, you buy it. It can happen very fast, unless you have a staff of 12 who are sitting around waiting for the next meeting so each of them can have a vote. I think a story chosen by a committee probably reads like a story written by a committee."

His commitment to new writers goes beyond his publishing routine, however. He has used *Tomorrow* as a forum of sorts for his views on writing. Every issue for a while contained an article by Budrys on writing (the only nonfiction in the magazine). "I've taught at a bewildering variety of places, and I know how tough it is for young writers. I know how many wrong things they are told. I suggest, frankly, writers send for back issues of *Tomorrow*, or the resulting book *Writing to the Point*.

Although his writing and hands-on editing of the magazine take up much of his time, Budrys still manages to attend a few conventions each year. "I used to do more. I like conventions in places like Vancouver, Moscow, Idaho or even Los Angeles. Western conventions have a certain style, less buttoned-up than those on the east coast." His favorites, however, are Constellation in Huntsville, Alabama, MosCon, in Moscow, Idaho, and you usually can find him at WindyCon in Chicago as well.

HOW TO CONTACT: Send your complete manuscript and SASE for reply or return of the manuscript. To find out if you should send a disk submission, send hard copy first. Budrys will report back within 2-3 days, except in September, when he goes on vacation. A sample copy is available for $5.

PAYMENT: Pays 4-7¢/word plus 3 contributor's copies.

TERMS: Pays between acceptance and publication for first North American serial rights.

ADDRESS: P.O. Box 6038, Evanston IL 60204 ✳

WORLDS OF FANTASY & HORROR

Terminus Publishing Company • Established: 1987 (as *Weird Tales*) • Circulation: 6,000 • Frequency: Quarterly • Pages: 66 • Size: 8½ × 11

Contact: Darrell Schweitzer, Editor

CATEGORIES
Dark Fantasy, High Fantasy, Traditional Fantasy

Recently Published: "A Cup of Honeysuckle," by Kevin Andrew Murphy; "Hollow Bones," by D. Christine Benders; "Neighborhood Watch," by Duncan Adams.

Worlds of Fantasy & Horror has a very unusual publishing history. Its first incarnation began as *Weird Tales* in 1923 and lasted until 1954. It was resurrected in 1973-74, again in 1981, again in 1984, and it began its fifth and current incarnation in 1987 as a quarterly publication under Editor Darrell Schweitzer and Publisher George Scithers. In the Spring of 1994, the publication was renamed *Worlds of Fantasy & Horror*.

Schweitzer describes the magazine as "what the original *Weird Tales* would have been if it had been published continuously to this day. We carry on the tradition of the first and most classic fantasy-horror magazine in the world." He elaborates, "We publish a broad range of fiction with an emphasis on the fantastic. We don't want 'mad killer stories' or crime fiction, and any science fiction submissions must have strong elements of weirdness or strangeness. I want vivid, gripping writing; an original voice; and original ideas and presentation—genuine imagination rather than recycled clichés.

"There is a trend toward nonsupernatural 'dark suspense' mixing with horror," Schweitzer continues, "We're against that. There is also a ten-

...cy toward more ambitious and thematically complex fantasy. We're in favor."

The magazine is 8½″ by 11″ with a color cover and black-and-white-interior. A typical issue contains 66 pages filled with author interviews, three to ten book reviews by regular columnists S.T. Joshi and Douglas Winter, a handful of poems, and six to eight short stories by such noted authors as F. Paul Wilson, Ian Watson, John Brunner, Robert Bloch and Brian Lumley. This mix has proven successful, as seen in a stable circulation of around 8,000, and the reception of a World Fantasy Award in 1992.

Though *WoF&H* has a backlog of stories to stock the magazine through the end of 1996, Schweitzer welcomes submissions. He prefers stories to be between 2,000 and 10,000 words in length and offers this advice: "Read the magazine. Be familiar with contemporary authors like Tanith Lee and Clive Barker, but also classic authors like H.P. Lovecraft and Lord Dunsany. Avoid reinventing the wheel." Schweitzer, Scithers and several first readers handle the 300 or so submissions they currently receive each month.

Schweitzer advises newer writers to keep their short stories around 3,000 to 5,000 words. "Stories of this length are much easier to fit into the magazine. Anything shorter requires a great deal of skill. We do publish novellas occasionally, but they must be of exceptional quality." He will print accepted manuscripts within two years, "often much sooner," and usually comments on rejected manuscripts.

Schweitzer is himself a prolific writer of short fiction, with over 150 published pieces at recent count. He has also written two novels, including *The White Isle*, a fantastical story of hubris set in an imaginary land. He has long been involved in the sf/fantasy field, serving as editorial assistant at both *Amazing Stories* and *Asimov's Science Fiction* magazines.

He is an avid convention goer, attending around eight each year. He generally hits the "East Coast Circuit"—Boskone, LunaCon, Disclave, BaltiCon, and is cochairperson of PhilCon. He also tries to attend World-Con, the World Fantasy Convention, and the World Horror Convention.

HOW TO CONTACT: Submit your complete manuscript with SASE or tell them they can discard it. Include a #10 SASE if you want their comments. A sample copy is available for $4.95 and guidelines for SASE.

They report back in 1-2 weeks.

PAYMENT: Pays 3-7¢/word.

TERMS: They purchase first North American serial rights plus a nonexclusive anthology option.

ADDRESS: 113 Deepdale Rd., Stafford PA 19087 ✳

Other Short Fiction Markets

T he magazines included in this section can be divided into roughly four groups. Here you will find small press publications that deal exclusively in science fiction, many with a focus on a particular subgenre such as military or sociological science fiction. Also you will find magazines that are mostly science fiction and fantasy, but that also include some horror (many of these consider themselves "speculative fiction" publications). We've also listed some horror magazines that include dark fantasy and some literary journals that accept literary science fiction.

Each listing starts with basic information such as the date of establishment, circulation, frequency, size and number of pages. Newer magazines and those published frequently are most open to the work of new writers. After this information is a list of the subgenres that interest the magazine's editors. Knowing these can help you target your work to those editors most likely to be open to the type of work you write.

Next you will find a profile of the magazine outlining its particular focus and approach to science fiction or fantasy. Some editors offer specific advice to writers wishing to publish with them. Story length and the number of sf stories published in each issue are also included. Whenever possible we indicate how many submissions the magazine receives for each issue. If you compare the number of submissions with the number of stories published, it'll give you a good idea of the degree of competition at that particular magazine.

Some listings also include the names of recent contributors. When studying back issues, take a look at the work by these people to find out the kinds of stories that interest the editor. Following this information are details on how to submit to the magazine, whether it takes disk submissions and whether simultaneous submissions are acceptable. Some editors work actively with beginning writers and they will critique rejected manuscripts, so we included that information.

Reporting times are given, too, but keep in mind these are estimates.

Editors at small publications often work alone or with a small staff, so it is easy for them to get behind in responding to queries and manuscript submissions. Allow some additional time before contacting the magazine about the status of your submission.

Payment and terms are given at the end of the listing. Many small publications pay only in copies, but they offer new writers publishing experience—and this can help lead to publication in the larger, paying markets.

For more on submitting to magazines, see **Marketing Your Short Fiction** starting on page 52.

ABERRATIONS

Established: 1991 • Circulation: 1,500 • Frequency: Monthly • Pages: 64 • Size: Digest

Contact: Richard Blair

> CATEGORIES
> Articles/Essays, Contemporary Fantasy, Convention/Workshop Listings, Cyberpunk, Dark Fantasy, Experimental Fiction, Hard Science Fiction, High Fantasy, Horror, Humorous, Interviews, Magic Realism, Military Science Fiction, Reviews, Science Fantasy, Sociological Science Fiction, Space Opera, Splatterpunk, Steampunk, Traditional Fantasy

"No one who reads manuscripts here brings preconceived notions of what the 'perfect' *Aberrations* story is, so I don't expect a writer to either. In fact, any attempt to make a piece an *Aberrations*-type story is probably not going to work due largely to the fact that the magazine was (in)famous for its first couple of years as being a magazine of extreme horror.

While we still have no restriction on subject matter, we're also just as inclined to like a story that doesn't make any use of explicit material. Toward that end, sf/fantasy that takes some innovative chances with plot, characterization, structure, and/or etc., will definitely win us over, as will fiction that is, for lack of a better term, fun to read.

"One look at our per word pay rate will show that we aren't yet in a position to make a writer rich (and I don't think there's any short genre fiction market that can do that), however, we can give a beginning writer exposure on the newsstands and make sure he gets his work reviewed by the sf/fantasy/horror world at large. We give new writers an even break in that we don't have a sliding payment scale and have proven ourselves many times over to be more impressed by a story's merit than an author's name. Given our frequency, we bring more new and unpublished writers into print each year than just about any other sf/fantasy/horror magazine around. But by the same token, we don't cater to new writers and therefore don't see *Aberrations* as being a magazine designed solely to publish them. So while the playing field is even for anyone sending a manuscript our way, the competition is no less fierce. Which is how it should be."

HOW TO CONTACT: Unsolicited manuscripts welcome. Send full manuscript. Receives approximately 200-250 manuscripts each month. 1% of accepted manuscripts are submitted through agents. Preferred word length: to 8,000. Reports on queries in 3 weeks, on manuscripts in 16 weeks. Sometimes comments on rejected manuscripts. Writer's guidelines available for SASE. Sample copy available for $4.50. Subscription cost is $31 for 12 issues.

PAYMENT: Pays ¼¢/word and 2 contributor's copies. Additional copies available at 25% discount. Pays upon publication.

TERMS: Purchases first English language serial rights. Manuscript published 6 months after acceptance.

ADDRESS: P.O. Box 460430, San Francisco CA 94146-0430

PHONE: (415)777-3909

ART: PHILIP H. WILLIAMS

ADVENTURES OF SWORD & SORCERY

Established: 1995 • Circulation: 8,000 • Frequency: Quarterly • Pages: 90 • Size: 8½ × 11

Contact: Randy Dannenfelser, Editor

> **CATEGORIES**
> Articles/Essays, High Fantasy, Reviews, Sword & Sorcery, Traditional Fantasy

"We are looking for sword & sorcery, high fantasy and heroic fantasy fiction. We want fiction with an emphasis on action and adventure, but that is still cognizant of the struggles within as they play against the struggles without. As examples, think of the fiction of J.R.R. Tolkien, Fritz Leiber and Katherine Kurtz, but with 90s sensibilities. Include sexual content only as required by the story, but not excessive/porn."

HOW TO CONTACT: Unsolicited manuscripts welcome. Send full manuscripts. Accepts electronic queries. Submissions on computer disk should be formatted as Word 6.0, RTF, ASCII. Receives approximately 240 unsolicited manuscripts each month. Preferred word length: 1,000-8,000. Reports on queries and manuscripts in 1 month. Always comments on rejected manuscripts. Writer's guidelines for SASE. Sample copy available for $5.50. Subscription cost is $15.95 for 4 issues (payable to Double Star Press).

PAYMENT: Pays 3-6¢/word and 3 contributor's copies. Additional copies available at 40% discount. Pays upon acceptance.

TERMS: Purchases first North American serial rights. Manuscript published 1 year after acceptance.

ADDRESS: Double Star Press, P.O. Box 285, Xenia OH 45385

E-MAIL: dspress@erinet.com
WEBSITE: http://www.erinet.com/dspress/

AMELIA

Established: 1984 • Circulation: 1,750 • Frequency: Quarterly • Size: Digest • Pages: 176-204

Contact: Frederick A. Raborg, Jr., Editor

> CATEGORIES
> Book Reviews, Dark Fantasy, Hard Science Fiction, High Fantasy, Humorous Science Fiction, Military Science Fiction, Poetry, Sociological Science Fiction, Traditional Fantasy

Amelia contains "fiction, poetry, criticism, belles lettres, one-act plays, fine pen-and-ink sketches and line drawings, sophisticated cartoons, book reviews, and translations of both fiction and poetry for general readers with eclectic tastes for quality writing. We put no limits on sf writers as to content or style or genre. Sf writers could probably get stories published by us which other sf magazines would consider too risky."

Only a small percentage of *Amelia*'s fiction is sf/fantasy, but Editor Raborg would like to include more. "I want unique, avant-garde stories that are strong on characterization and plot/conflict. I want stories with natural narrative flows and believable alien personalities that do not ape sf masters. I would like to see stories that approach subjects relative to present times but with a futuristic slant—subjects such as gay/lesbian lifestyles and how they fit into the future of alien cultures. We're not really interested in futuristic politics. We would like to keep our stories on the close personal level. Above all else, a story must allow us to willingly suspend that disbelief. Our readers like to feel involved."

Amelia receives 160-180 manuscripts per month and uses up to 9 in each issue. They prefer stories from 1,000 to 5,000 words in length. They will usually critique rejected manuscripts. *Amelia* also gives a science fiction genre award.

HOW TO CONTACT: Send your complete manuscript with a cover letter, including previous credits if applicable and a brief personal comment to show your personality and experience. Also include SASE. They report back in 1 week on queries and 2 weeks to 3 months on manuscripts. A sample copy is available for $7.95. Fiction guidelines are available for SAE and 1 first-class stamp.

PAYMENT: Pays $35-50 and 2 contributor's copies; extra copies are available at a 20% discount.

TERMS: Pays on acceptance for first North American serial rights. They send galleys to author "when deadline permits."

ADDRESS: 329 E St., Bakersfield, CA 93304

PHONE: (805) 323-4064

ART: MAG

Established: 1984 • Circulation: 100 • Frequency: Semiannually • Size: Digest • Pages: 60-90

Contact: Peter Magliocco

CATEGORIES
Articles/Essays, Experimental Fiction, Horror, Humorous, Interviews, Poetry, Reviews, Traditional Fantasy

Art: Mag would like to see work that transcends its genre and concentrates on "universal human themes" prevalent in all great fiction. "We are an ultra-small press offering creative alternatives to writers and readers dissatisfied with commercially oriented mass market publications."

HOW TO CONTACT: Unsolicited manuscripts welcome. Send full manuscript with cover letter and SASE. Considers simultaneous submissions. Receives at least 5 unsolicited manuscripts each month. Preferred word length: 100-2,000. Reports on queries in 1 month, on manuscripts in 3 months. Sometimes comments on rejected manuscripts. Writer's guidelines available for SASE. Sample copy available for $5. Subscription cost is $20 for 2 issues.

PAYMENT: Pays 1-5 contributor's copies. Additional copies available at 25% discount.

TERMS: Purchases first North American serial rights. Manuscript published within 1 year after acceptance.
ADDRESS: P.O. Box 70896, Las Vegas NV 89170
PHONE: (702)734-8121

BARDIC RUNES

Established: 1990

Contact: Michael McKenny, Editor

CATEGORIES
High Fantasy, Traditional Fantasy

Bardic Runes publishes "traditional and high fantasy set in a preindustrial society, either historical or of the author's choosing. We think this is one of the few places that people like Lord Dunsany, Francis Stevens and A. Merritt could sell a story to today." Stories should be 3,500 words or less.

HOW TO CONTACT: Send your complete manuscript with SASE (or IRCs). They report back in 2 weeks. A sample copy is available for $4 or 3 issues for $10. Make Canadian checks payable to Michael McKenny, U.S. checks payable to Cathy Woodgold.
PAYMENT: Pays ½¢/word.
TERMS: Pays on acceptance.
ADDRESS: 424 Cambridge St. S., Ottawa, Ontario K1S 4H5 Canada
PHONE: (613)231-4311

BLACK MOON MAGAZINE

Established: 1995 • Circulation: 3,000 • Frequency: 8 times/year • Pages: 60 • Size: 8½ × 11

Contact: Armand Rosamilia, Editor

CATEGORIES
Articles/Essays, Dark Fantasy, Horror, Interviews, Reviews, Traditional
Fantasy

"Black Moon Publishing, Inc. publishes *Black Moon Magazine*, a horror fiction/heavy music mag, *Carnifex*, a death metal mag, and has several horror book projects in the works. We're always looking for new projects (magazines, books, newsletters, etc.) to work with. We generally cater to the twenty-something crowd, and look for traditional horror pieces. We aren't looking for wordy, pompous pieces; we're looking to be scared."

HOW TO CONTACT: Unsolicited manuscripts welcome. Send full manuscript. Accepts faxed and electronic queries. Receives approximately 30 unsolicited manuscripts each month. 10% of accepted manuscripts are submitted through agents. Preferred word length: to 7,500. Reports on queries in 2-4 weeks, on manuscripts in 3-6 weeks. Always comments on rejected manuscripts. Writer's guidelines available for SASE. Sample copy available for $3.95. Subscription cost is $28 for 8 issues.

PAYMENT: Pays 1 contributor's copy. Additional copies available at 20% discount.

TERMS: Purchases first North American serial rights. Ms published 3 months after acceptance.

ADDRESS: 1385 Route 35, Suite 169, Middletown NJ 07748

FAX: (908)517-1409

E-MAIL: loublackmoon@delphi.com

BLUE LADY, THE

Established: 1995 • Circulation: 100 • Frequency: Quarterly • Pages: 68 • Size: 5½ × 8½

Contact: Donna T. Burgess

CATEGORIES
Contemporary Fantasy, Cyberpunk, Dark Fantasy, Experimental Fiction, Horror, Poetry, Science Fantasy, Sociological Science Fiction, Southern Gothic, Splatterpunk, Steampunk

"*The Blue Lady* is a dark fiction magazine. I will consider any style story, regardless of setting, as long as it is dark in tone. Always include cover letter and SASE. Would like to see a list of [your] publications, if any, however, it's optional. Don't tell me about the story in the cover letter; let it speak for itself."

HOW TO CONTACT: Unsolicited manuscripts welcome. Send full manuscript. Considers simultaneous submissions and reprints. Receives approximately 30-40 manuscripts each month. Preferred word length: to 8,000. Reports on queries in 1 month, on manuscripts in 3 months. Never comments on rejected manuscripts. Writer's guidelines available for SASE. Sample copy available for $4.75. Subscription cost is $16 for 4 issues.

PAYMENT: Pays 1 contributor's copy. Additional copies available at 20% discount.

TERMS: Purchases first North American serial rights, one-time or reprint rights. Manuscript published 3-9 months after acceptance.

ADDRESS: 408 Townes St., #18, Greenville SC 29601-1642

PHONE: (864)233-3087

BONES

Established: 1966 • Frequency: Quarterly • Size: Digest • Pages: 60

Contact: Paula Guran

CATEGORIES
Dark Fantasy, Experimental Fiction, Horror, Magic Realism, Poetry, Splatterpunk

Bones is not interested in traditional science fiction or fantasy. "We do want science fiction that is too 'horrorific' for other markets. Unusual, cutting edge horror, or that which breaks new ground is welcome. Not interested in gore or violence for the sake of it; make sure it is in context. This is not a great market for beginning writers. We love 'unknown' writers, but the quality has to be topnotch. The competition is tough."

HOW TO CONTACT: Unsolicited manuscripts welcome. Send full manuscripts. Accepts faxed or electronic queries. Considers simultaneous submissions and reprints. Preferred word length: 1,000-5,000. Reports on queries and manuscripts in 2-4 weeks. Sometimes comments on rejected manuscripts. Writer's guidelines available for SASE, but they prefer writers e-mail for them.

PAYMENT: Pays 2-3 contributor's copies.

TERMS: Purchases first North American serial rights. Manuscript published up to 4 months after acceptance.

ADDRESS: P.O. Box 5410, Akron, OH 44334

TELEPHONE: (330)864-3852

FAX: (330)864-1770

E-MAIL: bonesmail@aol.com

CABAL ASYLUM

Established: 1994 • Circulation: 500 • Frequency: Quarterly • Pages: 100 • Size: Digest

Contact: Ren Hayes

CATEGORIES
Articles/Essays, Horror, Interviews, Market Listings, Poetry, Reviews, Supernatural/Occult Fiction

Would like "less self-glorification. Don't try to impress me with who published you before. Impress me with your manuscript. Being published by a hundred other publications doesn't mean you're right for mine."

HOW TO CONTACT: Query first. Accepts electronic queries. Submissions on computer disk should be Windows 3.0 compatible. Receives approximately 20-30 manuscripts each month. Reports on queries in 1-2 weeks, on manuscripts in 3-4 weeks. Sometimes comments on rejected manuscripts. Writer's guidelines available for SASE. Sample copy available for $3. Subscription cost is $12 for 4 issues (payable to Ren Hayes).

PAYMENT: Pays in 1 year subscription. Pays upon publication. Additional copies are available at 10% discount.

TERMS: Purchases first North American serial rights.

ADDRESS: P.O. Box 24906, Denver CO 80224

E-MAIL: cabalism@aol.com

CEMETERY DANCE

Established 1988 • Circulation: 10,000 • Frequency: Quarterly • Size: 8½ × 11 • Pages: 104

Contact: Richard T. Chizmar

> CATEGORIES
> Articles/Essays, Dark Fantasy, Horror, Interviews, Reviews

Cemetery Dance is a slick, semipro horror and dark fantasy magazine with a color cover. It is looking for dark fiction with an edge. Horror can be psychological, supernatural, subtle or graphic as long as it is well done. *Cemetery Dance* has published the short fiction of Peter Straub and Stephen King. Editor Chizmar strongly advises prospective writers to at least look at an issue before submitting.

HOW TO CONTACT: Unsolicited manuscripts welcome (if under 5,000 words). Send full manuscripts. Query first for nonfiction and works more than 5,000 words. Considers simultaneous submissions and reprints if so noted. Receives approximately 400-500 unsolicited manuscripts each month. Preferred word length: to 5,000. Reports on queries in 1 month, on manuscripts in 1-3 months. Sometimes comments on rejected manuscripts. Writer's guidelines available for SASE. Sample copy available for $5. Subscription cost is $15 for 4 issues.

PAYMENT: Pays 3-5¢/story and 2 contributor's copies. Additional copies available at 50% discount. Pays upon publication.

TERMS: Purchases first North American serial rights. Manuscript published 3-9 months after acceptance.

ADDRESS: P.O. Box 858, Edgewood MD 21040

ART: REPRINTED BY PERMISSION

CHRYSALIS, JOURNAL OF THE SWEDENBORG FOUNDATION

Established: 1985 • Circulation: 3,000 • Frequency: Semiannually • Size: 7×10 • Pages: 128-160

Contact: Carol S. Lawson, Editor or Phoebe Loughrey, Fiction Editor

> CATEGORIES
> Articles/Essays, Book Reviews, Poetry, Traditional Fantasy

Chrysalis is filled with fiction, articles, poetry, and book and film reviews. "We publish for intellectually curious readers interested in spiritual topics. Our sf/fantasy content is related to personal spiritual growth." Each issue is centered around a theme. Upcoming themes are: "Play" for Autumn 1996 and "The Good Life" for Spring 1997.

They receive 40 manuscripts per month and publish 10-12 in each issue. Stories must be 2,500-3,500 words and will be published within 1 year after acceptance. They will sometimes critique rejected manuscripts and welcome submissions from new writers.

HOW TO CONTACT: Query first and request fiction guidelines. Include SAE and 1 first-class stamp. Then send your complete manuscript with SASE. They report back in 2 months. A sample copy is available for $10.

PAYMENT: Pays $75-250 and 5 contributor's copies.

TERMS: Pays on publication for one-time rights. They send galleys to author.

ADDRESS: Rt. 1, Box 184, Dillwyn VA 23936
PHONE: (804)983-3021
E-MAIL: lawson@aba.org

ART: DAVID J. HEATH

A COMPANION IN ZEOR

Established: 1978 • Circulation: 300 • Frequency: Irregularly • Size: 8½ × 11 • Pages: 60

Contact: Karen Litman, Editor

> CATEGORIES
> Humorous Science Fiction, Reviews, Traditional Fantasy

   A Companion in Zeor is a fanzine based on the various universe creations (Sime/Gen, Dushau, Kren, Kraith, Luren, etc.) of Jacqueline Lichtenberg. This publication also contains occasional features on *Star Trek* (due to Lichtenberg's authoring of *Star Trek Lives*), some convention reports and reviews of movies and books.

   Editor Karen Litman says, "*Companion in Zeor* has been the starting point of the career of Andrea Alton, the author of *Demon of Undoing* (Baen Books). Her earliest works appeared here, and she continues to contribute to us. We offer professional assistance to upcoming writers. I assist in early rewrites before Mrs. Lichtenberg critiques the works in progess, and sometimes others also work in the story development process."

   They accept as many manuscripts as they can afford to print. Publication of an accepted manuscript "can take years, due to limit of finances available for publication."

HOW TO CONTACT: Query first or send your complete manuscript with a cover letter. "We prefer cover letters about any prior writing experience or related interests toward writing aims." Also include SASE. Simultaneous submissions are acceptable. They report back in 1 month. "I write individual letters to all queries. No form letter at present." Price of a sample copy depends on individual circumstances. Fiction guidelines are available for SAE and 1 first-class stamp.

PAYMENT: Pays in contributor's copies.

TERMS: Acquires first rights.

ADDRESS: 307 Ashland Ave., Egg Harbor Township NJ 08234-5568

THE COSMIC UNICORN

Established: 1993 • Circulation: 100 • Frequency: Semiannually • Size: Digest • Pages: 150

Contact: Tricia Packard, Editor

CATEGORIES
Articles/Essays, Dark Fantasy, Hard Science Fiction, High Fantasy, Humorous Science Fiction, Military Science Fiction, Reviews, Sociological Science Fiction, Space Opera, Traditional Fantasy

"*The Cosmic Unicorn* is devoted to publishing new and established writers of science fiction, fantasy, science fantasy and poetry."

Editor Tricia Packard particularly likes "good characterization and the unusual introduction." She advises writers to "take your time with your writing. Be aware of your use of every word."

They receive 40-70 manuscripts each month and purchase 10-18 every issue. Manuscripts should be less than 10,000 words in length and will be printed within a year after acceptance. They critique rejected manuscripts as often as possible.

HOW TO CONTACT: Send your complete manuscript with a cover letter. Reading dates May 1-August 31 only. Reprint and electronic submissions are acceptable. They report back in 10 weeks. A sample copy is available for $7.50 (make payable to Tricia Packard).

PAYMENT: Pays ¼-½¢/word.

TERMS: Acquires one-time rights.

ADDRESS: Silver Creation Press, 451 Hibiscus Tree Dr., Lantana FL 33462

E-MAIL: t. packard@genie.com

CRAZY QUILT

Established: 1986 • Circulation: 175 • Frequency: Semiannually • Pages: 192 • Size: Digest

Contact: Marsh Cassady, Fiction Editor

CATEGORIES
Contemporary Fantasy, Experimental Fiction, Poetry, Science Fantasy

HOW TO CONTACT: Unsolicited manuscripts welcome. Send full manuscript. Considers simultaneous submissions. Submissions on disk should be formatted as WordPerfect file (Windows 95). Receives approximately 25 manuscripts each month. Preferred word length: to 4,000. Reports on manuscripts in 2 weeks. Sometimes comments on rejected manuscripts. Writer's guidelines available for SASE. Sample copy available for $6 current; $4.50 back issue. Subscription cost is $19 for 2 issues; $33 for 4 issues.

PAYMENT: Pays 2 contributor's copies. Additional copies available at 40% discount.

ADDRESS: P.O. Box 632729, San Diego CA 92163-2729

PHONE: (619)688-1023

FAX: (619)688-1753

DAGGER OF THE MIND, BEYOND THE REALMS OF IMAGINATION

Established: 1989 • Circulation: 5,000 • Frequency: Quarterly • Size: 8 × 11 • Pages: 62-86

Contact: Arthur William Lloyd Breach, Executive Editor

> CATEGORIES
> Dark Fantasy, Hard Science Fiction, High Fantasy, Interviews, Light Fantasy, Science Articles, Sociological Science Fiction, Traditional Fantasy

Recently Published: "Engines of the Night," by Kevin Michael Harris; "The Shattered Window," by Margaret Frastley.

Dagger of the Mind has around 80% of its content as sf or fantasy. Strong Lovecraftian influence. "Not only do we publish fiction, poetry and art relative to the genre, but we also publish science nonfiction, human interest, interviews and other scholarly works." Editor Breach continues: "I want to see stark realism created by the writer to the point where I can actually feel like I'm there caught up in the plot."

Receives 400 manuscripts each month and publishes 8-15 in every issue. Story length is open from short-short to novelette. Publishes 2 years after acceptance. "Read a copy of the magazine and memorize the guidelines. I don't have the time to read through inappropriate material. Send in only the finest work you can, highly polished. I always comment on rejected manuscripts."

HOW TO CONTACT: Send your complete manuscript with a cover letter. "Include a bio and list of previously published credits with tear sheets. I also expect a brief synopsis of the story." Reports back in 3 months on manuscripts sent with SASE. Simultaneous submissions are OK. A sample copy is available for $3.50, a 9×12 SASE and 5 first-class stamps. Fiction guidelines are available for a #10 SASE and 1 first-class stamp.

PAYMENT: ½-1¢/word plus 1 contributor's copy.

TERMS: Pays on publication for first rights (possibly anthology rights as well).

ADDRESS: K'yi-Lih Productions, 1317 Hookridge Dr., El Paso TX 79925

ART: DON SCHANK

DARK REGIONS

Established: 1985 • Circulation: 3,000 • Frequency: 3 times/year • Size: 8½ × 11 • Pages: 80-100

Contact: Joe Morey, Editor and Publisher

> **CATEGORIES**
> Cyberpunk, Dark Fantasy, Poetry, Science Fantasy, Science Horror

"We're dedicated to putting out a quality product, on time, that will entertain as well as make the reader think. We publish weird fantasy and horror and occasionally weird science fiction. Our magazine is intended for mature readers. We want inventive tales that push the boundaries of originality and invention. We dislike overused themes like Friday the 13th, Conan and invaders from Mars."

Dark Regions publishes 1-2 theme issues per year. A list of these themes is available for SASE. They receive 100 submissions each month and publish 8-10 in every issue. They publish manuscripts 6-12 months after acceptance. Story length should be around 3,000 words, but they will accept lengths of 1,000-5,000 words.

They also publish *The Year's Best Fantastic Fiction*. This publication is not open to unpublished writers; it is by invitation only and uses reprints only.

HOW TO CONTACT: Send your complete manuscript with a cover letter that includes estimated word count, brief bio and list of publications. Include SASE or tell them if it's a disposable copy. They report in 2 weeks on queries and on manuscripts. Fiction guidelines are available for SASE and a sample copy for $3.95 and 4 first-class stamps.

PAYMENT: Pays 1-6¢/word and 1 contributor's copy.

TERMS: Pays on publication for first North American serial rights.
ADDRESS: P.O. Box 6301, Concord CA 94524
PHONE: (510)254-7442
FAX: (510)254-6419
E-MAIL: j.rosenman@genie.geis.com

DARK TOME

Established: 1990 • Circulation: 100 • Frequency: 3 times/year • Pages: 32-48 • Size: Digest

Contact: Michelle Marr

CATEGORIES
Dark Fantasy, Horror, Splatterpunk

HOW TO CONTACT: Unsolicited manuscripts welcome. Send full manuscript. Accepts electronic queries and submissions via e-mail. No simultaneous submissions or reprints. Receives approximately 50 manuscripts each month. Preferred word length: to 4,000. Reports on queries and manuscripts in 1 month. Always comments on rejected manuscripts. Writer's guidelines available for SASE. Sample copy available for $2.75. Subscription cost is $7.50 for 3 issues (payable to Arabesque Publications).

PAYMENT: Pays $2-10 and 1 contributor's copy. Pays upon publication.
TERMS: Purchases first North American serial rights. Manuscript published 6-12 months after acceptance.
ADDRESS: P.O. Box 705, Salem OR 97308
PHONE: (503)390-9027
E-MAIL: dktome@cyberhighway.net
WEBSITE: http://wwide.com/darktome.html

ART: PAMELA MOORE

DAUGHTERS OF NYX, A MAGAZINE OF GODDESS STORIES, MYTHMAKING, AND FAIRY TALES

Established: 1993 • Circulation: 2,000 • Frequency: Semiannually • Size: 8½ × 11 • Pages: 32

Contact: Kim Antieau, Fiction Editor

CATEGORIES
Articles/Essays, Book Reviews, Fairy Tales, Myths

The editors describe *Daughters of Nyx* as "a woman-centered publication, interested in stories that retell legends, myths and fairy tales from a matristic viewpoint. We publish goddess-inspired fiction." They advise authors to "break free of patriarchal attitudes. Also, get away from high fantasy."

They receive 20 manuscripts per month and publish 7-10 in each issue. They accept lengths of 1,000-7,000 words, but prefer stories around 5,000 words.

HOW TO CONTACT: Send your complete manuscript with a cover letter. Also include SASE for reply or return of manuscript. Simultaneous and reprint submissions are acceptable, "but please tell us." They report back in 1-6 months. A sample copy is available for $5. Fiction guidelines are available for SAE and 1 first-class stamp. They review novels and short story collections.

PAYMENT: Pays ½ cent/word, $10 minimum, and 2 contributor's copies.

TERMS: Pays on publication for first North American serial rights.

ADDRESS: P.O. Box 1100, Stevenson WA 98648

DEAD LINES

Established: 1994 • Circulation: 200 • Frequency: Semiannually • Size: Digest • Pages: 70-80

Contact: Nancy Purnell

CATEGORIES
Experimental Fiction, Horror, Magic Realism, Poetry, Reviews (Books and Magazines), Sociological Science Fiction

Each issue of *Dead Lines* covers a different theme. Write for guidelines and upcoming theme.

HOW TO CONTACT: Unsolicited manuscripts welcome, but write for guidelines and upcoming themes before submitting. Receives 100 unsolicited manuscripts each month. Preferred word length: 3,500. Reports on queries in 1-2 weeks, on manuscripts in 2-8 weeks. Sometimes comments on rejected manuscripts. Writer's guidelines available for SASE. Sample copy available for $4.75. Subscription cost is $13 for 3 issues.

PAYMENT: Pays 1 contributor's copy and 10 32¢ stamps/story and 5 32¢ stamps/poem. Additional copies available at 10-20% discount.

TERMS: Purchases first North American serial rights. Accepted works published in following issue.

ADDRESS: Crash Landing Press, P.O. Box 907, Tolland CT 06084-0907

PHONE: (860)875-4524

DEAD OF NIGHT ™

Established: 1989 • Circulation: 3,200 • Frequency: Annually • Size: 8½ × 11 • Pages: 100

Contact: Lin Stein, Editor

CATEGORIES
Dark Fantasy, Horror, Humorous Science Fiction, Literary Criticism, Sociological Science Fiction, Traditional Fantasy

Editor Lin Stein says: *"Dead of Night™* publishes horror, fantasy, mystery, suspense, sf and vampire-related fiction. I prefer sociological and character-oriented stories as opposed to hard sf. I don't care for fantasy with an overabundance of elves, wizards, etc." Almost one third of the magazine is sf or fantasy.

Dead of Night™ has published work by Janet Fox, J.N. Williamson and Mort Castle. They receive 90 manuscripts per month and accept 8-12 each issue. Lengths of 2,500-3,500 words are preferred, and they also publish literary essays, book reviews and poetry. The editors do not read June through December. They will often critique rejected manuscripts.

HOW TO CONTACT: Send your complete manuscript with a cover letter, including estimated word count, a bio (1-2 paragraphs), Social Security number and list of publications (if available). Also include SASE for reply or return of manuscript, or send a disposable copy of your manuscript. "No reprints except novel/book excerpts." They report back in 3 weeks on queries and 4-6 weeks on manuscripts. A sample copy is available for $5 (current copy); $2.50 (back issue). Fiction guidelines are available for SAE and 1 first-class stamp.

PAYMENT: Pays 4-7¢/word and 1 contributor's copy (cover artists, two). Additional copies are available at a 10% discount off cover price.

TERMS: Pays on publication for first North American serial rights.

ADDRESS: P.O. Box 60730, Longmeadow MA 01116-0730

PHONE: (413)567-9524

E-MAIL: lstein1@genie.com

DEATHREALM, THE LAND WHERE HORROR DWELLS

Established: 1987 • Circulation: 4,000 • Frequency: Quarterly • Size: 8½ × 11 • Pages: 64

Contact: Mark Rainey

CATEGORIES
Dark Fantasy, Horror, Poetry

HOW TO CONTACT: Unsolicited manuscripts welcome. Send full manuscripts. Accepts electronic queries. Receives approximately 300-400 unsolicited manuscripts each month. Preferred word length: to 5,000. Reports on queries in 1 month, on manuscripts in 3 months. Sometimes comments on rejected manuscripts. Writer's guidelines available for SASE. Sample copy available for $4.95. Subscription cost is $17.95 for 4 issues.

PAYMENT: pays 1-3¢/word and 1 contributor's copy. Additional copies available at 50% discount. Pays upon acceptance.

TERMS: Purchases first North American serial rights. Manuscript published 1 year after acceptance.

ADDRESS: 2210 Wilcox Dr., Greensboro NC 27405

PHONE: (910)621-8160

E-MAIL: s.rainey@genie.com

WEBSITE: http://home.aol.com/markrainey

DOWNSTATE STORY

Established: 1992 • Circulation: 500 • Frequency: Annually • Pages: 70

Contact: Elaine Hopkins

CATEGORIES
Contemporary Fantasy, Cyberpunk, Dark Fantasy, Elfpunk, Experimental Fiction, Hard Science Fiction, High Fantasy, Horror, Humorous, Magic Realism, Military Science Fiction, Poetry, Science Fantasy, Sociological Science Fiction, Space Opera, Splatterpunk, Steampunk, Traditional Fantasy

Would like to see more political and social commentary in science fiction and fantasy submissions. "Write well. Give your story meaning and significance!" Not-for-profit organization. No pseudonyms used. Name and photo of author required.

HOW TO CONTACT: Unsolicited manuscripts welcome. Send full manuscript. Include SASE. Accepts electronic queries. Considers simultaneous submissions. Receives approximately 10 unsolicited manuscripts each month. Preferred word length: to 2,000. Never comments on rejected manuscripts. Writer's guidelines available for SASE. Sample copy available for $8. Subscription cost is $25 for 4 issues.

PAYMENT: Pays $50. Pays upon acceptance.

TERMS: Purchases first worldwide and electronic rights. Manuscript published 2-3 months after acceptance.

ADDRESS: 1825 Maple Ridge, Peoria IL 61614

PHONE: (309)688-1409

E-MAIL: ehopkins@prairienet.org

WEBSITE: http://www.wiu.bgu.edu/users/mfgeh/dss

DRAGON® MAGAZINE

Established: 1976 • Circulation: 70,000 • Published: Monthly • Size: 8½ × 11 • Pages: 120

Contact: Anthony J. Bryant, Editor

CATEGORIES
Articles/Essays, Dark Fantasy, High Fantasy, Humorous Fantasy, Traditional Fantasy

"*Dragon* contains primarily nonfiction—articles and essays on various aspects of the hobby of fantasy and science fiction role-playing games." Each issue, however, contains one fantasy story. "We are looking for all types of fantasy (not horror) stories. We are not interested in fictionalized accounts of role-playing sessions. It is essential that you actually see a copy before submitting."

Dragon has recently published fiction by Lois Tilton, Heather Lynn Sarik and Jean Lorrah. They receive 50-60 manuscripts per month. Stories should be between 3,000-4,000 words in length and will appear in the magazine 6-12 months after acceptance. They will occasionally critique rejected manuscripts.

HOW TO CONTACT: Send your complete manuscript, an estimated word count and list of publication credits within the genre. Also include SASE. They report back in 4-6 weeks. A sample copy is available for $4.50.

PAYMENT: Pays 5-8¢/word and 2 contributor's copies.

TERMS: Pays on acceptance for first world English language rights.

ADDRESS: TSR, Inc., 201 Sheridan Springs Rd., Lake Geneva WI 53147
PHONE: (414)248-3625
E-MAIL: tsrmags@aol.com

DREAMS & NIGHTMARES, THE MAGAZINE OF FANTASTIC POETRY

Established: 1986 • Circulation: 200 • Frequency: Semiannually • Size: Digest • Pages: 24

Contact: David C. Kopaska-Merkel, Editor

> CATEGORIES
> Cyberpunk, Dark Fantasy, Hard Science Fiction, High Fantasy, Humorous Science Fiction, Poetry, Sociological Science Fiction, Space Opera, Traditional Fantasy

Editor David C. Kopaska-Merkel says, "*DN* is mainly a poetry magazine, but I am looking for short shorts. They should be either fantasy, science fiction or horror. I dislike senseless violence, sappiness, misogyny or hatred (unreasoning) of any kind of people. Look at a copy of *Dreams & Nightmares* and then send me your best work that you think I might be interested in. Don't give up after one attempt and don't assume that one issue contains all the kinds of writing I'd like to publish."

They receive from 10-15 manuscripts per month and only print 1-2 short shorts each issue, in addition to a variable number of poems. Accepted submissions will be published 1-9 months after acceptance. They will sometimes critique rejected manuscripts.

HOW TO CONTACT: Send your complete manuscript with SASE. Electronic submissions are acceptable. They report back in 1-3 weeks on queries and 1-6 weeks on manuscripts. A sample copy is available for $2. Fiction guidelines are available for SAE and 1 first-class stamp.

PAYMENT: Pays $3 and 2 contributor's copies.

TERMS: Pays on acceptance for one-time rights.

ADDRESS: 1300 Kicker Rd., Tuscaloosa AL 35404

PHONE: (205)553-2284

E-MAIL: dkm.alageol@genie.com

DREAMS & VISIONS: NEW FRONTIERS IN CHRISTIAN FICTION

Established: 1989 • Circulation: 200 • Frequency: 3 times/year • Pages: 56 • Size: Digest

Contact: Steve Stanton

CATEGORIES
Contemporary Fantasy, Experimental Fiction, Hard Science Fiction, Magic Realism, Science Fantasy

"All work submitted should be based on orthodox Biblical norms or traditions, but should portray spiritual truths in new, innovative or unique ways. Skysong Press is a Christian publishing company."

HOW TO CONTACT: Unsolicited manuscripts welcome. Send full manuscript. Considers simultaneous submissions. Accepts submissions on computer disk; contact for preferred format. Receives approximately 30 unsolicited manuscripts each month. Preferred word length: 2,000-6,000. Reports on queries in 1 month, on manuscripts in 10 weeks. Never comments on rejected manuscripts. Writer's guidelines available for SASE. Sample copy available for $4.95. Subscription cost is $12 for 3 issues.

PAYMENT: Pays ½¢/word. Additional copies available at 50% discount. Pays upon publication.

TERMS: Purchases first North American serial rights. Manuscript published 3-6 months after acceptance.

ADDRESS: Skysong Press, 35 Peter St. S., Orillia, Ontario L3V 5A8 Canada

ELDRITCH TALES

Established: 1996 • Frequency: Quarterly • Size: Digest • Pages: 60

Contact: Crispin Burnham

CATEGORIES
Articles/Essays, Dark Fantasy, Horror, Interviews, Poetry, Splatterpunk

HOW TO CONTACT: Unsolicited manuscripts welcome. Send full manuscripts. Considers reprints. Receives approximately 20-30 unsolicited manuscripts each month. Preferred word length: to 10,000. Reports on queries and manuscripts in 1 week. Sometimes comments on rejected manuscripts. Writer's guidelines available for SASE. Sample copy available for $7.25. Subscription cost is $25 for 4 issues.

PAYMENT: Pays ¼-1¢/story and 1 contributor's copy. Additional copies available at 50% discount. Pays upon publication.

TERMS: Purchases first North American serial rights. Manuscript published 3-4 years after acceptance.

ADDRESS: 1051 Wellington Rd., Lawrence KS 66049-3030

ELF: ECLECTIC LITERARY FORUM

Established: 1991 • Circulation: 5,000 • Frequency: Quarterly • Size: 8½ × 11 • Pages: 56

Contact: C.K. Erbes, Editor

CATEGORIES
Hard Science Fiction, Humorous Science Fiction, Sociological Science Fiction, Traditional Fantasy

According to editor Erbes, *ELF* is "a publication of well-crafted short stories, poetry and essays on literary themes for a sophisticated audience." She continues, "We wish to include more sf, but our editorial board looks for a high quality of writing. We want to see stories that show an ability to use the language, not merely pyrotechnics or robotics." They do not want violence or horror.

They publish 4-6 manuscripts per issue and publish stories up to 1 year after acceptance. Preferred story length is 3,500 words, but they sometimes publish short shorts as well. They will sometimes critique rejected manuscripts.

HOW TO CONTACT: Send your complete manuscript; cover letter is optional. Also include SASE. Simultaneous submissions are acceptable if so indicated. They report back in 4-6 weeks on manuscripts. A sample copy is available for $5.50 ($6 foreign). Fiction guidelines are available for SAE and 1 first-class stamp.

PAYMENT: Pays contributor's copies.

TERMS: Acquires first North American serial rights.

ADDRESS: P.O. Box 392, Tonawanda NY 14150

PHONE: (716)693-7006

E-MAIL: neubauer@buffnet.net

WEBSITE: http://www.cais.net/aesir/fiction/elforum

ART: SCOTT A. BECKER

FANTASTIC WORLDS

Established: 1995 • Circulation: 1,000 • Frequency: Quarterly • Pages: 48 • Size: 8½ × 11

Contact: Scott Becker, Editor/Publisher

CATEGORIES

Articles/Essays, Contemporary Fantasy, Cyberpunk, Dark Fantasy, Elfpunk, Experimental Fiction, Hard Science Fiction, High Fantasy, Horror, Humorous, Interviews, Magic Realism, Military Science Fiction, Poetry, Reviews, Science Fantasy, Sociological Science Fiction, Space Opera, Splatterpunk, Steampunk, Traditional Fantasy

Needs shorter stories (under 5,000 words). "I would like to see more well-crafted horror stories in the future. I would also like to see a few more well-written heroic fantasy stories. There's lots of good sf and contemporary fantasy around, but for some reason most of the fiction I get in these two categories are gimmick-laden and could really use a bit more heart and soul (story-telling is not simply putting your latest dungeon crawl into narrative form). Writers really need to keep in mind that character is what drives a story, not high-tech toys or fire-breathing dragons. I'm also looking for stuff that's a little larger than life, stories that make you want to call a friend and say, 'I read the coolest story today.' I love fantastic fiction that manages to capture that feeling, and I think most other fans do, too.

"As far as advice goes, keep in mind that the name of the magazine is *Fantastic Worlds*. Buy a sample copy!"

HOW TO CONTACT: Unsolicited manuscripts welcome. Send full manuscript. On nonfiction, query with samples first. Considers simultaneous submissions and reprints, but query first. Receives approximately 200 unsolicited manuscripts each month. Preferred word length: 500-15,000. Reports on queries in 2 months, on manuscripts in 4 months. Writer's guidelines available for SASE. Sample copy available for $5. Subscription cost is $15 for 3 issues and $28 for 6 issues.

PAYMENT: Pays 1-5¢/word. Pays $25 minimum. Additional copies available at 50% discount. Pays upon publication.

TERMS: Purchases first North American serial rights. Reserves the right to publish story in a future "best of" collection at original rate (if chosen). Manuscript published 6-12 months after acceptance.

ADDRESS: 1644 S. 11th West, Missoula MT 59801

E-MAIL: fw@selway.umt.edu

FOR DICKHEADS ONLY

Established: 1991 • Circulation: 500 • Frequency: 1-3 times/year • Size: Digest • Pages: 40

Contact: David Hyde, Editor

> CATEGORIES
> Articles/Essays, Humorous Science Fiction, Reviews

Editor David Hyde says, "We are an internationally circulated magazine devoted to the work and life of the late master of the science fiction novel, Philip K. Dick. We publish essays, commentary, reviews, news, notes, etc. on the life and work of Philip K. Dick. We are open to anything related to PKD, including short humorous pieces and short fiction in which PKD is a character. We'll publish anything as long as it relates in some way to PKD. We are also looking for artwork."

They receive 1-2 manuscripts each month and publish 2 or 3 in each issue. Pieces should be under 3,000 words in length and will be published 3-4 months after acceptance.

HOW TO CONTACT: "Send a friendly letter showing interest in the writing of Philip K. Dick." Include SASE. Simultaneous and reprint submissions are acceptable. They report back in 2 weeks. A sample copy is available for $2.

PAYMENT: Pays contributor's copies—"as many as you want."

ADDRESS: Ganymedean Slime Mold Prods., P.O. Box 611, Kokomo IN 46903

THE FRACTAL

Established: 1992 • Circulation: 1,000 • Frequency: Semiannually • Pages: 60 • Size: 5½ × 8½

Contact: Sean Newborn

CATEGORIES
Contemporary Fantasy, Cyberpunk, Dark Fantasy, Experimental Fiction, Hard Science Fiction, High Fantasy, Horror, Interviews, Magic Realism, Military Science Fiction, Poetry, Reviews, Sociological Science Fiction, Space Opera, Splatterpunk, Steampunk, Traditional Fantasy

"*The Fractal* was founded to, among other things, provide a market for collegiate writers of genre literature whose school's lit mag would not consider sf or fantasy. We appreciate submissions from all sources, but we are particularly interested in college/university writers. Don't try to mimic what you find on the bookstore shelves; develop *your* stories about themes that *you* find interesting and deserving of comment. No matter whether you write about LGMs, BEMs, vampires or elves, make them people, understandable if not human." Would like to see more fiction for a literary audience. Less fiction for a commercial audience.

HOW TO CONTACT: Unsolicited manuscripts welcome. Send full manuscript. Accepts electronic queries. Considers simultaneous submissions and reprints. Submissions on computer disk should be formatted as ASCII. Receives approximately 50 unsolicited manuscripts each month. Preferred word length: to 15,000. Reports on queries in 2 weeks, on manuscripts in 2-3 months. Always comments on rejected manuscripts. Writer's guidelines available for SASE. Sample copy available for $5. Subscription cost is $8 for 2 issues.

PAYMENT: Pays $25 and 2 contributor's copies. Pays upon publication.

TERMS: Purchases first North American serial rights. Manuscript published 6 months after acceptance.

ADDRESS: MS 2D6 4400 University Dr., Fairfax VA 22030-4444

E-MAIL: fractal@gmu.edu

FREEZER BURN MAGAZINE

Established: 1995 • Circulation: 100 • Frequency: Quarterly • Pages: 50 • Size: Letter-sized Digest

Contact: David G. Rogers, Editor/Publisher or Teresa Cerrato, Fantasy Editor

> CATEGORIES
> Articles/Essays, Dark Fantasy, Experimental Fiction, Hard Science Fiction, High Fantasy, Horror, Humorous, Poetry, Science Fantasy, Sociological Science Fiction, Traditional Fantasy

"Regardless of genre I would like to see more stories that deal with human or nonhuman problems in a way that is socially motivated. Try to have your story be relevant. I would rather see a dull plot that has a message than an action-packed one that says nothing or very little about human nature. Be yourself. Try to be different. Please use cover letters!"

HOW TO CONTACT: Unsolicited manuscripts welcome. Send full manuscript. Considers simultaneous submissions and reprints. Receives approximately 40 unsolicited manuscripts each month. Preferred word length: 100-3,000. Reports on queries in 1 week, on manuscripts in 2-3 weeks. Always comments on rejected manuscripts. Writer's guidelines available for SASE. Sample copy available for $3. Subscription cost is $12 for 4 issues.

PAYMENT: Pays $5 and 1 contributor's copy; $20 after October 1, 1996. Pays upon publication.

TERMS: Purchases first North American serial rights. Manuscript published 9 months after acceptance.

ADDRESS: 10 Becket St., Salem MA 01970

PHONE: (508)745-7379

GOLDEN ISIS

Established: 1980 • Circulation: 3,600 • Frequency: Quarterly • Size: Digest • Pages: 32

Contact: Gerina Dunwich

CATEGORIES
Articles/Essays, Experimental Fiction, Interviews, Magic Realism, Occult/Pagan Fiction, Poetry, Reviews

Golden Isis is a mystical journal of goddess-inspired poetry, paganistic artwork and spellcraft. "We would like to see more work by Pagan and Wiccan writers. We would like to see less fiction portraying witches in a negative, evil or stereotypical fashion. Short stories containing magickal spells/rituals or Sabbat themes are most welcome." It is a good idea to read a sample copy first if you are unfamiliar with the magazine.

HOW TO CONTACT: Unsolicited manuscripts welcome. Send full manuscript. Considers simultaneous submissions and reprints. Receives 150 unsolicited manuscripts each month. Preferred word length: 1,000-3,000. Reports on queries and manuscripts in 3 weeks. Sometimes comments on rejected manuscripts. Writer's guidelines available for SASE. Sample copy available for $2.95. Subscription cost is $10 for 4 issues.

PAYMENT: Pays 1 contributor's copy.

TERMS: Purchases first North American serial rights. Manuscripts published within 6 months after acceptance.

ADDRESS: P.O. Box 525, Fort Covington NY 12937

GOTTA WRITE NETWORK LITMAG

Established: 1988 • Circulation: 200 • Frequency: Semiannually • Pages: 64-72 • Size: 8½×11

Contact: Denise Fleischer

> **CATEGORIES**
> Articles/Essays, Contemporary Fantasy, Convention/Workshop Listings, Dark Fantasy, Interviews, Hard Science Fiction, High Fantasy, Horror, Market Listings, Overseas Reports, Poetry, Reviews, Science Fantasy, Traditional Fantasy

Would like to see more "original fiction that lets the imagination soar, stories that you wish continued on, characters that are real and strive to achieve their goals. We may publish only twice a year, but it will take you months to review all the information printed on our pages."

Open to both beginning and established writers. "Behind the Scenes" interviews have included in-depth interviews with F. Pohl, Mickey Zucker Reichert, T. Winter Damon, Kevin Stein, *Next Phase* editor Kim Guarnaccia and the editor of *Death Realm* magazine.

HOW TO CONTACT: Unsolicited manuscripts welcome. Send full manuscript. Accepts faxed and electronic queries. Receives approximately 40-70 manuscripts each month. Reports on queries in 2-3 weeks, on manuscripts in 3-4 months. Sometimes comments on rejected manuscripts. Writer's guidelines available for SASE. Sample copy available for $5. Subscription cost is $12.75 for 2 issues.

PAYMENT: Pays $10/short story; $5/interview and 1 contributor's copy for poetry. Additional copies available at $3.75 for contributors. Pays upon publication.

TERMS: Purchases first North American serial rights. Manuscript published 6 months after acceptance.

ADDRESS: Maren Publications, 612 Cobblestone Circle, Glenview IL 60025

PHONE: (708)296-7631

FAX: (708)296-7631

E-MAIL: netera@aol.com

GRUE MAGAZINE

Established: 1985 • Circulation: 4,500 • Frequency: 1-2 times/year • Size: Digest • Pages: 96

Contact: Peggy Nadramia

CATEGORIES
Cyberpunk, Dark Fantasy, Experimental Fiction, Horror, Poetry, Splatterpunk, Steampunk

"I'd like to see less of the horror cliches: vampires, werewolves, serial killers," says Peggy Nadramia, publisher of *Grue Magazine*. "I'd like to use less of the old standby plotlines such as: Joe Average encounters Femme Fatale in smoky bar; she turns out to be one of the above. I'd love to see more work wherein the writer digs deep into her own fears, prejudices, experiences and puts together a well-plotted story with a beginning, a middle and an end, utilizing some real supernatural elements, instead of the 'psychological horror' we've all seen so much of lately. I've liked it; I've published it. But I'd like to publish more of the kind of stories that brought us all to horror in the first place."

Grue has garnered a small reputation over the past ten years for publishing "cutting edge" horror fiction. "Stories from our pages appear frequently in various Year's Best anthologies. We've even won a World Fantasy Award. But that doesn't mean the complete unknown, the total neophyte, doesn't have a chance here. You do; you just have to write well, and know what horror feels like. Then make me feel it, too."

HOW TO CONTACT: Unsolicited manuscripts welcome. Send full manuscript. Considers simultaneous submissions. Receives approximately 50-75 unsolicited manuscripts each month. Preferred word length: 5,000. Reports on queries and manuscripts in 6-9 months. Sometimes comments on rejected manuscripts. Writer's guidelines available for SASE. Sample copy available for $5. Subscription cost is $14 for 3 issues.

PAYMENT: Pays ½¢/word; $5/poem; and 2 contributor's copies. Additional copies available at 50% discount. Pays upon publication.

TERMS: Purchases first worldwide rights. Manuscript published within 1 year after acceptance.

ADDRESS: Hell's Kitchen Productions, P.O. Box 370, Times Square Station, New York NY 10108-0370

E-MAIL: nadramia@panix.com

ART: ERIC GENDELL

HEAVEN BONE

Established: 1987 • Circulation: 2,500 • Frequency: Semiannually • Size: 8½ × 11 • Pages: 48-96

Contact: Steven Hirsch or Kirpal Gordon, Editors

> CATEGORIES
> Articles/Essays, High Fantasy, Reviews, Sociological Science Fiction, Traditional Fantasy

The editors of *Heaven Bone* label their content as "new consciousness, expansive, fine literary, earth and nature and spiritual path. We use current reviews, essays on spiritual and esoteric topics, creative stories and fantasy. Our readers are spiritual seekers, healers, poets, artists, musicians and students."

Only 10-20% of the magazine is sf or fantasy, and they are looking for stories with "poetic linguistics and structure; attention to the music of the language; drama, emotion, innovation." Editor Hirsch says, "We have nothing to lose so we can take outrageous chances. No one can successfully define us. That points out both our ambiguities and passions for what we feel a literary magazine should be—a friendly challenge to live more fully and be more imaginative."

They receive from 45-110 manuscripts a month, and they are looking for lengths of 1,200-6,000 words, but will also publish short shorts and poetry. Works are published 2 weeks to 10 months after acceptance.

They will sometimes critique rejected manuscripts or recommend other markets.

HOW TO CONTACT: Send your complete manuscript with a cover letter, including a short bio of recent activities. Also include SASE. Reprint submissions are acceptable. Electronic submissions are acceptable via "Apple Mac versions of Macwrite, Microsoft Word version 5.1 or Writenow version 3.0." They report back in 2 weeks on queries and 2 weeks to 6 months on manuscripts. A sample copy is available for $6. Fiction guidelines are available for SAE and 1 first-class stamp.

PAYMENT: Pays in contributor's copies and charges for extras.

TERMS: Acquires first North American serial rights. They send galleys to author if requested.

ADDRESS: Heaven Bone Press, P.O. Box 486, Chester NY 10918

PHONE: (914)469-9018

HECATE'S LOOM

Established: 1986 • Circulation: 2,000 • Frequency: Quarterly • Pages: 60 • Size: 8½×11

Contact: Yvonne Owens

CATEGORIES
Articles/Essays, Experimental Fiction, Magic Realism, Mythology, Reviews

"Research your market well. Your chances of acceptance are far greater when you submit material appropriate to the market. Our market is Pagan/Wiccan/Goddess worship, submitting material on historic homes for instance, no matter how well-written, has a very small chance of getting published by us!

"We would like to see more good, historically-based fiction and transformational parables/fairytales with modern settings. Less material about ghosts and spirits etc., and less stories to do with 'good' witch versus 'bad' witch.

"Our magazine has themes for each issue. Please send for writer's guidelines for a list of up-coming themes."

Hobson's Choice

Established: 1974 • Circulation: 2,000 • Frequency: Bimonthly • Size: 8½ × 11 • Pages: 16-24

Contact: Susannah West, Editor

CATEGORIES
Hard Science Fiction, High Fantasy, Literary Criticism, Sociological Science Fiction, Traditional Fantasy

Hobson's Choice is a magazine of "science fiction and fantasy for young adults and adults with an interest in science, technology and sf/fantasy." Editor Susannah West says, "We like sf that shows hope for the future and protagonists who interact with their environment rather than let themselves be manipulated by it. We present stories that attempt to show the reader that science fiction and contemporary science and technology aren't so far apart after all."

She continues, "I want to see original stories that explore fresh new themes. I like an intriguing opening and a title that captures my interest." She advises new authors "to study the sf genre—movie and TV sf alone won't give you enough 'feel' for the genre."

They receive 50 manuscripts or more each month and publish between 2-4 in every issue. Stories should be 2,000-10,000 words and will appear 4 months to 2 years after acceptance. They will sometimes critique rejected manuscripts.

HOW TO CONTACT: Send your complete manuscript with SASE. Electronic submissions via disk for the IBM PC or PC compatible in ASCII format and Macintosh are acceptable. They report back in 2-3 months. "If an author hasn't heard from us by 4 months, he or she should feel free to withdraw." A sample copy is available for $2.50. Fiction guidelines are available for SAE and 1 first-class stamp. Tipsheet packet (all guidelines plus tips on writing science fiction) is available for $1.50 and SASE.

PAYMENT: Pays 1-4¢/word and contributor's copies.

TERMS: Pays 25% on acceptance and 75% on publication. "25% payment is kill fee if we decide not to publish the story." Rights are negotiable. They send galleys to the author.

ADDRESS: Starwind Press, P.O. Box 98, Ripley OH 45167
PHONE: (513)392-4549

ART: JEFFREY R. BROWN

I.E. MAGAZINE

Established: 1990 • Circulation: 1,000 • Frequency: Quarterly • Pages: 60 • Size: Digest

Contact: Yolande Gottlieb, Managing Editor or Frank Bayer, Science Fiction Editor

---

CATEGORIES
Articles/Essays, Contemporary Fantasy, Experimental Fiction, Hard Science Fiction, High Fantasy, Humorous, Magic Realism, Poetry, Science Fantasy, Sociological Science Fiction, Traditional Fantasy

---

"We look for crisp, vivid prose, well edited. We appreciate humor, satire, insight, a wry but benign exposition of our common human experience. Read your story aloud, see if it flows. We are now moving toward national distribution, and are planning to go international. We have consistently been able to attract quality submissions, indicating that there are many quality freelance writers who can use a service such as ours."

HOW TO CONTACT: Unsolicited manuscripts welcome. Send full manuscript. Receives approximately 200 manuscripts each month. Preferred word length: 100-4,500. Reports on manuscripts in 1-3 months. Sometimes comments on rejected manuscripts. Writer's guidelines available for SASE. Sample copy available for $6.10. Subscription cost is $20 for 5 issues.

PAYMENT: Pays $2-5/story and 1 contributor's copy. Pays upon publication.

TERMS: Purchases first North American serial rights. Manuscript published 3-12 months after acceptance.

ADDRESS: P.O. Box 73403, Houston TX 77273-3403

İNTERMİX

Established: 1995 • Circulation: 800 • Frequency: Monthly • Pages: 20

Contact: Mike Hicks

> CATEGORIES
>
> Advice Columns, Articles/Essays, Contemporary Fantasy, Cyberpunk, Convention/Workshop Listings, Dark Fantasy, Elfpunk, Experimental Fiction, Hard Science Fiction, High Fantasy, Horror, Humorous, Industry Reports, Interviews, Magic Realism, Market Listings, Military Science Fiction, Overseas Reports, Poetry, Reviews, Science Fantasy, Sociological Science Fiction, Space Opera, Traditional Fantasy

Intermix is an electronic publication. Distribution of publication is done via the Internet e-mail system. "We primarily focus on short stories and poetry. We also serialize larger pieces across issues. PG-13 rating or below, as our issue is read by many age groups."

HOW TO CONTACT: Unsolicited manuscripts welcome. Send full manuscript. E-mail submissions (strongly encouraged) to michael@intermix.com. Page specifications: ASCII text file, 70 characters wide. No margins, single spaced. No simultaneous submissions or reprints. Submissions on computer disk should be formatted on 3½″ disk as ASCII, 70 characters wide. Receives approximately 50 unsolicited manuscripts each month. Preferred word length: 4,000. Reports on queries in 6 months. Always comments on rejected manuscripts. E-mail for writer's guidelines at intermix@interaccess.com.

PAYMENT: Pays 0.1515¢/line of text. Pays upon publication.

TERMS: Purchases first North American serial rights. Manuscript published 6 months after acceptance.

ADDRESS: 1662-D Williamsburg Court, Wheaton IL 60187

PHONE: (708)871-0042
E-MAIL: michael@intermix.com

LACUNAE

Established: 1994 • Circulation: 3,000-5,000 • Frequency: Bimonthly •
Size: 6⅝ × 10¾ • Pages: 48

Contact: Pamela Hazelton

> **CATEGORIES**
> Contemporary Fantasy, Cyberpunk, Dark Fantasy, Experiemental Fiction,
> Hard Science Fiction, Horror, Humorous Science Fiction, Interviews,
> Market Listings, Poetry, Reviews, Splatterpunk, Traditional Fantasy

Lacunae would like to see more original ideas. "We're tired of retold
Star Trek stories and such. We want compelling stories that leave the
reader's mouth agape. We are daring in content. Make us squirm." *Lacunae* encourages new writers and states that it always gives "real" reasons
for rejection.

HOW TO CONTACT: Unsolicited manuscripts welcome. Send full manuscript. Accepts electronic queries. Considers simultaneous submissions
and reprints. Receives approximately 30 unsolicited manuscripts each
month. Preferred word length: 750-3,000. Reports on queries in 2
weeks, on manuscripts in 6 weeks. Always comments on rejected
manuscripts. Writer's guidelines available for SASE. Sample copy
available for $3.25. Subscription cost is $14 for 6 issues.

PAYMENT: Pays 5-30 contributor's copies (based on length). Additional
copies available at 60% discount.

TERMS: Purchases first North American serial rights. In some cases, however, creator may retain all rights.

ADDRESS: 32 Tallow Wood Rd., Clifton Park NY 12065
PHONE: (518)383-1856
FAX: (518)383-1781
E-MAIL: lacunaemag@aol.com

THE LAMP-POST: OF THE SOUTHERN CALIFORNIA C.S. LEWIS SOCIETY

Established: 1977 • Circulation: 200 • Frequency: Quarterly • Pages: 40 • Size: Digest

Contact: James Prothero, Senior Editor

CATEGORIES
Article/Essays, High Fantasy, Magic Realism, Poetry, Traditional Fantasy, Reviews (Books)

"We are a literary review devoted to C.S. Lewis and his thought. Read our influences (C.S. Lewis, Charles Williams, George MacDonald) before you submit." Would like to see "more fantasy like Williams's or MacDonald's or Lewis's, where the real world of Aslan's country or Faerie or whatever-you-call-it is about to break into our tawdry reality."

HOW TO CONTACT: Unsolicited manuscripts welcome. Send full manuscript with SASE. Considers reprints. Submissions on computer disk should be formatted in ASCII or be Microsoft Word compatible. Receives approximately 1-2 fiction and 4-5 nonfiction manuscripts each month. Preferred word length: to 4,500. Reports on queries in 1 week, on manuscripts in 6-8 weeks. Sometimes comments on rejected manuscripts. Writer's guidelines available for SASE. Sample copy available for $3. Subscription cost is $12 for 4 issues.

PAYMENT: Pays 3 contributor's copies.

TERMS: Purchases first worldwide rights. Manuscript published 1 year after acceptance.

ADDRESS: 29562 Westmont Court, San Juan Capistrano CA 92675

ART: BRIAN DURFEE

THE LEADING EDGE, MAGAZINE OF SCIENCE FICTION AND FANTASY

Circulation: 400 • Frequency: Semiannually • Size: Digest • Pages: 110-120

Contact: Alex Grover, Editor

> CATEGORIES
> Articles/Essays, Dark Fantasy, Hard Science Fiction, High Fantasy, Humorous Science Fiction, Literary Criticism, Military Science Fiction, Sociological Science Fiction, Space Opera, Traditional Fantasy

Editor Alex Grover describes *The Leading Edge* as "a magazine dedicated to the new and upcoming author, poet and artist involved in the sf/fantasy field. We have high production values and a commitment to providing comments, critiques and a forum for up-and-coming authors.

"We are very interested in sf/fantasy stories in unexpected settings. We're publishing more sf than fantasy recently. We do not want sex, profanity and violence nor do we want fannish/media stories."

The Leading Edge has recently published works by Jane Yolen and Ben Bova. Stories should be from 500-17,000 words, but those over 9,000 words "ought to be brilliant." They also publish poetry. They receive 80 manuscripts per month and publish 4-6 in each issue.

HOW TO CONTACT: Send your complete manuscript, including your name, address, phone number and SASE. They report back in 4-6 months. A sample copy is available for $4.50 and fiction guidelines for SASE.

PAYMENT: Pays 1¢/word up to $100 for fiction. Pays $10 for 1-4 published pages of poetry, $4.50 for each subsequent page.

TERMS: Pays on publication for first North American serial rights. They send galleys to the author.

ADDRESS: 3163 JKHB, Provo UT 84602

E-MAIL: tle@byu/edu

WEBSITE: http://humanities.byu.edu/tle/theleadingedge.html

LITERAL LATTÉ

Established: 1994 • Circulation: 20,000 • Frequency: Bimonthly • Pages: 24 • Size: 11×17

Contact: Jeffrey Michael Bockman, Science Fiction Editor or Erich Zann, Fantasy Editor

> CATEGORIES
> Contemporary Fantasy, Cyberpunk, Dark Fantasy, Experimental Fiction, Hard Science Fiction, High Fantasy, Horror, Humorous, Magic Realism, Poetry, Science Fantasy, Sociological Science Fiction, Traditional Fantasy

"Literal Latté publishes prose, poetry and art from the classic to the experimental in all genres. We print works by well-knowns (Harlan Ellison, Silvina Ocampo, Bruno Schulz, Allen Ginsberg, Carol Maso) alongside exciting newcomers."

HOW TO CONTACT: Unsolicited manuscripts welcome. Send full manuscript. Considers simultaneous submissions. Submissions on computer disk should be formatted as Word for Windows compatible file. Receives approximately 400 unsolicited manuscripts each month. 5% of accepted manuscripts are submitted through agents. Preferred word length: to 6,000. Reports on manuscripts in 10 weeks. Sometimes comments on rejected manuscripts. Writer's guidelines available for

SASE. Sample copy available for $3. Subscription cost is $15 for 6 issues.

PAYMENT: Pays $25 minimum and 10 contributor's copies. Offers 1 year subscription and 2 gift subscriptions as well. Additional copies available at 50% discount.

TERMS: Purchases first worldwide rights. Manuscript published within 1 year after acceptance.

ADDRESS: 61 E. 8th St., Suite 240, New York NY 10003

PHONE: (213)260-5532

E-MAIL: litlatte@pipeline.com

WEBSITE: http://www.literal-latte.com

LORE THE QUARTERLY DIGEST OF MADDENING FICTION

Established: 1995 • Circulation: 500 • Frequency: Quarterly • Size: Digest • Pages: 60

Contact: Rod Heather

CATEGORIES
Dark Fantasy, Horror, Traditional Fantasy

Lore would like to see more Lovecraft-like "cosmic fear" fiction and less vampiric gothic romances. "We think 'bastard/bitch gets his/her comeuppance' is a dead forumla. Be familiar with what we publish, and the market as a whole. We like what's been showing up in magazines like *Dearthrealm* and *Terminal Fright*."

Three of the tales that appeared in the first issue of *Lore* were nominated for the Bram Stoker Award, including Harlan Ellison's "Chatting with Anubis." In 3 issues, the publication has won the Dragon's Breath Small Press Award for Best New Title and the Deathrealm Award for Best Magazine.

HOW TO CONTACT: Unsolicited manuscripts welcome. Send full manuscripts. Considers reprints. Receives approximately 75 unsolicited manuscripts each month. Preferred word length: 1,000-5,000. Reports on queries and manuscripts in 1 month. Always comments on rejected manuscripts. Writer's guidelines available for SASE. Sample copy available for $4. Subscription cost is $15 for 4 issues. Make checks payable to Rod Heather.

PAYMENT: Pays 2-3 contributor's copies.

TERMS: Purchases first North American serial rights. Manuscript published up to 4 months after acceptance.

ADDRESS: P.O. Box 381, Matawan NJ 07747-9998

E-MAIL: loredigest@aol.com

LOST WORLDS, THE SCIENCE FICTION AND FANTASY FORUM

Established: 1988 • Circulation: 150 • Frequency: Monthly • Size: 8½ × 11 • Pages: 24

Contact: Holley B. Drye, Editor

> CATEGORIES
> Articles/Essays, Experimental Fiction, Hard Science Fiction, Light Horror, Psychic/Supernatural/Occult, Sociological Science Fiction, Traditional Fantasy

Lost Worlds is 35-45% fantasy and 35-45% sf. They publish "general interest sf and fantasy for broad-spectrum age groups and anyone interested in newcomers." Editor Holley B. Drye wants "more authors not afraid to experiment with old formulas that need new ingredients. I'd like to find more 'pure' science fiction, and less science fantasy."

She continues, "I like to think our magazine is unique for its value of the individual and our attitude that each author and story we receive has some value. We refuse to treat any of our potential contributors as one among the many—they are all individuals, and they all deserve respect. *Lost Worlds* is intent on being, above and beyond all things, a voice of encouragement to keep trying; with practice and patience, all things are possible."

Lost Worlds receives 30-40 manuscripts every month and uses 7-10 in each issue, so odds of getting published are relatively high. Lengths of 3,000 words are preferred, although they accept stories from 2,000-5,500 words. Stories are published 3 months after acceptance.

HOW TO CONTACT: Query first with SASE. "Cover letter should include where and when to contact the author, a pen name if one is preferred, as well as real name, and whether or not the author wishes real name to be kept confidential." Simultaneous, reprint and electronic (via disk or modem) submissions are acceptable. They report back in 4-6 months on queries and 6-8 months on manuscripts. A sample copy is available for $2. Fiction guidelines are available for SAE with 1 first-class stamp.

PAYMENT: Pays contributor's copies.

TERMS: Acquires one-time rights.

ADDRESS: HBD Publishing, P.O. Box 605, Concord NC 28025

PHONE: (704)933-7998

LYNX EYE

Established: 1994 • Circulation: 300 • Frequency: Quarterly • Pages: 120 • Size: Digest

Contact: Pam McCully or Kathryn Morrison

CATEGORIES
Contemporary Fantasy, Experimental Fiction, Horror, Humorous, Magic Realism, Poetry, Science Fantasy, Sociological Science Fiction

"*Lynx Eye* [a publication of the Scribble Fest Literary Group] is a mainstream, general-readership magazine. However, we discriminate against no genre, and in all issues published to date have included at least one piece that falls into the categories of fiction indicated above.

"Your ideas, even if they are the most original, imaginative and visionary, are sabotaged by the lack of attention to the basics."

HOW TO CONTACT: Unsolicited manuscripts welcome. Send full manuscript. Considers simultaneous submissions. Receives approximately 300 unsolicited manuscripts each month. Preferred word length: to 5,000. Reports on queries in 2 months, on manuscripts in 2-3 months. Always comments on rejected manuscripts. Writer's guidelines available for SASE. Sample copy available for $5. Subscription cost is $20 for 4 issues.

PAYMENT: Pays $10 and 3 contributor's copies. Pays upon acceptance.

TERMS: Purchases first North American serial rights. Manuscript published 3-6 months after acceptance.

ADDRESS: 1880 Hill Dr., Los Angeles CA 90041

PHONE: (213)550-8522

MAGAZINE OF SPECULATIVE POETRY

Established: 1984 • Circulation: 150 • Frequency: Irregularly • Pages: 20-24 • Size: Digest

Contact: Roger Dutcher, Co-Editor

CATEGORIES
Articles/Essays, Poetry, Reviews (Poetry)

HOW TO CONTACT: Unsolicited manuscripts welcome. Send full manuscript. Receives approximately 10-25 manuscripts each month. Will look at any length except epic. Reports in 4-6 weeks. Sometimes comments on rejected manuscripts. Writer's guidelines available for SASE. Sample copy available for $3.50. Subscription cost is $11 for 4 issues.

PAYMENT: Pays $3 minimum. Pays upon acceptance.

TERMS: Purchases first worldwide rights.

ADDRESS: P.O. Box 564, Beloit WI 53512

MEDUSA'S HAIRDO

Established: 1995 • Circulation: 50 • Frequency: Quarterly • Size 8½×11 • Pages: 45

Contact: Beverly Moore or Jason Chapman

CATEGORIES
Contemporary Fantasy, Experimental Fiction, Horror, Humorous, Modern Mythology, Poetry, Sociological Science Fiction, Traditional Fantasy

The theme of *Medusa's Hairdo* is modern mythology. "This does not mean we just want stories with references to classical myth. Rather, we are simply interested in good literature with a legendary feel, from virtually any genre. Include a cover letter with your submission. Also tell us a little bit about yourself, and be open to criticism. We just want to help new writers. We do not print sexually explicit or violent material at all. We are also looking for artists to illustrate stories."

HOW TO CONTACT: Unsolicited manuscripts welcome. Send full manuscripts. Accepts electronic queries. Considers simultaneous submissions. Receives approximately 60 unsolicited manuscripts each month. Preferred word length: to 4,000. Reports on queries in 1 week, on manuscripts in 3-4 weeks. Always comments on rejected manuscripts. Writer's guidelines available for SASE. Sample copy available for $4.50. Subscription cost is $18 for 4 issues.

PAYMENT: Pays $2-5/story and 1 contributor's copy. Pays upon publication.

TERMS: Purchases first North American serial rights. Manuscript published 6 months after acceptance.

ADDRESS: 5734 State Route 3, Catlettsburg KY 41129-9646

PHONE: (606)928-4631

E-MAIL: bymoor0@pop.uky.edu

WEBSITE: http://sac.uky.edu/~bymoor0/medusa.html

MINAS TIRITH EVENING-STAR: JOURNAL OF THE AMERICAN TOLKIEN SOCIETY

Established: 1966 • Circulation: 480 • Frequency: Quarterly • Pages: 35 • Size: 8½ × 11

CATEGORIES
Advice Columns, Articles/Essays, High Fantasy, Industry Reports, Interviews, Reviews

"All material must be rooted in and consistent with published works of J.R.R. Tolkien. In elaborating his works, avoid concepts which are foreign or too trendy to be consistent. We have rejected elves named Muffy and the unicorns of Valinor. Scholarly articles should be of professional demeanor and quality, with proper footnotes where needed. Avoid basing articles on someone else's analysis or conjecture; work from Tolkien."

HOW TO CONTACT: Unsolicited manuscripts welcome but prefers writers to query first. Accepts faxed queries. Considers simultaneous submissions and reprints. Receives approximately 12 unsolicited manuscripts each month. Reports on queries in 3 weeks, on manuscripts in 2 months. Sometimes comments on rejected manuscripts. Writer's guidelines available for SASE. Sample copy available for $1. Subscription cost is $10 for 4 issues.

PAYMENT: Pays in contributor's copies. Additional copies available at 20% discount.

TERMS: Purchases first worldwide rights. Manuscript published 1-2 years after acceptance.

ADDRESS: W.W. Publications, Box 373, Highland MI 48357-0373

PHONE: (813)585-0985

MIND IN MOTION

Established: 1985 • Circulation: 450 • Frequency: Quarterly • Pages: 64 • Size: Digest

Contact: Celeste Goyer, Editor

> CATEGORIES
> Contemporary Fantasy, Experimental Fiction, Humorous, Poetry, Science
> Fantasy, Sociological Science Fiction

"Would like to see more philosophical, satirical, analytical, fast-paced science fiction. Also interiority, original language, surrealism. Read the short stories of Alfred Bester's collection, *Starburst*, and send stories just as smart and entertaining."

HOW TO CONTACT: Unsolicited manuscripts welcome. Send full manuscript. Considers simultaneous submissions. Receives approximately 40 unsolicited manuscripts each month. Preferred word length: 500-3,500. Reports on queries in 1 week, on manuscripts in 1-2 months. Sometimes comments on rejected manuscripts. Writer's guidelines available for SASE. Sample copy available for $3.50. Subscription cost is $14 for 4 issues.

PAYMENT: Pays 1 contributor's copy.

TERMS: Purchases first North American serial rights. Manuscript published 1-3 months after acceptance.

ADDRESS: P.O. Box 1118, Apple Valley CA 92307

PHONE: (619)248-6512

MOBiUS: THE JOURNAL OF SOCiAL CHANGE

Established: 1989 • Circulation: 1,500 • Frequency: Quarterly • Pages: 24 • Size: 8½ × 11

Contact: Fred Schepartz

> CATEGORIES
> Contemporary Fantasy, Cyberpunk, Dark Fantasy, Experimental Fiction,
> Hard Science Fiction, Horror, Humorous, Magic Realism, Poetry, Science
> Fantasy, Sociological Science Fiction

"*Mobius* is subtitled 'The Journal of Social Change.' Please keep this in mind. We look for fiction that has social relevance, that offers various forms of social commentary. We look for good, solid writing, first and foremost, and we especially like writing that packs a punch. Remember that a short story should be like theater of the mind. A story that is mostly summary will not make the grade."

HOW TO CONTACT: Unsolicited manuscripts welcome. Send full manuscript. Considers simultaneous submissions and reprints. Receives approximately 20 unsolicited manuscripts each month. Preferred word length: to 5,000. Reports on queries in 2-4 weeks, on manuscripts in 3-4 months. Always comments on rejected manuscripts. Writer's guidelines available for SASE. Sample copy available for $3. Subscription cost is $10 for 4 issues.

PAYMENT: Pays 2 contributor's copies.

TERMS: Purchases first North American serial rights and one-time rights if reprint. Manuscript published 1-3 months after acceptance.

ADDRESS: 1250 E. Dayton, #3, Madison WI 53703

PHONE: (608)255-4224

E-MAIL: smfred@aol.com

NEXT PHASE

Established: 1989 • Circulation: 1,700 • Published: 3 times/year • Size: 8½ × 11 • Pages: 52

Contact: Kim Guarnaccia, Editor

> **CATEGORIES**
> Book Reviews, Environmentally/Socially Conscious Science Fiction/Fantasy, Humorous Science Fiction, Interviews, Poetry, Sociological Science Fiction, Traditional Fantasy

Editor Kim Guarnaccia describes *Next Phase* as a magazine of "impeccable design and commitment to offering positive solutions to the problems we all face, such as poverty, pollution, crime, acid rain, etc. We want stories that offer a positive solution to an environmental or social issue."

Next Phase prefers stories of 4,000 words or less and will always comment on rejected manuscripts. They receive 15-20 manuscripts each month and accept 6-8 per issue. Manuscripts are usually published from 6-12 months after acceptance. Authors are often asked to rewrite for clarity or to fit length requirements.

HOW TO CONTACT: Send your complete manuscript with a cover letter. Also include SASE. Simultaneous, electronic and reprint submissions are acceptable. They report back in 3 weeks. A sample copy is available for $3.95. Submission guidelines are available for SASE.

PAYMENT: Pays 3 contributor's copies.

TERMS: Acquires one-time rights.

ADDRESS: Phantom Press Publications, 5A Green Meadow Dr., Nantucket MA 02554

PHONE: (508)325-0411

E-MAIL: 76603.2224@compuserve.com

Night Songs

Established: 1991 • Frequency: 3 times/year • Pages: 8

Contact: Gary William Crawford

CATEGORIES
Poetry

"*Night Songs* publishes horror poetry that expresses some element of horror in the human condition. Poetry may be in strict forms, free verse, or prose poems. We are open to any theme, style, or approach, as long as the primary motive is horror." Beginning writers wishing to publish with *Night Songs* should read horror poetry as well as mainstream poetry.

HOW TO CONTACT: Unsolicited manuscripts welcome. Send full manuscript. Receives approximately 35 unsolicited manuscripts each month. Preferred word length: under 50 lines. Reports on manuscripts in 2 weeks. Sometimes comments on rejected manuscripts. Writer's guidelines available for SASE. Sample copy available for $1. Subscription cost is $3 for 4 issues.

PAYMENT: Pays $1/poem. Pays upon acceptance.

TERMS: Purchases first North American serial rights. Manuscript published 6 months after acceptance.

ADDRESS: Gothic Press, 4998 Perkins Rd., Baton Rouge LA 70808-3043

NiGHTMARES

Established: 1994 • Circulation: 725 • Frequency: Quarterly • Size: 8½ × 11 • Pages: 64

Contact: Ed Kobialka, Jr., Editor

CATEGORIES
Horror

HOW TO CONTACT: Unsolicited manuscripts welcome. Send full manuscripts with cover letter and SASE. Accepts faxed queries. Considers simultaneous submissions. Receives approximately 50 unsolicited manuscripts each month. Preferred word length: to 3,000. Reports on queries in 1 week, on manuscripts in 6-8 weeks. Sometimes comments on rejected manuscripts. Writer's guidelines available for SASE. Sample copy available for $2.95. Subscription cost is $11.80 for 4 issues.

PAYMENT: Pays $10/story and 2 contributor's copies. Additional copies available at $2 an issue. Pays upon acceptance.

TERMS: Purchases first North American serial rights. Manuscript published 1 year after acceptance.

ADDRESS: New Illiad Publications, P.O. Box 587, Rocky Hill CT 06067

PHONE: (860)721-0111

FAX: (860)832-4246

NOCTURNAL ECSTASY VAMPIRE COVEN JOURNAL

Established: 1990 • Circulation: 10,000 • Frequency: 3 times/year • Size: 8½×11 • Pages: 55

Contact: Darlene Daniels, Editor

> CATEGORIES
> Articles/Essays, Cyberpunk, Dark Fantasy, Hard Science Fiction, High Fantasy, Humorous Science Fiction, Interviews, Reviews, Sociological Science Fiction, Traditional Fantasy

In the words of editor and founder Darlene Daniels, *Nocturnal Ecstasy* is "a journal that includes stories; poetry; artwork; photos; reviews of vampire books, movies, music and other club journals; observations; essays; debate and letters with vampire researchers, authors, artists and real vampires; vampire news; advertisements; contests and more." All science fiction and fantasy submissions must be vampire-related. She continues, "We cater to the dark side of things—we like reality with a twist, vampirism connected with the underbelly of human nature.

"My best advice is to send in a manuscript. Without trying, you'll never know." They receive around 30 manuscripts each month and publish 5-8 in each issue. They prefer lengths of under 3,000 words and will often comment on rejected manuscripts. *Nocturnal Ecstasy* also actively solicits book reviews and other nonfiction articles.

HOW TO CONTACT: Send your complete manuscript with a cover letter. Include an SASE. Simultaneous and reprint submissions are acceptable. They report back in 2-6 weeks. A sample copy is available for $6.

PAYMENT: No payment.

ADDRESS: NEVC/Nocturnal Productions, P.O. Box 147, Palos Heights IL 60463-0147

E-MAIL: vampir4@aol.com

NOVA EXPRESS

Established: 1987 • Circulation: 750 • Frequency: Irregularly • Pages: 32 • Size: 8½ × 11

Contact: Lawrence Person

CATEGORIES
Articles/Essays, Cyberpunk, Experimental Fiction, Horror, Interviews, Poetry, Reviews (Books), Slipstream, Sociological Science Fiction, Splatterpunk, Steampunk

"We specialize in covering cutting-edge science fiction, horror, slipstream and weird fantasy, with a focus on authors and topics of the 1980s and 1990s. To that end, we can always use critical articles and reviews on these topics. We are especially interested in the British sf scene (specifically in new authors like Mary Gentle, Storm Constantine, Kim Newman, Iain Banks, Ian MacDonald, Paul J. McAuley, Geoff Ryman, etc.) and any articles or reviews on these authors would be particularly welcome. We have no use for 'traditional' (i.e. elf and unicorn) fantasy, nor anything unconnected to the sf/f/h/slipstream genre. We are also less interested in horror than in years past. Book reviews and critical articles are the best way to break in with us as we are being very selective with fiction these days.

"Our issues are usually structured around a long interview we conduct with a leading new writer·in the sf/f/h field. Past interview subjects have included Bruce Sterling, Joe R. Lansdale, Pat Cadigan, Howard Waldrop, and K.W. Jeter (among others). Though small, *Nova Express* is well thought of among sf professionals, and has been a Readercon Award nominee for Best Magazine. Though response times have lagged in the past, right now we have cleaned out the slush pile, so it's possible to get a quick response on submissions."

HOW TO CONTACT: Unsolicited manuscripts welcome. Send full manuscript. Accepts electronic queries. Submissions on computer disk should be formatted for Macintosh. Receives approximately 10 unsolicited manuscripts each month. Preferred word length: 3,000 (for fiction or articles); 1,000 (for reviews). Reports on queries and manuscripts in 2 weeks. Sometimes comments on rejected manuscripts.

Writer's guidelines available for SASE. Sample copy available for $4 (post-paid). Subscription cost is $10 for 4-issues.

PAYMENT: Pays in 2-5 contributor's copies plus a 4 issue subscription to the magazine. Additional copies available at 50% discount. Pays upon publication.

TERMS: Purchases one-time rights, all rights subsequently reverting to the writer. Manuscript published 6-12 months after acceptance.

ADDRESS: P.O. Box 27231, Austin TX 78755

E-MAIL: lawrencep@delphi.com

ON SPEC, THE CANADIAN MAGAZINE OF SPECULATIVE WRITING

Circulation: 2,000 • Frequency: Quarterly • Size: 13 × 20½cm • Pages: 96

CATEGORIES
Cyberpunk, Dark Fantasy, Hard Science Fiction, High Fantasy, Humorous Science Fiction, Military Science Fiction, Sociological Science Fiction, Traditional Fantasy

Recently Published: "Leaves," by L.R. Morrison; "Gone to Earth and Ashes," by William Southey; "Paper," by Marcel Gagné

On Spec is a small press literary magazine with a focus on stories by Canadian authors. Stories should not be longer than 6,000 words in length. They also accept poetry and black-and-white artwork. All submissions in competition format only. Artwork is commissioned. "We look for strong, thought-provoking character-driven work. Don't be afraid to push the envelope and show us innovative fiction, but be sure the story is the most important element, not the style."

HOW TO CONTACT: Send complete manuscript with a detailed cover letter and SASE with Canadian postage or IRCs. A sample copy costs $6.
PAYMENT: Pays 2½¢/word for fiction. Pays $15 for poems.
TERMS: Acquires first North American serial rights.
ADDRESS: The Copper Pig Writers' Society, P.O. Box 4727, Edmonton, Alberta T6E 5G6 Canada
WEBSITE: http://www.greenwoods.com/onspec/

OTHER WORLDS, THE PAPERBACK MAGAZINE OF SCIENCE FICTION-SCIENCE FANTASY

Established: 1988 • Circulation: 300 • Frequency: Annually • Size: 8½×11 • Pages: 100

Contact: Gary Lovisi, Editor

> CATEGORIES
> Cyberpunk, Hard Science Fiction, Military Science Fiction, Science Fantasy, Science Fiction Urban Horror, Sociological Science Fiction, Space Opera

Other Worlds consists of 80% sf and 20% science fantasy. Editor Gary Lovisi wants "hard-hitting, cutting-edge stories with impact. Science fantasy stories must have a rational basis for looking at the fantastic." He does not want traditional fantasy, the supernatural or outright horror.

They receive 24 manuscripts each month and print 4-6 in every issue. Stories must not be longer than 3,000 words. They also accept short shorts. Manuscripts will be published 1-2 years after acceptance. They will sometimes critique rejected manuscripts.

HOW TO CONTACT: Send your complete manuscript with a cover letter. Include SASE. "I suggest prospective contributors buy a copy of the latest issue." Simultaneous submissions are acceptable. They report back in 2 weeks on queries and 1 month on manuscripts. A sample copy is available for $9.95.
PAYMENT: Pays 1 contributor's copy.

TERMS: Acquires first North American serial rights. Copyright reverts to author.

ADDRESS: Gryphon Publications, P.O. Box 209, Brooklyn NY 11228

OZ-STORY

Established: 1995 • Circulation: 2,000 • Frequency: Annually • Pages: 128 • Size: 8½ × 11

Contact: David Maxine

> CATEGORIES
> Oz-related prose, comics and verse.

"All stories, comics, and verse must deal with the Land of Oz created by L. Frank Baum and his successors or with Oz characters, or else be otherwise strongly Oz-related. The Oz series is rich and varied, and we encourage a wide range of styles. Oz does not mean simply 'Over the Rainbow' or a mile-a-minute travelogue from one wacky country to the next. We would like to see imaginative new characters, rich characterization, and new ways of looking at America's greatest fairyland.

"We encourage writers to be at least passingly familiar with the Land of Oz and its characters. Established characters and locations must remain reasonably consistent with past appearance. If you are not an Oz expert, but are willing to work with an editor to establish consistency, we want to see your work. A story set in the Land of Oz doesn't need to have overt fantasy elements, but it must be convicing as an Oz story; it must not be possible to transplant the story to the real world and have the story remain essentially the same. A story set in the real world must have a firm and clear relation to Oz or the Oz books.

"*Oz-story* can't consider work based upon material still under copyright. Please send SASE for our guidelines detailing the Oz material that is in public domain. *Oz-story* can't consider work based upon the 1939 MGM film *The Wizard of Oz*. *Oz-story* is a publication for all ages. Please no explicit sex or extreme violence."

HOW TO CONTACT: Unsolicited manuscripts welcome. Send full manuscript. Accepts faxed queries. Considers simultaneous submissions and reprints. Receives approximately 1 unsolicited manuscript each month. Preferred word length: 5,000-7,000. Will publish up to 30,000 if story warrants such length. Reports on queries in 3 weeks, on manuscripts in 2 months. Sometimes comments on rejected manuscripts. Writer's guidelines available for SASE. Sample copy available for $17.95 postpaid.

PAYMENT: Stories: ½¢/word; verse: 25¢/line; comics: $40 first page, $20 each additional page up to 4 pages. Each contributor receives 3 contributor's copies. Additional copies available at 40% discount. Pays upon publication.

TERMS: Purchases first English language rights. Manuscript published within 1 year after acceptance.

ADDRESS: Hungry Tiger Press, 15 Marcy St., Bloomfield NJ 07003-3814

PHONE/FAX: (201)743-4749

PABLO LENNIS, THE MAGAZINE OF SCIENCE FICTION, FANTASY AND FACT

Circulation: 100 • Frequency: Monthly • Size: 8½ × 11 • Pages: 22

Contact: John Thiel, Editor

CATEGORIES
Hard Science Fiction, High Fantasy, Humorous Science Fiction, Literary Criticism, Poetry, Traditional Fantasy

Recently Published: "Reoccurence in Marylinville," by Mike D. Woodhouse; "Between a Rock and a Hard Place," by Bradley Everett Duncan; "George Says," by A.F. Sweeney.

Pablo Lennis is a fanzine packed with "sf, fantasy, science, research and mystic for scientists and science fiction and fantasy appreciators." Editor John Thiel wants fiction submissions with "optimism, real poetic qualities and a humanitarian attitude. I am willing to display a large variety of attitudes.

SF keeps moving toward the avant-garde in seeking expression, and is influenced by NASA in considering hard science. Writers are now tending to want to incorporate a wider world of experience into their writings. Fantasy is wanting a stronger mystical element and more self expression from fantastic characters. They are taking a turn back toward sheer magic."

Pablo Lennis receives about 40 manuscripts per year and needs only 35 every year. Stories should not exceed 3,000 words in length and 1,500 words is preferred.

HOW TO CONTACT: "The method of submission is author's choice but he or she might prefer to query. No self-statement is necessary." Include SASE. Reports back in 2 weeks.

PAYMENT: Pays 1 contributor's copy.

TERMS: Publication not copyrighted.

ADDRESS: Deneb Press, 30 N. 19th St., Lafayette IN 47904

PAPER RADIO

Established: 1986 • Circulation: 2,000 • Frequency: Monthly • Size: 8½ × 11 • Pages: 48-64

Contact: N.S. Kvern, Editor

CATEGORIES
Cyberpunk, Dark Fantasy, Humorous Science Fiction, Sociological Science Fiction, Surrealism, Traditional Fantasy

Paper Radio's readers are "mostly people who are interested in avant-garde, political, bizarre, surrealism, cyberpunk, literary/experimental writing and computers." Between 10 and 20% of *Paper Radio*'s content is sf or fantasy.

They receive 50 manuscripts per month and accept 4-5 for each issue.

Stories should not be longer than 3,500 words; 2,000 words is preferred. They also publish short shorts. Manuscripts are published 2-3 months after acceptance.

Editor N.S. Kvern offers this advice to aspiring writers: "Forget writing for money—you'd just spend it anyway. Write for love and fame!"

HOW TO CONTACT: Send your complete manuscript with a cover letter. "Some autobiographical information is helpful—1-2 paragraphs— and I like to know where they heard about our magazine." Also include SASE. Simultaneous submissions are acceptable if so advised. Reports back in 2 months. A sample copy is available for $4.

PAYMENT: Pays contributor's copies.

TERMS: Acquires first rights.

ADDRESS: P.O. Box 425, Bremerton WA 98337-0104

PHANTASM

Established: 1990 • Circulation: 1,000 • Frequency: Quarterly • Size: 8½ × 11 • Pages: 96

Contact: J.F. Gonzalez or Buddy Martinez

CATEGORIES
Contemporary Horror, Dark Fantasy, Horrific Science Fiction

Phantasm is primarily interested in horror/dark fantasy, or anything that contains horrific elements, including cross-genre work. Its main emphasis is on horror fiction in all its forms, from the subtle to the extreme.

HOW TO CONTACT: Send your complete manuscript with a cover letter and SASE. Considers simultaneous submissions. Preferred word length: 3,000-6,000. Guidelines available for SASE.

PAYMENT: Pays 1-3¢/word.

TERMS: Pays upon publication. Buys first North American serial rights.

ADDRESS: 235 E. Colorado Blvd., Suite 1346, Pasadena CA 91101

Established: 1958 • Frequency: Semiannually • Pages: 40 • Size: 8½ × 11

Looking for fantasy manuscripts that are mostly believable. "Learn grammar and punctuation. We prefer steady writers; no *one-timers*." Also publishes *Philae*, established 1947, and *Epic*, established 1995.

HOW TO CONTACT: Unsolicited manuscripts welcome. Send full manuscript. Receives approximately 50 unsolicited manuscripts each month. Preferred word length: 1,200-2,500. Reports on queries in 3 weeks, on manuscripts in 1 month. Sometimes comments on rejected manuscripts. Writer's guidelines available for SASE. Sample copy available for $3.75.

PAYMENT: Pays 2 contributor copies. Pays upon publication.

TERMS: Purchases first North American rights. Manuscript published 3 months after acceptance.

ADDRESS: P.O. 357, Lakewood CO 80214

ART: MICHAEL APICE

PRISONERS OF THE NIGHT, AN ADULT ANTHOLOGY OF EROTICA, FRIGHT, ALLURE AND ... VAMPIRISM

Established: 1987 • Circulation: 5,000 • Frequency: Annually • Size: 8½ × 11 • Pages: 50-80

Contact: Alayne Gelfand, Editor

> **CATEGORIES**
> Dark Fantasy, Futuristic Science Fiction, High Fantasy, Sociological Science Fiction, Space Opera, Time Travel, Traditional Fantasy

Recently Published: "The Wounding," by Linda Malm; "The Blooding Cage," by Rhonda Eikamp.

@

Prisoners of the Night is "an adult, erotic vampire anthology of original character stories and poetry. Heterosexual and homosexual situations included."

Editor Alayne Gelfand continues, "*POTN* is the only all-vampire annual anthology that publishes more than your basic 'evil count in the mysterious castle on the hill' story. *POTN* offers new writers, as well as established writers, an opportunity to flex their creative muscles in the vampire genre! The more daring the story, the more 'out there' the idea, the better your chances for acceptance in *POTN*. Be imaginative and daring not only in your plot but in your characterizations, settings and especially in your word usage. It is advisable to read an issue of *POTN* and mandatory that you send for guidelines before submitting."

They receive 50-60 unsolicited manuscripts per month and print 5-12 in every issue. Stories should be under 10,000 words in length and will be printed within 1 year after acceptance. They will sometimes critique rejected manuscripts.

HOW TO CONTACT: Send your complete manuscript with a short cover letter, including "a brief introduction of the author to the editor, name and address, and some past credits if available." Also include SASE. Electronic submissions via IBM WordPerfect (4.2 or 5.1) or a DOS ASCII file disk are acceptable. They report back in 1-3 weeks on queries and 1-2 months on manuscripts. They read *only* September-March. Sample copies are available: #1-4, $15; #5, $12; #6-10, $9.95. Fiction guidelines are available for SAE and 1 first-class stamp.

PAYMENT: Pays 1¢/word for fiction.

TERMS: Pays on publication for first North American serial rights.

ADDRESS: MKASHEF Enterprises, P.O. Box 688, Yucca Valley CA 92286-0688

PSYCHOTRAIN

Established: 1991 • Circulation: 200 • Size: 8½ × 11 • Pages: 25-35

Contact: Shannon Frach, Editor

> CATEGORIES
> Dark Fantasy, Darkly Humorous Science Fiction, Poetry, Sociological Science Fiction, Surreal Science Fiction, Traditional Fantasy

"*Psychotrain* is a journal of poetry, fiction and art that welcomes intense, earthy, decadent and often risqué work from a wide array of authors, including both beginners and more established writers. I publish for a generally left-of-center audience that appreciates humor noir, radical writing and tough, edgy fiction," says Editor Shannon Frach. At present, only a small portion of the magazine is sf/fantasy, "but with appropriate submissions, this could go higher."

Frach is very specific on the kind of fiction she wants: "I'd like to see more sf/fantasy manuscripts that are on the edge—sending me traditional genre pieces is a quick way to win your own free rejection slip. One thing that makes us unique is the variety of material we print. While we search for dark, edgy material, we place few other restrictions on the handling of such material. Send your strongest, most outrageous and bizarre material. Material should be as far out in left field as possible."

Psychotrain receives a huge number of submissions, somewhere around 250 each month, and only prints 5-7 in each issue. Stories should be between 50 and 3,000 words, while 1,000-2,500 words is preferred. Manuscripts are generally printed 1-2 years after acceptance. They will sometimes critique rejected manuscripts.

HOW TO CONTACT: Send your complete manuscript. "A cover letter is not necessary. If you send one, don't give me a mere list of credits or whine about how nobody understands you because you're a sensitive artist. A friendly note always beats a cold, pedantic, computerized form letter. And no plot synopses, please." Include an SASE. Simultaneous and reprint submissions are acceptable. They report back in 2-8 months on manuscripts. A sample copy is available for $4 and 4 first-class stamps. Fiction guidelines are available for SAE and 1 first-class stamp.

PAYMENT: No payment.

TERMS: Acquires one-time rights.

ADDRESS: Hyacinth House Publications, P.O. Box 120, Fayetteville AR 72702-0120

PLOT MAGAZINE

Established: 1994 • Circulation: 1,000-2,000 • Frequency: Quarterly • Size: 8 × 11 • Pages: 48

Contact: Christina C. Russell

> CATEGORIES
> Contemporary Fantasy, Dark Fantasy, High Fantasy, Horror, Humorous, Magic Realism, Science Fantasy, Sociological Science Fiction, Space Opera, Traditional Fantasy

Plot Magazine needs high fantasy, fairy tales and supernatural horror. Favorite authors include Ursula K. Le Guin, Stephen King and Eudora Welty. They do not want to see R-rated language or themes, mysogyny or "fat" equated with stupid/evil. "Understand what a plot is and make sure your story has one. Use a single point of view and write with a unique personal voice; not omniscient. We like to see your character face tough dilemmas and emerge a better person for it.

"We exist to encourage new and emerging writers in the genres of fantasy, science fiction, horror and suspense. We give personal feedback on every submission, so if you can't handle criticism submit elsewhere."

HOW TO CONTACT: Unsolicited manuscripts welcome. Send full manuscripts. Considers simultaneous submissions. Receives approximately 100 unsolicited manuscripts each month. Preferred word length: to 7,500. Reports on manuscripts in 3-4 months. Always comments on rejected manuscripts. Writer's guidelines available for SASE. Sample copy available for $5. Subscription cost is $14 for 4 issues.

PAYMENT: Pays $10/story and 1 contributor's copy. Additional copies available at 40% discount. Pays upon acceptance.

TERMS: Purchases first North American serial rights. Manuscript published within 1 year after acceptance.

RESS: Calypso Publishing, P.O. Box 1351, Sugar Land TX 77487-
-351
E-MAIL: 74542.1361@compuserve.com

PUCK, THE UNOFFICIAL MAGAZINE OF THE IRREPRESIBLE

Established: 1984 • Circulation: 8,000 • Frequency: Quarterly • Pages:
60 • Size: 4×9

Contact: Brian Clark, Publisher or Violet Riverrun, Fantasy Editor

> CATEGORIES
> Articles/Essays, Contemporary Fantasy, Cyberpunk, Experimental Fiction,
> Hard Science Fiction, High Fantasy, Horror, Humorous, Interviews, Magic
> Realism, Market Listings, Poetry, Reviews, Science Fantasy, Sociological
> Science Fiction, Splatterpunk, Steampunk, Traditional Fantasy

Would like to see "better continuity, less self-indulgence, more imagination, play, experiment. Check out our webpage or the print publications in order to get a feel for our idiosyncratic tastes in fiction."

HOW TO CONTACT: Unsolicited manuscripts welcome, but prefer writers
to query first. Accepts electronic queries. Accepts submissions on computer disk; contact for preferred format. Receives approximately 40-
50 unsolicited manuscripts each month. Preferred word length: 200-
2,000 for "short fiction." Reports on queries in 2 weeks, on manuscripts in 1 month. Sometimes comments on rejected manuscripts.
Writer's guidelines available for SASE. Sample copy available for $4.
Subscription cost is $12 for 4 issues.

PAYMENT: Pays ½¢/word and in copies. Additional copies available at
50% discount. Pays upon publication.

TERMS: Purchases first North American serial rights. Manuscript published 3-6 months after acceptance.

ADDRESS: 47 Noe St., #4, San Francisco CA 94114-1017

PHONE: (415)255-9765

E-MAIL: bcclark@igc.apc.org

WEBSITE: http://www.armory.com/jay~permeable.html

PULP: A FICTION MAGAZINE

Established: 1995 • Circulation: 100 • Frequency: Bimonthly • Pages: 40-50 • Size: Digest

Contact: Clancy O'Hara

> **CATEGORIES**
> Contemporary Fantasy, Cyberpunk, Horror, Magic Realism, Science Fantasy, Splatterpunk, Steampunk, Traditional Fantasy

"We will work with new unpublished writers; we like to. Buy at least a sample copy. Show some interest in the mag. Don't deluge an editor with multiple submissions."

HOW TO CONTACT: Unsolicited manuscripts welcome. Send full manuscript. Considers simultaneous submissions. Accepts submissions on computer disk; contact for preferred format. Receives approximately 100 unsolicited manuscripts each month. Preferred word length: 1,000-2,000. Reports on queries and manuscripts in 2 months. Always comments on rejected manuscripts. Writer's guidelines available for SASE. Sample copy available for $5 (includes postage). Subscription cost is $20 for 6 issues.

PAYMENT: Pays ½-1¢/word and 2 contributor's copies. Pays upon publication.

TERMS: Purchases first North American serial rights.

ADDRESS: 2023 Hermosa Ave., Hermosa Beach CA 90254

PHONE: (310)376-5959

RALPH'S REVIEW

Established: 1988 • Circulation: 35-100 • Frequency: Monthly • Pages: 20 • Size: 8½×11

Contact: R. Cornell

> **CATEGORIES**
> Contemporary Fantasy, Dark Fantasy, Experimental Fiction, Horror, Humorous, Poetry, Science Fantasy, Traditional Fantasy

"Just write what you feel. Keep it clean and clear everyday people talk. No heavy slang or racial slur type."

HOW TO CONTACT: Unsolicited manuscripts welcome. Send full manuscript. Accepts electronic queries. Considers simultaneous submissions and reprints. Accepts submissions on computer disk; contact for preferred format. Receives approximately 10 unsolicited manuscripts each month. Preferred word length: to 1,000. Reports on queries in 1 week, on manuscripts in 2-3 weeks. Always comments on rejected manuscripts. Writer's guidelines available for SASE. Sample copy available for $2. Subscription cost is $15 for 10-12 issues

PAYMENT: Pays 1-2 contributor's copies. Additional copies available at 50% discount.

TERMS: Purchases first North American serial rights. Manuscript published 2-3 months after acceptance.

ADDRESS: RC Publications, 97 Delaware Ave., Albany NY 12202-1333

PHONE: (518)434-0512

E-MAIL: ralco@ichange.com

REAL FRIGHT

Established: 1995 • Circulation: 50-100 • Frequency: Quarterly • Pages: 40 • Size: Digest

Contact: Rob MacKenzie

CATEGORIES
Dark Fantasy, Horror

"Scare me! Write well, and throw some likeable characters into a horrifying situation. See what happens. Use gore sparingly, for effect; I find casual use of obscenity distracting. Don't! My zine is an ideal place for new and developing writers to stretch themselves outside of the restrained word counts of most other magazines and practice for that novel!

"Each issue of *Real Fright* is devoted to a single long short story/ novella. I believe that this is the ideal form for horror fiction, long enough to develop atmosphere, character, and situation to the extent that the reader is drawn into the story, yet short enough to avoid diffusion of tension and loss of focus. History bears this out, yet the form is, as so many complain, 'neglected' and 'forgotten.' Hence, *Real Fright*.

"I would like to see horror fiction that makes an all-out attempt to scare the reader, to keep him or her turning pages while the tea-kettle whistles itself dry. Horror fiction that thrills, that chills, that fills the reader with vicarious terror."

HOW TO CONTACT: Unsolicited manuscripts welcome. Send full manuscript. Considers simultaneous submissions and reprints. Preferred word length: 10,000-40,000. Reports on queries and manuscripts in 2 weeks. Always comments on rejected manuscripts. Writer's guidelines available for SASE. Sample copy available for $3. Subscription cost is $5 for 2 issues.

PAYMENT: Pays 6 contributor's copies. Additional copies available at cost.

TERMS: Manuscript published 3-6 months after acceptance.

ADDRESS: Electric Druid Publications, 12 Ash Rd., Stafford Springs CT 06076

PHONE: (860)684-9952

RiVERSiDE QUARTERLY

Established: 1965 • Circulation: 1,100 • Frequency: Irregularly • Pages: 68 • Size: Digest

Contact: Leland Sapiro, Editor or Sheryl Smith, Poetry Editor

> CATEGORIES
> Articles/Essays, Contemporary Fantasy, Cyberpunk, Experimental Fiction, Hard Science Fiction, High Fantasy, Horror, Interviews, Poetry, Reviews, Science Fantasy, Sociological Science Fiction, Traditional Fantasy

"We print all types of sf and fantasy, but our critical emphasis is on the 20th century, rather than on Victorian fantasy or sf of the Gilded Age." Sample titles: "Science-Fiction and the Symbolist Tradition," "The Mystic Renaissance" (on Orlin Tremaines's *Astounding Stories*) and "The Monster God of Dreams" (on Kafka and H.P. Lovecraft).

"Writers are advised to inspect a copy of the publication to see the sort of thing we publish before sending in a manuscript. In the event of a negative decision, try to learn something from it. Do not send the editor a letter proving that he rejected your manuscript because he's too young, too old, too stupid or too neurotic."

HOW TO CONTACT: Unsolicited manuscripts welcome. Send full manuscript. Considers simultaneous submissions. Preferred word length: to 4,000 for fiction; no preferred word length on nonfiction. Send poetry to Sheryl Smith, 515 Saratoga, #2, Santa Clara CA 95050. Reports on queries and manuscripts in 2 weeks. Always comments on rejected manuscripts. Writer's guidelines available for SASE. Sample copy available for $2.50. Subscription cost is $8 for 4 issues.
PAYMENT: Pays in 4 contributor's copies.
TERMS: All rights released to author on publication. Manuscript published 9 months after acceptance.
ADDRESS: Box 12085, San Antonio TX 78212
PHONE: (210)734-5424

SAMSARA, THE MAGAZINE OF SUFFERING

Established: 1993 • Circulation: 300 • Frequency: Semiannually • Pages: 60 • Size: 8½×11

Contact: R. David Fulcher

CATEGORIES
Contemporary Fantasy, Cyberpunk, Dark Fantasy, Elfpunk, Experimental Fiction, Hard Science Fiction, High Fantasy, Horror, Humorous, Magic Realism, Military Science Fiction, Poetry, Science Fantasy, Sociological Science Fiction, Space Opera, Splatterpunk, Steampunk, Traditional Fantasy

"All submissions to *Samsara* must deal with the theme of suffering. Setting and genre are up to the author."

HOW TO CONTACT: Unsolicited manuscripts welcome. Send full manuscript. Accepts submissions on computer disk; contact for preferred format. Receives approximately 50 unsolicited manuscripts each month. Preferred word length: to 3,000. Reports on queries in 1 month, on manuscripts in 6 weeks. Sometimes comments on rejected manuscripts. Writer's guidelines available for SASE. Sample copy available for $5.50. Subscription cost is $12 for 2 issues.

PAYMENT: Pays 1 contributor copy.

TERMS: Purchases first North American serial rights. Manuscript published 3 months after acceptance.

ADDRESS: P.O. Box 367, College Park MD 20741-0367

PHONE: (703)222-3565

SENSATIONS MAGAZINE

Established: 1987 • Circulation: 2,000 • Frequency: Annually • Pages: 100-200 • Size: 8½ × 11

Contact: David Messineo

CATEGORIES
High Fantasy, Poetry, Science Fantasy, Sociological Science Fiction, Traditional Fantasy

Sensations won First Place, Design, in the 1994 American Literary Magazine Awards. "We would like more diversity of subject matter in our fiction, so we strongly encourage sf/fantasy writers to give us a try." Would like to see fantasy "set in medieval America, pre-1700s."

HOW TO CONTACT: SASE for writer's guidelines before submitting. Considers simultaneous submissions and reprints. Next deadline for receiving submissions is January 30, 1997. Reports on queries in 1-2 weeks, on manuscripts in 3-4 weeks from their deadline. Always comments on rejected manuscripts. Writer's guidelines available for SASE. Sample copy available for $12. Subscription cost is $20 for 1 issue.

PAYMENT: Pays $25-75. Pays upon acceptance.

TERMS: Purchases first worldwide rights. Manuscript published 1-2 months after acceptance.

ADDRESS: 2 Radio Ave., A5, Secaucus NJ 07094

SERENDIPITY'S CIRCLE

Established: 1994 • Circulation: 200 • Frequency: Semiannually • Pages: 44 • Size: Digest

Contact: Julie Hoverson

CATEGORIES
Advice Columns, Articles/Essays, Horror, Humorous, Reviews (Role playing games), Splatterpunk, Steampunk

"We accept only *very short* fiction, as our main focus is role-playing games in the horror and weird fantasy genres (anything which is not sf, sword & sorcery or superheroes). Write to us for a sample copy and writer's guidelines so you can get an idea of what we do and what we want."

HOW TO CONTACT: Unsolicited manuscripts welcome, but prefers writers to query first. Accepts electronic queries. Considers simultaneous submissions and reprints. Preferred word length: 800-1,000. Reports on queries and manuscripts in 2 weeks. Sometimes comments on rejected manuscripts. Writer's guidelines available for SASE. Sample copy available for $1.50. Subscription cost is $12 for 6 issues.

PAYMENT: Pays in 1 contributor's copy. Additional copies available at 50% discount.

TERMS: No purchase, but reserves the right to reprint the specific issue it appears in.

ADDRESS: 12345 Lake City Way NE, Suite 147, Seattle WA 98125

E-MAIL: serccircle@aol.com

SHADOW MAGAZINE

Established: 1995 • Circulation: 3,500 • Frequency: Quarterly • Pages: 35 • Size: Digest

Contact: Brian P. Murphy

> CATEGORIES
>
> Advice Columns, Articles/Essays, Contemporary Fantasy, Cyberpunk, Dark Fantasy, Experimental Fiction, Hard Science Fiction, High Fantasy, Horror, Humorous, Interviews, Magic Realism, Military Science Fiction, Science Fantasy, Sociological Science Fiction, Traditional Fantasy

"Basically, we just want work that's exciting, interesting and creative. We like to see work with strong, believable characters. We take new writers just as seriously as experienced writers. There's no reason to be shy about submitting. If nothing else, you'll probably get some useful comments."

HOW TO CONTACT: Unsolicited manuscripts welcome. Send full manuscript. Accepts electronic queries. Considers simultaneous submissions and reprints. Accepts submissions on computer disk; contact for preferred format. Receives approximately 30-40 unsolicited manuscripts each month. 5% of accepted manuscripts are submitted through agents. Preferred word length: to 10,000. Reports on queries in 2-4 weeks, on manuscripts in 1-2 months. Sometimes comments on rejected manuscripts. Writer's guidelines available for SASE. Sample copy available for $2.50. Subscription cost is $8 for 4 issues.

PAYMENT: Pays 2-3 contributor's copies. Additional copies available at 20% discount.

TERMS: Purchases first North American serial rights. Manuscript published 2-4 months after acceptance.

ADDRESS: P.O. Box 5464, Santa Rosa CA 95402

PHONE/FAX: (707)542-7114

E-MAIL: brianwts@aol.com
WEBSITE: http://nermal.santarosa.edu/~tmurphy/shadow.html

SIDETREKKED

Established: 1980 • Circulation: 200 • Frequency: Quarterly • Size: 7 × 8½ • Pages: 36-40

Contact: James Jarvis, Editor

> CATEGORIES
> Hard Science Fiction, Humorous Science Fiction, Sociological Science Fiction

Sidetrekked subscribes to "the high standards of a small cadre of intelligent but slightly eccentric sf enthusiasts." Within the sf genre, the editors are open to many ideas, but "the science fiction classification must be met, usually by setting the story in a plausible, futuristic universe."

Writers are advised to "concentrate on a background of careful extrapolation from the initial premise to its logical consequences, which the perceptive reader might discover in the subtext. Try to strike a balance between the exposition of an intriguing idea and the construction of a compelling story."

They receive 3-5 unsolicited manuscripts a month and publish 3-8 in every issue. Short story length should be from 1,000 to 5,000 words. They will critique rejected manuscripts if requested by author.

HOW TO CONTACT: Send your complete manuscript with a cover letter. Include an SASE (or IRCs). They report back in three weeks on queries and one month on manuscripts. A sample copy is available for $2 (Canadian) and 9 × 12 SAE.
PAYMENT: Pays in contributor's copies.
TERMS: Acquires first North American serial rights.
ADDRESS: Science Fiction London, Unit 78, 320 Westminster, London, Ontario N6H 2X9 Canada
PHONE: (519)434-9588

ART: PHIL REYNOLDS

THE SILVER WEB

Established: 1989 • **Frequency:** Semiannually • **Size:** 8½ × 11 • **Pages:** 64

Contact: Ann Kennedy, Editor

> CATEGORIES
> Dark Fantasy, Experimental Science Fiction, Hard Science Fiction, Poetry, Sociological Science Fiction, Surreal Science Fiction

Recently Published: "Last Rites: Resurrections," by Martin Simpson; "The Beekeepers," by Alan Casey; "Pieces of the Moon," by R.L. Rummel.

ⓔ

The *Silver Web* publishes "speculative fiction to dark tales and all weirdness in between, specifically works of the surreal." Editor Ann Kennedy says, "I publish stories that may be too bizarre for the mainstream, but are not standard genre fare. I look for plots that evolve from the character, rather than a neat idea." However, she says, "I do not want fantasy, sword and sorcery or quest-adventure stories. Unfortunately, I see too much 'dumbing down' of the field—too many stories that read like a TV episode."

They are currently receiving 20-25 manuscripts per day and only print 8-12 per issue. Stories should be from 500 to 8,000 words in length and will be published 6-12 months after acceptance.

HOW TO CONTACT: "Send for guidelines, or better yet, a copy of our magazine, and then submit." They report back in 6-8 weeks. A sample copy is available for $4.95 plus $1 for postage and handling. Fiction guidelines are available for SAE and 1 first-class stamp.

PAYMENT: Pays 2-3¢/word plus 2 contributor's copies; discount is available to writers for additional copies.

TERMS: Acquires first North American serial rights, reprint rights or one-time rights. All contributors receive galleys—even poets.

ADDRESS: Buzzcity Press, P.O. Box 38190, Tallahassee FL 32315

E-MAIL: annk@freenet.scri.fsu.edu

ART: JAMES ZIMMERMAN

SPACE & TIME

Established: 1966 • Circulation: 2,000 • Frequency: Semiannually • Pages: 64 • Size: 8½×11

Contact: Tom Piccirilli

> CATEGORIES
> Articles/Essays, Contemporary Fantasy, Cyberpunk, Dark Fantasy, Elfpunk, Experimental Fiction, Hard Science Fiction, High Fantasy, Horror, Humorous, Magic Realism, Military Science Fiction, Poetry, Science Fantasy, Sociological Science Fiction, Space Opera, Splatterpunk, Steampunk, Traditional Fantasy

Would like to see "less of the tired clichés with nothing new added—more risk taking. Most of our contributors *are* beginners—just be professional, proper manuscript format and SASE, all that."

HOW TO CONTACT: Unsolicited manuscripts welcome. Send full manuscript. Receives approximately 200 unsolicited manuscripts each month. Preferred word length: to 10,000 (but can be longer if *really* good). Reports on queries in 1-2 weeks, on manuscripts in 4-6 weeks. Sometimes comments on rejected manuscripts. Writer's guidelines available for SASE. Sample copy available for $6.35. Subscription cost is $10 for 2 issues.

PAYMENT: Pays 1¢/word and 2 contributor's copies. Additional copies available at 40% discount. Pays upon acceptance.

TERMS: Purchases first North American serial rights. Manuscript published within 1 year after acceptance.

ADDRESS: 138 W. 70th St., 4B, New York NY 10023-4468

SPECULATIVE FICTION & BEYOND

Established: 1996 • Frequency: Monthly • Pages: 150-200

Contact: John Bradt

> CATEGORIES
> Advice Columns, Articles/Essays, Contemporary Fantasy, Convention/ Workshop Listings, Cyberpunk, Dark Fantasy, Experimental Fiction, Horror, Humorous, Industry Reports, Interviews, Magic Realism, Market Listings, Reviews, Science Fantasy, Sociological Science Fiction, Splatterpunk, Steampunk, Traditional Fantasy

"*SFB* is a monthly e-zine devoted to bringing our adult readers a diverse selection of fiction and nonfiction relating to the speculative fiction field in general. Our aim is to offer something for everyone. The primary theme of the magazine deals with situations that explore society and the human condition; past, present and future. Speculative fiction that asks, 'What if?' Stories that examine the roles of culture, government, family, and the individual. Taking an existing situation to its extreme, and successfully suspending disbelief.

The following subjects have a very poor chance of being accepted: vampires, graphic sexual abuse of victims, generic serial killers, sword & sorcery (on any planet), stories where it's all just a dream, or where the character is dead and doesn't know it. "I also tend to buy more third person point-of-view stories than first person point-of-view stories.

"We want to give new and unpublished writers the chance they deserve. We're tired of magazines that play the name game. We won't buy a story just because it's written by someone everyone knows. Everyone that sends a story to us for submission will have an equal chance to make it out of 'The Slush Pile.' "

HOW TO CONTACT: Unsolicited manuscripts welcome. Send full manuscript. Due to an ongoing problem with receiving unreadable manuscripts via e-mail, we are only accepting submissions through the regular mail. Accepts electronic queries. Considers simultaneous submissions and reprints. Submissions on computer disk should be formatted in RTF or ASCII. Receives approximately 200 manuscripts each month. 1% of accepted manuscripts are submitted through agents. Preferred word length: to 5,000. Reports on queries in 1 month, on manuscripts in 3 months. Always comments on rejected manuscripts. Writer's guidelines available for SASE.

PAYMENT: Pays 3¢/word ($150/story maximum) and 1 contributor's copy on disk or download. Pays upon publication.

TERMS: Purchases first North American serial rights. Manuscript published 3-6 months after acceptance.

ADDRESS: 4 Tonada Dr., Irvine CA 92720

PHONE: (714)838-7886

E-MAIL: darkgenre@aol.com

SQUARE ONE, A MAGAZINE OF DARK FICTION

Established: 1984 • Circulation: 200 • Frequency: Irregularly • Pages: 60-80

CATEGORIES
Contemporary Fantasy, Cyberpunk, Dark Fantasy, Experimental Fiction, Horror, Magic Realism, Military Science Fiction, Science Fantasy, Sociological Science Fiction, Splatterpunk, Steampunk

Would like to see "less sword & sorcery, less hardboiled sf mystery, more disturbing (not necessarily graphic) fiction, more steampunk and more pure horror. We love genre-blending.

"Give us time! We're always behind, and we are currently reorganizing into possible anthology projects . . . but we're very slow."

HOW TO CONTACT: Unsolicited manuscripts welcome. Send full manuscript. Considers simultaneous submissions if so noted. Submissions on computer disk should be formatted for Macintosh Word or Word-

Perfect. Receives approximately 20-30 unsolicited manuscripts each month. Preferred word length: 3,000-5,000. Reports on queries in 4-6 months, on manuscripts in 1-16 months. Sometimes comments on rejected manuscripts. Writer's guidelines available for SASE. Subscription cost is $15 for 2 issues.

PAYMENT: Pays 2 contributor's copies. Additional copies available at 40% discount.

TERMS: Purchases first North American serial rights. Manuscript published 1-3 years after acceptance.

ADDRESS: Tarkus Press, P.O. Box 11921, Milwaukee WI 53211-0921

TALE SPINNER

Established: 1995 • Circulation: 200 • Frequency: Quarterly • Pages: 48 • Size: 8½ × 11

Contact: Joe Glasgow

CATEGORIES

Dark Fantasy, Experimental Fiction, Hard Science Fiction, High Fantasy, Horror, Humorous, Interviews, Military Science Fiction, Poetry, Reviews (Books), Traditional Fantasy

"I would just like to see some imagination. We are looking for more Military sf. Beginning writers should read a back issue of *Tale Spinner* to see what we have already published. We would also encourage beginning writers to send for a copy of our guidelines."

HOW TO CONTACT: Unsolicited manuscripts welcome. Send full manuscript. Accepts electronic queries. Considers simultaneous submissions and reprints. Receives approximately 50 unsolicited manuscripts each month. Preferred word length: to 3,000. Reports on queries in 2 weeks, on manuscripts in 1 month. Sometimes comments on rejected manuscripts. Writer's guidelines available for SASE. Sample copy available for $5. Subscription cost is $14 for 4 issues.

PAYMENT: Pays ½-3¢/word. Additional copies available at 40% discount. Pays upon publication.

TERMS: Purchases first North American serial rights. Manuscript published 3-6 months after acceptance.

ADDRESS: Glasgow Publishing, P.O. Box 336, Bedford IN 47421

PHONE: (812)279-8863

TALEBONES; FICTION ON THE DARK EDGE

Established: 1995 • Circulation: 200 • Frequency: Quarterly • Pages: 60 • Size: Digest

Contact: Patrick J. Swenson

> **CATEGORIES**
> Advice Columns, Dark Fantasy, Experimental Fiction, Humorous, Interviews, Magic Realism, Poetry, Reviews (Books and Science Fiction Music), Sociological Science Fiction, Space Opera

Would like to see "science fiction that has an edge to it—dark—'horror in space' (á la *Alien*) and other ideas that explore the human psyche, but in the context of a good story. Less straight slash 'n hack horror, more dark fantasy twists.

"Be aware of the guidelines, buy a sample copy if you can, and act in a professional manner. *Talebones* is continuing to grow. We are committed to putting out a professional product, and treating our readers and writers fairly."

HOW TO CONTACT: Unsolicited mss welcome. Send full manuscript. Accepts electronic queries. Receives approximately 100 unsolicited manuscripts each month. Preferred word length: to 5,000. Reports on queries in 1 week, on manuscripts in 1-2 weeks. Always comments on rejected manuscripts. Writer's guidelines available for SASE. Sample copy available for $4.50. Subscription cost is $16 for 4 issues.

PAYMENT: Pays 1¢/word and 1 contributor's copy. Additional copies available at 30% discount. Pays upon acceptance.

TERMS: Purchases first North American serial rights. Manuscript published 3-4 months after acceptance.

ADDRESS: 10531 S.E. 250th Place, Kent WA 98031

PHONE: (206)813-6814

E-MAIL: talebones@aol.com

WEBSITE: http://www.world-wide.com/talebones/default.ltm

TERMINAL FRIGHT, THE JOURNAL OF TRADITIONAL HAUNTS AND HORRORS

Established: 1983 • Circulation: 3,000 • Frequency: Quarterly • Pages: 76 • Size: 8½ × 11

Contact: Ken Abner

CATEGORIES
Dark Fantasy, Horror

HOW TO CONTACT: Unsolicited manuscripts welcome. Send full manuscript. Considers simultaneous submissions. Receives approximately 100 unsolicited manuscripts each month. Preferred word length: 1,500-10,000. Reports on manuscripts in 6-8 weeks. Sometimes comments on rejected manuscripts. Writer's guidelines available for SASE. Sample copy available for $5. Subscription cost is $18 for 4 issues.

PAYMENT: Pays ½-2¢/word. Additional copies available at 30% discount. Pays upon publication.

TERMS: Purchases first North American serial rights. Manuscript published within 1 year after acceptance.

ADDRESS: P.O. Box 100, Black River NY 13612

FAX: (315)779-8310

TERRA INCOGNITA

Established: 1996 • Frequency: Quarterly • Pages: 64 • Size: 8½ × 11

Contact: Jan Berrien Berends, Editor

> **CATEGORIES**
> Articles/Essays, Cyberpunk, Experimental Fiction, Hard Science Fiction, Humorous, Interviews, Poetry, Reviews (Books), Science Articles, Science Fantasy, Sociological Science Fiction

"*Terra Incognita* has a theme: Earth, both today and in the future. With that in mind, here are our needs: fiction: Earth-based science-fiction stories up to 15,000 words in length. By 'Earth-based science fiction' we mean stories set on or around Earth, now or in the future. Nonfiction: Reviews of books relevant to our theme; accessible science articles which will leave the reader with an understanding of how the topic relates to his or her life or to science fiction; articles about the genre; essays and features on the theme. Poetry: Really good Earth-based science-fiction poetry."

No misogyny, racism, or gratuitous sex or violence. "Observe our theme! Right now, we need to see more adventure stories which do not sacrifice quality of writing. A well-written adventure will be read very favorably. Here's stuff we like: cybertechnology, apocalypse and post-apocalypse settings, sociological extrapolations and alternative social systems, gender and race issues, biotech, infotech, human evolution, alien visitors, ecological disasters or triumphs, non-Western cultures in the future, the natural and applied sciences. Just remember: our theme is Earth-based science fiction."

HOW TO CONTACT: Unsolicited manuscripts welcome. Send full manuscript. Query for nonfiction. Accepts electronic queries. Receives approximately 60-80 unsolicited manuscripts each month. Preferred word length: to 15,000. Reports on queries in 1 week, on manuscripts in 2-3 weeks. Always comments on rejected manuscripts. Writer's guidelines available for SASE. Sample copy available for $5. Subscription cost is $15 for 4 issues

PAYMENT: Pays 1-2¢/word and 2 contributor's copies. Pays upon acceptance.

TERMS: Purchases first North American serial rights. Manuscript published 6-9 months after acceptance.
ADDRESS: 52 Windermere Ave., #3, Lansdowne PA 19050-1812
E-MAIL: terrincog@aol.com
WEBSITE: http://members.aol.com/terrincog

TERROR TIME AGAIN

Established: 1987 • Circulation: 500 • Frequency: Quarterly • Size: Digest • Pages: 40-60

Contact: Donald Miller

CATEGORIES
Horror

Terror Time Again would like to see original stories that really make the reader want to be involved. "I am looking for really good scary stories. Stay within word limit of 2,000 max!"

HOW TO CONTACT: Unsolicited manuscripts welcome. Send full manuscripts. Considers simultaneous submissions and reprints. Receives approximately 30-50 unsolicited manuscripts each month. Preferred word length: to 2,000. Reports on manuscripts in 6 weeks. Sometimes comments on rejected manuscripts. Writer's guidelines available for SASE. Sample copy available for $4.50. Subscription cost is $16 for 4 issues.
PAYMENT: Pays ¼-½¢/word and 1 contributor's copy. Additional copies available at 50% discount. Pays upon acceptance.
TERMS: Purchases first North American serial rights. Manuscript published 4 months after acceptance.
ADDRESS: Nocturnal Publications, 11 W. Winona St., St. Paul MN 55107-3354
TELEPHONE: (612)227-6958

THiRTEENTh MOON MAGAZiNE

Established: 1982 • Circulation: 600 • Frequency: Quarterly • Pages: 50 • Size: 8½ × 11

Contact: Jacob Weisman

> CATEGORIES
> Contemporary Fantasy, Humorous, Magic Realism, Poetry, Review (Books, Music), Science Fantasy, Sociological Science Fiction

"Thirteenth Moon Magazine is a quarterly literary magazine publishing fiction, book reviews and record reviews. We are primarily looking for short stories under 3,000 words, containing elements of magic realism or science fiction. Stories should not be too genre specific (space opera or cyberpunk, for example) and should lean, at least a little, toward the literary. We also accept poetry (under 32 lines including stanza breaks), shorts, and occasionally reprints. All material should be typed and double spaced. Writers should be cautioned to send only their best since space for fiction is limited."

HOW TO CONTACT: Unsolicited manuscripts welcome. Send full manuscript. Receives approximately 20 unsolicited manuscripts each month. 5% of accepted manuscripts are submitted through agents. Preferred word length: to 3,000. Reports on queries in 2-3 weeks, on manuscripts in 6 weeks. Sometimes comments on rejected manuscripts. Writer's guidelines available for SASE. Sample copy available for $4.95. Subscription cost is $24 for 4 issues.

PAYMENT: Pays 1-3¢/word for fiction; 5-10¢/line for poetry (to 32 lines). Pays upon acceptance.

TERMS: Purchases First North American serial rights. Manuscript published 1-6 months after acceptance.

ADDRESS: Tachyon Publications, 1459 18th St., #139, San Francisco CA 94107

PHONE: (415)285-5615

THRESHOLDS QUARTERLY, School of Metaphysics Associates Journal

Established: 1975 • Circulation: 5,000 • Frequency: Quarterly • Pages: 32 • Size: 7½×10

Contact: Dr. Laurel Clark

> **CATEGORIES**
> Articles/Essays, Contemporary Fantasy, Humorous, Interviews, Magic Realism, Poetry, Reviews, Science Fantasy, Traditional Fantasy

Would like to see "more inspirational, uplifting stories that stimulate imagination and hope. No dark, negative, brooding stories or ones with gory/sexual overtones. We publish only a small amount of poetry.

"We [the School of Metaphysics Associates—SOMA] are a nonprofit educational and spiritual organization with members in 27 countries and across the United States."

HOW TO CONTACT: Unsolicited manuscripts welcome. Send full manuscript. Receives approximately 5-10 unsolicited manuscripts each month. Preferred word length: 1,000-3,000. Reports on manuscripts in 6 weeks. Sometimes comments on rejected manuscripts. Writer's guidelines available for SASE. Subscription cost is $35 for 4 issues (cost of membership in SOMA).

PAYMENT: Pays 5 contributor's copies.

TERMS: Purchases all rights.

ADDRESS: School of Metaphysics National Headquarters, HCR 1, Box 15, Windyville MO 65783

PHONE: (417)345-8411

TIME PILOT

Established: 1993 • Frequency: Monthly

Contact: Gary Bryant, Editor

> **CATEGORIES**
> Hard Science Fiction, Humorous Science Fiction, Military Science Fiction, Sociological Science Fiction

Time Pilot is an electronic publication on the world wide web. *Time Pilot* is all science fiction and fantasy, but it is presented in a unique "news story" format. It looks like a newsletter, and story titles are set like headlines. For example, stories have had headline titles such as "We Have Contact! India VII Receives Communication from Oran!" and "Nocturnia Opens Subterranean Resort."

The best way to get a feel for how these fictional news stories are presented is to find *Time Pilot* on the web and read it. Says Editor Gary Bryant, "Read it and project yourself."

Manuscripts should be between 300 and 3,000 words and will be published 2-4 months after acceptance. The editor sometimes critiques rejected manuscripts.

HOW TO CONTACT: Prefers queries and submissions via e-mail, but considers faxed and conventionally mailed queries with SASE. Reports in 6-8 weeks.

ADDRESS: The New Legends Group, P.O. Box 2567, Bellingham WA 98227

FAX: (360)734-1346

E-MAIL: timepilot@gnn.com

WEBSITE: http://members.gnn.com/timepilot/

ART: ALLEN KOSZOWSKI

TWISTED

Established: 1985 • Circulation: 300 • Frequency: Irregularly • Size: 8½ × 11 • Pages: 100

Contact: Christine Hoard, Editor

CATEGORIES
Articles/Essays, Dark Fantasy, Horror, Poetry

One-fourth of the stories published in *Twisted* are dark fantasy (the rest are horror). "We pride ourselves on having published stories and poems by authors now under book contracts," says Editor Christine Hoard. "We were one of the first magazines to run 'splatterpunk' fiction, and we welcome experimental work."

Hoard is looking for "an interesting premise and thoughtful execution." Stories featuring familiar themes, such as vampires, must take an original approach, she says.

Twisted receives 30 manuscripts per month and publishes 10 stories per issue. Manuscripts should be 2,000-5,000 words long and will be published 2 months to 2 years after acceptance. Hoard sometimes critiques rejected manuscripts.

HOW TO CONTACT: Send your complete manuscript with SASE. "Cover letters are not necessary, but appreciated." They do not accept simultaneous or multiple submissions. Reporting time varies; they usually report back in 1-3 months. A sample copy is available for $6. Fiction guidelines are available for SAE and 1 first-class stamp.

PAYMENT: Pays in contributor's copies.

TERMS: Acquires first rights.

ADDRESS: P.O. Box 1249, Palmetto GA 30268-1249

PHONE: (770)463-1458

2 AM MAGAZINE

Established: 1986 • Circulation: 2,000 • Published: Quarterly • Size: 8½×11 • Pages: 60

Contact: Gretta M. Anderson, Editor

CATEGORIES
Cyberpunk, Dark Fantasy, Hard Science Fiction, Humorous Science Fiction, Mystery-Related Science Fiction, Psychological Horror, Sociological Science Fiction, Space Opera, Traditional Fantasy

2 AM publishes fiction for "a sophisticated, adult audience." They want "tight stories that should not be read as though they were meant to be a screenplay. We also do not publish slice 'n dice horror."

They receive 400 manuscripts per month and publish around 12 in every issue. Stories should be from 500-5,000 words in length, with 3,000 words as an average. Accepted manuscripts will be published 6-9 months after acceptance. They have published Avram Davidson and Darrell Schweitzer.

HOW TO CONTACT: Send your complete manuscript with a cover letter and SASE. Simultaneous submissions are acceptable. They report in 1 month on queries and 3 months on manuscripts. A sample copy is available for $4.95 and fiction guidelines for an SASE.

PAYMENT: Pays ½¢/word minimum plus 1 contributor's copy.

TERMS: Pays on acceptance for one-time rights with a nonexclusive anthology option.

ADDRESS: P.O. Box 6754, Rockford IL 61125-1754

THE ULTIMATE UNKNOWN

Established: 1995 • Circulation: 100 • Frequency: Quarterly • Pages: 64 • Size: 8½ × 11

Contact: David D. Combs

CATEGORIES
Articles/Essays, Fan Club Articles, Hard Science Fiction, Horror, Humorous Science Fiction, Military Science Fiction, Poetry, Science Fantasy, Sociological Science Fiction, Space Opera

Would like to see "science fiction with a hard science foundation and a unique story line. I do not accept gratuitous violence nor do I solicit bad language or sexual situations."

HOW TO CONTACT: Unsolicited manuscripts welcome. Send full manuscript. Considers simultaneous submissions and reprints. Receives approximately 5-10 unsolicited manuscripts each month. Preferred word length: 3,000. Reports on queries in 1 week, on manuscripts in 6 weeks. Always comments on rejected manuscripts. Sample copy available for $4. Subscription cost is $14 for 4 issues.

PAYMENT: Pays 1 contributor's copy.

TERMS: Purchases first North American serial rights.

ADDRESS: P.O. Box 219, Streamwood IL 60107-0219

THE URBANITE

Established: 1991 • Circulation: 500 • Frequency: 3 times/year • Pages: 64-92 • Size: 8½ × 11

Contact: Mark McLaughlin, Editor

> **CATEGORIES**
> Articles/Essays, Contemporary Fantasy, Dark Fantasy, Experimental Fiction, Horror, Humorous, Interviews, Magic Realism, Poetry, Reviews, Slipstream, Surrealism

"We see too many stories with cardboard characters and predictable plots. We encourage originality, innovation, eccentricity—everything that makes a story unique. Don't write because you want to see your name in print. Write because you have something to communicate." Fiction from *The Urbanite* has been reprinted in *The Year's Best Fantasy & Horror* from St. Martin's Press.

HOW TO CONTACT: Unsolicited manuscripts welcome. Send full manuscript. Query first for reprints. Submissions on computer disk should be formatted for Mac as ASCII. Receives approximately 400 unsolicited manuscripts each month. Less than 5% of accepted manuscripts are submitted through agents. Preferred word length: to 3,000. Reports on queries in 2 weeks, on manuscripts in 1 month. Sometimes comments on rejected manuscripts. Writer's guidelines available for SASE. Sample copy available for $5. Subscription cost is $13.50 for 3 issues.

PAYMENT: Pays 2-3¢/word and 2 contributor's copies. Additional copies available at 20% discount. Pays upon acceptance.

TERMS: Purchases first North American serial and non-exclusive rights for public readings. Manuscript published 6 months after acceptance.

ADDRESS: Urban Legend Press, P.O. Box 4737, Davenport IA 52808

VB Tech Journal

Established: 1995 • Circulation: 30,000 • Frequency: Monthly • Pages: 80 • Size: 8 × 10¾

Contact: Dean Wesley Smith, Fiction Editor

> **CATEGORIES**
> Contemporary Fantasy, Cyberpunk, Hard Science Fiction, Humorous, Magic Realism, Science Fantasy

VB Tech Journal is a technical publication for Visual Basic programmers. However, each issues features a "Techtales" section with 2-3 short works of fiction. This section is edited by Dean Wesley Smith, formerly of *Pulphouse*.

HOW TO CONTACT: Unsolicited manuscripts welcome. Send full manuscript. No simultaneous submissions or reprints. Receives approximately 100 unsolicited manuscripts each month. Preferred word length: 1,000-5,000. Reports on manuscripts in 2 months. Sometimes comments on rejected manuscripts. Subscription cost is $24.95 for 12 issues.

PAYMENT: Pays 10¢/word and 3 contributor's copies. Pays upon acceptance.

Other Short Fiction Markets

TERMS: Purchases first North American serial rights. Manuscript published 3 months after acceptance.
ADDRESS: P.O. Box 419, Lincoln City OR 97367

VIRGIN MEAT

Established: 1986 • Circulation: 5,000 • Frequency: Irregularly

Contact: Steve Blum

> CATEGORIES
> Dark Fantasy, Experimental Fiction, Horror, Magic Realism, Poetry, Reviews

Virgin Meat is an electronic publication. Request guidelines before submitting. "All submissions of fiction *must* be made electronically."

HOW TO CONTACT: Unsolicited manuscripts welcome. Send full manuscript. E-mail submissions to virginmeat@aol.com. Accepts electronic queries. Considers simultaneous submissions and reprints. Receives approximately 60 unsolicited manuscripts each month. Preferred word length: 1,000-2,000. Reports on queries in 1 week, on manuscripts in 6 months. Sometimes comments on rejected manuscripts. Writer's guidelines available for SASE. Sample copy available for $5 (softcopy, Macintosh only) or $2 hardcopy.
PAYMENT: Pays 1 contributor's copy.
TERMS: Purchases first worldwide rights. Manuscript published 6 months after acceptance.
ADDRESS: 2325 W. K-15, Lancaster CA 93536
PHONE: (805)722-1758
E-MAIL: virginmeat@aol.com

WICKED MYSTIC

Established: 1990 • Circulation: 10,000 • Frequency: Quarterly • Size: 8½×11 • Pages: 86

Contact: Andre Scheluchin, Editor

Recently Published: "Virtually Red," by Christine Braunberger; "Eating Out," by Russell A. Calhoun; "Bone Heap," by Chris Heller.

Wicked Mystic publishes dark fantasy focusing on "common topics with new twists," says Editor Andre Scheluchin. Topics include "horror, gothic, gore, vampires, violence, blood and death," he says.

The magazine receives 100 manuscripts per month and publishes 40 per issue. Manuscripts should be 500-3,000 words maximum, and the time between acceptance and publication varies. Poetry is also accepted.

HOW TO CONTACT: Send your complete manuscript with a cover letter, including estimated word count, a short and basic bio and list of your publications. Include SASE for reply or return of manuscript, or send a disposable copy of your manuscript. Electronic submissions are acceptable. They report back in 2-8 weeks. A sample copy is available for $6.50 (payable to Andre Scheluchin). Fiction guidelines are available for SAE and 1 first-class stamp.

PAYMENT: Pays 1¼¢/word.

TERMS: Acquires first rights.

ADDRESS: Dept. SF, P.O. Box 3087, Astoria, NY 11103

E-MAIL: scheluchin@wickedmystic.com

WEBSITE: http://www.wickedmystic.com

WORLD OF H.P. LOVECRAFT

Established: 1993 • Circulation: 200 • Frequency: Annually • Pages: 50-150 • Size: 8½×11

Contact: Leslie Thomas

World of H.P. Lovecraft is one of the few magazines devoted to the works of Lovecraft. "I would like to see more women and minorities venture into the field of Lovecraft and weird fiction. Also, more writers willing to take a chance on something new, daring and experimental in the way of dark fiction. What I would like to see less of is 'crap sf,' stuff pumped out by mindless editors. Be bold and direct, and follow your dreams and write, write, write, never stop writing. The more you do the better you'll get.

When submitting stories/nonfiction—please check and edit yourselves, make sure you're satisfied with the work before sending manuscript. We also publish stories and special edition chapbooks by known and unknown authors (Clark Ashton Smith, Cotton Mather)."

HOW TO CONTACT: Unsolicited manuscripts welcome. Send full manuscript. Considers reprints. Submissions on computer disk should be formatted as Word Perfect file (IBM). Receives approximately 3-5 unsolicited manuscripts each month. Preferred word length: 1-10 double spaced pages. Reports on queries in 2 weeks, on manuscripts in 3 weeks. Sometimes comments on rejected manuscripts. Writer's guidelines available for SASE. Sample copy available for $5.

PAYMENT: Pays 2-3 contributor's copies. Additional copies available at 10% discount.

TERMS: Purchases first worldwide rights. Manuscript published 2-4 months after acceptance.

ADDRESS: 13th Hour Books, 5714 Fenwich Dr., Alexandria VA 22303

PHONE: (703)960-3461

ART: SHEILAH LUCAS

WRiTER'S BLOCK MAGAZiNE

Established: 1994 • Circulation: 25,000 • Frequency: Quarterly • Pages: 52 • Size: Digest

Contact: Shawn Donnelly

> **CATEGORIES**
> Advice Columns, Articles/Essays, Contemporary Fantasy, Dark Fantasy, Hard Science Fiction, High Fantasy, Horror, Humorous, Interviews, Magic Realism, Poetry, Reviews, Science Fantasy, Space Opera, Traditional Fantasy

Would like to see "more straight sf and fantasy and less mixed with other genres (e.g. horror, romance). Because we pay, we've become a very difficult market [to break in to]. Authors are advised to send only their best."

HOW TO CONTACT: Unsolicited manuscripts welcome. Send full manuscript. Considers simultaneous submissions and reprints. Receives approximately 200 unsolicited manuscripts each month. 5% of accepted manuscripts are submitted through agents. Preferred word length: 2,000-5,000. Reports on queries in 2 weeks, on manuscripts in 4-6 weeks. Sometimes comments on rejected manuscripts. Writer's guidelines available for SASE. Sample copy available for $5. Subscription cost is $12 for 4 issues.

PAYMENT: Pays 5¢/word and 3 contributor's copies. Additional copies available at 50% discount. Pays upon publication.

TERMS: Purchases first North American serial rights. Manuscript published 6 months after acceptance.

ADDRESS: 9944-33 Ave., #32, Edmonton, Alberta T6N 1E8 Canada

Overseas Short Fiction Markets

In this section we've included science fiction and fantasy magazines from overseas. Science fiction and fantasy are very popular in the United Kingdom, Europe and other parts of the world, and many authors are interested in expanding their readership to learn how readers in other cultures respond to their work.

Selling rights to your fiction abroad can bring added income. Most U.S. and Canadian magazines buy first North American serial rights, which means you can sell other rights, such as first British rights, to magazines overseas and increase your income from the sale of a single story. In this section we've listed some of the largest publications, those most interested in working with writers from North America.

At the start of the listing you will find the date of establishment, circulation, frequency, size and number of pages. These will help you determine the nature of each publication, as well as give you a clue to its openness to new writers. This information is followed by a list of the subgenres that most interest the editors.

Next, we've included a profile to give you an idea of the magazine's niche in the market and an insight into each editor's needs. An in-depth interview with David Pringle, the editor of *Interzone*, England's major commercial magazine, also appears with the magazine's listing in this section.

After the profile, you will find information on how to contact the magazine. When sending submissions to a country other than your own, you must include International Reply Coupons (IRCs) instead of stamps for a reply. These are available at most main post office locations. Many writers prefer to save money by sending a disposable copy of their manuscript and a #10 self-addressed envelope with one IRC. Allow the editor an additional two or three weeks on his stated reporting time to accommodate for overseas mail time.

Since it is often more difficult to find copies of overseas magazines in North American bookstores, you may want to send for a sample copy first. Whenever possible we've included U.S. sample copy rates, but you may want to write to the magazines for more information and their guidelines before submitting. For more information on submitting to magazines, see **Marketing Your Short Fiction**, starting on page 52. For more information on the listings in this section see the introduction to **Primary Short Fiction Markets**, beginning on page 59. Additional listings for overseas magazines can be found under **Nonfiction Magazines/Publications of Interest** in the **Resources** section.

AUSTRALIA

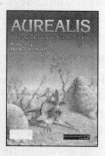

AUREALIS, AUSTRALIAN FANTASY AND SCIENCE FICTION

Established: 1990 • Circulation: 3,000 • Frequency: Semiannually (June and December) • Size: Digest • Pages: 96

Contact: Dirk Strasser and Stephen Higgins, Editors

> **CATEGORIES**
> Cyberpunk, Dark Fantasy, Hard Science Fiction, High Fantasy, Humorous Science Fiction, Military Science Fiction, Sociological Science Fiction, Space Opera, Traditional Fantasy

Recently Published: "Schrödinger's Fridge," by Ian Gunn; "The View From His Window," by Tracey Rolfe; "The Unspoken Puppet," by Kynan Hale.

According to the editors, *Aurealis* is "Australia's only professional

Australian sf magazine." They publish all types of science fiction and fantasy, but the emphasis is clearly on Australian writers, and they publish many who have become known in the United Kingdom, Europe and North America. Recent contributors include Greg Egan, Sean McMullen, Terry Dowling and Stephen Dedman.

"*Aurealis* was from its inception designed to be a large-scale magazine," Editor Dirk Strasser wrote in a recent editorial. "We want to force back the boundaries. We want to reach the widest audience, to give everyone a chance to discover the passion [for science fiction]." That passion for the field shows in each tightly packed issue, which includes a color cover and black & white interior art.

The editors receive about 250 submissions and publish 6 short stories an issue. Stories range in length from 1,500-6,000 words. The editors look for "conflict, character, voice—especially strong characters in unique situations and settings."

In addition to fiction, the magazine also includes essays, reviews and articles related specifically to Australian fantasy, science fiction and horror. From issue #15, *Aurealis* incorporates marketing and publishing news for writers of fantasy, science fiction and horror.

HOW TO CONTACT: Send SASE (or SAE and IRC) for guidelines first. Then send complete manuscript. The editors will report in 3 months. Accepted work is published within 6-8 months. A sample copy is available for a credit card (VISA, Mastercard) payment of A$8 (sea mail) and A$10 (air mail). Do not send personal checks.

PAYMENT: Payment is $20-$60 (Australian)/1,000 words.

TERMS: Buys first Australian serial rights and anthology rights.

ADDRESS: Chimaera Publications, P.O. Box 2164, Mt. Waverley, Victoria 3149, Australia

FAX: 011 613 95341530

GERMANY

ALIEN CONTACT

Established: 1990 • Circulation: 700-1,000 • Frequency: Quarterly • Size: 163mm × 229mm • Pages: 60

Contact: Hardy Kettlitz

> CATEGORIES
> Advice Columns, Articles/Essays, Contemporary Fantasy, Cyberpunk, Hard Science Fiction, Horror, Humorous Science Fiction, Interviews, Market Listings, Reviews, Science Fantasy, Sociological Science Fiction, Space Opera

"Alien Contact is a semiprofessional science fiction magazine. We usually publish German writers, sometimes translations."

HOW TO CONTACT: Unsolicited manuscripts welcome. Send full manuscript. Considers simultaneous submissions and reprints. Receives approximately 15 unsolicited manuscripts each month. Preferred word length: 3,000-3,500. Reports on queries in 2 weeks, on manuscripts in 2 months. Always comments on rejected manuscripts. Writer's guidelines available for SASE. Sample copy available for 5 deutshe mark (DM). Subscription cost is 20 DM plus postage for 4 issues.
PAYMENT: No payment.
ADDRESS: Kopenhagener Str. 28, 10437 Berlin, Germany

KOPFGEBURTEN

Established: 1992 • Circulation: 200-350 • Frequency: Semiannually • Pages: 80 • Size: 210mm × 297mm

> CATEGORIES
> Articles/Essays, Cyberpunk, Experimental Fiction, Hard Science Fiction, Horror, Interviews, Magic Realism, Poetry, Sociological Science Fiction, Space Opera

"*Kopfgeburten* works on a nonprofit base. Submissions will be translated. If possible, send printouts with computer disk."

HOW TO CONTACT: Unsolicited manuscripts welcome. Send full manuscript. Accepts electronic queries. Considers simultaneous submissions and reprints. Submissions on computer disk should be formatted as ASCII (Mac). Receives approximately 2 unsolicited manuscripts each month. Preferred word length: 3,000-5,000. Reports on queries and manuscripts in 2-4 weeks. Always comments on rejected manuscripts. Sample copy available for $6 (sea mail). Subscription cost is $16 for 3 issues.

PAYMENT: Pays 2 contributor's copies. Additional copies available at 25% discount.

TERMS: Purchases first German rights. Mansucript published from 1 month to 1 year after acceptance.

ADDRESS: Breslauer Str. 18, % Jurgen Thomann, Weil am Rheim D-79576 Germany

E-MAIL: thomann@hbi-stuttgart.de

UNITED KINGDOM

ART: DAVID A. HARDY

INTERZONE: SCIENCE FICTION AND FANTASY

Established: 1982 • Circulation: 8,000 • Frequency: Monthly

Contact: David Pringle, Editor and Publisher

In 1982 there were no commercial outlets for short science fiction in England. David Pringle and seven other people, all with some editing or publishing experience, got together to fill this void with *Interzone*. Over the years, the magazine went from a quarterly publication to monthly and Pringle became the sole publisher. Today the magazine boasts a circulation approaching 10,000. It also includes a stellar lineup of authors whose work has been published throughout its pages.

Even though *Interzone* is still the only commercial science fiction magazine published in England, Pringle says his magazine must compete with those published in the U.S. and elsewhere. So far, this hasn't been a problem. The list of authors whose work has appeared in the magazine reads like a who's who of the international science fiction scene with names like Brian Aldiss, J.G. Ballard, Terry Pratchett, David Brin, Greg Bear and Frederik Pohl.

Pringle says he's open to the work of new writers as well. Of the five or six stories he publishes each issue, usually one or two are from new writers. "We've always prided ourselves on including new writers, but it is terribly competitive. I'd say most of the submissions we receive are from new writers, but it's not easy. You've got to be good."

Although it is tough to break in here, *Interzone* has an excellent record of "discovering" new talent. "We're delighted, of course, to find promising new British writers, but we don't exclude anyone. While the majority of writers we've published are from Britain or America, we've also published writers from Japan, Czechoslovakia, Canada, Australia and continental Europe." Among those writers whose work was first published in *Interzone*, Pringle lists Geoff Ryman from the U.S., Scott Bradfield from Canada, Stephen Baxter from England, and Greg Egan from Australia.

Pringle says he "contracted the science fiction bug at age 12 or 13," and he can name a different favorite for each year of his adolescence, among them H.G. Wells, Arthur C. Clarke and Ray Bradbury. J.G. Ballard, however, is the author he credits with having influenced his tastes the most. To find out more about his personal tastes, writers may want to check out his 1985 book, *Science Fiction: The 100 Best Novels* (published by Carroll & Graf), which summarizes each book and explains why each made it onto the list. He's also written and edited a number of other books on the field including *Imaginary People*, published in 1987 in the United Kingdom, which is a reference book to fictional characters, and the *Ultimate Guide to Science Fiction*, another sourcebook and reference on science fiction novels and story collections, published in 1990 by Grafton in the United Kingdom and in 1991 by Pharos Books (now part of Funk & Wagnalls, Inc.) in the U.S.

Between these projects and his role as editor of *Interzone*, Pringle keeps busy. He has not been to science fiction conventions in the U.S., but he has been to the last three WorldCons on his side of the ocean (Britain in 1987 and 1995 and one in the Netherlands in 1990).

Pringle is heavily involved in the nonfiction aspect of the magazine, selecting articles and working with contributors on *Interzone*'s review columns. In addition to fiction, each issue includes an interview or interviews with science fiction writers, reviews, short articles on the field, and a science fiction news column. The news column is written by the Hugo Award-winning author David Langford. The head book reviewer is John Clute, whose reviews have appeared in the *Washington Post* and several other places internationally. Nick Lowe, a well-known United Kingdom film critic, writes reviews of science fiction films.

Interzone receives 200 fiction submissions each month. "I'm helped by a number of people. We have three assistant editors who very valiantly go through the slush pile, and Deputy Editor Lee Montgomerie goes through and selects our fiction." While fiction is Montgomerie's responsibility, she passes all of her selections to Pringle to review.

Stories published in *Interzone* range from 2,000-7,000 words. "We publish both science fiction and fantasy," Pringle says. "The two genres seem to be published side by side everywhere these days and it would seem foolish to bar fantasy. It would be very difficult to get enough good science fiction to fill the magazine, but you could say we tend to favor science fiction.

"One thing about publishing both science fiction and fantasy," he adds, "is it gives us the freedom to publish things that don't fit neatly into a category—anything weird or borderline, anything ranging across the spectrum of the imagination."

Interzone is open to most subgenres, Pringle says, but he tends to avoid space opera and what he considers slam-bam adventure stories. "One of the biggest mistakes writers make is sending us hackneyed, clichéd, old-fashioned stories or stories that we would consider too juvenile. The best advice for all writers is to research your market. Read a few issues or you may send something just totally wrong for the magazine. We reject a majority of otherwise competent stories because they are off the wavelength of our readership."

It takes a little more effort to obtain copies of *Interzone* in the U.S., but several specialty science fiction stores carry it and recently *Locus* has been selling copies through an advertisement in its pages. Writers can also subscribe of course (U.S. rates are $30 for 6 issues, $56 for 12 issues), or they may obtain a sample copy for $5.50 (U.S.).

"I want stories of ideas, of characters," Pringle says. "With science fiction, it's more than just good writing—good characters, plot and dialogue. I want those things, but more. There has to be the use of ideas, inspiration from science. With fantasy, the idea is important too, and it must have an original twist. Both need a strong element of imagination."

How can he tell when a story is right for *Interzone*? "I heard this rule of thumb a long time ago, and it's still the best test of a good story. If you can get lost in it and forget you're reading it for a purpose and it carries you away, you've got a good story."

HOW TO CONTACT: Send a disposable copy of the manuscript, if you are sending an overseas submission. Writer's guidelines are available.
PAYMENT: Pays £30/1,000 words, plus 2 contributor's copies.
TERMS: Pays on publication.
ADDRESS: 217 Preston Drove, Brighton BN1 6FL England

PREMONITIONS

Established: 1992 • Frequency: Annually • Pages: 80 • Size: Digest

Contact: Tony Lee

CATEGORIES
Contemporary Fantasy, Cyberpunk, Graphic Poems, Hard Science Fiction, Horror, Military Science Fiction, Science Fantasy, Splatterpunk, Science Fictional Horror

"We are looking for futuristic thrillers, dark sf satire, psychological and surreal sf shockers. We do not want any supernatural fantasy or horror. Please read our magazine before sending us your stories or poetry. We publish a variety of magazines and newsletters. Catalogs are available for SAE/IRC."

In the USA, send $7 for sample copy to New SF Alliance, % Anne Marsden, 31192 Paseo Amapola, San Juan Capistrano, CA 92675-2227 (checks payable to "Anne Marsden"). "All stock is held in the UK, and your magazine will be dispatched to you by air mail, so please allow 28 days for delivery. Send SAE to Anne for full catalog of UK titles available."

HOW TO CONTACT: Send full manuscript. Considers reprints. Submissions on computer disk should be formatted in ASCII on 3½″ disk. Preferred word length: 500-5,000. Reports on queries in 1-2 weeks, on manuscripts in 2 months. Writer's guidelines available for SASE. Subscription cost is $36 for 4 issues.

PAYMENT: Pays 1 contributor's copy.

TERMS: Purchases first British rights. Manuscript published 1-2 years after acceptance.

ADDRESS: 13 Hazely Combe, Arreton, Isle of Wight P030 3AJ UK

PHONE: 01983 865668

PSYCHOTROPE

Established: 1994 • Circulation: 250 • Frequency: Semiannually • Pages: 48 • Size: Digest

> CATEGORIES
> Dark Fantasy, Experimental Fiction, Horror

"I don't tend to publish 'conventional' horror stories: those dealing with the supernatural, the gruesome or the gothic. *Psychotrope* favors the darkly psychological—preferably contemporary settings—the fears and secrets and horrors that lie beneath the surface of the 'real' world. I am happy to consider both experimental/surreal pieces and more traditional prose stories. If possible, I'd advise potential contributors to read a copy of the magazine before submitting, to get a feel for the mood, but if in doubt, send it anyway. I'll at least give it a read. Remember to enclose SASE with all submissions."

HOW TO CONTACT: Unsolicited manuscripts welcome. Send full manuscript. Submissions on computer disk should be formatted as ASCII. Receives approximately 10-20 manuscripts each month. Preferred word length: 500-5,000. Reports on queries in 2 weeks, on manuscripts in 2 months. Always comments on rejected manuscripts. Writer's guidelines available for SASE. Sample copy available for $5.50. Subscription cost is $20 for 4 issues.

PAYMENT: Pays in 1 contributor's copy. Additional copies available at 50% discount.

TERMS: Purchases first British rights.

ADDRESS: Flat 6, 17 Droitwich Rd., Worcester WR3 7LG UK

PHONE: 01905 22622

WORKS, A MAGAZINE OF SPECULATIVE & IMAGINATIVE FICTION

Established: 1987 • Circulation: 4,000 • Frequency: Biannually • Size: 8½×11

Contact: Dave W. Hughes, Editor

CATEGORIES
Cyberpunk, Humorous Science Fiction (occasionally), Military Science Fiction (occasionally), Poetry, Surreal/Mood Science Fiction

This British "magazine of mood-oriented fiction and prose" was redesigned, going from a digest-sized publication to a full-size format. It also just switched to a biannual publishing schedule. "The beauty of this new format," writes Editor Dave Hughes in a recent edition, "is that I can allow myself more freedom with regard to design and layout; secondly, it just seems to give more credibility to the fiction." He describes "mood fiction" as a cross between surreal and science fiction. The best way to get a feel for the work included here is to read a recent copy.

The magazine includes 10-13 short stories and 4 or 5 poems. Fiction should be 5,000 words maximum. Past contributors include Brian Aldiss,

Garry Kilworth and John Brunner. This magazine is almost entirely fiction with occasionally 1 or 2 book reviews. Artwork is black-and-white and appears throughout.

HOW TO CONTACT: Send a complete manuscript with a cover letter and SAE with IRCs. Submissions may be made on disk (IBM compatible). The editor will report within 1 month. A sample copy is available for 3.50 (U.K. Sterling only).

PAYMENT: Payment is 1 contributor's copy.

TERMS: All rights remain with the author.

ADDRESS: Works Publishing, 12 Blakestones Rd, Scaithwaite, Huddersfield HD7 5UQ UK

THE ZONE

Established: 1994 • Frequency: 2-3 times/year • Pages: 44 • Size: 210mm × 297mm

Contact: Tony Lee

CATEGORIES
Articles/Essays, Contemporary Fantasy, Cyberpunk, Elfpunk, Experimental Fiction, Hard Science Fiction, Humorous, Interviews, Magic Realism, Military Science Fiction, Overseas Reports, Poetry, Reviews, Science Fantasy, Sociological, Space Opera, Splatterpunk, Steampunk

"We are in urgent need of high quality, speculative fiction with plenty of ideas and imagination—but it does not have to be 'hard-sf'. Please read our magazine before sending your stories or nonfiction. We publish a variety of magazines and newsletters. Catalogs are available for S.A.E/ I.R.C."

In the USA, send $7 for sample copy to New SF Alliance, % Anne Marsden, 31192 Paseo Amapola, San Juan Capistrano CA 92675-2227 (checks payable to "Anne Marsden"). "All stock is held in the UK, and your magazine will be dispatched to you by air mail, so please allow 28 days for delivery. Send SAE to Anne for full catalog of UK titles available."

HOW TO CONTACT: Unsolicited manuscripts welcome. Send full manuscript. Submissions on computer disk should be formatted in ASCII on 3½" disk. Preferred word length: 1,000-5,000. Reports on queries in 1-2 weeks, on manuscripts in 2 months. Sometimes comments on rejected manuscripts. Writer's guidelines available for SASE. Subscription cost is $45 for 5 issues.

PAYMENT: Pays $10 and 1 contributor's copy. Pays upon publication.

TERMS: Purchases first British serial rights. Manuscript published 6-12 months after acceptance.

ADDRESS: 13 Hazely Combe, Arreton, Isle of Wight, P030 3AJ UK

PHONE: 01983 865668

NON-RESPONDING MARKETS

The following magazines did not respond to our requests for information. Those marked with an asterisk (*) are, to our knowledge, no longer in business.

*Abrupt Edge
Albedo One (Ireland)
Amazing Stories (suspended publication)
*Argonaut
Artemis Magazine
Bahlasti Papers
*Ball Magazine
Beyond (UK)
Black October Magazine
Blis Magazine
Blood & Midnight
Cosmic Landscapes
Cyber-Psycho's AOD
Dream International
Eidolon (Australia)

Escape
Fantastic Collectibles Magazine
Fantasy Macabre
Free Worlds
*Full Clip
Galactic Bard, The
*Galaxy (exploring possibility of E-zine format)
Gaslight
Gateways
Horizons
Kaleria
Magic Realism
*Mindsparks
Non-Stop SF Magazine

nu real
Parlour Papers
Playboy
*Pulphouse Magazine
Scorched Productions
Shadow Sword (moving)
Southern Gothic
Tails of Wonder
A Theater of Blood
Thunder's Shadow
Transversions
Unreality
Valkyrie
ViperBlue
Whisper
WonderDisk
Year 2000

SECTION IV

SECTION IV

Novel Markets

$\ast$ $\ast$ $\ast$

Marketing Your Novel

Marketing your fantasy or science fiction novel is very similar to marketing your short fiction. In both cases, you must complete and polish a well-crafted story, research the publisher and then send your manuscripts to the best markets for your work. The "three Ps"—preparation, professionalism, persistence—apply to marketing your novel as well as your short stories, and you can research novel markets and network through the same online resources, trade journals and conventions. Since we've already covered that (see **Marketing Your Short Fiction,** page 52), let's take a look at the differences of marketing a novel.

Agents

Unlike a short story, you don't have to market a novel yourself—you can hire an agent to do the legwork for you. Finding a good agent, however, can sometimes be tougher than finding a publisher. Professional literary representative Russell Galen gives you tips on **Finding and Getting the Most Out of an Agent** on page 325.

Publishers

No two publishers are exactly alike in the type of sf and fantasy they buy. Some prefer single-book stories while others prefer trilogies or series. Some publish novels based on TV shows, movies or role-playing games; others prefer completely original, experimental fiction. A few want juvenile and young adult books. This is one reason knowing the market is so important. Sending a X-Files novel to a company not licensed to publish X-Files novels wastes your time and tells the editor you didn't do your homework.

If you are a new writer or your work is highly experimental or literary, don't ignore the small press. The advantages to working with small press publishers include a more personal relationship, more freedom and more opportunity. The financial rewards may not be high—advances tend to be lower and royalties more modest—but many writers find small press publication can be a springboard to more commercial publication.

Before submitting a novel or series to a publisher, take a trip to the bookstore and invest in three or four of their most recent titles in your subgenre. While you read those books, look for clues to the editor's taste. Does he like explicit violence or is the violence usually off-stage? How many of the books are by new writers? Are they single-title books or part of a series? The answers can tell you generally what appeals to an editor. And, of course, make sure that editor is still with the publisher. Careful research can go a long way.

Approaching Publishers

It cannot be emphasized enough that a complete and polished manuscript is essential. No matter how good your story is, a sloppy or poorly presented submission will only earn you a rejection slip. The same rules that apply for short story submission are true of novel-length manuscripts as well—dark 12-point type (laser-printed if possible), double-spaced on paper that will withstand heavy handling.

How you submit your manuscript depends on what the publisher wants. Most publishers ask for queries before you submit a complete manuscript. Some like an outline and sample chapters. A few want to see the entire manuscript up front. We've noted how the editor wants you to submit your manuscript in the listings.

Query only

For those publishers who only wish to see a query letter initially, keep your query letter to a single page, preferably only a few paragraphs (see **Sample Query Letter**, page 224). Mention what type of science fiction or fantasy novel you've written, giving a brief capsule of the story.

Keep the personal information to a minimum. A rule of thumb here is to include only information that lends credibility to what you have written. If your novel is about a civilization of genetically altered humans and you happen to be a genetic researcher, by all means, mention it. If your story is a retelling of a Russian myth and this is an area you studied in graduate school, include that. Avoid personal details that have nothing to do with your story or your publishing history. Remember, when writing a query letter, you are simply asking a publisher if she would be interested in seeing your manuscript.

Query with outline/summary/synopsis

Often you will be asked to include a brief outline, a summary or a synopsis of your book. Unfortunately, these terms have sometimes been used interchangeably throughout the industry, so when in doubt about what publishers want, check their guidelines.

- An *outline* usually follows the chapters in the book and can run from 5 to 20 pages, depending on the depth and length of your book. List chapter headings and a few lines about what happens in each chapter.
- A *summary* can be a few paragraphs or a few pages—it depends on the particular publisher's definition. Again, check the guidelines first.
- A *synopsis* is usually a brief summation of your story, a page or a page and a half, single-spaced.

Sample chapters

In fiction, however, queries are usually accompanied by some example of your work—usually the first three chapters of your novel. Note that we said the *first* three chapters; since this is what readers will initially see, it is also what the editors want to see. And they want to see three chapters to get a feel for how your work flows from one chapter to the next.

When sending a partial or a complete manuscript, include a title page (see **Sample Title Page**, page 222). Type your name, address and daytime phone number in the upper left-hand corner and the word count on the right. Agented authors often leave the right-hand corner open so the agent can stamp or type in her name and address. (Check your agent's preferences; some agents prefer that their address information be the only such material included on the title page.) Center your title and byline about half-way down the page and start your first chapter on the next page. If your chapter has a title, place it about a third of the way down the page. Be sure to number and include your last name on each page. Carry page numbers all the way to the end of the manuscript; don't start renumbering at the start of each chapter.

Complete manuscripts

For publishers wishing to see a complete manuscript, include a cover letter (see **Sample Cover Letter**, page 223). Keep it as brief as you would a query. Avoid retelling the story beyond one or two sentences since it's all there for the editor to read. And of course, send a clean copy, not your original manuscript.

Other Considerations

Some publishers will look at simultaneous queries, but do not send a simultaneous manuscript submission unless the publisher has indicated a willingness to accept it. If you do send to more than one publisher at a time, however, it's common courtesy, should your work be accepted by one of them, to inform all the publishers who are considering it when it is no longer available.

Response times vary and are generally slow. The times given in the listings and in writer's guidelines are estimates, so allow an additional three to four weeks beyond the stated reporting time before you check on the status of your submission. A follow-up letter should be courteous and brief and should include a SASE for reply.

As with any submission, be sure to include a self-addressed, stamped envelope or a label and the proper amount of postage stamps so that your manuscript can be returned to you. If you are submitting a disposable manuscript, note it in your cover letter and include a #10 SASE or stamped postcard for the editor's correspondence.

Established writers will tell you—the hardest part of the whole process is the waiting. Most agree, too, that the best way to combat "submission anxiety" is to get busy on your next writing project.

Geoff Sanders
433 Main St.
Norwood OH 45212
(513)555-5555

60,000 words

Dipping into the Gene Pool
by Geoff Sanders

Sample Title Page

Geoff Sanders
443 Main St.
Norwood OH 45212

September 3, 1997

John Anderson
Zone Publishing
Suite 2B
897 Broadway
New York, NY 11001

Dear Mr. Anderson:

I am a published science fiction writer whose short fiction has appeared in *Starfire Magazine* and *Morgan's SF Adventures*. As a professional anthropologist, I often find a wealth of ideas for my stories in my studies of ancient South American and West African cultures. In my recent research I have come across a tale passed down through generations of a visitation by "otherworld beings."

In my enclosed 60,000-word science fiction novel, *Dipping into the Gene Pool*, I take a sociological approach to such an ancient visitation. If a remote tribe were visited by extraterrestrials and they intermarried, what effect would this have on future generations? How would these half-alien, half-human people be affected when someone from their ancestors' home planet returns?

Your successful trilogy, *Wander Far*, by Ann Coyne, and best-selling *The Beginning Land*, by Pat Smyth, attest to readers' strong interest in novels that explore alien contact with future earth societies. *Dipping into the Gene Pool* would make a strong addition to your science fiction line.

I look forward to hearing from you.

Sincerely,

Geoff Sanders
(513)555-5555

Encl.: Manuscript
      SASE

Sample Cover Letter

Geoff Sanders
443 Main St.
Norwood OH 45212

September 3, 1997

John Anderson
Zone Publishing
Suite 2B
897 Broadway
New York, NY 11001

Dear Mr. Anderson:

I am a published science fiction writer whose short fiction has appeared in *Starfire Magazine* and *Morgan's SF Adventures*. As a professional anthropologist, I often find a wealth of ideas for my stories in my studies of ancient South American and West African cultures. In my recent research I have come across a tale passed down through generations of a visitation by "otherworld beings."

If a remote tribe were visited by extraterrestrials and they intermarried, what effect would this have on future generations? How would these half-alien, half-human people be affected when someone from their ancestors' home planet returns? In *Dipping into the Gene Pool*, my 60,000-word novel, I take a sociological approach to answering these questions as well as the effect of such a visitation on the visitor. When life on his planet is threatened by the spread of a deadly virus, my protagonist, Medical Defense Researcher Urch Lan, is convinced the key to the cure lies with the descendants of a legendary colony in the Ra System. First, he must find them, and second, he must convince them to return home with him.

Your successful trilogy, *Wander Far*, by Ann Coyne, and best-selling *The Beginning Land*, by Pat Smyth, attest to readers' strong interest in novels that explore alien contact with future earth societies. *Dipping into the Gene Pool* would make a strong addition to your science fiction line.

Enclosed are the first three chapters of my novel and a brief synopsis. May I send you the complete manuscript?

I look forward to hearing from you.

Sincerely,

Geoff Sanders
(513)555-5555

Encl.: Manuscript
          SASE

Sample Query Letter

About the Author

Geoff Sanders

Geoff Sanders's short fiction has appeared in several publications including *Starfire Magazine, Morgan's SF Adventures, Soaring* and *Ohio Literary Review*. His work has also been published in professional scientific journals including *The Anthropologist,* and several of his travel articles have been included in *Ohio Living* and *Travels Abroad*.

An expert on medicine in ancient cultures, Sanders has done extensive field work in South America, West Africa and Australia. He is also an avid art collector with a special interest in pre-Colombian artifacts and African textiles.

Dipping into the Gene Pool is Sanders's first full-length novel. He is currently working on a sequel featuring his protagonist, Urch Lan.

Sanders lives in Norwood, Ohio, with his wife and two sons.

Sample Bio

Primary Novel Markets

In this section you will find those book publishers who publish science fiction and fantasy exclusively, those who have a strong science fiction/fantasy imprint, and those who maintain a strong science fiction presence in their fiction lines. Since these are the primary markets for science fiction and fantasy novels, we've included in-depth interviews with senior editors at each of these companies.

We asked the editors about the history of their companies or science fiction book lines. We've included information on how many books they publish each year, as well as how many of these are science fiction and fantasy. Editors also detailed how many hardcover and how many paperback books are published by their companies each year and the criteria for publishing a book in hardcover. We also asked about each publisher's openness and willingness to work with new writers and how hard it is to break in. Each interview includes examples of some of the publisher's well-known authors and books, as well as examples of work from new writers who broke out of the "slush" with their first publication.

The editors told us a little about their own publishing experiences, their influences, and what authors or books got them interested in science fiction. We also asked what they look for in a manuscript, what they dislike, and the best way for new writers to grab their attention. These personal inside glimpses will help you choose an editor and publishing house and pitch your manuscript effectively.

Before each profile, there is a brief list of subgenres that most interest the publisher. These will help you find the publishers most likely to be interested in the type you write. Read the interview and some of the publisher's recent books, however, to get a more in-depth feel for the material they publish.

After the profile, you'll find a short listing outlining how to contact the publisher, including specifics on how to submit and how long it usually takes for the publisher to reply (the reporting time). Keep in mind these times are only estimates. Give the publisher three or four weeks in addition to the stated reporting time before writing to check the status of your submission. Keep careful records in order to keep track of when you sent your material and of your responses.

If a publisher is open to simultaneous submissions, we've noted it. While some will accept queries sent to more than one publisher at a time, most prefer to look at manuscripts that aren't being considered simultaneously by someone else. If you do send a simultaneous submission, and it is accepted by one publisher, it is a courtesy to inform other publishers who may still be looking at your book of this fact.

Always include a self-addressed, stamped envelope (SASE) with your submission. Some writers send a #10 SASE or a stamped, addressed postcard for a reply along with a disposable copy of their manuscript. If you do want your manuscript back, however, be sure to send a mailer large enough for that purpose. If you are expecting a reply from a publisher not in your own country, include International Reply Coupons instead of stamps. These are available at the main location of most post offices. In this section you will find North American publishers. Many more North American novel markets can be found in **Other Novel Markets**, and, following that section, you will find listings for overseas publishers.

For more on how to prepare a manuscript for submission, see **Marketing Your Novel**, starting on page 218. There you will find a more detailed description and examples of how to prepare query or cover letters and manuscripts for submission to a publisher.

We also provide a brief description of the publisher's payment and terms. The publishers in this section are all "royalty" publishers—they pay a lump sum called an advance, and then, once the advance is paid back from book sales, authors also receive additional payments based on a percentage of sales. Royalties typically range from 10 to 15 percent.

Once a writer and publisher agree to work together, they will negotiate a contract. Terms for rights and other details can be very complex. Contract negotiation is a primary part of an agent's job, if you have one. On contract negotiations, unagented writers often seek the advice of an agent or a publishing lawyer. See Russell Galen's article **Finding and Getting the Most Out of an Agent** on page 325. For more information on contracts, see *The Writer's Legal Companion*, by Brad Bunnin and Peter Beren, published by Addison-Wesley.

ACE SCIENCE FICTION AND FANTASY

The Berkley Publishing Group, Subsidiary of G.P. Putnam's Sons

Contact: Ginjer Buchanan, Executive Editor

> **CATEGORIES**
> Cyberpunk, Dark Fantasy, Hard Science Fiction, High Fantasy, Military Science Fiction, Sociological Science Fiction, Space Opera, Traditional Fantasy

Recently Published: *Freedom's Landing*, by Anne McCaffrey; *The Godmother*, by Elizabeth Ann Scarborough; *Tek Money*, by William Shatner.

@

Above Ginjer Buchanan's desk at Ace Science Fiction and Fantasy hangs a framed, black-and-white photograph of actress Katherine Hepburn, a publicity photo from around 1940. "I'm a big fan," Buchanan explains. And upon first meeting her, one detects certain Hepburnish qualities. She's a genial, open person, well-read and well-spoken and a little feisty. In describing the tastes of the three acquiring editors, she notes with a certain pride, "Most of the tougher stuff is mine.

"I like fairly straightforward stuff," she says. "I don't like flowery, dense or convoluted writing." Spoken like a true Hepburn fan. Originally from Pittsburgh, Buchanan pursued a career in social work before moving into publishing. She's been an editor at Ace for the past ten years and a science fiction fan since childhood. C.S. Lewis was an early favorite—especially the Narnia series—as was Mary Norton. From there she graduated to Robert A. Heinlein and H.P. Lovecraft. Since then, her tastes have continued to evolve.

"I prefer things that are more toward fantasy," she says, citing Tad Williams as a particular favorite. "A well-done, well-grounded adventure rather than traditional hard science fiction." She also likes near-future, earth-setting narratives, such as those by William Gibson. But she is quick to add that her editorial tastes are varied, and Ace publishes all types of science fiction and fantasy.

Ace, founded in 1953, publishes more sf/fantasy books per month than any other publisher, usually 80 books a year: 70 in mass market paperback, 10 in hardcover. Thus, in a given year, Ace offers books in every category. They are, however, much less interested than they used to be in humorous science fiction, which for years has played a key role in their line. The market for this brand of sf has waned, she explains, and Ace had become so well-known among sf writers as a market for humor that Ace editors saw too much of it.

Otherwise, they are open to anything as they try to reach the diversifying and fragmenting sf market. Buchanan sees this diversity as a trend in sf publishing. In her view, publishers are losing a clear sense of identity. The days when a reader could count on a certain stamp from a publisher are, at least for the moment, gone. While this trend blurs a reader's and a writer's sense of the marketplace, it has decreased the old pigeonholing of publishers, allowing editors greater freedom to choose a variety of projects.

"What we want is a good story, well-told," Buchanan says in describing what Ace now looks for, "not graphically violent, not graphically sexual." She adds that the hot commodity at Ace and elsewhere is media-related science fiction and fantasy. Ace has licensing rights to tie-ins to young adult *Star Wars*, *Quantum Leap*, *Hercules* and *Xena*. They have enjoyed great success with these series. Though they don't own the rights to *Star Trek*, one of their most popular authors is William Shatner, whose Tek Wars series has done well.

Shatner, of course, is well-known to sf fans, and his name lends considerable cachet to his books, but Buchanan also notes, "Bill is a relentless promoter," always taking time for public appearances that may draw new fans to his fiction.

Though well-known authors such as Shatner, Piers Anthony, Anne McCaffrey and John Varley anchor the list, Ace is open to new writers. They publish an average of six new writers per year. New writers, Buchanan says, are important to the line. They inject new ideas and voices, and they replace authors who, after four or five books, do not show a growing readership. The media-related books, however, are not a good point of entry for the beginner, since all such books must be approved by the group that holds the license for the series. A writer usually must have a track record to win approval for a media-related project.

New writers, however, especially unagented ones, face a difficult road in publishing their first novel at Ace. "The chances are not good," Buchanan says, "but they're not impossible." She adds with a sympathetic shrug, "Editors are looking for track records. But that's always been true." Neither Susan Allison, editor-in-chief of Ace, or Buchanan read unagented material. Other editors, however, still dip into the slush pile. Ace receives 30 to 40 unagented submissions per week, all of which are read.

Buchanan receives many strong submissions, but most lack "that extra spark that makes you think this could build." Work by a new writer must fill a need in the list (so timing is crucial) or must, as Buchanan puts it, "blow us away" with a strong writing style or original ideas.

New writers, she says, must know the market well. She recommends that they read the trade journals, especially *Publishers Weekly, Locus* and *Science Fiction Chronicle*. She also feels that writers should attend writer's conferences, where they can develop contacts with editors and agents. Most of the big writer's conferences have at least one sf editor or publisher on their guest staff, and it's important for aspiring writers to meet them. These contacts, she feels, are crucial. "It's just human nature to choose the known commodity," she says. "In the best of all possible worlds, it wouldn't be like that, but it really is just like that." She puts less stock in the sf conventions, noting that, "They've gotten so diffuse. They're not really about writing anymore."

Buchanan also believes new writers should read more. They should not limit their reading to science fiction, but they definitely should read science fiction. Buchanan feels many beginning sf writers don't read as assiduously as those in other genres. These new writers come to the field through watching television and movies. They aren't really interested in reading and writing.

"An editor can tell immediately," she says. Novels in which *Star Trek* characters appear, under new names, are frequent denizens of the slush pile and are just as frequently rejected. She states emphatically, "Don't think you can write science fiction if you don't read science fiction."

Other frequent slush pile habitués? Religious allegories. And novels that don't fit the Ace line because they aren't really science fiction. "The authors have written something they know isn't Chandler and they know isn't Cheever, that has some fantastical elements, but it isn't science fiction or fantasy either," Buchanan says. "We get a lot of those."

When submitting to Ace, keep the cover letter short, simple and direct. And let the work speak for itself. Too many writers oversell the work and themselves, Buchanan says. If you have publication credits, it doesn't hurt to list them. Since Ace tends to publish short novels, especially by new writers, manuscripts should be no longer than 75-80,000 words. Once a writer is established, longer lengths are acceptable.

Though the odds are long for unknown writers, Buchanan insists that Ace is always looking for new voices. Other recent sales to Ace by first-time novelists include *The Shapechanger's Wife*, by Sharon Shinn; *Looking for the Mahdi*, by N. Lee Ward and *Branch Point*, by Mona Clee.

These success stories make Buchanan optimistic, if guardedly so, about the chances for new writers in the field. Guarded optimism, a wily yet upbeat view—pretty much what you'd expect from a diehard Hepburn fan.

HOW TO CONTACT: Submit a cover letter with the first 50 or 60 pages of the manuscript and a summary of the rest. No submissions by disk or by fax. Please include SASE. They report back in 3 or more months on manuscripts, while queries are answered immediately if SASE is enclosed.

PAYMENT: Pays in royalties, with a competitive advance.

ADDRESS: 200 Madison Ave., New York NY 10016

PHONE: (212)951-8800

WEBSITE: http://www.berkley.com ✳

AVONOVA BOOKS

Division of Avon Books

Contact: Jennifer Brehl, Senior Editor

> CATEGORIES
> Cyberpunk, Dark Fantasy, Hard Science Fiction, High Fantasy, Humorous Science Fiction, Military Science Fiction, Sociological Science Fiction, Space Opera, Traditional Fantasy

Recently Published: *An Exchange of Hostages*, by Susan R. Matthews.

"Story is all," Jennifer Brehl says. "You can't throw in a few spaceships and have a science fiction story and you can't throw in a few dragons and have a fantasy story. Those are just trappings." As the new senior editor at AvoNova books, Brehl works with such award winning authors as Tim Powers, Nancy Kress and Michael Swanwick—story-driven writers that also have what Brehl refers to as a high "what-if factor?"

Nancy Kress's *Beggars in Spain* is a beautiful example of "what-if?," the premise being "What if humans did not need to sleep?" Kress extrapolates from this simple idea sweeping societal changes over several hundred years. It's this type of creativity and skill that Brehl is looking for from new writers.

Unlike the previous senior editor at AvoNova, Brehl recommends that a writer send only the first couple of chapters, with an outline, synopsis and query letter. Even better is to have an agent send the package. Agents save time by being first readers, and by knowing which editors might be interested in a client's work. Even if an agent is not used, however, and your manuscript winds up in the slush pile, there is a chance it will be read. AvoNova is in the process of publishing just such a book by Susan Matthews; her sf novel, *An Exchange of Hostages*, made it out of the slush pile. (For more about Susan Matthews's first sale, see page 386.)

When sending a manuscript to AvoNova, Brehl says, "Do not address a submission to Avon Books. It will not get to me." Address submissions to Brehl care of AvoNova Books. Brehl's assistant, Amy Goldschlager, usually acts as first reader, although Brehl sees some works first. Goldschlager says that she looks for something "fresh" to pass on to Brehl and she does not want to see New Age masquerading as science fiction or fantasy. "Reincarnation, the astral plain, and other New Age terminology are warning flags, and I don't want to see them."

With the diversity of writers and styles published under the AvoNova banner, Brehl has not noticed any current trends, nor does she have any specific sub-genres she wants to see more of. Well-written stories will catch her attention more surely than any particular subject. And within reason, there are no taboos. Tim Powers's *Last Call* contains graphic violence and some sex, both necessary to the story without detracting from it.

Brehl has always been interested in science fiction, as a reader and an editor. Though her last job at Bantam Doubleday Dell was not with its science fiction line, she was Isaac Asimov's editor for the last ten years of his life. She has recently helped Asimov's brother, Stanley Asimov, assemble a book of Isaac's correspondence.

From Bantam Doubleday Dell, Brehl moved to AvoNova as senior editor, taking the place of John Douglas, who had been senior editor since the 1991 inception of the AvoNova imprint. Brehl has been at AvoNova since December of 1995. She is easing back into the science ficiton scene by attending Lunacon and other conventions, which she attended frequently when working with Asimov. She recommends that beginning writers attend conventions, also, as a way to meet editors and other writers.

It may come as no surprise to learn that Brehl's advice to writers is to read—especially Isaac Asimov, Ray Bradbury and Arthur C. Clarke. Maureen McHugh, Neil Stephenson, Dan Simmons, Tim Powers and Ursula K. LeGuin are other writers with strong narrative voices whose works cross genres, stretch bounderies, and always flirt with "what-if?"

HOW TO CONTACT: Send complete manuscript with a SASE.
PAYMENT: Pays a "negotiable, competitive" advance against royalties.
ADDRESS: 1350 Avenue of the Americas, New York NY 10019
PHONE: (212)261-6800 ✳

BAEN BOOKS

Contact: Toni Weisskopf, Executive Editor

> **CATEGORIES**
> Cyberpunk, Hard Science Fiction, High Fantasy, Humorous Science Fiction, Military Fantasy, Military Science Fiction, Sociological Science Fiction, Space Opera, Traditional Fantasy, Urban Fantasy

Recently Published: *Mirror Dance*, by Lois McMaster-Bujold; *Paths to Otherwhere*, by James P. Hogan; *The Fire Rose*, by Mercedes Lackey.

Toni Weisskopf joined Baen Books in 1987 straight out of college. In fact, she started there as an editorial assistant on the Monday after graduation. She had a keen interest in science fiction while growing up and taught classes on the subject in college. Her interest in the subject matter led her to a growing participation in science fiction fandom, attending conventions where she met some of her favorite authors and editors. When she was about to graduate from college, a friend suggested she use her interest (and the contacts she had made) to try to get a job in publishing. She had met one of the Baen editors at a convention and when she sent the company her résumé, they gave her a call and subsequently the job.

The advantage to working for a small, independent company like Baen, she says, is that you get hands-on experience in the entire operation and you get it fairly quickly. Now she's executive editor, a position that enables her to have a hand in advertising, promotion, author contracts and management as well as editing.

The regular editorial staff is headed by Publisher and Editor-in-Chief Jim Baen. Baen has the final say on all acquisitions. This explains Weisskopf, helps Baen Books to offer a flexible but consistent line. "There are things that we are known for publishing well, and I think Baen as a line has a distinct flavor, a consistency of taste from book to book. If you like one Baen author, chances are good you'll like the work of someone else we publish too. As the editor-in-chief, Jim Baen's tastes guide the entire line. In this way we're more like an old-fashioned publishing company—the name on the spine means something.

"With that said, Jim's tastes are very eclectic, so we're not restricted to any subgenre. We publish science fiction. It can be time travel, planet stories, space adventure, near-future, alternative societies. . . . We also publish high fantasy, low fantasy, epic fantasy, just about anything you might term fantasy."

There are a few things Weisskopf says the company does very well. Space adventure, the kind of thing Poul Anderson and Robert A. Heinlein have written, she says, is one area for which the publisher is well-known. She names David Weber, who has done several books for Baen, including his Honor Harrington series, as a major new author in this subgenre.

Military science fiction is another strong area for Baen, with well-known authors like David Drake and Jerry Pournelle leading the list. Here, Weisskopf makes a clear distinction between "military" and "militaristic" science fiction. "Militaristic science fiction tends to use war and violence as plot without really exploring it. In military science fiction, war and its implications are a theme. Drake's work deals with tactics and the soldier's-eye view of war. Pournelle takes a philosophical approach to war and its impact on society. A lot of people have tried to imitate these writers because they've been so successful. These days people are labeling any novel that has a battle in it whatsoever as 'military.' Just because a novel includes a battle does not mean it is concerned with the implications of war.

"On the fantasy side, something we really like to publish is urban fantasy," says Weisskopf. "It's an old idea tracing back to John W. Campbell's *Unknown* magazine. The premise is simple. A fantasy character—an elf, a dwarf, a vampire—exists in the real world, and the story goes on from there. Mercedes Lackey has done several urban fantasies for us."

Baen publishes a number of top names in the science fiction field. Books are published in both hardcover and softcover, depending on the book and the author's clout (on some hardcovers, the author's name is as large as the book's title). Yet, out of about 60 titles a year, about a tenth are from new writers. Weisskopf is particularly proud of the success of these writers, especially those whose work first came in through the slush pile.

Lois McMaster Bujold's first manuscript was "discovered" in the slush pile, and it was so well received by Baen that the author was able to sell them two more sight unseen on the strength of that one. Since that time, says Weisskopf, Bujold has gone on to do 11 novels with the company and has won several awards. Her novel, *Falling Free*, received a Nebula and three of her books, *The Vor Game*, *Barrayar* and *Mirror Dance*, have received Hugos. She also won a Hugo for part of a novel, "Mountain of Madness," which appeared in a Baen collection of her work, *Borders of Infinity*.

Weisskopf says the first work of critically acclaimed author Elizabeth Moon was also an unsolicited manuscript. Moon's first novel, which became the trilogy, *The Deed of Paksenarrion*, was a "high-heroic fantasy" that, unlike most fantasy, became known for its gritty realism. "Some have called it the first book of military fantasy," says Weisskopf, and Baen has become known as a pioneer of this type of fantasy in which magic and strategic low-tech warmaking play a role as opposed to mere thud and blunder.

Baen is also known for its creative pairings or collaborations of new authors and their more established colleagues. Moon joined with Anne McCaffrey to help with writing *Sassinak*, a book from "The Planet Pirates" series. "The Ship Who" is another popular series featuring authors in pairs including McCaffrey, Mercedes Lackey and others. The idea originated, says Weisskopf, with McCaffrey. "*Sassinak* was part of a series she wanted to continue, but couldn't because she didn't have the time, so we matched her with Moon and then with another author, Jody Lynn Nye, and let her rip. When you get the right combination of authors, there's a special synergy. This way we got some really great novels that wouldn't otherwise have been written." On many collaborations, Baen works with well-known packager Bill Fawcett, who was instrumental in the McCaffrey deals.

When asked why series books have been so popular (Baen Books does several three-book and a few multibook series), Weisskopf says it's the nature of the beast. "In science fiction more than any other type of fiction, the reader invests a lot of time learning about a world and what the rules are of that world. They want to go on from there. And a lot of authors, once they've set up a world, feel they have more than one story to tell about it."

If an author has an idea for a series, they should mention it when submitting, but, says Weisskopf, "We insist that any novel in a series be a complete novel in itself, not dependent on other volumes in the series for a sense of closure or completeness. We want a series in which you can start anywhere, not necessarily in chronological order."

New writers must be especially mindful of this, she says. "I want to stress that, although there are a few exceptions, in general, new writers should concentrate on writing one novel. There are really very few stories that can't be told in one volume."

One thing that ties all Baen writers together regardless of subgenre is their desire and ability to make a statement with their stories. It's important, says Weisskopf, for writers to have something to say. "You have to know how to formulate sentences and put a story together, of course, but that isn't enough for us. There must be something behind your work other than smooth prose. The idea is essential. Without it you're not doing science fiction. Sometimes I have my writers do a little exercise like they did in freshman English. I ask them to write a paragraph on the theme of their novel. It helps them to clarify their thinking and see where they want the story to go. If it's good copy, of course we steal it for our packaging of the novel."

Editing for Baen keeps Weisskopf busy, but she still manages to keep active in the larger science fiction world. She still attends some conventions, but warns writers, "Conventions can be a double-edged sword. They're primarily for fans. As a published author it's good to meet part of your audience and talk to other writers, but it's not something you need to do to get published. You can't write at a convention. What you need is a quiet room and a word processor and that's about it."

Weisskopf is hesitant to say which subgenres or trends are most popular right now. She cautions writers (and publishers) not to fall prey to the trap of writing and publishing only the things they think will be popular. The next "trend" has not been written yet. "I think today's science fiction publishers are having trouble meeting the field's potential. Science fiction today should be dealing more with technology, telling people about the future and helping them explore it. That's a challenge that all science fiction publishers will face for at least the next ten years."

HOW TO CONTACT: Send submissions to Executive Editor Toni Weis-skopf. Send your complete manuscript or an outline/synopsis and 3 consecutive chapters along with SASE. They will report in 4-6 weeks on partials, 6-10 weeks on complete manuscripts. They will look at simultaneous submissions, but "grudgingly and not as seriously as at exclusives."

PAYMENT: Pays in royalties and offers an advance, but they vary depending on project. Authors receive galleys. Writer's guidelines are available for a SASE.

ADDRESS: P.O. Box 1403, Riverdale NY 10471

PHONE: (718)548-3100

WEBSITE: http://www.baen.com ✳

BANTAM SPECTRA BOOKS

Division of Bantam Doubleday Dell Publishing Group, Inc.

Contact: Tom Dupree, Senior Editor

> CATEGORIES
> Cyberpunk, Hard Science Fiction, High Fantasy, Humorous Science Fiction,
> Military Science Fiction, Sociological Science Fiction, Space Opera,
> Traditional Fantasy

Recently Published: *Endymion*, by Dan Simmons; *Brightness Reef*, by David Brin; *Royal Assassin*, by Robin Hobb.

When the U.S. space program was taking off, Tom Dupree was being transported to worlds and galaxies unknown via the young-adult space exploration novels of Andre Norton and Robert A. Heinlein and, along the way, developing a sense of wonder about what might exist beyond earth. Dupree still has a "thrill at wondering what's out there," which is partly the reason for his arrival at the post he holds today: a senior editor at one of the oldest paperback publishing houses in America, Bantam Books, where he edits for the Spectra imprint.

"I never thought while growing up about being an sf editor, and I never thought I would actually edit science fiction," Dupree says. "I've just always been a reader and a fan. But when I first got to Bantam Books, that's what I wanted to do. A series of good fortunes has given me that chance."

Dupree began editing for Spectra in July 1993. Before that he spent a year editing historical novels and westerns for Bantam and a year and a half managing Bantam's hardcover and trade books. Prior to that he was head writer of the house's cover copy department.

Founded in 1985, the Spectra imprint seeks to publish science fiction of high quality and commercial success as well as attract readers who don't normally read sf. "We're trying to publish works of such quality that they transcend the field," Dupree says. "We don't always hit it, but that's what we're looking for. We prize writing ability higher than anything else."

Several bestsellers and award winners are proof Spectra is hitting the mark. *Hyperion*, by Dan Simmons, was a 1990 Hugo Award winner and Ursula K. Le Guin's book, *Tehanu*, won the Nebula Award in 1991. In 1993 three of the five Hugo Award nominees were books published by Spectra, and among the two that tied for the award that year was Spectra's *Doomsday Book*, by Connie Willis. The summer of 1993 brought more accolades when Spectra published *Virtual Light*, and it became William Gibson's first book to hit the *New York Times* best-seller list. "That's pretty amazing for a science fiction book," Dupree says. That summer Spectra came out with a tie-in book with DC Comics, *The Death and Life of Superman*, which also hit the *New York Times* bestseller list.

"We've had a good deal of commercial success and we're very proud of the fact that our books are on most people's short list for the annual awards year after year, so that's very gratifying," Dupree says.

Spectra publishes 60 to 70 paperbacks and 20 to 30 hardcovers and trade paperbacks a year, mainly literary hard sf. Other categories include high fantasy (two of the biggest names in this field, Margaret Weis and Tracy Hickman, are Spectra authors), space adventure, sociological sf, space opera (the *Star Wars* books Spectra publishes in conjunction with Lucasfilm) and cyberpunk. Cyberpunk "deals with the vast amounts of information our culture is forcing on us—computers and modems have a lot to do with cyberpunk, but not everything," Dupree explains. Spectra shies away from dark fantasy. "Dark fantasy is usually a code word for horror, and we don't do too much horror anymore," he says.

On the bookshelves, Spectra paperbacks and hardbacks have a professional look. Glossy covers, colorful artwork and concise, lively copy invite readers inside the paperbacks, where a wealth of quotes from prominent reviewers across the country grab attention. Hardbacks, such as *Virtual Light*, present a different design style for readers with longer cover copy inside and pointed reviews by highly acclaimed authors on the outside back cover. Typefaces selected to tell the story are typically easy to read. In the case of *Virtual Light*, the typeface reminds readers of a computer-generated readout, which may take readers some getting accustomed to.

Most of the work Spectra handles is agented, but that doesn't necessarily mean beginning writers have to have an agent to approach Spectra. "Having an agent helps," Dupree says, "but first-time authors sell books all the time without them." Recent sales to Spectra by first-time novelists include *Luck in the Shadows*, by Lynn Flewelling; *Quasar*, by Jamil Nasir and *Lethe*, by Tricia Sullivan. "We strongly believe in finding new writers," he says.

Spectra editors prefer seeing a three-page, double-spaced synopsis describing a fresh, compelling idea for a novel, along with a cover letter briefly stating publication credits that are pertinent, such as publication in any of the sf magazines—*Asimov's*, *Analog*, *Magazine of Fantasy and Science Fiction* or *Amazing Stories*. Sending an entire manuscript is highly discouraged because of the time constraints editors must deal with every day, but these are still reviewed by editorial assistants.

Story ideas that are a departure from what's been published before are what Spectra is looking for. "Science fiction is really a literature of ideas," Dupree says. "We're tired of stories that have been told again and again. A lot of writers, especially young ones who are starting off and want to write science fiction, fall into the trap of telling a story that's been told. For example, two astronauts, a man and a woman, crash on a planet. They're stranded; they're going to live out the rest of their lives there, and their names are Adam and Eve. That's the old type of *Twilight Zone* or O. Henry story. You tend to see these stories told again and again."

Spectra reports within six to eight weeks on queries, and writers fortunate enough to have their manuscripts considered can expect their work in print one to three years after acceptance. As far as length is concerned, "under about 50,000 words is a little too short for us, but beyond that it's the length that the book wants to be," Dupree says.

An active imagination and a knack for observing real science are the best prerequisites for becoming a successful sf author. "Most people assume that William Gibson, who writes about computers and information exchanges, must be a computer whiz and plugged into a number of computer networks," Dupree says. "Actually, I found when I met him that he wrote his first book on a manual typewriter. What he created was all in his imagination. To me, that's truly astounding. Science fiction writers are also usually one step ahead of the scientific discoveries we read about almost on a weekly basis. Some of these writers could be great science journalists themselves."

On the outlook for science fiction, Dupree says, "Science fiction publishing is well enough entrenched in the pop culture that it is assured a rosy future. *TV Guide* even began a science fiction column about all the sf shows that are on TV." Science fiction readers are highly selective now and will be even more discerning in the future, Dupree adds. "Readers will still require a higher level of invention and writing ability," he says, "and as long as the readership still has a sense of wonder and still wants to escape, the best writers will always have an audience."

Dupree declines to elaborate on questions of average royalty and the lowest/highest advance offered to beginning writers. "Payments to a first-time novelist depend on the book," Dupree says. "If a first-time novelist had written a book like *Virtual Light*, there would probably be an auction for it among three or four publishing houses because they would all see how fantastic it is and then who knows how much it would fetch. Authors are individual artists, and their books are individual creations. We don't have a standard contract."

Dupree offers these last words of advice for writers who would like to publish with Spectra: "Look to the magazine marketplace first to publish your short stories. That's really my highest recommendation for somebody wanting to break into the field. When you come up with a proposal and you tell us you've been published in *Asimov's* a couple of times, we perk up."

HOW TO CONTACT: The editors prefer to see a 3-page, double-spaced synopsis with a cover letter listing publication credits. They will reluctantly accept complete manuscripts. They report back on queries as soon as possible.

PAYMENT: Pays an advance against royalties depending on the author.

ADDRESS: 1540 Broadway, New York NY 10036

WEBSITE: http://www.bdd.com ✳

DAW BOOKS, INC.

Contact: Sheila Gilbert, Copublisher

CATEGORIES
Dark Fantasy, Hard Science Fiction, High Fantasy, Military Science Fiction, Sociological Science Fiction, Traditional Fantasy

Recently Published: *The Silver Gryphon,* by Mercedes Lackey and Larry Dixon; *Exiles: Volume 1-The Ruins of Ambrai,* by Melanie Rawn; *Inheritor,* by C.J. Cherryh.

❦

"We were the first company devoted solely to science fiction and fantasy," says Sheila Gilbert of DAW Books, Inc. She and Betsy Wollheim share the job of publisher at DAW, a company started by Wollheim's father in 1971 (the company name is derived from Don Wollheim's initials). He was editor-in-chief at Ace before he started his own company, and Gilbert, who has known the Wollheims since she was 13, took her first job in publishing with the elder Wollheim at Ace.

Less than a year after Wollheim left to start DAW, Gilbert went to work at New American Library and eventually became editor of the Signet science fiction line (Roc's predecessor). In July, 1985, Don Wollheim became very ill, and the family asked Gilbert to come work with them. "So I guess you could say I was heading here since I was 13," she says.

Betsy Wollheim and Sheila Gilbert are also the only editors at DAW who work directly with authors on manuscripts. They are aided by Assistant Editor Peter Stampfel and Gilbert's husband, Michael, who read through slush pile submissions. "We're possibly the last family company—or, actually, two-family company—in existence [working in this field]," says Gilbert, and there are many advantages in this for authors.

"It's really true we consider authors a part of our family, and I think they consider us family, too. There are a lot of things we can offer authors that a bigger company can't. For instance, at a larger publisher you may have your first book published and find out that the editor you started with is two editors removed from the one who is the editor when your book comes out. So we can offer more continuity. And when authors have a problem, we can sometimes help them out in ways that someone in a larger corporate structure would not be free to do. We have a personal investment in the company, the books and the authors."

One thing smaller companies seem to be able to do well is keep the backlist accessible, and DAW is no exception, says Gilbert. This is very important in science fiction and fantasy, she says, where so many books are done in series. In fact, DAW has a policy of reissuing other books in a series each time a new book comes out. If an author has started something new, the publisher will even reissue that writer's earlier work. "It's good for the authors and the readers," Gilbert says.

DAW publishes in both hardcover and paperback. They always publish three original paperbacks a month and sometimes one hardcover volume as well. "I would say we publish between three and six hardcovers a year, usually four or five. We don't do them on a specific schedule. Instead, we base the decision [to publish a book in hardcover] on whether we feel the work belongs in hardcover. We know it will sell well because we've built the author's career up to the point where we know he or she is ready for it. This is why we have such a successful hardcover line— we don't have to fill predetermined slots."

Rarely does DAW launch a new writer in hardcover, but it has happened. When they found author Tad Williams, for instance, the editors felt his cat fantasy, *Tailchaser's Song*, was such a strong book it would do well in hardcover, and it was one of the books with which they started their hardcover line. Williams's books have gone on to make both the *New York Times* and the *Los Angeles Times* bestseller lists, as well as numerous bestseller lists in the U.S. and abroad. Yet, for the most part, Gilbert says the best indication of whether an author's work is really ready for hardcover treatment is how well the work has sold in paperback first.

Although DAW has a very active and strong fantasy line, Gilbert says it's not because of any personal preference for fantasy over science fiction. Instead, she says, it's simply become much easier to find commercially strong fantasy than it is to find good science fiction. In science fiction's early days, people were less technologically sophisticated. Writers could "get away with" more. Today writers must be very technologically aware, and the writing must be much more polished.

"In the late 1960s and early 1970s, there started becoming more social science fiction published dealing with cultural development—building worlds and societies. I'd say we do more of that type of science fiction here, yet we also do a certain amount of straight adventure science fiction as well."

DAW does just about any type of fantasy with the exception of what might be called straight "barbarian-type" fantasy. "I would say there is no one type we do over another type," Gilbert says. "I think what fuels the books that we do is really good characters. A gripping plot is important, too, but you have to have believable characters, people you can really care about, whether it's the hero, the heroine or even the villain. When an author says to me 'This character came alive and, even though I had the intention of him doing this, he did this,' that's when I know it's going to be a really good book.

"We tend to do bigger books than a lot of other companies," says Gilbert. "We're sort of going against tradition because large books are not very economical. I think people like a 'big read,' and when it's a good story with a lot to say, we shouldn't cut it down to 300 pages just to meet some length requirement."

This is not to say that new writers should approach DAW with a 1,000 plus-page manuscript. "We wouldn't be interested unless it was just an incredible book. To launch somebody new, you don't want to price them too high and with a 500- or 600-page book, you can only price it so low. You want a first book to be priced so the readers are going to be willing to risk the money on someone whose work they don't know."

Gilbert says new writers should aim for between 70,000 and 125,000 words (DAW does not publish short novels under 65,000 words). While DAW publishes one or two new writers each year who are not represented, many of the their new authors have come to them through agents, and several have published short fiction first.

In addition to novels, DAW publishes several original and a few reprint anthologies. In recent years this sector of their publishing program has grown from only a handful to eight or ten a year. Some are ongoing series such as the Sword and Sorceress series, edited by Marion Zimmer Bradley, and Bradley's Darkover story anthologies. Many are individual theme anthologies.

DAW mostly works with outside anthologists, including people like Martin Greenberg and science fiction author Mike Resnick. The anthologist will usually approach the publisher with an idea for a project. They will also be responsible for commissioning, selecting and editing the work. All anthologists have their own way of soliciting work, Gilbert explains.

Although she grew up reading science fiction, Gilbert hesitates to name authors she is currently reading. "Frankly, I have very little time to read any novels but those I am publishing or manuscripts I am considering buying," she says.

"It's easy to spot a bad book, but it's much more difficult to say what makes a certain book work. Strong characters and plot and, of course, convincing dialogue are the basic elements, but I think you just develop a kind of intuition when you've been in the business for awhile. You just know when something's good. When you pick up a book and start to read it, you can tell fairly quickly if you are going to want to finish it. There are so many submissions, and we are a small company. You have to feel there's a lot of promise there."

Gilbert notes that many times the first book she publishes by an author is not the first thing from the author she's seen. In fact, the manuscript submitted by Melanie Rawn, one of DAW's now established authors, was not her highly successful first book, *The Dragon Prince*. Gilbert says something in Rawn's first submission, however, made her want to work with the author, and she asked if Rawn had anything else. The same goes for another DAW author, Mickey Zucker Reichert. After rejecting Reichert's first submission, Gilbert accepted and published another. Later the author reworked her original manuscript, and it was published as the *Renshai* trilogy.

DAW does publish a lot of trilogies, as well as single books, and sometimes authors will write sequels to books they've done earlier. "The best fantasy is that which is most fully developed," explains Gilbert. "There's an investment in time and creativity building a world and characters, and sometimes it seems a shame to use it all up in one book. In fact, it's often very hard to do if the fantasy is well done. Fantasies tend to be generational. It's one thing to follow the adventures of a hero, heroine, or a small group of characters, but a lot of these books build their worlds so completely there is interest in following them through generations and even going back into the past history of a world."

One way to write a really good fantasy story, she says, is to start with reality. "It's certainly not a new concept, but one thing people can do to make their work stronger is to draw upon their own experiences and transform them to use in their story. You can get a much better emotional content and more believability if you do that. We don't want to hear everybody's life story, but drawing from the world around you can bring realism to what you are writing."

Although Gilbert does not have much time to go to conventions (she does attend the World Science Fiction and the World Fantasy conventions), she has had the opportunity to speak with many new writers. "It's funny the things some new or would-be writers focus on. Some think there's a magic formula—the right type, the right margins, the right number of lines on a page. But it's really not that—you have to grab an editor with your story."

Too much trend watching can be dangerous, too, she says. "To write what you're not comfortable with because it's a 'hot topic' is crazy. You're not going to write a good book. It's the quality of the book that counts, not the particular subject matter."

HOW TO CONTACT: Submit your complete manuscript with SASE. Submit to: Peter Stampfel, assistant editor. They usually report in 3-5 months, but in some cases may take longer.
PAYMENT: Pays an advance and royalties.
ADDRESS: 375 Hudson St., New York NY 10014
PHONE: (212)366-2096 ✳

DEL REY BOOKS

Subsidiary of Ballantine Books

Contact: Shelly Shapiro, Executive Editor

> **CATEGORIES**
> Cyberpunk, Dark Fantasy, Hard Science Fiction, High Fantasy, Humorous Science Fiction, Military Science Fiction, Sociological Science Fiction, Space Opera, Traditional Fantasy

Recently Published: *First King of Shannara,* by Terry Brooks; *Worldwar: Upsetting the Balance,* by Harry Turtledove; *The Wind After Time,* by Chris Bunch.

@

"It's hard to say what I'm tired of because a really good book can make any subject not seem tired—that's one of the ways you can recognize a really good book," says Shelly Shapiro, executive editor of Del Rey, an imprint of Ballantine Books. Del Rey publishes books in all areas of science fiction without paying much attention to which segment they fall into, according to Shapiro. "We don't care overmuch about subgenre labels. We publish books that we like. We always used to say that we didn't publish 'Atlantis' books, or UFO books, or New Age books, for example, but the fact is that if something comes in and wows us, we'll publish it."

What sets Del Rey apart, according to Shapiro, is a strong tradition of creating best-sellers. "In terms of mass market, we basically created the field of fantasy best-sellers. Not that it didn't exist before, but we put the mass into mass market," she says. Some of the great successes are books by Terry Brooks and Stephen R. Donaldson, which appeared in the mid to late 1970s. "The *Sword of Shannara* was, I believe, the first time that a fiction book—forget fantasy or sf, but a fiction book—hit the *New York Times* bestseller trade book list."

Some of Del Rey's bestselling authors are Anne McCaffrey, David Eddings, and the aforementioned Terry Brooks. Del Rey also publishes Katherine Kurtz and is working on some collaborations between McCaffrey and Elizabeth Ann Scarborough, a 1989 Nebula Award winner for *The Healer's War*.

Del Rey publishes from 36 to 48 mass market paperbacks each year, eight to twelve of which are reprints of their own hardcovers. Trade paperbacks average two to three per year, but there's no set amount. The ten to twelve hardcovers Del Rey publishes each year are reserved for well-established authors or books they want reviewed by major publications.

To submit to Del Rey, writers should send a detailed outline and a query letter. They no longer accept unsolicited manuscripts. Del Rey receives about 4,000 submissions a year. The preferred length of manuscript is 60,000-120,000 words. Del Rey pays an advance against royalties that is standard within the industry. The average time before a writer can expect a reply is three to six months, and the average time before the book is published is 18 months to two years. "That depends on the list and the state of the manuscript," according to Shapiro. She and Editor Ellen Harris deal with all sf manuscripts sent to Del Rey. Fantasy manuscripts are largely read by Senior Editor Veronica Chapman and Associate Editor Deborah Hogan.

New authors don't necessarily need to get an agent, Shapiro says. "It used to guarantee your manuscript would be looked at faster, but 10 to 15 percent of very little money is a lot to pay to have the agent be persistent." Some new authors have trouble with agents because the cut is so small the agent might not necessarily put as much into it as they would with a book they sold for $100,000, says Shapiro. If a writer is very uncomfortable doing the negotiating for a book, then an agent can be helpful, she said. "For a first novel, an agent is extremely unlikely to get an author anything more than the usual first novel payments and agreements and rights arrangements."

The number of beginning authors published by Del Rey varies: 1994 lists feature five first novels and 1993's, seven. "That's unusual—it's a lot. Each time we publish a first novel we hope to follow it up the next year with a second novel and go on from there." Previously unpublished novelists for 1995/1996 include Roby James for *Commencement*, Scott G. Gier for *Genellan: Planetfall* and Nancy McKenzie for *The Child Queen*.

The Del Rey Discovery Program was created specifically for new authors. "This is, in essence, our attempt to cash in on the fact that these are new authors. We are trying to combat the view in the marketplace that it is detrimental to be called a new author. I feel it ought to be used as a commodity. Any new author that gets published by us, at the moment anyway, gets published as a Del Rey Discovery and gets a bit more of a marketing push than they might get otherwise."

Shapiro has been at Del Rey for fourteen years and has been a fan of science fiction since she was a child. Shapiro's favorite books growing up included those by Andre Norton, Robert A. Heinlein and Frank Herbert, and Marilyn Zimmer Bradley's Darkover books. "As a child, the wonderful thing about science fiction was that everything was new except for Arthur C. Clarke and Isaac Asimov and Robert A. Heinlein. Everything was a risk because you never heard of them. That was one of the things that was so exciting about it—always finding some new author to experience and explore. Now in today's market, a market of so many known quantities, it seems that it's not going that way anymore and it's getting hard for us to sell new authors. So we just decided to turn that around to remind people that science fiction has always been about new things and seeing something new is reason for celebration—not something to hide. The reason we don't make too big a thing about it [the Del Rey Discovery Program] is the fact that we've always published new authors—we've always been very big on publishing new authors. We're not doing something new—we're just calling attention to it." Her advice to new authors is to keep trying: "Be persistent and flexible."

As for the future trends of science fiction publishing, Shapiro says she tries to ignore trends because the success of a book is longevity, not timeliness. "I think the success of a book is measured generally by its long life. And I think that paying too close attention to trends is a mistake because it means that you may get wide readership now, but you may not get it later for that book."

HOW TO CONTACT: Send a detailed outline or synopsis and query letter to the attention of Jill Benjamin, at Del Rey Books. The editors will report in 2 weeks on queries, 2-10 months on manuscripts. No simultaneous submissions.

PAYMENT: Pays in royalties, with a competitive advance. Send a #10 SASE for writer's guidelines.

ADDRESS: 201 E. 50 St., New York NY 10022

PHONE: (212)572-2677

E-MAIL: delrey@randomhouse.com

WEBSITE: http://www.randomhouse.com/delrey/ ✳

HARPERPRISM

HarperCollins Publishers

Contact: John Douglas, Executive Editor

> **CATEGORIES**
> Cyberpunk, Dark Fantasy, Hard Science Fiction, High Fantasy, Humorous Science Fiction, Military Science Fiction, Sociological Science Fiction, Space Opera, Traditional Fantasy

"But will it get read?" is one of the questions certain to cross a writer's mind when the manuscript is sent out the door. With John Douglas, executive editor at HarperPrism, the answer is yes. "We look at everything, open all of the packages," says Douglas, stressing that he and his fellow editors John Silbersack and Caitlin Blasdell read all submissions—even from unestablished writers. In fact, they're always looking for something new.

HarperPrism itself is somewhat of a new story. Founded in 1994, this division of Harper Paperbacks was a "natural outgrowth" of Harper's desire to expand into mass markets. "These days, to be competitive you have to be 'vertical'," Douglas says. "You have to be willing to explore new markets." This attitude is borne out in HarperPrism's extreme flexibility in the science fiction/fantasy genre. "We probably would favor the broadest possible definition of what fits into a genre company," he admits. From a series of novels tied to the popular *Magic: The Gathering* card game to those related to such television series and movies as *The X-Files*, *Space: Above and Beyond*, *12 Monkeys* and the upcoming *Independence Day*, HarperPrism has grown quickly to match the merchandising opportunities available in the market today. "The rollout for *Independence Day* is the first I've ever heard of which is this extensive," Douglas says.

HarperPrism is also, of course, heavily involved with novels that are solely reliant on author and story. Currently in the works are extensions of Isaac Asimov's Foundation series, including novels written by Greg Benford, Greg Bear and David Brin. HarperPrism has also published novels by such writers as Stephen Baxter, Greg Egan, and Ursula K. LeGuin. Douglas joined HarperPrism in November of 1995, after 12 years working at Avon. Given this recent move, the most current new fiction writer he's worked with, Jane Lindscold, is being published by Avon. "Over the past year, we've worked on three paperback originals for publication," he says. "I think she's going to be one of the brightest new stars in the field."

Douglas most often meets new writers by going to conventions and writer's conferences, handing them his business card, and encouraging them to submit stories that sound interesting. He says he tries to "spread himself around" to various events, to meet the greatest cross-section of people. This year, he plans to attend the Southwest Writers Conference in Albuquerque, New Mexico. Last year, he attended the Pacific Northwest Conference.

While Douglas edges away from discussing current trends in the market, he stresses the importance of market knowledge. "It's absolutely vital for writers to know what's out there, to know what's been done and how" before they begin writing their own work. Finding an agent, however, is something new writers shouldn't worry about "until after they have an offer by a publisher," says Douglas. At that point, he says, you need someone to represent you, and agents will be interested in representing anyone who has an offer on the table.

What does Douglas himself look for? "The exciting thing about fantasy and science fiction is that it constantly reinvents itself. So I look for a really creative twist on a common theme, or an old story redone, something that's either brand new or made new— maybe a wildly original plot or a good variation on a standard scene." Good, appealing writing is also essential to the genre, and Douglas points to the art of "storytelling" as being the most critical aspect to a science fiction/fantasy reader.

Douglas immediately rejects manuscripts "if I feel like I've seen it before, if it's a routine variation on an old theme." Additionally, the cover letter plays a role in his decision. "If a new writer comes on too strong, saying he or she is going to be the next Michael Crichton, that's a bad impression for me. Based on my experience, the odds are they probably won't be. I try not to let that prejudice my opinion of the writing, but . . ."

Douglas often asks for a plot summary as well as three chapters of the manuscript, but he generally "starts with the text." He says, "I like to read the chapters first before the author tells me where it's going to go. I have to be hooked, so that I can turn around and hook someone else on the story." Incidentally, it's the first three chapters he's looking for. "It's almost worthless to me to receive chapters 7, 42 and 68. I need the first three chapters to be certain that the author has a strong opening for the work."

According to Douglas, both the science fiction and fantasy markets remain strong. "Despite the temporary ups and downs of the market, both of these genres have enjoyed steady growth. Over the past ten years, the fantasy genre has grown more quickly, but science fiction is absolutely holding its own." A tip for writers: writing your novel as part of a continuing series—two books, a trilogy or more—or with common characters or settings. "It's certainly the easiest way to target and work toward commercial success," Douglas says, "more so in fantasy than science fiction. And after all, commercial success is the goal."

But the key, especially for new writers, is to write what's in your heart. "Don't try to imitate someone just because they're successful. You have to write with an inner conviction, and stick with it until the market finds you. Unfortunately, there are a lot of people who want to be writers, who don't have this vision, who aren't terribly original in their work, and so don't succeed. The toughest and best way is to synthesize all that you see and like and come up with your own version. Write what compels you."

HOW TO CONTACT: Submit a query letter with a brief synopsis of your book. If interested, the editors will request the complete manuscript. Reporting time on queries is 2 weeks to 1 month; on manuscripts it's usually 1 to 4 months. Send a SASE with all correspondence. Harper-Prism will not take responsibility for return of material.

PAYMENT: Pays in royalties, with a competitive advance.

ADDRESS: 10 E. 53rd St., New York NY 10022-5299

PHONE: (212)207-7000 ✳

POCKET BOOKS

Contact: John Ordover, Editor or Kevin Ryan, Senior Editor

CATEGORIES
Media-Related Science Fiction

Recently Published: *Star Trek: The Next Generation: Rogue Saucer*, by John Vornholt; *Star Trek: Voyager: Ghost of a Chance*, by Mark Garland and Charles McGraw; *The Return*, by William Shatner (with Judith and Garfield Reeve-Stevens).

@

Books based on the hit television series *Star Trek* have been published since 1979, says Editor John Ordover of Pocket Books. "We picked up the book line from Ballantine after the first *Star Trek* movie came out." Thanks in part to the popularity of the movie and subsequent films, interest in *Star Trek* has never waned. Today there are three related television series, *Star Trek: The Next Generation, Deep Space Nine* and *Star Trek Voyager*.

As the family of *Star Trek* media has grown, so has Pocket's line of *Star Trek* books. They now publish five books a year in each series: the original *Star Trek* (which the editors refer to as TOS); *The Next Generation* (TNG); *Deep Space Nine* (DS9); and *Star Trek Voyager* (STV).

Ordover has been editing the *Star Trek* line for Pocket for a little more than three years, but he had been reading manuscripts for the line on a freelance basis while he was an assistant editor at Tor Books. He and Senior Editor Kevin Ryan, who has been with the line for about seven years, make up the line's editorial staff.

Most of the books in the various series are paperback, but Pocket publishes one hardcover a year in each series. Ordover and Ryan choose the strongest book in each line to fill that slot. Pocket distributes books for Baen, and so by agreement does not publish other science fiction and fantasy paperbacks. The company, however, will publish a hardcover science fiction novel occasionally if they feel the book will be a very important book by a well-known author, one considered a very "big" book sure to have sales outside the genre.

Each series uses characters from the television show, says Ordover, and Paramount (Pocket's parent company), which owns the rights to the original characters and material, has approval on all book projects. "Other characters may appear in the novels, but only as foils for the main characters," explains Ordover. "Writers must, of course, be familiar with the shows—if you don't watch them, you can't write about them," he says. "But we provide a 'bible' to anyone who feels they need it." This bible covers the basics of the series—its history and characters.

Interested authors should send for guidelines first, says Ordover. Usually, the idea for the book comes from the writer, he says. Writers must submit through an agent with a query letter, three sample chapters and a detailed synopsis. Books are handled one at a time, but some authors have written several books for the line. Work is produced on a work-for-hire basis, meaning Pocket buys all rights to the work, but authors are paid on a limited royalty basis.

"We are not generally a good market for a first novel," says Ordover. "We are looking for professional novelists." However, he says, less-experienced agented writers may have a shot if they've published short stories in the commercial science fiction magazines or have a completed, but unpublished, novel and feel they have a good story for one of the series.

HOW TO CONTACT: Write first for guidelines. Submit through an agent only.

PAYMENT: Buys all rights to the work and pays limited royalties.

ADDRESS: 1230 Avenue of the Americas, New York NY 10020

PHONE: (212)698-7000

E-MAIL: ordover@aol.com ✳

ROC BOOKS

Penguin USA

Contact: Laura Anne Gilman, Executive Editor

> **CATEGORIES**
> Cyberpunk, Hard Science Fiction, High Fantasy, Military Science Fiction, Sociological Science Fiction, Space Opera, Traditional Fantasy

Recently Published: *The Hollowing*, by Robert Holdstock; *The Knight of the Black Earth*, by Margaret Weis and Don Perrin; *The Forest House*, by Marion Zimmer Bradley.

"Don't omit the fantasy," stresses former Executive Editor Amy Stout when describing Roc Books, the six-year-old science fiction and fantasy imprint of Dutton/Signet. (Stout has left Roc, and as this book was going to press, a replacement had yet to be named.) "When people say 'science fiction,' they usually always mean 'science fiction and fantasy.' The 'and fantasy' is referred to only by its absence, which sort of annoys fantasy writers," Stout says, "Fantasy has traditionally been thought of by science fiction writers as the lesser twin, the poor stepsister."

Stout has grounds for defending the genre. Asked to name the imprint's most successful authors, she lists fantasy writers Marion Zimmer Bradley, Anne McCaffrey and Peter S. Beagle. She includes in that list Guy Gavriel Kay, whose fantasies have been compared by critics to J.R.R. Tolkien's *The Lord of the Rings*, and who worked with Christopher Tolkien on the best-selling hardcover fantasy *The Silmarillion*. "This probably means that we've had better fortunes with fantasy over the years," she says.

"Fantasy is generally thought of as not well-researched, sloppy, easy— 'yeah, you can tell this story because you've got all the easy ways out . . . and you just whip up a spell and it goes away,' " Stout says. "In fact, fantasies are not written like that at all . . . if you cannot tell what the rules of the fantasy—the magic—are, there's something wrong with the

---

EDITOR'S NOTE: At interview time, Amy Stout was executive editor at Roc. By our press time, Laura Anne Gilman was named the new executive editor.

way they've written it, because that is sloppy."

Established in March of 1990 to replace Signet's science fiction line, Roc Books, named for a powerful mythical bird of prey, was launched to better position the company in the field of science fiction and fantasy publishing, Stout says.

Roc will consider manuscripts in any genre of science fiction and fantasy. Space opera, hard science fiction, adventure science fiction and cyberpunk submissions are welcome because "the minute you say (you won't read it), the one that's brilliant will pass you by." But Stout does keep an eye out for a story with broad implications, full-bodied characters, and a strong story line—mainstream science fiction and fantasy in the tradition of Asimov, Heinlein and Clarke.

"To me, a good story is both strong in adventure and pacing, but also it comes to something when you get done with it," she says. "So when you've finished reading 300 pages or 900 pages, you don't say 'oh, that was nice,' and close the book. . . . For somebody who's looking for a bit more meat, it's there all along. I think that can be done a number of ways, whether that's by fresh ideas or a different take on an idea that's been floating around in the field for a long time."

Repetition of theme is one pitfall common to beginning science fiction writers, says Stout, who edited for *Asimov's* magazine and Bantam Science Fiction before coming to Roc. Young, enthusiastic and anxious to get their stories published, new writers don't familiarize themselves with the work of their predecessors, she says, and can alienate editors in the process. "Beginning writers are doing one of two things: They're either looking at that old material and thinking 'I could write that stuff,' or more likely they've never seen the original stuff, and everybody, when starting out writing, wants to reinvent the wheel," Stout says. "And you have to have read enough to get past the point where (writers) were 15 or 20 years ago."

Top-quality hard science fiction novels, much sought-after by publishers, are particularly challenging to writers because they require a strong background in science and the ability to craft a good story, said Stout, who herself majored in biology and English literature in college. ("Maybe they should call it hard science fiction because it's hard to find," she jokes.)

"Hard sf, more than any other (subgenre), is working with the science of ideas or the ideas of science," Stout says. "Many of these science fiction writers are scientists of a sort themselves, whether self-taught or actually working in some scientific area. You have that coupled with the fact that you can't just be a scientist to write one of these things. . . . This is a novel, not an academic treatise. So you need somebody who's got a good, accessible voice, but at the same time understands scientific principles."

While Roc does consider submissions in all genres, unsolicited submissions are not accepted. With roughly 100 to 200 manuscripts coming in monthly, and about 50 hardcovers and paperbacks published each year, Roc accepts manuscripts through agents or by query only. Stout has one in-house assistant and two freelance readers reviewing incoming manuscripts, and reporting time averages about one to two months. Advances and royalties are "competitive," based on an author's experience, Stout says.

The story should dictate the length of the manuscript, although with "anything under 300 manuscript pages, I'm extremely suspect that you've got a novel and with anything over 700 pages, I'm extremely suspect that it's good enough to be 700 pages long."

An agent can be helpful beyond just getting his client in the door, Stout says, although she concedes finding an agent and selling a novel for the first time can be equally difficult. As a business manager, the agent can negotiate the fine points of contracts, which vary from publishing house to publishing house.

Another way agents prove invaluable to beginning writers is in the time they save both writers and publishers during the submission process, says Stout. A good agent has been around long enough to know market trends and editors' tastes and can steer certain types of subject matter to editors at specific publishing houses. "I will never tell an author to his face 'you're writing the kind of thing that makes me want to run screaming into a closet,' " Stout says, "but an agent would know that."

Beginning authors who choose not to work with an agent should be aware that Stout considers query letters as attentively as agented material. Stout explains, "Some publishers do still read unsolicited manuscripts, but, since we don't, you have snowball's chance of selling me your book without an agent. The snowball's chance is the query letter."

Another way beginning authors can increase their chances of publication with Roc is by cutting their teeth in short fiction, Stout says. Science fiction and fantasy magazines such as *Asimov's* not only give writers the chance to sharpen their skills, but also help them develop an audience, which is important to publishers when considering promotion of a new author, Stout says.

Although Roc published no beginning authors in 1994, it contracted with three first-time novelists in 1995 and three more in 1996, including Kim Antiezv for *The Jigsaw Women* and Charles Barnitz for *The Deepest Sea.* "We expect to publish several first novels in 1997 as well," Stout says.

Despite the fact that Roc has limited room to publish first-time authors ("We've turned away some very fine first novels because they were just that close," Stout says), Stout is committed to keeping the door open: "I think we should all be interested in fresh new voices that have something to say that hasn't been said already. That's most likely to come from people who haven't been published yet. You get a certain depth of development from established writers, but . . . certainly new writers are a lot of where the lifeblood comes from."

HOW TO CONTACT: The editors prefer agented submissions. Otherwise query and include previous publishing credits. They report back in 1-2 months.

PAYMENT: Pays variable advance against negotiable royalties.

ADDRESS: 375 Hudson St., New York NY 10014

WEBSITE: http://www.penguin.com/usa/ ✳

ST. MARTIN'S PRESS

Macmillan Publishers Ltd. (England)

Contact: Gordon Van Gelder, Editor

CATEGORIES
Cyberpunk, Dark Fantasy, Hard Science Fiction, Humorous Science Fiction, Sociological Science Fiction, Space Opera, Traditional Fantasy

Recently Published: *Lunatics*, by Bradley Denton; *Zod Wallop*, by William Browing Spencer; *Panda Ray*, by Michael Kandel.

At the ripe old age of 16, Gordon Van Gelder placed a short story in an anthology titled *100 Great Fantasy Short Short Stories*, published by Doubleday in 1984. In his own words: "My career has gone down steadily from there." This sort of self-effacing humor seems characteristic of him, a laid-back guy with an easy smile. As he sits in his office at St. Martin's Press—where he edits science fiction, fantasy, mystery and horror—his soft voice is sometimes tough to hear over the traffic noise outside. But he has strong opinions about science fiction in general and the books he publishes in particular.

The St. Martin's sf and fantasy line is an upscale, literary one. They publish only 12 to 15 titles per year, all in hardcover. And these books tend to be written by established writers who possess high-powered, sophisticated styles. They have published Kate Wilhelm, Marc Laidlaw, Brian Aldiss, J.G. Ballard, Jonathan Carroll and Geoff Ryman, among an impressive number of the genre's top stylists.

Van Gelder feels that this is the publisher's niche. "We publish experimental upper-echelon science fiction," he says. "Our writers are out to try different things." He cites Marc Laidlaw's *Kalifornia*, a satirical postcyberpunk novel, as a recent example of the type of book he's always looking for. "I like the wild extrapolations, the daring concept, the prose."

St. Martin's is open to most types of science fiction and fantasy, though Van Gelder is not interested in military sf or high fantasy. He is especially interested in novels that "don't fit into any easy genre categories," a philosophy that departs from that of many sf publishers, who want manuscripts to fill specific slots in their line. Van Gelder understands this thinking, especially with mass market publishers, but feels that St. Martin's plays a different role in the marketplace, one more concerned with crossing boundaries than with enforcing them.

"What I'm trying to do here," he explains, "is publish influential books that will stand up better than a lot of other stuff that's around, books that people will still be talking about in ten years. I want the reader to expect an entertaining story, very well told, both in content and prose style." More specifically, he prefers novels that are character-driven rather than plot-driven. And he wants the main character established quickly.

He also likes a vivid and engaging sense of place. The setting should be multidimensional, the societies complex and varied, and the setting should be tied to character. Too often he sees manuscripts that rely on a succession of plot twists with settings that merely supply one-dimensional backgrounds for those twists. His other pet peeve? Wooden dialogue—especially when aliens or machines engage in what he calls "Tarzan talk." This type of dialogue indicates that the writer has not read extensively in the field and is ignorant of the established traditions.

If you're sensing that this is a tough market for the unpublished novelist, you're right. Van Gelder has been at St. Martin's since the summer of 1988 and only had his first two first novels come out in 1995: *The Unnatural* by David Prill and *Dead Girls* by Richard Calder. "I'm very eager to do them," he says, "but it's hard to justify when you're coming out in hardcover."

Still, he is always searching for fresh voices in the field, a search aided by his role as in-house editor on *The Year's Best Science Fiction* (edited by Gardner Dozois) and *The Year's Best Fantasy and Horror* (coedited by Ellen Datlow and Terri Windling), the annual anthologies that anchor the sf/fantasy line at St. Martin's. The short fiction field, Van Gelder believes, is a fertile one, pumping new ideas and new voices into the genre. Though many of the writers featured in these anthologies have published a novel or two, many have not been published in the hardcover, prestige format, or to as wide an audience as St. Martin's can offer them.

Van Gelder also regularly wades into the slush pile. Though he receives 35 to 40 manuscripts per month, he tries to respond quickly, usually within three months. Having been on the writer's side of the process, he knows the frustration of waiting. He pays little attention to whether or not a manuscript is represented by an agent. Cover letters mean little to him. His only advice in composing them: "Be forthright."

Manuscript lengths can vary widely, though those less than 60,000 words are tough to publish in hard cover. They're simply too short to be published and marketed profitably. "Length depends upon what the story calls for," he says. "People who have read a lot in the field have a much better sense of what length the material will sustain than those who haven't."

His advice to aspiring writers is to do just that: Read a lot in the field. Read the anthologies. Read the classics. And study what you read. Analyze your reaction to a story or novel and examine how the writer evoked this reaction. And don't limit your reading to one genre. He believes that reading other genres broadens a writer's background and creates a keener sense of story possibilities.

As you might expect from this prestige line, St. Martin's has won a number of awards in recent years. James Morrow's *City of Truth*, a satirical novella, won the Nebula Award in 1993 while John Kessel's alternate history, "Buffalo," won the Theodore Sturgeon Award. Fred Chappell's *More Shapes than One*, a literary dark fantasy, took a World Fantasy Award in 1992 as did *The Year's Best Fantasy and Horror* anthology in 1993. Van Gelder firmly believes that such awards, along with good reviews, are crucial in maintaining the publisher's upper-echelon niche.

He is less firm in his sense of where the genre is headed. He likes the current energy in the field, and though he cannot detect a clear trend, he does not feel this lack of focus or direction suggests a fallow period. He does feel that science fiction is entering a kind of middle age. "The first generation is passing away, and the second generation is getting old," he says. But this situation, too, does not concern him. New blood continues to invigorate the genre. "Science fiction has always been a young person's field," he explains. "It's all about finding limits—what's taboo, what's acceptable."

HOW TO CONTACT: Submit a cover letter with the complete manuscript or send a 1-page query. The editors will report in less than 3 months on a manuscript, less than 1 month on a query.

PAYMENT: Pays in royalties, with a competitive advance.

ADDRESS: 175 Fifth Ave., New York NY 10010

PHONE: (212)674-5151

E-MAIL: gordonsmp@aol.com (But please, *no* submissions or queries by e-mail.) ※

TOR BOOKS

Contact: Patrick Nielsen Hayden, Senior Editor

> **CATEGORIES**
>
> Cyberpunk, Dark Fantasy, Hard Science Fiction, High Fantasy, Humorous Science Fiction, Military Science Fiction, Sociological Science Fiction, Space Opera, Traditional Fantasy

Recently Published: *Expiration Date*, by Tim Powers; *Legacy*, by Greg Bear; *A Crown of Swords*, by Robert Jordan.

"I've been involved in the subculture of reading fanzines and going to conventions and being a pushy nuisance since I was a teenager," says Patrick Nielsen Hayden. Although his tone is light, his involvement in the science fiction community is anything but. His "hanging around the subculture" for a few years led to writing reviews and then to some freelance work for various publishing houses in a process Hayden calls "a kind of gradual osmosis." The end product was his current position as senior editor of Tor Books, where he has been now for five years.

Tor was founded in 1981 by Tom Doherty, the current president and publisher. After working for years at other publishers in the sf field, Doherty decided to start a mass market publishing company of his own. He named it Tor, which, according to Hayden, is not an acronym. "Tor is a somewhat obscure English word basically meaning a hill."

Nielsen Hayden and Doherty work with a large staff of editors and consultants including Beth Meacham, Jim Frenkel, Terri Windling, David Hartwell, Claire Eddy and Greg Cox. Tor publishes between 60 and 75 paperbacks a year and publishes a roughly equal number of hardcovers. Tor also publishes trade paperback books each month, some under its Orb imprint, which was formed in 1993 to keep Tor's backlist titles in circulation.

Tor has certainly had its share of bestsellers. Several examples include Vernor Vinge's *A Fire Upon the Deep*, one of the two Hugo Award winners for Best Novel of 1993, and Robert Jordan's Wheel of Time series, which regularly makes the *New York Times* bestseller list.

"We've never wanted to be seen as a niche publisher in science fiction," Nielsen Hayden says. Tor has a company policy that keeps them from focusing on any one area. "We publish extremely literary and audacious and avant-garde work, and we also publish Conan.

"One of the basic questions that people who want to submit to us always ask is 'What in particular are you looking for?' " Nielsen Hayden says. His answer is that, in all honesty, they are looking for something they didn't know was out there. "We're looking to be startled by something really fresh and new."

New writers do not have to have agents to get Nielsen Hayden and his staff to read their manuscripts. They should submit the first three chapters (or 150 pages) and a detailed outline. A team of assistants, headed by Micole Sudberg, assists Nielsen Hayden with the slush pile. If writers can't boil their novel down to an outline, they may submit the entire work, but first reading priority goes to those with just the three chapters and an outline. "By outline, we basically mean a coherent piece of prose writing that gives some sense of the overall shape of the book." Recent first novelists who were given a chance at Tor include Raphael Carter (*The Fortunate Fall*), Sage Walker (*Whiteout*) and Elizabeth Kerner (*Song in the Silence*).

With an open submissions policy, Tor doesn't require query letters. "Don't send us query letters asking for permission to submit to us, because the answer is inherently yes," Nielsen Hayden comments. "We really don't know whether we want to see your manuscript until we see your manuscript." Once they receive a manuscript, Tor might contact the writer in anywhere from "ten minutes to four months," although they usually average a turnaround of about three months.

After acceptance, seeing the book in print is a different story. Although the minimum wait is about a year, Nielsen Hayden does not want that to stand as an average. "We're going to put it in print when there's an appropriate spot in the schedule . . . in order to get the book tied in with some appropriate anniversary or media event that may tie in with their subject matter or just so their book is not being shipped up against two other books that are nominally similar types. We pay attention to a lot of little details."

As for advances and royalties, Nielsen Hayden says Tor is competitive. "We're right in there with everyone else . . . we don't nickel and dime people. We don't offer bottom dollar. It varies with the book."

Another thing that sets Tor apart from other publishers is that they are more willing to do a book in hardcover. "We don't do hardcovers only for writers who have proved themselves to be paperback bestsellers," Nielsen Hayden says. "We do hardcovers as a way of building a writer's career." Publishing first in hardcover, Tor has found, helps later paperback sales by attracting more attention and reviews. "We think there are a lot of middle tier science fiction and fantasy writers who have a definite small hardcover audience. We find it modestly profitable to publish to that audience."

Nielsen Hayden's ultimate advice to new writers seeking to publish with Tor is to know the building blocks, but do something new with them. "The people at Tor who are going to be reading your material are tremendously savvy in the history of the genre, tremendously sensitive to cliché, and tremendously hungry to have that old childlike sense of wonder reawakened. We want those youthful reader receptors restimulated."

HOW TO CONTACT: Though agented manuscripts are preferred, authors may submit first 3 chapters and a detailed outline or the complete manuscript. Address manuscripts to "Editorial" and include SASE. No simultaneous submissions accepted.

PAYMENT: Pays in royalties and advance, which vary according to the author. Sends galley to the author. Free book catalog available on request.

ADDRESS: 175 Fifth Ave., New York NY 10010

PHONE: (212)388-0100

WEBSITE: http://www.tor.com ✳

TSR

Contact: Brian Thomsen, Executive Editor

> **CATEGORIES**
> Cyberpunk, Dark Fantasy, Hard Science Fiction, High Fantasy, Horror, Humorous Science Fiction, Military Science Fiction, Sociological Science Fiction, Space Opera, Traditional Fantasy

Recently Published: *Dragons of Summer Flame*, by Margaret Weis and Tracy Hickman; *Buck Rogers: A Life in the Future*, by Martin Caidin; *Daughter of the Drow*, by Elaine Cunningham.

TSR has long been known as one of the leading publishers of role-playing games and game world materials. The company got its start in 1974 and has steadily expanded its line of products to include magazines, computer games and books. According to Executive Editor Brian Thomsen, the company started its book publishing program with a series of "Endless Quest" books, interactive fiction in which readers could choose their own adventure. Yet, it wasn't until 1985, with the success of the *Dragonlance Chronicles*, which told the story behind one of their game worlds, that TSR became much more actively involved in book publishing.

Thomsen joined TSR in 1992 after 12 years in various editorial positions at Warner Books. He started his career at Warner as a student intern and had moved up to senior editor in charge of the publisher's science fiction, fantasy, movie tie-in and graphic novel lines. At TSR he actually holds three positions—associate publisher of the magazine division, director of books and periodicals, and executive editor of books.

As executive editor, Thomsen is in charge of the company's several book lines. In the "TSR Books" imprint, novels are handled in the traditional manner. Books in this line are original science fiction and fantasy novels not based on any game world product. As with most commercial book publishers, authors retain the copyright to the work and are paid standard royalties. TSR publishes one book in this line every other month, says Thomsen.

"The other lines of books that we publish are set within the worlds we've established our gaming systems around, and they are no different in concept than novels spun off from television shows such as *Star Trek* or *Quantum Leap*," Thomsen explains. The books in these lines are published as work-for-hire with TSR retaining all rights to the work, much the same as a book packager. Payment is not a flat fee as it is for many packagers, however. Writers are paid through a royalty arrangement.

Although these books are set in game worlds, it is not necessary for readers to be role-game players. And Thomsen says there is lots of room within the broad parameters of each world for writers to explore different areas and time frames within the particular gaming universe.

Writers interested in writing for one of the game-inspired lines should be familiar with them, says Thomsen. Dungeons and Dragons is the best known of the games, but the publisher has four other lines. Says Thomsen, "Forgotten Realms is medieval fantasy of the hack and slash variety, for lack of a better phrase. Robin Hood and Conan would feel at home in Forgotten Realms. Dragonlance is epic, chivalric fantasy in the tradition of *Lord of the Rings*. Dark Sun is a gladiatorial, dark, desert fantasy. If *Dune* were a fantasy world, it would probably be Dark Sun. Ravenloft is gothic horror."

Each year TSR publishes four to six books in the Dungeons and Dragons series, three in Dark Sun, three or four in Ravenloft, and ten each in Dragonlance and Forgotten Realms. It's important, says Thomsen, that the company keeps much of the backlist in stock and in stores. Most large bookstores stock whole shelves of each series, and each line is easily identified by its colorful borders on the cover art and spine, and by specially designed series logos.

The number of submissions TSR receives for the various lines varies greatly from week to week, says Thomsen. "Some weeks we may get 20 or more, others we'll get none. We have a staff of seven plus myself with both in-house and out-of-house editors. The unsolicited manuscripts are divided up among everyone."

A variety of people write for each line and many have written more than one book for TSR. "We have a lot of writers who have published work elsewhere and some who are homegrown here—staff people who have written books for the company on their own time," says Thomsen.

Thomsen names just a few of the better known TSR authors, such as

Margaret Weis and Tracy Hickman, who wrote the original *Dragonlance* trilogies. There are several who write regularly for Forgotten Realms, he says, including Doug Niles, Troy Denning and R.A. Salvatore. As with book packagers, writers for the various series can choose to keep their own names or may use pseudonyms. "For example, Richard Allinson, who is, on paper, the author of Forgotten Realms's *Avatar* trilogy, is actually several people, but Simon Hawke, who writes for Dark Sun, is Simon Hawke."

Although a complete "bible" of the game universe in each series is available, most of the time authors receive a more condensed core of material for the particular game world in which their story is based. Yet each book in the series is independent from the previous book, so authors need not know everything going on in other books in the series. "They will receive all the information necessary for the completion of a project," Thomsen says.

Some of the books are published as trilogies. Says Thomsen, "Sometimes a book will turn into a trilogy if the author feels the whole story hasn't been told yet. Each book, however, is contracted separately." The average length of most TSR books is 90,000-100,000 words.

Although most of the TSR lines are paperback, the company has published a few hardcover volumes. "So far we've done one Dragonlance, two Forgotten Realms and one Ravenloft book in hardcover." The decision on whether a book should be hardcover, he says, depends on the subject matter as well as the strength of the author.

Most authors approach TSR with an idea for a book, but sometimes the company has an idea and then seeks an author. "What I want to see from authors is evidence that they are able to write well and they are able to complete a project. Obviously, if they've had something published, that is good, but, if they've never been published before, they should at least have a written body of work they feel is representative of their abilities. We've had authors who sent us book manuscripts that we could not publish, but, based on their work, we asked them to write something else for us."

TSR publishes both science fiction and fantasy and Thomsen says the breakdown just depends on what they've received. "Basically the work has to fall within the confines of what might be called middle-of-the-road science fiction or fantasy. If it's something along the lines of someone like John Gardner or the magic realism of someone like Gabriel Garcia

Marquez, we're probably not the right publisher for it. We want more traditional work."

Thomsen has been reading science fiction and fantasy works since he was very young, starting with Ray Bradbury, Robert A. Heinlein and J.R.R. Tolkien. "I also read my fair share of page turners, everything from the historicals like *Captain Blood* to contemporaries like the *Guns of Navarone*," he said. "The thing that continually drives my reading habits is the storytelling."

This carries over into Thomsen's philosophy on what makes good writing. "Get down your storytelling skills," he says. "I think it's better to be an author for the masses, one most people enjoy reading. There's a place in this world for Dostoevsky, Sartre and Henry Miller, but not as part of the TSR program. I like to think that if Rafael Sabatini or Alexandre Dumas were writing today, they'd be writing for TSR."

HOW TO CONTACT: First, if you are interested in submitting for any of the series based in game worlds, you must familiarize yourself with that product. Query first and include publication experience. If you have not had a book published, you must be able to provide a completed book or other evidence of your ability to complete a book project.

PAYMENT: Commissioned work (all lines except TSR) is done on a work-for-hire basis with TSR holding the copyright. TSR books are purchased under standard contract terms. Pays royalties on all projects (both TSR books and work-for-hire contracts), and these are negotiable.

ADDRESS: 201 Sheridan Springs Rd., Lake Geneva WI 53147
PHONE: (414)248-3625 ✳

WARNER ASPECT BOOKS

Contact: Betsy Mitchell, Editor-in-Chief

CATEGORIES
Cyberpunk, Epic Fantasy, Hard Science Fiction, High Fantasy, Military
Science Fiction, Sociological Science Fiction, Space Opera

Recently Published: *Fisherman's Hope*, by David Feintuch; *The Baker's Boy*, by J.V. Jones; *The Sword of Bedwyr*, by R. A. Salvatore.

When Warner Books felt their sf/fantasy list, under the imprint of Warner Questar, needed to be changed, they brought in Betsy Mitchell in July of 1993. The new line has taken on a very different tone from that of its predecessor, which did more fantasy and light fantasy. Mitchell renamed the imprint Aspect, an astronomical term meaning the position of a body in the solar system with respect to the sun. The term also symbolizes the new image of the book line, which is being revamped with new cover designs and logos. "I want to establish an identity as the house that does big science fiction ideas, books similar to *Dune* or *2001* if they were being written today. That's the sort of book that appeals most to me personally, and that's the identity I would like to gain for Aspect," Mitchell says.

An example is *Encounter With Tiber*, cowritten by astronaut Buzz Aldrin and writer John Barnes and published in July 1996. "It's a story Buzz Aldrin has been wanting to write all his life, about how humanity has to get off of Earth and into space permanently, or we run the risk of race extinction. That's a big science fictional idea that is going to be an important book for Aspect.

"I'll be doing all kinds of books," Mitchell continues. "I'll be doing fantasy; I'll be doing movie and comic book tie-ins, cyberpunk—all different kinds of books. It will be a very balanced list, but I'd like to become known for that type of big science fiction novel." There are no actual taboos, but Mitchell says she "won't be doing any light fantasy for a while."

Recent novels from Aspect include *Batman: The Ultimate Evil*, by Andrew Vachss, *The Resurrectionist*, by Thomas F. Monteleone, and the hardcover chain bestseller *Luthien's Gamble*, by R.A. Salvatore.

Mitchell has no qualms about working with beginning authors. Published in May 1996 was *Reclamation*, by Sarah Zettel, the first novel to be published under the New Aspects program. "New Aspects is being created strictly to focus on new authors, who otherwise can get lost in the monthly crowd of new releases," Mitchell says. "I'll only designate a first novel as a New Aspects selection when the writing is truly outstanding. But if it is, that first novel will get as much attention as I can attract for it from booksellers."

She also advises new writers to be familiar with the field and not just dabble in science fiction. "I think it's difficult to be a science fiction or fantasy writer these days if you don't know what's already been done. A tremendous amount is being written. To be competitive you really have to know what's coming out. Read the best-sellers and then come out with a new idea. Both 1990 and 1991 were bad years for new writers to break in due to the recession," she says, "but the situation is improving."

For 1996 Mitchell published 24 mass market paperbacks, four trade paperbacks and six hardcovers. She prefers potential books to fall between 80,000 and 120,000 words. Her assistant, Wayne Chang, reads the slush pile and passes along noteworthy manuscripts.

On trends in science fiction publishing, Mitchell says, "Right now epic fantasy is the hot thing—Robert Jordan, Mercedes Lackey, people like that—but these things come and go. Right now, fantasy seems to be more popular than science fiction, but no one would ever say it's always going to be that way. Also the media tie-ins are having a powerful effect on the field. It seems to work to cross over to the comic book audience or the television audience or the movie audience, so I think those books are part of the landscape now. They won't be going away."

Some of Mitchell's favorite science fiction novels are *Ringworld*, by Larry Niven; *Gateway*, by Frederik Pohl; *Downbelow Station*, by C.J.

Cherryh; *Doomsday Book*, by Connie Willis; and *Riddley Walker*, by Russell Hoban. Ursula K. Le Guin is also a longtime favorite of Mitchell's. "I was a second-generation reader. My father had Asimov, van Vogt, Heinlein and Clarke. After reading kids' fantasy until age ten, I shifted over to my father's library. He subscribed to some of the fiction magazines, so I was exposed to short stories."

Before her current position with Warner, Mitchell spent five years at Bantam Books as associate publisher of Spectra. Prior to that, she was senior editor at Baen Books, preceded by the position of managing editor at *Analog*. Mitchell herself doesn't write, due to lack of time, but does go to conventions, including the World Science Fiction Convention.

HOW TO CONTACT: Agent is required. Please include a cover letter detailing publishing credits and relevant background information. She will report back within 2 months.

PAYMENT: Pays advance against royalties; amount varies with author.

ADDRESS: 1271 Avenue of the Americas, New York NY 10020

PHONE: (212)522-7200

WEBSITE: http://pathfinder.com/twep/aspect ✳

✳ ✳ ✳

Other Novel Markets

The following listings are of publishers who do some science fiction and fantasy novels, but who do not generally have a line devoted to them. Also included are small presses who publish only a few books a year, but who include science fiction and fantasy in their lists.

The profiles in this section are shorter than the interviews with editors in the "Primary Novel Markets" section, but you will find specific details about the publisher, including information from editors on the types of material they are seeking and how best to approach them.

Many of the smaller markets in this section are very open to the work of new writers and, in fact, some list "publishing new writers" as a philosophy. Although many do not have the large distribution networks that are available to large publishing houses, distribution for small presses has been improving steadily over the years. At the same time, small press editors are becoming more savvy about marketing and promotion. As a result, trade journals and book reviewers have begun to take notice.

And in a few cases, books published by small presses have gotten such rave reviews that they have been picked up by larger houses. The most recent occurrence of this is Jeff Noon's *Vurt*, which was originally published by Britian's Ringpull Press. *Vurt* won the Arthur C. Clarke Award, and Noon won the John W. Campbell Award for Best New Writer. Shortly thereafter, *Vurt* was picked up by HarperCollins (See Jeff Noon's **First Sale** story on page 409.)

Writers who work with small presses say they particularly like the personal attention they receive. Small presses tend to keep their backlist in stock a long time and divide their promotion budgets evenly among the books they publish. On the other hand, many do not have a lot of money for promotion and rely heavily on help from the author. Authors, therefore, tend to have more say in the way their books are handled and promoted in the small press.

At the start of each listing, you will find a list of subgenres that most interest the publisher. Read the profile and a few of the publisher's books to get a more complete feel for the types of material they publish. You'll find several publishers in this section who are open to shorter books, such as novellas and novelettes. Others publish chapbooks for poets and short fiction authors. This information is outlined in the profile.

After each profile there is information on how to approach the publisher. In addition to details on how to submit your work, we've included reporting times. Reporting times are estimates, so be sure to allow an additional three or four weeks before checking on the status of your submission. Editors at small presses will often work alone or with a staff of only a few people, and, at certain times throughout the year, they may get behind in response time.

Payment and terms for each publisher are also included. Some pay advances and royalties, a percentage on sales of the book. This is particularly the case with the large publishers we've included in this section, i.e., those who do a limited amount of science fiction, but who are considered major publishing houses. Others pay no advance, but do pay royalties, while a few pay a flat fee.

The listings also include a very small number of subsidy publishers that are open to science fiction. These publishers split the cost of publication with writers. When offered a subsidy arrangement, make sure you know exactly how much is expected from you. Check the publisher's references and carefully consider the situation before entering into an agreement in which you are asked to spend your own money.

For more on how to prepare a manuscript for submission, see **Marketing Your Novel**, starting on page 218.

AGELESS PRESS

Established: 1992

Contact: Hope Day

CATEGORIES
Contemporary Fantasy, Cyberpunk, Dark Fantasy, Experimental Fiction, High Fantasy, Horror, Humorous, Science Fantasy

HOW TO CONTACT: Unsolicited manuscripts welcome but prefers writers to query first. Accepts faxed and electronic queries. Considers simultaneous submissions. Accepts submissions on computer disk; contact for preferred format. Reports on queries and manuscripts in 1 week. Always comments on rejected manuscripts. Writer's guidelines available for SASE.

PAYMENT: No royalties. Each contract negotiated individually. Pays on acceptance.

TERMS: Purchases first North American, foreign and electronic rights. Author receives a bio note on jacket or in book. 1 free copy of the book goes to the author; additional copies available at 50% discount.

ADDRESS: P.O. Box 5915, Sarasota FL 34277-5915

PHONE: (941)952-0576

E-MAIL: irishope@ix.netcom.com

WEBSITE: http://www.books.com

Arkham House

Established: 1939

Arkham House is the "oldest of the sf/fantasy small presses." Arkham House specializes in short story collections in trade hardcover. They only take submissions by invitation, as they are very small.

HOW TO CONTACT: A query letter may be useful in introducing yourself to the editors.

ADDRESS: P.O. Box 546, Sauk City WI 53583

Black Heron Press

Established: 1984

Contact: Jerry Gold, Publisher

CATEGORIES
Sociological Science Fiction

Recently Published: *The Rat and the Roses*, by Arnold Rabin; *The Prisoner's Son*, by Jerome Gold; *Terminal Weird*, by Jack Remick.

"We do not want fantasy that has a mass market appeal. We are not exclusively sf/fantasy publishers; in fact, we're pretty contemptuous of most of it published today. We do like intelligent, speculative, social science fiction, say, in the tradition of Orwell and Anthony Burgess. We also like some stuff in the alternate reality subgenre.

"An agent said that Black Heron publishes stuff that pushes the edge of acceptability, and a bookseller said the characters in our novels have no moral center. I hope both are right."

Black Heron Press is a one-person operation. It publishes paperback and hardback originals with an average print run of 1,000-1,500 books. They average 4 fiction titles each year. Some of their fiction is agented.

HOW TO CONTACT: Send a query and sample chapters or "first 30-50 pages." They report on queries in 3 months, and simultaneous submissions are OK.

PAYMENT: Authors are paid standard royalty rates, with no advance.

ADDRESS: P.O. Box 95676, Seattle WA 98145

BLUESTAR PRODUCTIONS

Established: 1994

Contact: Barbara Debolt, Editor

> CATEGORIES
> Contemporary Fantasy, Magic Realism, Science Fantasy, Traditional Fantasy

Bluestar Productions publishes 1 fantasy trade paperback and 1 mass market paperback each year. Averge print run for a first novel is 500-1,000.

HOW TO CONTACT: Query with first 3 chapters and SASE. Accepts faxed and electronic queries. Considers simultaneous submissions. Receives

approximately 40-45 unsolicited manuscripts each month. Reports on queries in 1-2 months, on manuscripts in 6-8 months. Never comments on rejected manuscripts. Writer's guidelines available for SASE.
PAYMENT: Pays royalties 10% of retail price.
TERMS: Purchases all rights. Manuscript published 2 years after acceptance. Author reviews galleys and copyedited manuscript. Author receives a bio note. 5 free copies of book go to author. Additional copies available at 40% discount; 50% if bought in quantities of 100.
ADDRESS: 9666 E. Riggs Rd., #194, Sun Lake AZ 85248
PHONE/FAX: (602)895-7995
E-MAIL: bdebolt@aol.com

CARROLL & GRAF PUBLISHERS, INC.

Established: 1983

Contact: Kent Carroll, Editor

CATEGORIES
Fantasy, Science Fiction

Carroll & Graf has an average first novel print run of 7,500 copies. They do not accept unsolicited manuscripts.

They have published *Anno Dracula*, by Kim Newman; *Sineater*, by Elizabeth Massie; and *The Carnival of Destruction*, by Brian Stableford.

HOW TO CONTACT: They prefer agented manuscripts, but writers may query first or submit an outline/synopsis and sample chapters. They report back in 2 weeks.
PAYMENT: Pays a negotiable advance against royalties of 6-15%. They send galleys to the author. A free book catalog is available on request.
ADDRESS: 260 Fifth Ave., New York NY 10001
PHONE: (212) 889-8772

ART: ANDII BRIGGS

CIRCLET PRESS, INC.

Established: 1992

Contact: Cecilia Tan, Editor

CATEGORIES
Erotic Science Fiction and Fantasy

Recently Published: *S/M Futures*, edited by Cecilia Tan; *Earthly Pleasures: Stories by Reed Manning*; *Selling Venus*, edited by Cecilia Tan.

"I want to see more *positive* depictions of sex and sexuality—no murder, dismemberment, castration or rape. I want to see authors using sf/f to explore arousing erotic possibilities. I want to see intelligently-crafted fiction. Don't send us your novel. We publish short stories *only*. Each year we choose a list of anthology topics, and accept manuscripts only between April 5 and August 31. Get our guidelines (for SASE)—they are very detailed. We seek high quality sf/f stories that cannot be published in other markets merely because their sexual content is too much for the average publication." Publishes 8 trade paperbacks per year.

HOW TO CONTACT: Unsolicited manuscripts welcome. Send full short story. Accepts electronic queries. Considers simultaneous submissions. Receives approximately 60-75 unsolicited manuscripts each month. 10% of accepted manuscripts are submitted through agents. Reports on queries in 2 weeks, on manuscripts in 3-6 months. Always comments on rejected manuscripts. Writer's guidelines available for SASE.

PAYMENT: Pays flat fee.

TERMS: Purchases one-time reprint rights or first-time anthology rights. Manuscript published 6-12 months after acceptance. Author reviews galleys. Author receives a bio note on jacket or in book. 2-5 free copies of the book go to the author; additional copies available at 40% discount.

ADDRESS: 1770 Massachusetts Ave., Suite 278, Cambridge MA 02140

PHONE: (617) 864-0492

FAX: (617) 864-0663

E-MAIL: circlet-info@circlet.com

WEBSITE: http://www.circlet.com/circlet/~

DRAGON MOON PRESS

Established: 1995

Contact: Gwen Gades or Christine Mains

> CATEGORIES
> Contemporary Fantasy, Dark Fantasy, High Fantasy, Humorous Fantasy, Magic Realism, Traditional Fantasy

Recently Published: *Daughter of Dragons*, by Kathy Nelson; *Communicators: Inflection*, by Valerie Kirkwood; *Twilight of the Fifth Sun*, by David Sakmyster (books under contract and scheduled for Christmas 1996).

Dragon Moon is a new fantasy publisher. "We publish mini-hardcovers, a mass market-sized book with a hardcover binding. We feel that this fits in with our stand on the environment and offers an alternative to larger, more expensive hardcovers which many book buyers can no longer afford.

"For fantasy manuscripts, we'd like to see tighter, better-planned plots more lyrical writing when the type of story requires it. We'd like to see fewer talking animal stories, and no more 'craft of the wise,' explanations for modern Wicca—we've already seen too much of it."

In its first year, Dragon Moon intends to publish 3-10 hardcovers, with 2-6 being first novels. Averge print run of a first novel is 2,500.

HOW TO CONTACT: Query first with 3 sample chapters and SASE. Accepts faxed and electronic queries. Considers simultaneous submissions. Receives approximately 10 unsolicited manuscripts each month. Reports on queries and manuscripts in 1-3 months. Sometimes comments on rejected manuscripts. Writer's guidelines available for SASE.

PAYMENT: Pays royalties of 8-12% on list price.

TERMS: Purchases first North American rights. Manuscript published within 1-2 years after acceptance. Author reviews copyedited manuscript and jacket copy. Author receives a bio note. 15 free copies of book go to author.

ADDRESS: 4 St. NW, Box 64312-5512, Calgary, Alberta T2K 6J0 Canada

PHONE: (403)277-2140

E-MAIL: cmains@freenet.calgary.ab.ca

DELL PUBLISHING

Bantam Doubleday Dell Publishing Group, Inc.

> CATEGORIES
> Cyberpunk, Dark Fantasy, Hard Science Fiction, Offbeat Fantasy, Offbeat Science Fiction, Psychological Horror, Sociological Fantasy, Sociological Science Fiction, Technological Horror, Traditional Fantasy

Dell has all but eliminated its science fiction and fantasy line, Abyss. They still accept the occasional sf/f submission, but writers are advised to query first before sending any materials.

HOW TO CONTACT: Query. They report back in several months.

PAYMENT: Offers an advance against royalties. Sends galleys to author. Book catalog available for SAE plus $1.30 postage.

ADDRESS: 1540 Broadway, New York NY 10036

PHONE: (212)354-6500

E.M. PRESS, INC.

Established: 1991

Contact: Ellen Beck

CATEGORIES
Contemporary Fantasy, High Fantasy, Science Fantasy

Recently Published: *The Search for Archerland* and *The Golden Haze*, by H.R. Coursen.

Would like to see more "positive, uplifting" themes. "Experience is not an issue. Quality is our only concern." Publishes 2 trade paperbacks per year. Publishes 90% first novels each year. Average print run for a first novel is 500-1,000.

HOW TO CONTACT: Unsolicited manuscripts welcome, but prefers writers to query first. Considers simultaneous submissions. Receives approximately 250 unsolicited manuscripts each month. Reports on queries in 1 month. Sometimes comments on rejected manuscripts. Writer's guidelines available for SASE.

PAYMENT: Pays average advance of $500 and royalties of 6-12%.

TERMS: Purchases all rights. Manuscript published 1 year after acceptance. Author reviews galleys. Author receives a bio note on jacket on in book.

ADDRESS: P.O. Box 4057, Manassas VA 20108

PHONE: (540)439-0304

FASA CORPORATION

Imprint: Rock • Established: 1982

Contact: Donna Ippolito, Editor

CATEGORIES
Cyberpunk, Dark Fantasy, Game Fiction, Military Science Fiction

Recently Published: *Who Hunts the Hunter, Tactics of Duty, House of the Sun.*

"FASA Corporation publishes only sf/fantasy manuscripts based in our Battle Tech, Shadowrun and Earthdawn Universes." They are fully integrated in other storytelling media and offer this advice: "Beginning writers need to prove writing ability by writing a game product."

FASA Corporation publishes 12 mass market paperbacks each year. The average print run is 70,000 books. About 50% of the manuscripts they accept are submitted through agents, and they receive an average of 12 unsolicited manuscripts each month. They publish 2 first novels each year.

HOW TO CONTACT: Send query letter and SASE to receive submission guidelines. They do not accept unsolicited manuscripts. They report back in 4-6 weeks. Writer's guidelines are available for SASE. Write for a catalog, including $1 for postage and handling.

PAYMENT: Authors are paid in royalties of 4% and receive an average advance of $4,500. They purchase foreign, gaming, movie and television rights. The manuscript is published 1 year after acceptance. Author reviews galleys and copyedited manuscript. The author receives 24 copies of the book, and additional copies are available at a 60% discount.

ADDRESS: 1100 W. Cermak, B305, Chicago IL 60708

PHONE: (312)243-5660

FAX: (312)243-4847

FC2 Black Ice Books

Established: 1990

CATEGORIES
Cyberpunk, Experimental Fiction

Recently Published: Titles by Samuel Delany, Kit Reed, John Shirly and Don Webb.

"We do not publish traditional sf. We are interested in sf with an experimental edge." Publishes 3 first novels each year. Average print run for a first novel is 2,500.

HOW TO CONTACT: Does not accept unsolicited manuscripts. Query first. Considers simultaneous submissions. Receives approximately 5-10 unsolicited manuscripts each month. Few accepted manuscripts are submitted through agents. Reports on queries in 2 weeks. Sometimes comments on rejected manuscripts. Writer's guidelines available for SASE.

PAYMENT: Pays average advance of $100 and royalties of 7½-10%.

TERMS: Purchases various rights. Manuscript published 1 year after acceptance. Author reviews galleys, copyedited manuscript and jacket copy. Author receives a bio note on jacket or in book. 20 free copies go to the author; additional copies available at 50% discount.

ADDRESS: Unit for Contemporary Literature, Illinois State University, Normal IL 61790-4241

PHONE: (309)438-3582

FAX: (309)438-3523

FEDOGAN & BREMER

Established: 1989

Contact: Philip J. Rahman

> **CATEGORIES**
> Contemporary Fantasy, Dark Fantasy, High Fantasy, Humorous Fantasy, Magic Realism, Traditional Fantasy

Fedogan & Bremer is very interested in pulp authors—living or deceased—and works of a similar vein. It publishes 2-3 hardcovers annually. Averge print run of a first novel is 1,500-2,000.

HOW TO CONTACT: Query first with SASE. Accepts faxed and electronic queries. Considers simultaneous submissions. Receives approximately 1 unsolicited manuscript every other month. Reports on queries in 1 month, on manuscripts in 6 months. Sometimes comments on rejected manuscripts.

PAYMENT: Pays straight royalty. Each contract negotiated individually.

TERMS: Purchases various rights. Manuscript published 2 years after acceptance. Author reviews galleys. Author receives a bio note. 5 free copies of book go to author. Additional copies available at 40% discount.

ADDRESS: 603 Washington Ave., Minneapolis MN 55414

PHONE/FAX: (612)721-8848

E-MAIL: fedogan@aol.com

Four Walls Eight Windows

Established: 1986

Contact: John Oakes, Publisher

CATEGORIES
Alternate History, Cyberpunk, Steampunk

Recently Published: *Ribofunk*, by Paul DiFilippo

The publishers are interested in "offbeat, witty and original submissions with dark humor. We would like to see fewer vampires, and more weird Ellison-types." They describe themselves as "small, aggressive, progressive and editorially driven."

They offer this advice: "Look for the house that has your taste. Don't submit everything to everyone."

Four Walls Eight Windows publishes 2 sf/fantasy hardcovers annually with a print run of 5,000-15,000. Around 50% of their fiction is agented.

HOW TO CONTACT: Send a query letter and a few pages of the manuscript with SASE. Include a previous publishing history in your cover letter. They report back in 2 months, and simultaneous submissions are acceptable. A book catalog is free on request.

PAYMENT: Authors are paid a variable advance against standard royalties. They send galleys to the author.

ADDRESS: 39 W. 14th St., #503, New York NY 10011

PHONE: (212) 206-8965

DONALD M. GRANT, PUBLISHER

Established: 1964

This publisher, one of the oldest active small presses, was founded in 1964. They are currently overstocked and will not be accepting submissions until the end of 1996.

ADDRESS: P.O. Box 187, Hampton Falls NH 03844
PHONE: (603)778-7191

GRYPHON PUBLICATIONS

Established: 1983

Contact: Gary Lovisi, Owner and Editor

> CATEGORIES
> Cyberpunk, Dark Fantasy, Hard Science Fiction

Recently Published: *Clay Drew Mars Quartet,* by John Russell Fearn (4 book series); *Pandoras Box* and *Saturn Patrol,* by E.C. Tubb.

The publishers are interested in "good characters in believable situations." They would like to see "more originality and a harder edge" to sf/fantasy manuscripts. Gryphon publishes "a lot of good material and offers a unique opportunity to new writers."

Gryphon publishes a variety of publications: magazines, chapbooks and books. They publish hardcover and original trade paperbacks with a total of 5-10 titles each year. The average print run is 500-1,000 books. They publish some first novels and often comment on rejected manuscripts. About 5% of the manuscripts they accept are submitted through agents.

HOW TO CONTACT: "Send a 1-page synopsis for anything longer than 3,000 words." Include estimated word count, 50-word bio, short list of publishing credits, and "how you heard about us." Send SASE for reply or return of manuscript. Reports back in 2-6 weeks. Simultaneous and electronic submissions are OK (with hard copy and ASCII disk).

PAYMENT: For magazines, they pay $5-45 on publication plus 2 contributor's copies; for novels or collections, payment varies and "is much more."

TERMS: They usually send galleys to author for review. Publishes 1-3 years after acceptance. Writer's guidelines and book catalog are available for SASE.

ADDRESS: P.O. Box 209, Brooklyn NY 11228

PHONE: (718) 646-6126, after 6 P.M. EST

HARMONY BOOKS-CROWN PUBLISHERS, INC.

Established: 1972

> CATEGORIES
> Fantasy, Science Fiction

Harmony Books "is not really seeking or soliciting science fiction/fantasy per se, only as a story line." Harmony Books publishes 1 sf/fantasy hardcover annually. The average print run is 10,000 books. Nearly 95% of the manuscripts they accept are submitted through agents, and they receive an average of 50 unsolicited manuscripts each month. They publish 1 first novel each year. They published *Mostly Harmless*, by Douglas Adams.

HOW TO CONTACT: Send a short proposal consisting of summary and sample chapter. They report back in 1 month. They will accept simultaneous submissions. Writer's guidelines are available for SASE.

PAYMENT: Authors are paid a variable advance against royalties. The manuscript is published 9 months to 1 year after acceptance. The author reviews galleys, copyedited manuscript and jacket copy and does receive a bio note. The author receives 25 copies of the book, and additional copies are available at a 40% discount.

ADDRESS: 201 E. 50th St., New York NY 10022

PHONE: (212) 751-2600

FAX: (212) 572-6192

Hollow Earth Publishing

Established: 1983

Contact: Heilan-Yvette Grimes

> **CATEGORIES**
> Contemporary Fantasy, Cyberpunk, Dark Fantasy, Experimental Fiction, Hard Science Fiction, High Fantasy, Horror, Humorous, Magic Realism, Science Fantasy, Steampunk, Traditional Fantasy

Would like to see fewer derivative stories. "Tolkien has been done. Also interested in potential multimedia stories." Publishes 4 mass market paperbacks per year. Average print run for a first novel is 5,000.

HOW TO CONTACT: Does not accept unsolicited manuscripts. Query first. Accepts electronic queries. No simultaneous submissions. Submissions on computer disk should be formatted in ASCII. Receives approximately 100 unsolicited manuscripts each month. Reports on queries and manuscripts in 1 week. Writer's guidelines available for SASE.

PAYMENT: Pays royalties of 10-15%. Royalties are on net.

TERMS: Purchases all rights. Manuscript published 6 months after acceptance. Author reviews galleys, copyedited manuscript and jacket copy. Author receives a bio note on jacket or in book. 10 free copies of book go to the author, additional copies available at 50% discount.

ADDRESS: P.O. Box 1355, Boston MA 02205-1358

PHONE: (617)746-3130

FAX: (603)433-8735

E-MAIL: hep2@aol.com

Horse Latitudes Press

Established: 1982

Contact: Michael P. Jones

CATEGORIES
Contemporary Fantasy, Cyberpunk, Dark Fantasy, Elfpunk, Experimental Fiction, Hard Science Fiction, High Fantasy, Horror, Humorous, Magic Realism, Military Science Fiction, Poetry, Science Fantasy, Sociological, Space Opera, Splatterpunk, Steampunk, Traditional Fantasy

"Don't get in the I'm-gonna-write-like-everyone-else rut. Don't be a copycat! Be yourself and your ability will shine. I am very tired of reading the boring, run-of-the-mill, everyone-could-have-written-this manuscript. Be patient and flexible. We want to work with writers who can take advice without having to destroy their creativity.

"We are just getting into sf/f under this imprint. Being so new, we are a good place for beginners. Also, since we have other imprints, writers will have additional opportunities for publishing."

HOW TO CONTACT: Unsolicited manuscripts welcome. Send full manuscript with SASE. Considers simultaneous submissions. Receives approximately 10 unsolicited manuscripts each month. 1% of accepted manuscripts are submitted through agents. Sometimes comments on rejected manuscripts. Writer's guidelines available for SASE.

PAYMENT: Pays royalties of 20-50%. Each contract negotiated individually.

TERMS: Purchases first North American rights. Manuscript published 12-16 months after acceptance. Author reviews galleys, copyedited manuscript and jacket copy. Author receives a bio note on jacket or in book. Negotiated number of free copies of the book go to the author.

ADDRESS: P.O. Box 294, Rhododendron, OR 97049

PHONE: (503)622-4798

isf–iNTEGRA SPECULATIVE FICTION

Established: 1990

Contact: Frank Wagner, Publisher

CATEGORIES
Dark Fantasy, Hard Science Fiction, High Fantasy, Space Opera, Traditional Fantasy

"Integra will consider cross-genre works. Also we will consider first-time authors. We are in the process of exploring electronic publishing. We hope this will allow us to handle more titles soon."

Integra Press publishes 1-2 sf/fantasy hardcovers and 1-2 paperbacks annually. The average print run is 3,500 books. About 40% of the manuscripts they accept are submitted through agents, and they receive 10-20 unsolicited manuscripts each month. They publish 1-2 first novels every year.

They published *The Charm* and *The Serpent Slayers*, by Adam Niswander.

HOW TO CONTACT: Send manuscript or have agent contact publisher. They report back in 2-6 weeks. They will accept fax queries and simultaneous and disk submissions. They sometimes comment on rejected manuscripts. Writer's guidelines are available for SASE.

PAYMENT: Authors are paid an advance (average $2,000) against royalties of 20-50%. They purchase all rights. The manuscript is published approximately 1 year after acceptance. The author reviews galleys, copyedited manuscript and jacket copy and does receive a bio note. Number of copies of book received by author is negotiated in contract.

ADDRESS: Integra Press, 1702 W. Camelback Rd., Phoenix AZ 85015

PHONE: (602) 996-2106

THE NAIAD PRESS, INC.

Established: 1973

Contact: Barbara Grier

CATEGORIES
Contemporary Fantasy, Dark Fantasy, High Fantasy, Traditional Fantasy

"As a lesbian publishing company, we look for the marriage between fantasy and the lesbian orientation of the major characters without artifice . . . difficult to find but not impossible. Think in terms of complete titles, not in series, and think in terms of a 50,000 word manuscript. We are genuinely interested in good fantasy and absolutely unable to market science fiction . . . so we are reading no science fiction at all."

Publishes at least 2 trade paperbacks per year. Publishes 4-5 first novels each year. Average print run for a first novel is 6,000-8,000.

HOW TO CONTACT: Does not accept unsolicited manuscripts. Query first. Receives approximately 40 manuscripts each month. Reports on queries in 1 week, on manuscripts in 5 months. Sometimes comments on rejected manuscripts. Writer's guidelines available for SASE.

PAYMENT: No advance, royalties of 15%. Royalties are on net.

TERMS: Purchases all rights. Manuscript published 8-15 months after acceptance. Author receives a bio note on jacket or in book. 20 free copies of the book go to the author; additional copies available at 40% discount.

ADDRESS: P.O. Box 10543, Tallahassee FL 32302

PHONE: (904)539-5965

FAX: (904)539-9731

NEW VICTORIA PUBLISHERS

Established: 1976

Contact: Claudia Lamperti

> CATEGORIES
> Contemporary Fantasy, Humorous, Magic Realism, Science Fantasy, Sociological Science Fiction.

Recently Published: *Shadows of Aggar* and *Fires of Aggar*, by Chris Anne Wolfe.

"We are committed to publishing works with lesbian or strong female protagonists, with priority given to writings by women authors." Would like to see fiction set in believable alternate worlds, complete with atmosphere, language and cultures. Publishes 8-10 trade paperbacks per year. Average print run for a first novel is 5,000.

HOW TO CONTACT: Unsolicited manuscripts welcome but prefers writers to query with 1-2 sample chapters (50 pages). Accepts electronic queries. Receives approximately 30-40 unsolicited manuscripts each month. Reports on queries in 1-2 weeks, on manuscripts in 3-4 weeks. Writer's guidelines available for SASE.

PAYMENT: No advance, royalties of 10%.

TERMS: Manuscript published 1 year after acceptance. Author reviews galleys and copyedited manuscripts. Author receives a bio note on jacket or in book. 5 free copies of the book go the author; additional copies available at 40% discount.

ADDRESS: P.O. Box 27, Norwich VT 05055

PHONE: (802)649-5297

E-MAIL: newvic@aol.com

OBELESK BOOKS

Imprint: Triangle Titles • Established: 1993

Contact: Gary Brown, Editor

> CATEGORIES
> Dark Fantasy, Erotica, Hard Science Fiction, High Fantasy, Horror, Humorous Science Fiction, Military Science Fiction, Sociological Science Fiction, Traditional Fantasy

Recently Published: *Worthy Foes: Differently Abled Heroes*; *Winter of the Soul: Gay Vampire Fiction*; *Cyber Magick: Lesbian SF*; *Green Echo: Ecological SF*.

"We want more ethnic sf/f/h, especially Oriental, Native American, African and other nonwhite cultures. We want to see more women characters, racial, ethnic and sexual minorities, as well as differently abled characters.

"We publish fiction from 500-5,000 words in length, firm. We do not publish novels or book length works. We do not publish poetry. We publish adult short fiction—thoughtful, mature, sensual and imaginative. We are constantly looking for manuscripts that explore the (in)human mind through magic, science, human relationships, sex, culture, etc. Our Triangle imprint publishes sf/f/h about gay, lesbian, bisexual and trans-gendered characters. This imprint has been well received and will be expanded."

Obelesk Books/Triangle Titles publishes an average of 4 sf/f/h trade paperbacks per year. "We receive approximately 60 manuscripts per month. Stories appearing in our books have won awards and been re-printed around the world."

HOW TO CONTACT: Authors should request guidelines before submitting. Reports back in 2 weeks. Accepts simultaneous manuscripts and usu-ally comments on rejected manuscripts. Writer's guidelines are avail-able for SASE with first-class postage or 2 IRCs.

PAYMENT: Pays flat fee $10-20.

TERMS: Buys one-time nonexclusive anthology rights. The author reviews galleys and receives a bio note. The author gets 1 copy of the work, and additional copies are available at 40% off cover price.

ADDRESS: P.O. Box 1118, Elkton MO 21922-1118

PHONE: (410) 392-3640

E-MAIL: obelesk@tantalus.clark.net

THE OVERLOOK PRESS

Established: 1972

Contact: Tracy Carns, Editor

CATEGORIES
Cyberpunk, Dark Fantasy, Feminist Science Fiction, Traditional Fantasy

Recently Published: *Horripilations*, by J.K. Potter; *The Gods Are Thirsty*, by Tanith Lee; *Still Life With Volkswagens*, by Geoff Nicholson.

The Overlook Press recommends that writers "try to find an agent while submitting to publishers." The Overlook Press is a small-staffed, full-time publisher. They publish 2 hardcover and 2 paperback sf/fantasy books each year.

HOW TO CONTACT: Send a query letter or submit an outline/synopsis with SASE. Reports back in 6 months and simultaneous submissions are OK. Occasionally they will comment on rejected manuscripts.
PAYMENT: Payment varies.
ADDRESS: 149 Wooster St., New York NY 10012
PHONE: (212)477-7162

PERMEABLE PRESS

Established: 1984

Contact: Brian Clark, Editor

> CATEGORIES
> Apocalyptic Science Fiction, Avant-Pop Science Fiction, Cyberpunk, Hard Science Fiction, Humorous Science Fiction, Post-Modern Science Fiction, Sociological Science Fiction, Traditional Fantasy

Recently Published: *The Final Dream*, by Daniel Pearlman; *Time Famine*, by Lance Olsen; *Elements of Style*, by Sarah Hafner.

Permeable Press is interested in a "provocative synopsis." Submissions should be from an "unusual perspective, e.g., narrator(s) is queer, of color, or ethically difficult situation, e.g., using AIDS as a weapon, nano-technology.

"We do not publish mainstream genre fiction. We love the stuff too dangerous for the big houses, but too good to leave unpublished."

Permeable is a small literary press established in 1984. They publish

2 hardcover and 6-8 paperback sf/fantasy books each year with a print run of 3,500 books. Around 10% of their fiction is agented. They publish several first novels each year.

HOW TO CONTACT: Send query with synopsis and, if applicable, three sample chapters with SASE. Reports back in 4-6 weeks on queries and 3 months on manuscripts. They accept electronic and unsolicited manuscripts. Writer's guidelines and book catalog are available for a 9 × 12 SAE and 4 first-class stamps.

PAYMENT: Authors are paid royalties of 5-20%. Author's copies vary. They send galleys to the author.

ADDRESS: 2336 Market St., #14, San Francisco CA 94114-1521

PHONE: (415)255-9765

E-MAIL: bcclark@igc.apc.org

PiNNACLE BOOKS-KENSiNGTON PUBLiSHiNG CORP.

Contact: Denise Little, Senior Editor or Karen Haas, Consulting Editor

> CATEGORIES
> Dark Fantasy, Futuristic Romance, Traditional Fantasy

Pinnacle Book publishes very little sf/fantasy. Although Senior Editor Denise Little does like what's being done with genre-mixing, i.e., futuristic romance.

They published *Lady of the Forest*, by Jennifer Roberson.

HOW TO CONTACT: Send a proposal with SASE. They will accept simultaneous submissions and comment on rejected manuscripts.

PAYMENT: Authors are paid in variable royalties. They purchase world rights. The author reviews galleys. Author's copies vary.

ADDRESS: 850 Third Ave., 16th Floor, New York NY 10022

PHONE: (212)407-1500

FAX: (212)407-1590

ART: LEE BOOJAMRA

RiSiNG TiDE PRESS

Established: 1990

Contact: Lee Boojamra

> **CATEGORIES**
> Contemporary Fantasy, Cyberpunk, Dark Fantasy, Hard Science Fiction, High Fantasy, Horror, Humorous, Magic Realism, Military Science Fiction, Science Fantasy, Sociological, Steampunk, Traditional Fantasy

Recently Published: *Warriors of Isis*, by Jean Stewart; *Heartstone & Saber*, by Jacqui Singleton; *Nightshade*, by Karen Williams.

"Rising Tide Press publishes lesbian fiction. We are interested in all of the above categories, but the protagonists *must* be lesbian and the story must have a lesbian sensibility. Story must contain supportive subplots, well developed characters and not be predictable. Avoid longwinded narratives that slow the story down, and most of all, study the craft of writing good fiction." Would like to see better research pertaining to period, place, technology and society. Publishes 3-6 trade paperbacks per year. Average print run for a first novel is 5,000-7,000.

HOW TO CONTACT: Unsolicited manuscripts welcome. Send full manuscript. Receives approximately 50 unsolicited manuscripts each month. Reports on queries in 1 week, on manuscripts in 2 months. Always comments on rejected manuscripts. Writer's guidelines available for SASE.

PAYMENT: No advance, royalties of 10-15%. Royalties are on net.

TERMS: Manuscript published 6 months to 2 years after acceptance. Author reviews galleys and copyedited manuscript. Author receives a bio note on jacket or in book. 15-30 free copies of the book go to the author; additional copies available at 40% discount.
ADDRESS: 5 Kivy St., Huntington Station NY 11746
PHONE: (516)427-1289
E-MAIL: rtpress@aol.com

RIVERBEND PRESS

Imprint: Alien Vistas • Established: 1995

Contact: Lynn Jenny, Editor

> CATEGORIES
> Cyberpunk, Hard Science Fiction, Military Science Fiction, Sociological Science Fiction, Space Opera

"RiverBend is a new company. We plan to establish ourselves firmly in the marketplace by mid 1998. We are looking for authors who will help take us where we want to be." RiverBend Press needs "high quality writing, original ideas, unique settings." Would like to see more "characters from different cultural backgrounds, characters that have depth and elicit strong emotional responses from the reader." Less: telepathy and all female societies. "Polish your manuscript before you send it. Get people to read it and give you feedback; join a writer's critique group. Present your manuscript in a professional manner."

Publishes 4-10 hardcovers and/or 4-10 mass market paperbacks per year. Publishes 2-6 first novels each year. Average print run for a first novel is 1,000-10,000 copies.

HOW TO CONTACT: Unsolicited manuscripts welcome, but prefers writers to query with 3 sample chapters. Considers simultaneous submissions. Receives approximately 25-40 unsolicited manuscripts each month. 10% of manuscripts are submitted through agents. Reports on queries in 3 months, on manuscripts in 6 months. Sometimes comments on rejected manuscripts.
PAYMENT: Pays small advance with royalties of 6-15%.

TERMS: Purchases first North American rights. Manuscript published 1-2 years after acceptance. Author reviews galleys and jacket copy. Author receives a bio note on jacket or in book. 15 free copies of the book go to the author; additional copies available at 40% discount.

ADDRESS: Box 75064, Cambrian P.O., Calgary, Alberta T2K 6J8 Canada

PHONE: (403)282-5206

SERENDIPITY SYSTEMS

Established: 1986

Contact: John Galuszka

> CATEGORIES
> Experimental Fiction, Hard Science Fiction, Humorous

Recently Published: *Sideshow*, by Marian Allen; *D.A.I.S.Y.*, by Joe Dacy II; *Silicon Karma*, by Tom Easton.

"We only publish electronic editions for IBM-PC compatible computers, (and soon on the Internet). Submissions must be on IBM PC computer disks. We cannot use manuscripts on paper. Explore the literary potential of your computer. Use hypertext, multimedia and/or interactivity. Hard science fiction in computer-enhanced form (with hypertext, interactivity and/or multimedia)." Publishes 2-3 first novels each year. Books are "printed" to order.

HOW TO CONTACT: Unsolicited manuscripts welcome, but prefers writers to query first with SASE. Accepts electronic queries. Considers simultaneous submissions. Receives approximately 25 unsolicited manuscripts each month. Reports on queries and manuscripts in 2-3 weeks.

PAYMENT: Pays no advance, royalties of 30% minimum. Royalties are on net.

TERMS: Purchases electronic rights. Manuscript published 1-4 months after acceptance. Author receives a bio note on jacket or in book. 10 free copies of the book go to the author; 50 additional copies available at cost.

ADDRESS: P.O. Box 140, San Simeon CA 93452

PHONE: (805)927-5259

E-MAIL: j.galuszka@genie.geis.com

Thistledown Press Ltd.

Established: 1975

Contact: Jesse Strothers

> CATEGORIES
> Contemporary Fantasy, Cyberpunk, Experimental Fiction, High Fantasy, Humorous, Magic Realism, Poetry, Science Fantasy, Traditional Fantasy

Recently Published: *The Fungus Garden*, by Brian Brett; *Wind Shifter*, by Linda Smith; *Dance of the Snow Dragon*, by Eileen Kernaghan.

"Only Canadian authors published (or co-publications with American publishers)." Would like to see "more quality short stories, better quality writing and submissions with publication history in journals and magazines enclosed. Query first with SASE."

Publishes 1-2 trade paperbacks and 1-2 mass market paperback per year. Publishes 1-4 first novels each year. Average print run for a first novel is 2,000.

HOW TO CONTACT: Does not accept unsolicited manuscripts. Query first. Receives approximately 50 unsolicited manuscripts each year. 1% of accepted manuscripts are submitted through agents. Reports on queries in 1 month, on manuscripts in 2 months. Always comments on rejected manuscripts. Writer's guidelines available for SASE.

PAYMENT: Each contract individually negotiated.

TERMS: Manuscript published 6-12 months after acceptance. Author reviews galleys. Author receives a bio note on jacket or in book.

ADDRESS: 633 Main St., Saskatoon, Saskatchewan S7H 0J8 Canada

PHONE: (306)244-1722

FAX: (306)244-1762

ULTRAMARINE PUBLISHING

Established: 1970

Contact: Christopher P. Stephens

A small, selective publisher with more than 200 books in print, Ultramarine publishes only a "few" fantasy and science fiction titles each year. It does not want or accept unsolicited manuscripts.

HOW TO CONTACT: Accepts agented manuscripts only. Considers simultaneous submissions. Sometimes comments on rejected manuscripts.

TERMS: Purchases various rights. Each contract negotiated individually.

ADDRESS: P.O. Box 303, Hastings-on-Hudson NY 10706

PHONE: (914)478-1339

FAX: (914)478-1365

THE VIRTUAL PRESS

Established: 1994

Contact: William Stanek, Publisher

> CATEGORIES
> Contemporary Fantasy, Cyberpunk, Dark Fantasy, Hard Science Fiction, High Fantasy, Science Fantasy, Space Opera, Traditional Fantasy

Recently Published: *The Paliy Crisis; Dreamers and Mystics.*

"The Virtual Press is a nontraditional press forging the rules for those that will follow us. A local reporter recently called me the father of the electronic press. While others are talking and writing about this new movement, we are actually producing, marketing and helping to direct this nontraditional medium into the mainstream.

"The best way to preview our electronic books is on the world-wide web. On the web, we have fully interactive demos. We've even set up a virtual tour of the *World of the Paths*, which is the fantasy world from the *Destiny Chronicles* series. Users who have access to the Internet can point their web browser at http://tvp.com/. A fully interactive catalog on floppy disk will also be available shortly. The catalog will feature sample chapters from new and upcoming releases.

"We are seeking works from 50,000 to 90,000 words in length. While we do not pay advances (normally), we do pay royalties of up to 25%. Our terms may look very generous to writers. However, we want to ensure all our potential authors understand fully what publishing on this new medium means. Until electronic books become a part of the mainstream, they will not sell as well or as briskly as traditional books. A typical e-book may sell only a few hundred copies a year. We are working to change this and hope the success of our first release, *At Dream's End*, will help to legitimize the medium."

HOW TO CONTACT: Does not accept unsolicited manuscripts. Query first. Accepts electronic queries. Considers simultaneous submissions. Submissions on computer disk should be formatted as ASCII text. Receives approximately 20-25 manuscripts each month. 10% of accepted manuscripts are submitted through agents. Reports on queries and manuscripts in 2 months. Sometimes comments on rejected manuscripts. Writer's guidelines available for SASE.

PAYMENT: Pays 8-21% on net.

TERMS: Purchases first North American and first worldwide rights. Manuscript published 8-12 months after acceptance. Author reviews copyedited manuscripts. Author receives a bio note. 5-10 free copies go to the author; additional copies available at 50% discount.

ADDRESS: 408 Division St., Shawano WI 54166

E-MAIL: publisher@tvp.com

WEBSITE: http://tvp.com/

WHITE WOLF PUBLISHING

Imprint: Borealis • Established: 1984

Contact: Ms. Staley Krause, Editor-in-Chief

> **CATEGORIES**
> Contemporary Fantasy, Cyberpunk, Dark Fantasy, Experimental Fiction, Horror, Magic Realism, Science Fantasy, Sociological, Splatterpunk, Traditional Fantasy

Recently Published: Titles by Harlan Ellison, Michael Moorcock and Nancy Collins.

@

"Sf and fantasy should be a venue for cutting edge, speculative fiction. There is no room in the category for rehashed plots and generic settings. Follow the standard submission protocol! Tell us what is unique about your submission. Why should we consider this project above all others? Don't call us!"

Publishes 10 hardcovers, 10 trade paperbacks and 20 mass market paperbacks per year. Publishes 6 first novels each year. Average print run for a first novel is 10,000-20,000.

HOW TO CONTACT: Unsolicited manuscripts welcome. Send full manuscript. Considers simultaneous submissions. Receives approximately 60 unsolicited manuscripts each month. 80% of accepted manuscripts are submitted through agents. Reports on manuscripts in 6 months. Sometimes comments on rejected manuscripts. Writer's guidelines available for SASE.

PAYMENT: Standard professional rates.

TERMS: Purchases various rights. Manuscript published 18 months after acceptance. Author reviews galleys, copyedited manuscript and jacket copy. Author receives a bio note on jacket or in book. 25 free copies of the book go to the author; additional copies available at 40% discount.

ADDRESS: 780 Park North Blvd., Suite 100, Clarkston GA 30021

WRITE WAY PUBLISHING

Established: 1993

Contact: Dorrie O'Brien

> **CATEGORIES**
> Contemporary Fantasy, High Fantasy, Horror, Magic Realism, Science Fantasy, Space Opera, Traditional Fantasy

Recently Published: *The Tenant*, by Charles West; *Roadkill*, by Richard Sanford; *The Time Fount Project*, by Steve Vance.

"Make sure you are submitting a manuscript that has been edited (or at least looked at) by a professional, so that you're not submitting a work that *looks* amateur."

Publishes 10-12 hardcovers per year. Publishes 8-10 first novels each year. Average print run for a first novel is 2,000.

HOW TO CONTACT: Query with 2 sample chapters. Considers simultaneous submissions. 10-20% of accepted manuscripts are submitted through agents. Reports on queries in 1 month. Sometimes comments on rejected manuscripts. Writer's guidelines available for SASE.

PAYMENT: Pays royalties of 8-10%.

TERMS: Purchases all rights. Manuscript published 2-3 years after acceptance. Author reviews galleys. Author receives a bio note on jacket or in book. 10 free copies of the book go the author; additional copies available at 40% discount.

ADDRESS: 3806 S. Fraser, Aurora CO 80014

PHONE: (800)680-1493

FAX: (303)680-2181

JANE YOLEN BOOKS

Established: 1989

Contact: Jane Yolen, Editor-in-Chief

CATEGORIES
Juvenile Science Fiction/Fantasy

Jane Yolen Books is looking for "more middle grade and young adult fiction." They are the "high-quality trade imprint for young readers from Harcourt and Brace and Co."

Jane Yolen Books publishes 6 hardcover books each year with a print run of 5,000 to 10,000 books. About 90% of the manuscripts they accept are submitted through agents.

They have published *River Rats*, by Caroline Stevermer (Golden Duck Award); Enchanted Forest Chronicles: *Dealing with Dragons* (ALA Best Book for Young Readers), *Searching for Dragons* (ALA Best Book for Young Readers), *Calling on Dragons* and *Talking to Dragons*, by Patricia Wrede; *Jeremy Thatcher, The Dragon Hatcher*, by Bruce Coville; *A Wizard's Dozen: Stories of the Fantastic*, edited by Michael S. Stearns.

HOW TO CONTACT: Authors should contact through an agent or by query. They report back in 2 months and comment on rejected manuscripts. Writer's guidelines are available for SASE.

PAYMENT: Payment and rights vary. The manuscript is published 1 year after acceptance. The author reviews galleys, copyedited manuscript and jacket copy and does receive a bio note. The author receives 20 copies of the book, and additional copies are available at a 40% discount.

ADDRESS: 525 B. St., San Diego CA 92101
PHONE: (619)699-6810

MARK V. ZIESING BOOKS

Established: 1980

Contact: Mark Ziesing, Editor and Publisher

CATEGORIES
Cyberpunk, Dark Fantasy, Hard Science Fiction, Sociological Science Fiction, Traditional Fantasy

Recently Pulished: *Hunger and Ecstasy of Vampires*, by Brian Stableford; *Lunching with the Antichrist*, by Michael Moorcock.

@

Mark V. Ziesing Books is looking for manuscripts reflecting social, religious, and/or psychological viewpoints. They produce quality books, often in limited editions.

Mark V. Ziesing Books publishes 4 hardcover sf/fantasy books each year, with an average print run of 2,000 books. About 50% of the manuscripts they accept are submitted through agents, and they receive an average of 15 unsolicited manuscripts each month.

HOW TO CONTACT: Send a query and SASE. They report back in 1 month. Simultaneous submissions are OK.

PAYMENT: Authors are paid an advance against royalties of 10%.

TERMS: Rights vary by project. The manuscript is published 18 months after acceptance. The author reviews galleys and does receive a bio note. The author receives 10-20 copies of the book, and additional copies are available at a 50% discount.

ADDRESS: P.O. Box 76, Shingletown CA 96088

PHONE/FAX: (916)474-1580

E-MAIL: 103633.2555@compuserve.com or ziesing@bigchair.com

WEBSITE: http://www.bigchair.com/ziesing

Overseas Novel Markets

Science fiction and fantasy are truly international fields. The SFWA has international membership, and the trade magazines regularly review books from all over the world. If publishing overseas interests you, check the publishers in this section. We've included some of the largest publishers here, but due to the complexity of working with overseas publishers, we list only those that particularly welcome submissions from North Americans. Almost all prefer to work with agented writers. The best way to break into the overseas market for science fiction novels is, therefore, to work through an agent who deals with foreign publishers.

We've included a list of subgenres at the top of the listing. Each listing includes a profile, followed by information on how to contact the publishers, payment and terms. Whenever possible, we've indicated if currency is in U.S. dollars or another denomination. Check with the publisher for more on their specific terms for overseas authors.

Things to keep in mind when approaching an overseas publisher: Allow more time for your manuscript to reach an overseas market and for you to receive a response. When approaching an overseas market, use International Reply Coupons for return mail rather than stamps; these are available at most post offices. For more information on the listings, see the introduction to the **Primary Novel Markets** section starting on page 226.

BIBLIOTECA DI NOVA SF, FUTURO, GREAT WORKS OF SF

Established: 1979

Contact: Claudio Del Maso or Ugo Malaguti, Editor

> **CATEGORIES**
> All categories of science fiction and fantasy

They publish approximately 25 hardcover sf/fantasy books each year, with an average print run of 2,000-4,000 books. Approximately 70% of the manuscripts they accept are submitted through agents, and they receive 30-50 unsolicited manuscripts each month. They publish 8-10 first novels each year.

HOW TO CONTACT: Send complete manuscript with SASE. They report back in 2-3 months. They usually comment on rejected manuscripts.

PAYMENT: Authors are paid an advance of $1,000 against royalties of 7%. They purchase Italian rights. The manuscript is published in 12-15 months after acceptance. Only Italian authors review galleys, and all authors usually receive a bio note. The author receives 5 copies of the book, and additional copies are available at a 25% discount.

ADDRESS: Perseo Libri s.r.l., Box 1240, Bologna, Italy I-40100

MIRAGUANO EDICIONES

Imprint: Futuropolis • Established: 1979

Contact: José Ma Arizcun

> **CATEGORIES**
> Cyberpunk, Hard Science Fiction, Military Science Fiction, Science Fantasy, Sociological Science Fiction, Space Opera, Splatterpunk, Steampunk

Recently Published: *Sonrisa del Gato*, by Rodolfo Martinez; *Memorias Merodeador Estelar*, by Carlos Saiz Cidoncha; *Consecuencias Naturales*, by Elia Barceló.

Publishes science fiction/fantasy 2 trade paperbacks per year. Publishes 8 first novels each year. Average print run for a first novel is 2,000.

HOW TO CONTACT: Does not accept unsolicited manuscripts. Accepts agented manuscripts only. Receives approximately 3 manuscripts each month. Never comments on rejected manuscripts.

PAYMENT: Pays royalties of 7-10%.

TERMS: Purchases Spanish language rights. Manuscript published 6 months after acceptance. Author reviews galleys. 10 free copies of the book go to the author; additional copies available at 30% discount.

ADDRESS: Hermosilla 104, 28009 Madrid, Spain

UNITED KINGDOM

MILLENNIUM

Imprint: Orion Books • Established: 1992

Contact: Caroline Oakley, Editor

CATEGORIES
Dark Fantasy, High Fantasy, Humorous Science Fiction, Space Opera, Traditional Fantasy

Millennium offers excellent author/editor contact and excellent marketing innovations. They offer this advice to writers: "Never despair! Put your manuscript in a drawer on completion for a minimum of three weeks before rereading."

Millennium publishes 12-15 hardcover, 10-15 trade paperback and 15-20 mass market paperback sf/fantasy books each year. The print runs vary according to book type and average between 1,000-20,000 books. Some of the manuscripts they accept are submitted through agents, and they receive about 50 unsolicited manuscripts each month. They publish several first novels each year.

They published *Iron Dragon's Daughter*, by Michael Swanwick and *A Fire Upon the Deep*, by Vernor Vinge.

HOW TO CONTACT: Send a synopsis and 50 pages of text. They report back in 2 months. They will accept simultaneous submissions, if stated. They will accept fax queries and e-mail queries. When possible, they comment on rejected manuscripts.

PAYMENT: Advances and royalties negotiated on book-by-book basis. Rights vary. Manuscript is published 1-2 years after acceptance. The author reviews galleys, copyedited manuscript and jacket copy and does receive a bio note (on trade books only). The author receives sample copies of the book (variable by contract), and additional copies are available at a 50% discount.

ADDRESS: Orion House, 5 Upper St. Martin's Ln., London, WC2M9EA UK

NEL

Hodder & Stoughton Publishers Ltd. • Established: 1868

Contact: Humphrey Price, Editor

> CATEGORIES
> Cyberpunk, Hard Science Fiction, High Fantasy, Humorous Science Fiction, Space Opera, Traditional Fantasy

NEL is looking for something other than "futuristic detective novels."

NEL publishes 6 hardcover sf/fantasy books each year. Nearly 99% of the manuscripts they accept are submitted through agents. They receive approximately 20 unsolicited manuscripts each month. They publish a couple first novels each year.

They have recently published C.J. Cherryh, Joe Haldeman, Jack Vance, Gene Wolfe and Piers Anthony.

HOW TO CONTACT: Send cover letter, synopsis and sample chapters with SASE. They report back in one to three months. They will sometimes comment on a rejected manuscript.

PAYMENT: Payment and terms vary on a book-by-book basis. They purchase U.K. and Commonwealth rights. The manuscript is published one year after acceptance. The author reviews galleys, copyedited manuscript and jacket copy and does receive a bio note.

ADDRESS: Hodder & Stoughton Publishers Ltd., Mill Rd., Dunton Green, Seven Oaks, Kent TN13 2YA UK

PAN MACMILLAN LTD.

Established: 1843

Contact: Simon Spanton, Editor

> CATEGORIES
>
> Cyberpunk, Dark Fantasy, Hard Science Fiction, High Fantasy, Humorous Science Fiction, Sociological Science Fiction, Space Opera, Traditional Fantasy

Pan Macmillan would like to see more "good characterization, original use of language and large scope" manuscripts. "We wish to build British authors aggressively backed by big U.S. names."

They offer this advice to beginning writers: "Practice, practice, practice. Get an agent. Read around your area of interest. Check the competition and try to get a new angle."

Pan Macmillan publishes 3 hardcover, 2 trade paperback and 19 mass market paperback sf/fantasy books each year. The average print run is 10,000 books. About 95% of the manuscripts they accept are submitted through agents, and they receive about 15 unsolicited manuscripts each month. They publish a couple first novels each year.

They published *The Positronic Man*, by Isaac Asimov and Robert Silverberg; *The Little Country*, by Charles de Lint; and *Mindstar Rising*, by Peter Hamilton.

HOW TO CONTACT: Send a letter, synopsis and 3 sample chapters. They report back in 2-3 weeks. They accept simultaneous and disk submissions and unsolicited manuscripts. They accept fax queries. They usually comment on rejected manuscripts.

PAYMENT: Payment and terms vary by project. The manuscript is published 12-18 months after acceptance. The author reviews galleys, copyedited manuscript and jacket copy and does receive a bio note. The author receives 12 copies of the book, and additional copies are available at a 50%.

ADDRESS: 18-21 Cavaye Place, London SW10 9PG UK

ROBINSON PUBLISHING LTD.

Imprint: Raven • Established: 1993

Contact: Mark Crean

> **CATEGORIES**
>
> Contemporary Fantasy, Cyberpunk, Dark Fantasy, Erotic Fantasy and Horror, Hard Science Fiction, Horror, Magic Realism, Science Fantasy, Sociological Science Fiction, Space Opera, Splatterpunk, Traditional Fantasy

Recently Published: *Celestial Dogs*, by Jay Russell; *California Gothic*, by Dennis Etchison; *Bride of the Rat God*, by Barbara Hambly.

Publishes 12 trade paperbacks per year. Publishes 2 first novels per year "Do not send unsolicited manuscripts if you want prompt attention."

HOW TO CONTACT: Unsolicited manuscripts welcome but prefers writers to query with 1 sample chapter. Accepts faxed and electronic queries. Considers simultaneous submissions. Receives approximately 20 manuscripts each month. 90% of accepted manuscripts are submitted through agents. Reports on queries in 1 month, on manuscripts in 10 weeks. Sometimes comments on rejected manuscripts. Writer's guidelines available for SASE.

PAYMENT: Pays an advance against royalties that reflects the book's potential and the author's experience.

TERMS: Purchases various rights. Manuscript published 1 year after acceptance. Author reviews galleys, copyedited manuscript and jacket copy. Author receives a bio note on jacket or in book. 10 free copies of the book to the author; additional copies available at 35% discount.

ADDRESS: 7 Kensington Church Ct., London W8 4SP UK

E-MAIL: 100560.3511@compuserve.com

SCHOLASTIC CHILDREN'S BOOKS

Imprint: Point Fantasy/Point Science Fiction • Established: 1993/1994

CATEGORIES
Young Adult Fantasy, Young Adult Science Fiction

Recently Published: *Elgift*, by Susan Price; *Firefly Dreams*, by Jenny Jones; *Strange Invaders*, by Stan Nicholas.

@

"We publish widely for children from 3-16, so our sf/fantasy list is necessarily a small part of our general list. We are therefore unable to take on vast numbers of new authors in this area—if it is exceptional, we will publish it. Ensure that what you have written is suitable for the age range and fits into our list. Research thoroughly! Don't overburden editors with lengthy manuscripts they don't have time to read." Would like to see "a great deal more originality, and fresh new storylines. Exciting stories, well told, that are accessible for the age group."

HOW TO CONTACT: Unsolicited manuscripts welcome but prefers writers to query with 3 sample chapters. Accepts faxed queries. Considers simultaneous submissions. Receives approximately 30 manuscripts each month. 90% of accepted manuscripts are submitted through agents. Preferred word length: to 8,000. Reports on queries in 6 weeks, on manuscripts in 3 months. Sometimes comments on rejected manuscripts. Writer's guidelines available for SASE.

PAYMENT: Pays variable advance with royalties of 7½%.

TERMS: Purchases all rights. Manuscript published 18 months after acceptance. Author reviews galleys and jacket copy. 6 free copies of the book go to the author; additional copies available at 30% discount.

ADDRESS: 6th Floor, Commonwealth House, 1-19 New Oxford St., London WC1A 1NU UK

PHONE: 0171 421 9000

FAX: 0171 421 9001

SEVERN HOUSE PUBLISHERS

Established: 1974

Contact: Julie Stevens, Editor

Recently Published: *Space Movies I & II*, by Peter Haining (Editor); *Green Thieves*, by Alan Dean Foster; *A Dusk of Idols*, by James Blish.

@

Severn House Publishers publishes 10-12 hardcover sf/fantasy books each year, with an average print run of 1,500 books. Nearly 99% of the manuscripts they accept are submitted through an agent. They publish an average of 15 first novels each year. "Because of our hardcover specialization for the library market, the author's previous book publishing history counts more than anything when it comes to sales. We publish very little original sf/fantasy, preferring to buy in from agents or mass-market houses."

HOW TO CONTACT: Authors should contact Severn House through an agent. They accept fax queries, and simultaneous submissions are OK. They report in 2 weeks for a query and 6 weeks for a manuscript. They usually comment on rejected manuscripts.

PAYMENT: Authors are paid an advance of $1,000 to $3,000 against royalties of 7½-15%. They purchase world English hardcover rights plus subsidiary rights. The manuscript is published 6-9 months after acceptance. The author reviews galleys and copyedited manuscript and oftentimes receives a bio note. The author receives 6 copies of the book, and additional copies are available at a 40% discount.

ADDRESS: 9-15 High St., Sutton, Surrey, SM1 1DF UK

VIRGIN PUBLISHING LTD.

Contact: Peter Darvill-Evans, Editor

"We publish *only* in series—no stand-alone books. Most of our books are tied into licensed characters, from Doctor Who to Sonic the Hedgehog. We publish strongly branded, character-led fiction."

They offer this advice to beginning writers: "Read good, even classic authors, and see how they do it. Then familiarize yourself with the imprint you're writing for. Develop your own style, don't mimic. And follow the guidelines."

Virgin Publishing publishes 1 hardcover (nonfiction), 1 trade paperback and about 40 mass market paperback sf/fantasy books each year. About 20% of the manuscripts they accept are submitted through an agent, and they receive an average of 50 unsolicited manuscripts each month. They publish about 10 first novels each year.

They published *Doctor Who: Conundrum*; *Judge Dredd: The Medusa Seed*; *Sonic the Hedgehog in Castle Robotnik*; *Doctor Who: Timeframe*; and *The Avenger Programme Guide*.

HOW TO CONTACT: Request for series guidelines with a large SAE. Subsequently send 3 sample chapters and synopsis. They report on queries in 2 weeks and manuscripts in 3-4 months. They will accept simultaneous submissions and oftentimes comment on rejected manuscripts. Writer's guidelines available for a large SASE.

PAYMENT: The author is paid in royalties of 7½-10%. Royalties depend on licensing agreement. Sometimes payment is a flat fee. They purchase all/world rights. The manuscript is published 6-10 months after acceptance. The author reviews galleys and sometimes jacket copy. The author receives a bio note. The author receives 6 copies of the book, and additional books are available at a 35% discount.

ADDRESS: 332, Ladbroke Grove, London W10 5AH UK

VOYAGER (formerly HarperCollins SF and Fantasy)

HarperCollins Publishers Ltd.

Contact: Jane Johnson, Editorial Director

CATEGORIES
Cyberpunk, Dark Fantasy, Hard Science Fiction, High Fantasy, Humorous Science Fiction, Sociological Science Fiction, Space Opera, Traditional Fantasy

Recently Published: *Red Mars* and *Green Mars,* by Kim Stanley Robinson; *The Broken God,* by David Zindell; *Belgarath the Sorcerer,* by David Eddings; *Rise of a Merchant Prince,* by Raymond E. Feist.

☙

Voyager would like to see more space opera and "heroic fantasy with strong characterization. Voyager is the U.K.'s leading publisher in the genre with strengths in all areas: excellent marketing, long publishing history and experience."

They offer this advice to beginning writers: "Persevere. Find a distinctive voice. Revise, revise, revise."

Voyager publishes 12 hardcovers, 12 trade paperbacks and 48 mass market paperbacks each year. About 90% of the manuscripts they accept are submitted through agents, and they receive 40-50 unsolicited manuscripts each month. They publish several first novels every year.

HOW TO CONTACT: Send a letter, 2 sample chapters and a synopsis. They report back in 6 weeks for queries and 2 months for manuscripts. They accept fax queries, and simultaneous submissions are OK. They occasionally comment on rejected manuscripts.

PAYMENT: All payments vary by project.

TERMS: Purchases world, world-England, Commonwealth rights. The manuscript is published 18 months after acceptance. The author reviews proofs and jacket copy and does receive a bio note. The author receives 12 (hardcover) or 20 (paperback) copies of the book, and additional copies are available for a 33% discount.

ADDRESS: 77-85 Fulham Palace Rd., London W6 8JB UK

NON-RESPONDING MARKETS

The following publishers did not respond to our requests for information. Those marked with an asterisk (*) are, to our knowledge, no longer in business.

Clothespin Fever Press
Incunabula
Lion Publishing Company

Pyx Press
Walker & Company (declined)

Opportunities for Writers in the Comic Book Market

MARK CLARK

Just a few years ago, the comic book industry was a publishing boom town. In the early 1990s, dozens of new companies appeared in the market to cash in on unprecedented sales. Since that peak, however, the industry has suffered an implosion. Last year, industry leader Marvel slashed its line, canceling nearly half its titles. Most smaller companies followed suit, eliminating all but their most successful properties. Others sold their characters to other publishers or closed shop entirely.

Now, in an attempt to bring new fans into the fold and return revenues to former heights, several comic book companies are trying something a little different: science fiction. Marvel, in conjunction with Paramount Pictures, announced it will launch Paramount Comics. The new imprint will publish a refurbished line of *Star Trek* comics with a built-in readership in the tens of thousands. Arch-rival DC Comics announced plans for a new imprint of its own, Matrix, envisioned as the science fiction equivalent of the company's hugely successful line of dark fantasy titles, Vertigo. The new line will include work by comics veterans as well as established science fiction writers new to comics, such as Christopher Hinz and Lucius Shepard.

Meanwhile, companies like Dark Horse and Topps are cashing in with comics based on science fiction movies and TV series—*Star Wars* and *Aliens* at Dark Horse, *The X-Files* and *Jurassic Park* at Topps. And both companies publish other science fiction, as well. Dark Horse publishes *Harlan Ellison's Dream Corridor* and has, in the past, published several quirky, creator-owned science fiction stories. Topps published *Ray Bradbury Comics*, as well as *Mars Attacks*, based on a card series the company issued in the 1960s.

All this activity indicates that even in a flagging market, there are plenty of opportunities for science fiction writers in comics. "I think there are a lot of opportunities coming from the science fiction realm crossing over into writing comics," says Charles Novinskie, sales and promotions manager at Topps. Most comic book readers are also science fiction readers, and many science fiction readers are also comic book readers, Novinskie says. "I think if we look at it, and take comic book readers as a whole, comic book readers are very well read, period. They spend more time reading than the national average and less time watching TV. I've always found comic book fans to be voracious readers, and not just of comics. It's the same way with science fiction readers."

A Look Back

Science fiction and comic books have been Siamese twins joined at the imagination as long as comic books have been around. Longer, really. Strips like *Buck Rogers* and Alex Raymond's seminal "Flash Gordon" appeared in newspapers alongside fare like Krazy Kat, Little Orphan Annie and Mickey Mouse before the concept of a "comic book" ever caught on.

It could be argued that the most influential comic book character of all time, Superman, was in fact a science fiction creation. Kal-El is, after all, a "strange visitor from the planet Krypton." And, while some of the superheroes who flew to fame on Superman's capetails had origins which were more hard-boiled (Batman), gothic (The Spectre) or mystical (Captain Marvel), most were rooted in science (Captain America, The Human Torch, Hawkman, etc.). When, after a decade-long hiatus, superheroes returned to popularity in the 1960s, almost all the costumed do-gooders were products of atomic-age mishaps (Spider-Man, The Fantastic Four, the Hulk, The Flash, etc.).

Does this mean we should consider all superhero comics works of science fiction? Hardly. For one thing, the "science" in these stories was laughable. Comic book companies shied away from true science fiction stories because the prevailing opinion was that comics readers wouldn't appreciate more cerebral material. In fact, the finest science fiction comics ever produced, William Gaines's 1950s classics *Weird Science* and *Weird Fantasy* were among his company's weakest selling titles.

Comic books became a sort of four-color ghetto in publishing. Anyone old enough to have facial hair who admitted to reading comics was assumed to be intellectually stunted. And comic book writers were seen as a bunch of talentless hacks with chronic adolescent power fantasies.

That Was Then, This Is Now

While some still cling to those old prejudices, comics have gained new respectability in the last decade or so. Neil Gaiman won a World Fantasy Award for his acclaimed comic, *The Sandman,* beating out competitors whose dialogue wasn't delivered in balloons. And big names from the "legit" publishing world have crossed over to write projects for comics— legends like Bradbury and Ellison, as well as stalwarts like Larry Niven and hot new names like Kevin J. Anderson, among many others. Perhaps most importantly, Hollywood has purchased and produced a long series of comic book properties since Tim Burton's "Batman" smashed box office records in 1989.

"More of the general public are accepting that comics aren't just for kids anymore," Novinskie says. "When people stopped thinking of comics as just for kids, which they weren't really in the first place, that's when you start to bring in top talent from outside the industry. It doesn't hurt that so many comic book properties are being turned into big blockbuster movies. When Hollywood takes notice of something, I think that's when other industries will take notice."

So You Want To Write Comic Books

You can stop reading right now if:

1. You want to write comics to make Big Money. Comic book writers, on average, are compensated even more poorly than writers in most other fields.

2. You want to write comics as an avenue into "legitimate" publication. Even the biggest names in comics (such as Chris Claremont and John Byrne) have struggled trying to translate their success into sales of novels or short stories. As a result of lingering prejudices, publishing in comics might actually hurt your chances, says Brian Cunningham, editor of *Wizard,* a leading comic industry publication. "Book publishers sometimes frown on comic books as childish or without literary value," Cunningham says. "Comic book writers who want to get into writing novels or short stories have a tough time of it."

3. You are unfamiliar with terms like "splash page," "three-point perspective" and "breakout panel." Read more comics and read more about comics. (Scott McCloud's essential *Understanding Comics, How to Draw Comics the Marvel Way* by Stan Lee and magazines like *Wizard*

are good starting points.) Just as you wouldn't begin writing a screenplay until you knew terms like "close-up" and "dolly shot," don't try writing comic books without knowing that industry's terminology and techniques.

Still with us? Good. Then it's time to face up to another unpleasant reality: that it's harder to break into writing than into any other job in the comic book industry. "Writers have to take a much more difficult avenue than artists," says Jamie S. Rich, submissions editor at Dark Horse. "You can show an editor your artwork and in a second he can say yes or no. With a writer, you have to take the time to read something." Plus, a good writer can be more prolific, Novinksie adds. "Writers can write three, four, five books per month. Artists can do maybe two. So you need more artists than writers."

Just like publishers elsewhere, comic companies know books by established writers will likely sell better than those by newcomers. "Not only do you have to be as good as somebody already doing that, you have to be better," Novinskie says. "If your stuff is equally as good as somebody we're already working with, we're going to take the person we already have a rapport with." And, just like in other publishing fields, it helps to know somebody. Cunningham, Novinksie and Rich all recommend making contacts at science fiction conventions or by writing letters to comics you enjoy. "Blind submissions, unsolicited writing probably don't have much of a chance," Cunningham says. "The best way to get into writing comic books is to go to a convention and meet with the editors. Show them writing samples there and (later) mail work to them directly. They will remember the name."

What To Send (And What Not To Send)

A few basic rules should be obvious, but writers ignore them every day: First off, write for submission guidelines before you submit. Dark Horse, for instance, won't even read your submission unless you write for guidelines first and return a signed agreement (which arrives with the guidelines) along with your manuscript. Secondly, mind your Ps and Qs: Make sure your name, address and phone number appear on every page of your submission and make sure to send a self-addressed, stamped envelope along so the editor can reply. And finally, don't submit anything that isn't a comic book story to a comic book company. "I don't want novels, short stories or screenplays. I want a comic book," Rich says.

Actually, at first, most editors don't even want that. "They prefer a straight plot, a one- or two-page typewritten synopsis of a story, without dialogue or visual aids," Cunningham says. "Concisely explain what the story is about. From that, they can gauge a little of your talent. They might ask you to submit a plot and a full script (with dialogue)."

"We need a synopsis and an initial teaser of your script to tell if we need more," Rich says. "Don't waste time with your submission. The first page is going to sell you or not. Be as up front as you can. Tell me what your story is about and why I want to read it right off the bat. Then I look for whether or not you pulled it off, page to page, that you have the knowledge of how to write a comic book story and that you can write dialogue."

He says that some of the sage advice often given to aspiring comic book writers can actually work against them. For instance, writers are often advised to send their work to every editor at a given comic book company, in hopes that one of them will like it. That's a waste of time and postage, Rich says. Send to the submission editor only unless you know an editor personally. Other editors don't have the time or interest in wading through submissions. Also, writers are often advised to submit frequently, the logic being that persistence will wear down an unreceptive editor. Just the opposite may happen, Rich warns. If an editor sees one poor submission after another from you, he may stop taking you seriously after a while. Mail with your name on it will automatically move to the bottom of the pile.

"Quality of submissions is favorable over quantity of submissions," says Rich, who is frustrated with " 'stories' that are just a series of events with no rhyme or reason and characters that serve as a function of those events, not as characters. . . . I don't think we get enough quality science fiction proposals. As with most genre things, we get mostly retreads."

To improve their chances of getting in, writers sometimes hook up with an artist collaborator. That was the case when Mike Baron and Steve Rude sold their offbeat science fiction opus "Nexus" to First Comics, for instance. But think carefully when selecting a collaborator. For one thing, you will have to share rights (and royalties) from any creator-owned property with your collaborator. And your artist had better make your story look terrific. If the publisher likes your concept but feels the art is weak, you will have lost a sale.

"It definitely can be helpful but you have to be sure the person you're finding is really strong," Rich says. "Compare the person's artwork with the comics you like. Would you pay three bucks for a book with this guy's artwork, even if the story stinks?"

And one more word of caution: It can be especially difficult to get into writing for licensed properties, such as the *Star Trek* and *Star Wars* comics. Dark Horse won't even review unsolicited manuscripts for its licensed properties. Topps will look at them, but prefers to work with established creators on those projects. Your best bet is to pitch an idea for a one-shot or a mini-series. It's also tough to sell higher cost projects, like a new ongoing series or a graphic novel, if you're an unknown writer. "Show how talented you are and we might offer you something else," Rich says.

Success Stories and Other Pleasantries

Breaking into the comics market is difficult, but not impossible. "If something comes along and it's the greatest thing we've ever read, there's not a chance in hell we're going to pass it up," Rich says.

That was the case last year when a proposal arrived from Croatia in a battered envelope. Inside was a blind submission for a *Grendel Tales* story from two unknown Croats, writer Darko Macan and artist Edvin Biukovic. The story knocked out Dark Horse Editor-in-Chief Diana Schutz, who purchased it immediately. The duo went on to win the Russ Manning Award for Best Newcomer and was nominated for comics' highest honor, the Eisner Award, at last year's San Diego ComiCon. Macan and Biukovic are now working on one of Dark Horse's best selling titles, *Star Wars: X-Wing*.

Novinskie tells the story of Stefan Petrucha, who had been in comics a few years without really establishing a name for himself. Then one day the writer called Topps Editor Jim Salicrup, excited about a new TV show he had seen the night before. Petrucha loved the show and wanted desperately to write a comic book based on it. The show was *The X-Files*. Based in part on Petrucha's raw enthusiasm, Topps obtained the license—and gave the assignment to Petrucha. *The X-Files* has since become Topps's most popular title.

"There's always a need for new talent, for someone who can tell a story," Rich says.

Selected Comic Book Markets

Dark Horse Comics (Publishers of *Star Wars*, *Aliens* and *Harlan Ellison's Dream Corridor*. The company has published creator-owned science fiction and fantasy titles.) Submissions Editor: James S. Rich. Write for guidelines. Address: 10956 S.E. Main St., Milwaukee, OR 97222. Phone: (503) 652-8815.

DC Comics (Publishers of Vertigo, a line of dark fantasy titles; Matrix, a new line of science fiction titles; and of course superhero comics such as *Superman* and *Batman*.) Submissions Editor: Varies according to type of submission. Write for guidelines. Address: 1700 Broadway, New York NY 10019. Phone: (212) 636-5400.

Fantagraphics Books (Publishers of an eclectic line of titles, including *Hate* and *Love and Rockets*, as well as some genre pieces.) Submissions Editor: Ezra Mark. Address: 7563 Lake City Way NE, Seattle WA 98115. Phone: (206) 524-1967.

Kitchen Sink Press (Publishers of virtually all new and reprinted work by industry legend Will Eisner, as well as an assortment of other offbeat titles). Submissions Editor: Phil Amara Address: 320 Riverside Dr., Northampton MA 01060. Phone: (413) 586-9525.

Marvel Entertainment Group (Publishers of several comic lines, including the new Paramount Comics imprint, which will include revamped *Star Trek* comics. Home of old warhorses like *The Amazing Spider-Man* and *The Incredible Hulk*.) Submissions Editor: Varies according to type of submission. Write for guidelines. Address: 387 Park Ave. South, New York NY 10016. Phone: (212) 696-0808.

Topps Comics (and Cards) (Publishers of many different titles based on movies and TV shows, such as *The X-Files* and *Jurassic Park*. Also publishes original science fiction comics like *Mars Attacks*. Published *Ray Bradbury Comics* and will publishes a series based on Michael Moorcock's *Elric* saga.) Submissions Editor: Editors take turns reading unsolicited manuscripts. Address: One Whitehall St. New York NY 10004. Phone: (212) 376-0300.

MARK CLARK is a freelance journalist and lifelong comic book fan originally from Louisville, Kentucky. He now lives in Cincinnati with his wife, Donna, and cat, Stewart.

Finding an Agent

Finding and Getting the Most Out of an Agent

RUSSELL GALEN

Two stylistic points for starters:

1. Science fiction and fantasy are two very different literary forms, but are handled by the same publishing personnel and therefore regarded in publishing as a single field, which I'll call science fiction/fantasy here.

2. I prefer the convention of using the male pronoun to refer to representative members of a group. However, the many references here to literary agents as "he" do not mean most agents in this field are male or that most of the good ones are male. In fact the division is roughly equal.

You can get rich writing science fiction and fantasy these days. The audience has grown so large that it's possible for a single such book to earn more money than an ordinary family spends in a lifetime. While such occurrences are rare, hundreds of authors *are* able to support families and put children through college just from their science fiction/fantasy income; writing in this genre is now a legitimate career choice.

In the wake of all this commerce have come abstruse contracts loaded with booby traps; killer competition, with more and more writers fighting for recognition and market share; rich spin-off opportunities in movie, audio, multimedia, foreign and other rights; and a high-stakes, merciless retail marketplace in which a failed book can forever sour the bookstore chains on a writer and doom his career.

Where there is so much money to be made, agents are madly attracted, and where ignorance and bad strategy can have such catastrophic consequences, authors are made to have them. Today dozens of agents handle science fiction/fantasy. Several, including some of the finest practitioners in the field, handle little or nothing else, building their entire professional lives around this one corner of the publishing world. With no more than a handful of exceptions, every writer in this field has or wants an agent.

SF/Fantasy Agents: A Different Breed?

The single most important element to weigh when looking for your first agent or switching to a new one is the agent's enthusiasm for your work. As in any field of writing, having a brilliant agent who doesn't care about your material can be catastrophic, since his brilliance will rarely be deployed on your behalf. For most science fiction/fantasy writers, this means finding an agent who, whatever else he may be, is a fan, someone who enjoys reading science fiction and fantasy. Science fiction/fantasy is a peculiar, rare taste; no field is more cleanly divided into those who get it and those who don't. Those who aren't fans often don't understand the field at all and can't recognize a major book when it's shoved under their noses.

There are readers who read nothing but science fiction/fantasy, those who read a lot of it but also like other things, those who read only a sprinkling of the more famous books, and those who loathe the stuff. Agents fall into the same categories, and there are arguments to be made on behalf of each of the first three kinds. Which kind you choose to approach will depend on your own needs and goals as a writer.

The agents who handle nothing but science fiction/fantasy include some of the finest working today; their narrow specialization doesn't mean they are any less talented or effective than agents with lists of mainstream stars. If you have little or no interest in writing other than science fiction/fantasy, these agents will do the job for you, and in fact several of the best agents in the field fall into this category.

I'm in the middle group myself. About a third of my client list writes science fiction or fantasy. Of these, a large fraction has published or would someday like to publish fiction in other genres or nonfiction. The flexibility of the agents in this group is crucial for writers with such ambitions, unimportant for others.

There are agents who rarely read science fiction but have one or two clients in the field. Such agents usually are a bad choice for a writer just starting out; they lack the passion for the material that is necessary to sustain interest in a writer who is years away from producing highly profitable books. But for some established writers, they can be a legitimate option (a writer whose books are already profitable will always excite passion in an agent). You may feel it's not important to have an agent who knows the field particularly well if:

- you don't care about having an agent who has a deep understanding of science fiction or fantasy literature;
- you plan to stay with one publisher and therefore don't need an agent with good contacts throughout the science fiction industry;
- you want the agent to stick to the business side and not worry about literary matters.

Where to Look

There are several ways to identify the agents who are science fiction/fantasy insiders:

- Read *Locus* and/or *Science Fiction Chronicle* (see pages 460 and 468 for listings). These publications report many of the new deals, usually identifying the agent who handled the deal. A few months of this and you'll know the names of most of the agents who are active in the field.

- Track down the agents of your favorite authors. This is easy to do: just call the publisher, request the contracts or subsidiary rights departments and ask. There are two important advantages to this method: First, you'll now that the agent must be at least reasonably honest and competent—either that or this writer you admire is a jerk (which is unlikely, since science fiction/fantasy writers are the savviest in publishing and there aren't many of them that would stay with a lousy agent long). Second, this gives you a good, effective opening line with which to approach the agent: "I know you represent X, and if you like his or her work, there's a good chance you'll like mine."

- Science fiction/fantasy is unique in publishing for its hundreds of conventions (known as "cons") throughout the year during which fans, professional writers and agents mingle. At the very least you should attend local cons; if at all possible, go to the major ones, such as the World Science Fiction Convention, referred to as WorldCon (alternating each year between North American and overseas locations); the North American Science Fiction Convention (held in North America when the WorldCon is overseas); and the World Fantasy Convention. (See page 430 for more information about cons.)

- If you're a new writer but are bold, gutsy and personable, you might walk up to an agent cold and make a pitch for your work. I don't recommend doing this because frankly, not many writers have the kind of salesman's charm it takes to pull off this kind of presentation. Still, I've found a few clients this way, some of whom became major stars.

- More likely to be useful are not the agents you meet directly but the writers, who will in turn steer you to agents. While science fiction/fantasy writers, like any pros in any field, are not burning with desire to take newcomers and wannabes under their wings, they are more approachable than, say, famous surgeons are to medical students. Most were fans themselves and in any case are, like most people, receptive to approaches that begin with "I think you walk on water." At the very least they will often give you their agent's name just to be rid of you, but it's not at all uncommon for real friendships and even mentor/protégé relationships to develop. Needless to say, you have a much better chance of interesting an agent if your manuscript is recommended by one of the agent's clients.

- Once you've made some professional sales, you can join the Science-fiction and Fantasy Writers of America (SFWA), whose publications and newsletters are among the finest primers available on the role of agents, representation contracts, etc.

- Science fiction/fantasy is also unique in its early and enthusiastic use of online communications. The service that is the most used by pros in this field is GEnie, whose Science Fiction Roundtable bulletin board has become, in effect, a 24-hours-a-day, 365-days-a-year con in which pros and fans can exchange messages on hundreds of different topics. The most useful areas are closed to non-SFWA members, but even the open areas are frequented by pros and are a place to establish relationships with writers and share information. (See page 417 for more information concerning online conferencing.)

- In many cases you'll look for an agent only after you've made at least a few sales, in which case you'll know an editor or two. Editors are always a good source of recommendations of and introductions to agents, but this is especially so in science fiction/fantasy. This is a small world, dominated by perhaps 20 to 25 major editors and agents all of whom have known one another for years. Any major magazine or book editor in the field will know all the top agents and know them well enough to know their strengths, weaknesses, special tastes and current needs and thus be able to suggest a handful of agents who would make a good match with you and your work.

When to Look

Science fiction/fantasy is unique in its healthy short fiction market, consisting of not only several successful magazines, but also a steady stream of anthologies, many of which are open to new writers.

The ideal time to hook up with an agent is when you've sold three to five stories to any of the better short fiction markets in the field and have completed your first novel. The great majority of science fiction/fantasy agents will agree to look at your novel under those circumstances and to represent it if they think it'll sell; the only exception would be an agent whose client list is literally full and is not taking on new ones under any circumstances.

What if you simply don't like to write short fiction? There are certain book markets that, because of their financial or creative restrictions, seldom attract big-name writers and thus are more open to newcomers than traditional markets. A sale or two of this type of book is often enough to convince an agent that your own work is worth a look. These books are usually based on copyrighted material created and owned by third parties. For instance, there are the ongoing series of books based on television programs and movies, such as *Star Trek*, *Space Above & Beyond* and *seaQuest* DSV; role-playing games, such as those of the TSR Corporation (makers of *Dungeons and Dragons*); interactive computer games such as *King's Quest*, *Bard's Tale* and *Wing Commander*; and the works or ideas of established science fiction/fantasy writers, such as the Robot City novels based on an idea by Isaac Asimov.

Similarly, established writers sometimes collaborate with brand-new writers, and such a credit is often enough to get an agent to read the new writer's solo work. The established writer is going to get most of the credit, but we're not talking here about agents rolling out the red carpet for you—just getting them to notice you enough to agree to read your manuscript.

Failing that, you have to complete your first novel: Don't even think about trying to do anything with no track record and no completed manuscript. You can then try to interest a publisher and plan to bring in an agent once it's clear you have serious interest from a major house (a lure few agents can resist). Or you can approach agents directly and hope to persuade one of them to make submissions for you.

Either way, your weapon is to write the most effective query letter you can and hope an agent or editor is sufficiently impressed to offer to read your manuscript. After that the script will have to sell itself. If you've heard discouraging statistics about the odds against selling a first novel in this way, with no track record or connections, take heart: inside the narrow world of science fiction and fantasy the odds are more encouraging. In fact, science fiction/fantasy has a spectacular tradition of editors and agents carefully combing through submissions from unpublished writers (known as "slush") and finding not just books to publish, but, in some cases, hot properties that are then marketed and promoted aggressively.

Unfortunately, this tradition is in decline these days, and there are even some science fiction imprints that are absolutely closed to submissions from writers who lack a sponsor of some kind or a track record. Other houses remain open but have response times so slow that if you gave birth on the day you made your submission, your child might well be able to read the first edition by the time it is published. And agents who are raking in commissions on six- and seven-figure deals are hard to persuade to read a novel from an unpublished unknown with a 99 percent chance of being unsaleable. I urge you to avoid the slush pile if at all possible: Get some short story credits, work the cons and make connections, do something to make yourself an insider before you go agent-hunting. But if none of those routes make sense for you, write the best query letter you can and bang away.

Developing a Career in Partnership With Your Agent

The ghastly companion to the bigger sales of the lucky authors is the spectacle of authors who, when their sales plateau and then begin to fall, are cast aside by the science fiction/fantasy publishing industry altogether. The higher expectations of readers, booksellers and publishers mean that mediocre sales are far more disappointing and unforgivable than they might have been in a less ambitious era. If a career fails to take off after the first few books, or if an established author has a couple of consecutive failures, it often becomes impossible for that author to get a sale ever again.

Good books fail all the time for preventable reasons; the authors who succeed are not always more talented than the failures, but sometimes merely more canny, lucky or better guided by their agents.

A good agent will not merely sell your work and negotiate good contract terms. He'll also help you design a long-term career plan and work out the thousand midcourse corrections that will come up as the market, your editors and you go through unexpected changes during the course of a lifetime—all of which is especially tricky in science fiction/fantasy.

Think of the audience as a series of concentric circles, like a target. At the center ring—call it Ring A—is a small group of intense fans who read nothing but science fiction/fantasy. An ordinary novel that doesn't get noticed outside this group cannot, from the author's point of view, turn a profit. That is, the amount of money the author will earn from it will be far less than what he spent to write it, if you count the author's time as being worth what he might have earned at a modestly paying white-collar profession. The author is being paid minimum wage or less, in effect.

In the next ring is an additional group of readers whose basic interest is science fiction/fantasy, but who do read other things and won't read a science fiction/fantasy novel unless it appears special in some way. Only by writing a book that satisfies the audiences in Rings A and B can you make this your career; payment might be roughly on the level of a schoolteacher.

In Ring C are readers who only read the top science fiction/fantasy books of the year, and when you reach this level, you're making what a doctor makes. In Ring D you've got people who read maybe one such book a year, and there are Fortune 500 CEOs who do worse.

Navigating these rings is perilous. Few writers are able to find one and settle into it for life; most careers will be cut short unless they show outer movement to progressively larger audiences. But if you make the leap for the next ring and don't make it, you're often tossed out of the game altogether rather than allowed to fall back to a more comfortable level.

If your long-term goal is to survive and overcome this four-ring circus, you need a close partnership with an agent who knows how to work at all four levels. An agent whose clients are all in levels C and D might not have the patience to work with you while you spend years generating the low commissions of levels A and B. One whose clients are all in A and B levels might not know how to get you beyond it: Is this agent stuck at this level because of his own shortcomings or because he's young and will grow as you do? Does the agent know the field well enough to sense when you're ready to make a leap to a higher level, and is he inspiring enough to help you make it even when your own confidence is lacking?

The ideal agent in this field is adept at and interested in working on all of these levels and has a history of moving clients steadily out from the smaller rings. If I were a science fiction or fantasy writer, I would not be swayed by a client list filled with big names, nor put off by one devoid of them; I would not care about the number of clients an agent represented or the raw number of years of experience. I would look for a track record of, and continued commitment to, improving the lot of his clients; I would look for the one who is never satisfied with how I'm doing, but always looking to move me to the next level.

✳ ✳ ✳
SF/Fantasy Agent Listings

Even though most publishers in the science fiction and fantasy field are open to unsolicited submissions, only a small percentage of the work submitted directly to publishers sees print. The rest find their way to the editors' desks either through personal contact or through an agent (or through both, which is quite often the case).

Having an agent can give you an advantage—helping to get your work noticed and into the hands of the "right" editor. Once you've interested an editor, too, an agent acts as your business partner and career counselor, taking care of contracts and other business to leave you more time to write.

Before you start your search for an agent, read agent Russell Galen's piece, **Finding and Getting the Most Out of an Agent**, starting on page 325. In his article he gives tips on finding and working with an agent and discusses the particulars of the science fiction/fantasy field.

Approaching an Agent

Approach an agent as you would a publisher. Make sure your manuscript is polished and neat—typed or computer-printed, double-spaced and free of typos or cross-outs. Use a dark typewriter or printer ribbon, and use heavy bond white paper. A professional presentation tells the agent you are serious about your work and ready to work on your publishing career.

Many agents require a query letter with sample chapters, an outline or synopsis. Your query letter should be brief (keep it to one page) and direct. Mention what type of science fiction novel you've written, as well as details about your publishing history. Some agents want to see the entire manuscript, which should include a short cover letter introducing yourself and your work. It is generally accepted to query more than one agent at a time, but avoid sending complete manuscripts to more than one agent for consideration. Include a SASE for a reply, and, if you send a manuscript and want it returned, be sure to include a large enough mailer and the right amount of postage. (For more on queries, cover letters and manuscript presentation see **Marketing Your Novel**, starting on page 218.)

The Agents Listed in This Section

The listings in this section include both agents who are very active in the field and those who represent smaller numbers of science fiction/fantasy clients. Many of the most active agents are also the hardest to approach, and a few of these do not take unsolicited queries or manuscripts from new writers. The best way to interest these agents is to have some work published either in one of the commercial magazines or in the small press—and keep networking. Some of these hard-to-reach agents will take recommendations from clients, editors and established authors, so it may help to cultivate a sponsor. We've identified those agents or agencies most active in the science fiction/fantasy field with an (*).

Most of the agents included in this section handle some science fiction and fantasy in addition to fiction in other fields and nonfiction. The larger agencies designate specific agents to handle science fiction and fantasy, but agents at other agencies "do it all."

Each listing starts with the name of the agent or agents to whom you should address your manuscript, the date the agency was established and the number of clients. This gives you an idea of the size of the agency. Newer agencies are more likely to be open to less-experienced clients. After this information, we've included a list of science fiction and fantasy subgenres to help you determine which agents are most likely to be interested in the type of work you write.

The "profile" section gives a brief description of the agency, including the percentage of science fiction and fantasy clients, how much of their business comes from the sales of fiction manuscripts, and what other properties they may handle. Whenever possible, we've listed a few of the publishers the agents work with and any science fiction/fantasy conventions they regularly attend.

If the agent is a member of the Association of Authors' Representatives (AAR) or a signatory of the Writers Guild of America (WGA), we've noted it in the profile. While there are good agents who do not belong to AAR, membership in this national organization for agents means that the agent has signed a code of ethics, has had recent sales, is active in the publishing market and does not charge a fee for considering you as a client (called "reading fees"). The WGA also asks that agents meet similar criteria before becoming signatories (only writers can be full members in WGA).

Following this information are "Notable Titles or Clients" in which we list a few of the agent's recent science fiction/fantasy sales or a few of the writers who are clients of the agency. One way to find out what interests a particular agent is to read a few of the works they've handled.

Listings also include information on how to contact the agent and how long it will take for you to receive a reply. Agents tend to be slow to respond despite their best intentions, so add three weeks or so to their stated reporting time before checking on the status of your query or submission.

At the end of the listing, you'll find the agent's terms. This is a percentage commission taken from the sale of the work. Payment from the publisher will go to the agent, who will take out his or her share before sending it to the author. Keep in mind that a number of agents generally take out excessive office expenses (photocopying, phone calls, etc.) over and above their commission, but most will check with you first. The agent usually receives a higher percentage on foreign sales because the commission is split with a foreign agent. While there are agencies that charge writers reading and critique fees, nearly all the agents listed here do not.

Above all, remember your agent is your business partner. Take your time when looking for an agent, and feel free to ask questions and ask for references. A good agent will not only get you the best deal, but will also act as a liaison between you and your publisher. (For more on working with agents see *The Guide to Literary Agents*, published by Writer's Digest Books.)

AGENTS INC. FOR MEDICAL AND MENTAL HEALTH PROFESSIONALS

Established: 1987 • 50 clients

Contact: Harriet, Sydney H., Ph.D.,

> SPECIALIZES IN
> Dark Fantasy, Hard Science Fiction, Military Science Fiction, Sociological Science Fiction, Traditional Fantasy,

While Agents Inc. deals primarily with nonfiction books on health, medicine, nutrition, psychology, science, technology, reference and scholarly books (about 75% of their business), the rest of their business derives mostly from science fiction and fantasy (20-25%). Mostly due to their nonfiction interests, they specialize in handling writers with education and experience in the medical and mental health professions. About 45% of their clients are new writers. The staff attends writer's conferences in California and, upon invitation, in other states. They work with most publishers of science fiction and fantasy, including small presses, and they'd like to see more health-related science fiction. "Please note—we can only accept published fiction writers at this time."

HOW TO CONTACT: Query first with a vita and SASE. The agency will report in 3 weeks on queries or 1 month on manuscripts.

TERMS: The agent receives 15% commission on domestic sales and 20% on foreign sales. A written contract is offered and is binding for 6-12 months.

ADDRESS: Director, P.O. Box 4956, Fresno CA 93744-4956

PHONE: (209)438-1883

*JAMES ALLEN, LITERARY AGENT

Established: 1974 • Signatory of WGA • 40 clients

Contact: James Allen

> SPECIALIZES IN
> Dark Fantasy, Hard Science Fiction, High Fantasy, Humorous Science Fiction, Sociological Science Fiction, Space Opera, Traditional Fantasy

Recent Sales: *Cataract* and *Greyheart*, by Tara K. Harper to Del Rey; *As the Wolf Loves Winter*, by David Poyer to Tor.

@

This agency specializes in science fiction and fantasy, and about 60% of the work Allen handles comes from science fiction and fantasy authors. Most of his other clients write in other fiction genres such as mystery and romance. He works with all commercial fiction houses and is a signatory of WGA. About 10% of his clients are new writers.

HOW TO CONTACT: Send a query letter with a 2 or 3-page synopsis. Allen will reply in 1 week on queries. If interested, he will then ask for the first 4 chapters and will reply in 3 weeks on those. Then he may request the complete manuscript and will stipulate a reply date in his letter.

TERMS: The agent receives 10% commission on domestic sales (print), 20% commission on film sales, and 20% commission on foreign sales (in the 20% split 10% goes to him, 10% to his film or foreign affiliate).

ADDRESS: P.O. Box 278, Milford PA 18337

MARCIA AMSTERDAM AGENCY

Established: 1969 • WGA signatory • 30 clients

Contact: Marcia Amsterdam

> SPECIALIZES IN
> Dark Fantasy, Horror, Science Fantasy, Space Romance

Recent Sales: *Free Fall*, by Joyce Sweeney to Dell; *Dark Morning*, by William H. Lovejoy to Pinnacle; *Killing Suki Flood*, by Robert Leininger to Davis Co.

@

Agency seeking both new and established writers. Usually obtains new clients through recommendations from others, conferences and conventions, and queries. 25% of clients are new writers. 5% of represented titles are science fiction or fantasy. Query first. Standard fees will be charged to author. Would like to see more characters with a humorous perception of the world in science fiction and fantasy.

TERMS: Standard commission is 15% domestic. Offers a written contract. Contract binding for 1 year. Author must give 60 days notice to terminate contract.
ADDRESS: 41 W. 82 St., New York NY 10024-5613
PHONE: (212)873-4945

The Josh Behar Literary Agency

Established: 1993 • 12 clients

Contact: Josh Behar

> SPECIALIZES IN
> Contemporary Fantasy, Dark Fantasy, Experimental Fiction, High Fantasy, Horror, Science Fantasy, Traditional Fantasy

Agency prefers to work with established writers, mostly through referrals, although it does obtain some clients from unsolicited manuscripts. 85% of clients are new writers. 20% of the titles represented are science fiction or fantasy. Query first.

TERMS: Standard commission 10% domestic; 15% foreign.
ADDRESS: Empire State Building, 350 Fifth Ave., Suite 3304, New York NY 10118
PHONE: (212)826-4386

*Blassingame Spectrum Corp.

50 clients

Contact: Eleanor Wood or Lucienne Diver

Dark Fantasy, Hard Science Fiction, High Fantasy, Military Science Fiction, Space Opera, Traditional Fantasy

Well-known in the field, about 60% of this agency's clients are science fiction and fantasy writers, and they deal with all the major houses. Almost all their clients write fiction, with the exception of a handful who write about biography, health/medicine and history topics.

HOW TO CONTACT: Send a query letter with SASE. The agency will report in 2 months on queries.

TERMS: The agency receives 10% commission on domestic sales (other terms not disclosed).

ADDRESS: 111 Eighth Ave., Suite 1501, New York NY 10011

PHONE: (212)691-7556

*THE BARBARA BOVA LITERARY AGENCY

Established: 1974 • 30 clients

Contact: Barbara Bova

Hard Science Fiction, Sociological Science Fiction, Traditional Fantasy

Although only about 10% of this agency's clients are science fiction and fantasy writers, it's important to note 30% of Bova's clients are nonfiction writers in the science, technology and social science fields. Bova is the wife of science fiction author, Ben Bova, and she works with all the major houses. In addition to science fiction, she also handles mystery, suspense and mainstream fiction. She looks for science fiction that "sticks to the category and is well-written." She also looks for "originality, not a rehash of television." Notable clients include Ben Bova, David Gerrold and Orson Scott Card.

HOW TO CONTACT: Query with SASE. Bova will report in 1 month on queries.

TERMS: The agent receives 15% commission on domestic sales and also handles foreign, electronic, audio and other rights (percent commission not disclosed).

ADDRESS: 3951 Gulf Shore Blvd. N., Apt. PH1B, Naples FL 33940

PHONE: (813)649-7237

*JANE BUTLER, ART AND LITERARY AGENT

Established: 1981 • 15 clients

Contact: Jane Butler

> SPECIALIZES IN
> Dark Fantasy, Hard Science Fiction, Military Science Fiction, Traditional Fantasy

Recent sales: *Epona I*, by Judith Tarrto Forge; *Raven*, by S. Andrew Swann to DAW; *Hound & Falcon*, by Judith Tarrto to Easton Press.

About 80% of this agent's clients are science fiction and fantasy writers, and she works with all the major publishers in the field including Bantam, DAW, Tor, Avon, Berkley, Baen, Harcourt Brace, Little, Brown and Zebra. In addition to science fiction, she also handles romance, horror, young adult and juvenile fiction and some nonfiction. Butler prefers to work with authors that have publishing credits, but all queries are welcome. She looks for "lead title potential."

HOW TO CONTACT: Query first with SASE.

TERMS: The agent receives 10% commission on domestic sales, 15% commission on dramatic sales, and 25% commission on foreign sales. United Kingdom, translation and dramatic rights are handled in association with the Scovil Chichak Galen Literary Agency, Inc. and Baror International, Inc.

ADDRESS: P.O. Box 33, Matamoras PA 18336

CANTRELL-COLAS INC., LITERARY AGENCY

Established: 1980 • Represents: 80 clients

Contact: Maryanne C. Colas

> SPECIALIZES IN
> Cyberpunk, Hard Science Fiction, High Fantasy, Humorous Science Fiction, Military Science Fiction, Sociological Science Fiction, Space Opera, Traditional Fantasy

From 10 to 15 percent of this agency's clients are science fiction and fantasy writers, and 25 percent of the work they handle overall is fiction (some of the other fiction areas they handle are mainstream, mystery, family saga, historical and literary). Another quarter of their clients write juveniles. The agent works with most of the major houses including Tor, Random House, Bantam Doubleday Dell and Ballantine.

Colas says what makes science fiction and fantasy salable is "the story and characters that readers can identify with even though they may be out of time and place." The agent attends the Golden Triangle Conference in Texas each year.

Notable Titles or Clients: *Phoenix*, by Anne Reynolds, and *Out of the Blue*, by Kasey Michaels (time travel).

HOW TO CONTACT: Query with an outline plus two sample chapters and SASE. Also include some (brief) information about the author. The agent will report in two months on queries.

TERMS: The agent receives 15 percent commission on domestic sales, and commission varies on foreign sales. A written contract is offered.

ADDRESS: 229 E. 79th St., New York, NY 10021

PHONE: (212)737-8503

MARIA CARVAINIS AGENCY, INC.

Established: 1977 • Member: AAR • Signatory of WGA • 30 clients

Contact: Maria Carvainis

About 7% of the clients Carvainis handles are fantasy. "But we would love to increase this," she says. Carvainis does not handle science fiction. Overall, about 55% of her clientele are fiction writers, and, in addition to fantasy, they write literary and mainstream fiction, contemporary women's fiction, mystery, suspense, historicals, children's books and young adult novels. The agent is a board member and treasurer of AAR, a member of the Authors Guild and a signatory of WGA. About 10% of the agent's clients are new writers and she works with fantasy book publishers including Ace, Avon and TSR. In fantasy manuscripts, she looks for "compelling plot line and detailed research."

HOW TO CONTACT: Query first with SASE. The agent will report in 2-3 weeks on queries, 6-10 weeks on manuscripts.
TERMS: The agent receives 15% commission on domestic sales and 20% commission on foreign sales. A written contract is offered and is binding for 2 years on a "book-by-book basis."
ADDRESS: 235 West End Ave., Suite 15F, New York NY 10023
PHONE: (212)580-1559
FAX: (212)877-3486

CIRCLE OF CONFUSION LTD.

Established: 1990 • WGA signatory • 60 clients

Contact: Rajeev Agarwal

SPECIALIZES IN
Contemporary Fantasy, Cyberpunk, Dark Fantasy, Elfpunk, Experimental Fiction, Hard Science Fiction, High Fantasy, Horror, Humorous, Magic Realism, Military Science Fiction, Poetry, Science Fantasy, Sociological Science Fiction, Space Opera, Splatterpunk, Steampunk, Traditional Fantasy

Agency seeking both new and established writers. Usually obtains new clients through queries. 50% of clients are new writers. 60% of represented titles are science fiction or fantasy. Query first.

TERMS: Standard commission is 10%. Offers a written contract. Contract binding for 1 year. Author must give 60 days notice to terminate contract.
ADDRESS: 666 Fifth Ave., Suite 303L, New York NY 10103
PHONE: (212)969-0653
FAX: (212)975-7748

*FRANCES COLLIN LITERARY AGENT

Member: AAR • 90 clients

Contact: Frances Collin

> SPECIALIZES IN
> Anthropological and Genetic Science Fiction, High Fantasy

More than half of this agent's fiction clients are science fiction and fantasy writers. Fiction clients make up about 33% of those she represents. She works with all the major science fiction and fantasy publishers and is a member of AAR. About 2% of those she represents are new writers. When considering science fiction and fantasy manuscripts, the agent looks for "a strong, usable plot," as well as good writing and characterization.

HOW TO CONTACT: Query first with SASE. The agent will report in 1 week on queries, 6-8 weeks on manuscripts.
TERMS: The agent receives 15% commission on domestic sales and 20% commission on foreign sales. A written contract is offered.
ADDRESS: P.O. Box 33, Wayne PA 19087-0033

*RICHARD CURTIS ASSOCIATES, INC.

Established: 1969 • Member: AAR • Signatory of WGA • 150 clients

Contacts: Richard Curtis, Laura Tucker or Amy Victoria Meo

Recent Sales: *Legacy*, by Greg Bear; *Ignition*, by Kevin Anderson and Doug Beason; and *Endymion*, by Dan Simmons.

Richard Curtis is well-known in the science fiction and fantasy field. He's also a regular conference speaker, writes regularly for publishing trade journals and his book, *Beyond the Bestseller: A Literary Agent Takes You Inside the Book Business* (published by NAL Dutton in 1990), is an invaluable resource for any writer.

About 40% of his company's business is derived from science fiction and fantasy projects, and he's worked with all the commercial science fiction publishers. He is president of AAR and a signatory of WGA. About 5% of his clients are new writers.

HOW TO CONTACT: Query first. The agency will respond in 2 weeks on queries.

TERMS: The agent receives 15% commission on domestic sales and 20% commission on foreign sales.

ADDRESS: 171 E. 74th St., New York NY 10021

PHONE: (212)772-7363

FAX: (212)772-7393

DOYEN LITERARY SERVICES, INC.

Established: 1988 • 50 clients

Contact: B.J. Doyen or Susan Harvey

Open to previously published authors only.

HOW TO CONTACT: Send a query letter first with SASE. Doyen will report in 1-2 weeks on queries, 6-8 weeks on manuscripts.

TERMS: The agent receives 15% commission on domestic sales and 20% commission on foreign sales. A written contract is offered and is binding for 1 year.

ADDRESS: 1931 660th St., Newell IA 50568-7613

PHONE: (712)272-3300

ETHAN ELLENBERG LITERARY AGENCY

Established: 1983 • 70 clients

Contact: Ethan Ellenberg

> **SPECIALIZES IN**
> Cyberpunk, Dark Fantasy, Hard Science Fiction, High Fantasy, Humorous Science Fiction, Military Science Fiction, Space Opera, Traditional Fantasy

Recent Sales: *Archangel*, by Sharon Shinn to Berkley; Novelization of *Forever Knight*, by Susan Sizemore to Berkley; *Heritage* series (3 books), by Bill Keith to Avon.

About 10% of Ellenberg's clients are science fiction and fantasy writers. He works with all the major houses including NAL Dutton, Avon, Baen, Berkley and HarperCollins, and 75% of the works he handles are novels.

One-fourth of the agency's clients are new writers. Says Ellenberg, "We're actively seeking new clients and are happy to work with writers without charge if we believe they have potential. It's harder to break in now, but everyone is looking for books that sell and exciting writers. We welcome new submissions and writers looking for better representation."

HOW TO CONTACT: Send an outline with 3 sample chapters. Ellenberg will report in 10 days on queries, 3-4 weeks on manuscripts.

TERMS: The agent receives 15% commission on domestic sales and 10%

commission on foreign sales. A "flexible" written contract is offered.

ADDRESS: 548 Broadway, #5E, New York NY 10012

PHONE: (212)431-4554, Fax: (212)941-4652

GRAHAM LITERARY AGENCY, INC.

Established: 1994 • 30 clients

Contact: Susan L. Graham

SPECIALIZES IN
Cyberpunk, Hard Science Fiction, High Fantasy, Science Fantasy,
Sociological Science Fiction, Space Opera, Traditional Fantasy

Recent Sales: *Living Real* (working title) by James C. Bassett to HarperPrism; *Ladylord*, by Sasha Miller to Tor; *Kingmaker's Sword*, by Ann Marston to HarperPrism.

@

Agency seeking both new and established writers. Usually obtains new clients through queries. 95% of clients are new writers. 65% of represented titles are science fiction or fantasy. Send query, 3 sample chapters, SASE. "No phone calls."

"Thoroughly know or research the genre and information you are writing. Spend a lot of time perfecting your query letter. *Never* call an agent, unless you have an offer." Would like to see "professional formatting of a fresh, innovative idea or approach, with engaging characters, all within realistic and appropriate settings." Attends the following conferences: World Fantasy Con, DragonCon, Magic Carpet Con, NYC SFWA.

TERMS: Standard commission is 15% domestic, 20% foreign/subsidiary. Offers a written contract. Author must give 30 days notice to terminate contract.

ADDRESS: P.O. Box 1051, Alpharetta GA 30239

PHONE: (770)569-9755

E-MAIL: slg@atl.mindspring.com

WEBSITE: http://www.mindspring.com/~slgraham

SUSAN HERNER RIGHTS AGENCY

Established: 1987 • 45 clients

Contact: Susan Herner or Sue Yuen

> **SPECIALIZES IN**
> Cyberpunk, Dark Fantasy, Hard Science Fiction, High Fantasy, Military Science Fiction, Traditional Fantasy

About 10% of this agency's clients are science fiction and fantasy writers. The agency handles about 40% fiction, including thrillers, romance, mystery, literary and mainstream, as well as science fiction. About 25% of the agency's clients are new writers. The agency is actually divided into two sections, one handles the work of writers and one handles subsidiary rights for small publishers and packagers. The agent has worked with DAW, Berkley, Del Rey, Bantam and Roc.

HOW TO CONTACT: Send a query letter with an outline and sample chapters. The agent will report in 1 month on queries.

TERMS: The agent receives 15% commission on domestic sales, 20% commission on dramatic and foreign sales.

ADDRESS: P.O. Box 303, Scarsdale NY 10583

PHONE: (914)725-8967

IEVLEVA LITERARY AGENCY

Established: 1991 • 25 clients

Contact: Julie Ievleva

> **SPECIALIZES IN**
> Contemporary Fantasy, Science Fantasy, Traditional Fantasy

Recent Sales: *In Pursuit of Reality*, by Charles Giordan to Sunlight Press; *Russkie Business*, by Janet Applethorn to Johnson and Associates; *Broken Bones*, by Tony Kondo to Perestroika Press.

Agency seeking both new and established writers. Usually obtains new clients through recommendations from others, conferences and conventions, and queries. 50% of clients are new writers. 38% of represented titles are science fiction or fantasy. Query first with outline. Photocopying and overseas postage will be charged to author. Any expense must be approved by client.

"We look for a certain sense of realism in the alternative futures or worlds you create in your fiction. If we can answer the question, 'Do we feel that we are actually living in his strange, new world?' with a resounding 'yes!' than your project is for us. We are very interested in hearing from new writers. We know how hard it is to break in, but if you have a fresh voice and a unique slant, you can make it. Whatever you do, don't give up. Send us your material with confidence."

TERMS: Standard commission is 15%. Offers a written contract. Author must give 30 days notice to terminate contract.
ADDRESS: 7095 Hollywood Blvd., Suite 832, Hollywood CA 90028
PHONE: (213)993-6048

Jabberwocky Literary Agency

Established: 1994 • 40 clients

Contact: Joshua Bilmes

SPECIALIZES IN
Contemporary Fantasy, Cyberpunk, Dark Fantasy, Elfpunk, Hard Science Fiction, High Fantasy, Horror, Humorous, Magic Realism, Military Science Fiction, Science Fantasy, Sociological Science Fiction, Space Opera, Steampunk, Traditional Fantasy

Recent Sales: *Remnant Population*, by Elizabeth Moon to Baen; *Deathstalker Rebellion*, by Simon R. Green to Roc; *Blood Debt*, by Tanya Huff to DAW.

@

Agency seeking both new and established writers. Usually obtains new clients through queries. Query first. No manuscripts or sample chapters unless requested. Photocopying, some long distance calls and overseas mailings will be charged to author. All charges deducted from sale proceeds.

"Succeeding as an sf/fantasy author almost requries a personal familiarity with, fondness for, and understanding of the genres. The sf/fantasy readership has strong ideas of what it likes and dislikes. Rarely does it work to violate the expectations of the readers, but it is always possible (and often vital) to bring to your work a distinct quality that will bring new life to the reading experience." Attends the following conferences: World SF Convention, ICON.

TERMS: Standard commission is 10%. Offers a written contract. Contract binding for 1 year. Author must give 60 days notice to terminate contract.

ADDRESS: P.O. Box 4558, Sunnyside NY 11104-0558

PHONE: (718)392-5985

*Virginia Kidd, Literary Agent

Established: 1965 • 60 clients

Contact: Virginia Kidd

> **SPECIALIZES IN**
> Cyberpunk, Dark Fantasy, Hard Science Fiction, High Fantasy, Humorous Science Fiction, Military Science Fiction, Sociological Science Fiction, Space Opera, Traditional Fantasy

Virginia Kidd only represents published authors. Known as one of the most active agents in the science fiction field, about 80% of her clients are science fiction and fantasy writers. She works with all the major houses and many well-known authors in the field. In science fiction manuscripts, she looks for "good rationale and good style." Virginia Kidd is affiliated with the William Morris Agency.

HOW TO CONTACT: This agency is closed to unsolicited queries or submissions.

TERMS: The agent receives 10% commission on domestic sales and 20%

commission on foreign and dramatic sales. A written contract is offered.

ADDRESS: 538 E. Harford St., P.O. Box 278, Milford PA 18337
PHONE: (717)296-6205
FAX: (717)296-7266
E-MAIL: compuserve73107.3311

MiCHAEL LARSEN/ELiZABEETH POMADA, Literary Agents

Established: 1972 • AAR member • 100 clients

Contact: Elizabeth Pomada

> SPECIALIZES IN
> Contemporary Fantasy, Experimental Fiction, Horror, Humorous, Magic Realism, Space Opera, Traditional Fantasy

Recent Sales: *Pangaea*, by Lisa Mason to Bantam; *A Time of Magic*, by Katharine Kerr to Bantam; *Drum Warning*, by Jo Clayton to Tor.

Usually obtains new clients through recommendations from others. 50% of clients are new writers. 10% of represented titles are science fiction or fantasy. Send synopsis and first 30 pages of polished work with SASE and phone number. Photocopies will be charged to author.

Looking for a great, page-turning plot, characters readers can relate to or care about, whether or not they're human. Must believe that the world created is real. "We like new ideas and fresh voices in fantasy and science fiction. We also seek new worlds."

TERMS: Standard commission is 15%. Offers a written contract. Author must give 60 days notice to terminate contract.
ADDRESS: 1029 Jones St., San Francisco CA 94109
PHONE: (415)673-0939

DONALD MAASS LITERARY AGENCY

Established: 1980 • Member: AAR • 55 clients

Contact: Donald Maass or Jennifer Jackson

> SPECIALIZES IN
> Cyberpunk, Dark Fantasy, Game/Media Tie-Ins, Hard Science Fiction, High Fantasy, Historical Fantasy, Humorous Science Fiction, Military Science Fiction, Sociological Science Fiction, Space Opera, Traditional Fantasy, Urban Fantasy

Recent Sales: *God's Fires*, by Patricia Anthony to Ace; *Voices of Hope*, by David Feintuch to Warner Aspect; *Fairyland*, by Paul McAuley to AvoNova.

@

This is a very active agency in the field—75% of their clients are science fiction and fantasy writers (the rest write other types of fiction). Maass works with all the major houses and many well-known authors. He attends the World Science Fiction Convention and is a member of AAR. About 5% of the agent's clients are new writers.

In science fiction and fantasy manuscripts, the agent looks for "gripping openings, strong protagonists, detailed world building, sweeping plot, multiple points of view, distinctive style." He also looks for "strong storytelling. A short-story track record, advance quotes and other hype, good timing and luck are all useful, but in the end it all comes down to storytelling skill. I sell 50 to 75 novels per year, the majority of them science fiction and fantasy."

HOW TO CONTACT: Query with SASE. The agent will report in 2 weeks on queries, 2-3 months on manuscripts (if sent on request, after query).
TERMS: The agent receives 15% commission on domestic sales and 20% commission on foreign sales.
ADDRESS: 157 W. 57th St., Suite 1003, New York NY 10019
PHONE: (212)757-7755

HELEN MCGRATH

Established: 1977 • 80 clients

Contact: Helen McGrath or Doris Johnson

> SPECIALIZES IN
> Cyberpunk, Dark Fantasy, Hard Science Fiction, High Fantasy, Humorous
> Science Fiction, Military Science Fiction, Sociological Science Fiction, Space
> Opera, Traditional Fantasy

About 20% of this agent's clients write science fiction and fantasy, and McGrath works only with published writers in this field. Overall, half of the agent's clients write fiction. She works with all major publishers and attends the World Science Fiction Convention each year. In science fiction manuscripts, she looks for "a reasonable length, 'different' theme and a fast-moving plot."

HOW TO CONTACT: Query with a proposal and SASE (published authors only).

TERMS: The agent receives 15% commission on domestic sales. She sometimes offers a written contract.

ADDRESS: 1406 Idaho Ct., Concord CA 94521

PHONE: (510)672-6211

E-MAIL: dfrf05a@prodigy.com

THE ROBERT MADSEN LITERARY AGENCY

Established: 1992 • 5 clients

Contact: Robert Madsen (Agent) or Kim Van Nguyen (Senior Editor)

> SPECIALIZES IN
> Cyberpunk, Dark Fantasy, Hard Science Fiction, High Fantasy, Humorous
> Science Fiction, Military Science Fiction, Sociological Science Fiction, Space
> Opera, Traditional Fantasy

This young agency's clientele are all new writers, and they are currently marketing 2 science fiction and fantasy titles. About 25% of the work the agency handles is fiction. They work with all the major publishers and have contact with science fiction publishers in Commonwealth and United Kingdom countries as well. Senior Editor Kim Van Nguyen advises science fiction writers, "Manuscripts that are obviously derivative or overly imitative of television programs, films or other books rarely result in success."

HOW TO CONTACT: Query first with SASE. The agent will report in 1 month on queries, 2-3 months on manuscripts.

TERMS: The agent receives 10% commission on domestic sales and 20% commission on foreign sales. A written contract is offered and is binding for 3 years.

ADDRESS: 1331 E. 34th St., #1, Oakland CA 94602

PHONE: (510)223-2090

*MARTHA MILLARD LITERARY AGENCY

Although this agency has been mentioned as one that handles the work of a number of science fiction clients, Millard is closed to unsolicited submissions, but will accept a query letter *only* if the author has previously been published.

HOW TO CONTACT: Query with SASE (published authors only). Responds in approximately 1 month.

ADDRESS: 204 Park Ave., Madison NJ 07940

PHONE: (201)593-9233

JEAN V. NAGGAR LITERARY AGENCY

Established: 1978 • Member: AAR • 100 clients

Contact: Jean Naggar

Recent Sales: *Nadja*, by Pat Murphy to Tor; *Fair Peril*, by Nancy Springer to Avon; *The Serpent Garden*, by Judith Merkle Riley to Viking.

This well-established New York agency is not interested in hard-core science fiction or fantasy, but may look at futuristic fiction that crosses over into mainstream. About 10-15% of their clients write this type of material. A member of AAR, the agency works with all the major publishers including Berkley, Bantam, Del Rey and Ballantine. 10% of clients are new writers.

HOW TO CONTACT: The agency will only accept queries on finished manuscripts and tries to report within 24 hours on queries. They report in approximately 4 months on manuscripts.

TERMS: The agent receives 15% commission on domestic sales and 20% commission on foreign sales. A written contract is offered.

ADDRESS: 216 E. 75th St., 1E, New York NY 10021

PHONE: (212)794-1082

Perkins Associates

Established: 1989 • Member: AAR • 100 clients

Contact: Lori Perkins or Peter Rubie

Agency prefers to work with established writers, mostly through referrals. Obtains new clients through recommendations from others, conferences and conventions, queries, solicitation. 30% of clients are new writers. 10 % of titles represented are science fiction or fantasy. Query first with outline and first 2 sample chapters. Also include a brief bio. Sometimes fees for foreign mailings and photocopying will be charged to author.

TERMS: Standard commission 15% domestic; 20% foreign.

ADDRESS: 5800 Arlington Ave., Riverdale NY 10471-1419

PHONE: (718)543-5344

FAX: (718)543-5354

Susan Ann Protter Literary Agent

Established: 1971 • Member: AAR • 45 clients

Contact: Susan Ann Protter

SPECIALIZES IN
Contemporary Fantasy, Cyberpunk, Hard Science Fiction, Traditional
Fantasy

Recent Sales: *Door Number Three,* by Patrick O'Leary to Tor; *Pirates of the Universe,* by Terry Bisson to Tor; *Freeware,* by Rudy Rucker to AvoNova.

❦

About 35% of this agency's clients write science fiction and fantasy, and, overall, fiction makes up about 65% of the work the agency handles. The agency is a member of AAR and works with all the major publishers in the field. A small number of their clients are new writers.

HOW TO CONTACT: Query with a brief letter, including a description of the work, the author's publication background, and any other information on the author that might be helpful. Writers querying this agency must have a finished book-length work available. The agent will report in 2-3 weeks on queries, 6 weeks on solicited manuscripts.

TERMS: The agent receives 15% commission on domestic sales, 15% commission on dramatic sales, and 25% commission on foreign sales.

ADDRESS: 110 W. 40th St., Suite 1408, New York NY 10018

PHONE: (212)840-0480

*scovil chichak galen literary agency, inc.

Established: 1992 • Member: AAR • 300 clients

Contact: Russell Galen

SPECIALIZES IN
Cyberpunk, Dark Fantasy, Hard Science Fiction, High Fantasy, Humorous
Science Fiction, Military Science Fiction, Sociological Science Fiction, Space
Opera, Traditional Fantasy

Although this agency is relatively new, the staff includes 3 former executives from the Scott Meredith Literary Agency. They handle the work of several well-known authors in the field. About 25% of their clients write science fiction and fantasy. The agency is a member of AAR and works with all the major houses worldwide. Already a strong presence in the field, the agents attend the World Science Fiction Convention and the World Fantasy Convention. See Galen's article, **Finding and Getting the Most Out of an Agent**, on page 325.

Notable titles and clients include: *The Hammer of God*, by Arthur C. Clarke; *Forest House*, by Marion Zimmer Bradley; *The Last Command*, by Timothy Zahn; *The Far Kingdoms*, by Chris Bunch and Allan Cole; *In the Balance*, by Harry Turtledove; and *Sacred Ground*, by Mercedes Lackey.

HOW TO CONTACT: Query first with SASE.
TERMS: The agent receives 15% commission on domestic sales and offers a written contract.
ADDRESS: 381 Park Ave. S., Suite 1020, New York NY 10016
PHONE: (212)679-8686
FAX: (212)679-6710

VALERIE SMITH, LITERARY AGENT

Established: 1978 • 30 clients

Contact: Valerie Smith

SPECIALIZES IN
Contemporary Fantasy, Cyberpunk, Dark Fantasy, Hard Science Fiction, High Fantasy, Horror, Humorous, Science Fantasy, Sociological Science Fiction, Space Opera, Traditional Fantasy

Recent Sales: *The Fortunate Fall*, by Raphael Carter to Tor; *Lightpaths*, by Howard Hendrix to East Books; *The Book of Enchantment*, by Patricia Wrede to Harcourt Brace

Agency prefers to work with established writers, mostly through referrals. Less than 1% of clients are new writers. 85% of the titles represented are science fiction or fantasy. Send outline with 3 sample chapters.

TERMS: Standard commission 15%. Offers a written contract. Author must give 7 days notice to terminate contract.

ADDRESS: 1746 Rt. 44/55 Modena NY 12548-5205

PHONE: (914)883-5848

TOAD HALL, INC.

Established: 1983 • Member: AAR • WGA signatory • 55 clients

Contact: Sharon Jarvis or Anne Pinzow

> SPECIALIZES IN
> Contemporary Fantasy, Dark Fantasy, Hard Science Fiction, High Fantasy, Horror, Science Fantasy, Traditional Fantasy

Recent Sales: *True Names*, by Vernor Vinge to Tor; *Children of Enchantment*, by Anne Kelleher Bush to Warner; one untitled novel by Camille Bacon-Smith to DAW.

Usually obtains new clients through recommendations from others, conferences and conventions, and queries. 20% of clients are new writers. 15% of represented titles are science fiction or fantasy. Query first. Client must provide manuscript copies and extra copies of published books for subsidiary rights.

Looking for manuscripts that are "unique and wonderful," but they must also be commercial. "We have to love it." Attends the following conferences: World-Con, Luna-Con.

TERMS: Standard commission is 15%. Offers a written contract. Contract binding for 1 year. Author must give 30 days notice to terminate contract.

ADDRESS: R.R. 2, Box 16B, Laceyville PA 18623

PHONE: (717)869-2942

FAX: (717)869-1031

E-MAIL: toadhall@epix.net

*RALPH M. VICINANZA LTD.

Established: 1982 • Member: AAR • 70 clients

Contact: Ralph Vicinanza, Christopher Lotts or Sharon Friedman

> SPECIALIZES IN
> Cyberpunk, Dark Fantasy, Hard Science Fiction, High Fantasy, Humorous Science Fiction, Military Science Fiction, Sociological Science Fiction, Space Opera, Traditional Fantasy

Recent Sales: *The Green Mile*, by Stephen King to NAL; *Cosm*, by Greg Benford to Avon; *Nothing but the Rent*, by Sharon Mitchell to Dutton.

@

This agency is well-established in the field, and 60% of the work they handle comes from science fiction and fantasy writers. The agency has several well-known sf clients and works with all the major houses in the field. They attend the World Science Fiction Convention and the World Fantasy Convention. The agency is a member of AAR.

HOW TO CONTACT: This agency only works with writers they contact through professional references (no unsolicited queries or submissions).

TERMS: The agent receives 10% commission on domestic sales, 15% commission on dramatic sales and new writers, and 20% commission on foreign sales.

ADDRESS: 111 Eighth Ave., Suite 1501, New York NY 10011
PHONE: (212)924-7090

THE VINES AGENCY, INC.

Established: 1995 • WGA signatory • 42 clients

Contact: Jimmy Vines

Agency seeking both new and established writers. Usually obtains new clients through recommendations from others and queries. 5% of clients are new writers. 15% of represented titles are science fiction and fantasy. Query first. Postage, photocopying and messengers will be charged to author.

Would like to see manuscripts featuring memorable, lovable characters engaged in dramatic conflict from beginning to end in science fiction and fantasy submissions.

TERMS: Standard commission is 15% domestic and 20% foreign. Offers a written contract. Contract binding for 1 year. Author must give 30 days notice to terminate contract.

ADDRESS: 409 E. Sixth St., No. 4, New York NY 10009

PHONE: (212)777-5522

FAX: (212)777-5978

CHERRY WEINER LITERARY AGENCY

Established: 1977 • 40 clients

Contact: Cherry Weiner

Recent Sales: Novels by Gael Bardino (Roc); Damien Broderick (Avon); Diann Thornley (Tor).

About 20% of this agency's clients are science fiction and fantasy writers. Almost all the work the agent handles is fiction. The agency works with all the major houses in the field, including Avon, Tor and Roc, and attends the World Science Fiction Convention and the World Fantasy Conventions. 10% of the agency's clients are new writers. In science fiction manuscripts, Weiner looks for "something different, funny, exciting, adventurous."

HOW TO CONTACT: This agency only accepts queries through professional recommendations (no unsolicited queries).

TERMS: The agent receives 15% commission on domestic sales and 15% commission on foreign sales.

ADDRESS: 28 Kipling Way, Manalapan NJ 07726

PHONE: (908) 446-2096

*WRITERS HOUSE

Established: 1974 • Member: AAR • 35 clients

Contact: Merrilee Heifetz

SPECIALIZES IN
Cyberpunk, Dark Fantasy, Humorous Science Fiction, Sociological Science Fiction, Space Opera, Traditional Fantasy

About 67% of this established agency's clients are science fiction and fantasy writers. The agency works with all the major science fiction and fantasy publishers and attends the World Science Fiction and World Fantasy Conventions. About half of their clients are new writers. The agency is a member of AAR. Notable clients include: Joan D. Vinge, Bruce Sterling, Pat Cadigan and Octavia Butler.

HOW TO CONTACT: Query first with SASE. The agency will report in 1 month on queries.

TERMS: The agent receives 15% commission on domestic sales and 20% commission on foreign sales. A written contract is offered.

ADDRESS: 21 W. 26th St., New York NY 10010

PHONE: (212)685-2400

FAX: (212)685-1781

Success

Stories

❋ ❋ ❋

Anatomy of a Sale: "Pacifica" to *Realms of Fantasy*

SHAWNA MCCARTHY

Given that this is a sourcebook for serious writers of science fiction and fantasy, I might as well be honest. Regardless of how much better your story was than the one I ran, I don't pick the fiction I run at random from the slushpile. Every story submitted is given its fair chance at publication—though, I must admit, some have a better stab at it than others. Following this essay is one such story—a short story called "Pacifica"—and I'll try to tell you why it beat the odds.

First of all, while not a Really Famous Writer, Julie Stevens has been at this for a while—she's a professional and knows how to properly submit a story, so she easily made the first cut. And the first cut begins, oddly enough, at the post office. When I come, as I do twice a week, to collect the mail from the box, what I really don't want to do is stand on a half-hour long line to collect a postage-due manuscript. So I don't do it. If your manuscript comes to me postage-due, it goes back to you, unopened, the same way. Petty? Perhaps at first glance it is. But when you consider that I get some 100-130 manuscripts *per week*, you have to realize that the postage-due rates can add up pretty darn fast.

The other thing you have to consider is the number I just gave you—yes, you read it correctly: I do get 100-130 manuscripts per week. Keep that number in mind when I mention that I publish only six issues per year, each of which contains six or seven stories. Now do the math: At most, I can publish 42 stories per year. If they're all really, really short, then maybe we can push that number up to a nice round 50. I have submitted to me for publication, on the low end of the estimate, *5,200 stories per year.* So, your best possible odds on getting published in *Realms of Fantasy* are slightly more than 10 to one against. And that's assuming that the playing field is entirely even—that no stories from Really Famous Writers have jumped in there to take up space that should rightfully go to your story.

So, okay, you groan, *how do I get you to pick my story out of the teeming multitudes?* Well, the first thing you do is: Don't give me an excuse to reject you. That's all I'm looking for, you know. I've got manuscripts up to my hips in my office and enough stories already in inventory to publish another four complete issues. I don't *want* to buy any more stories, I don't *need* to buy any more stories, and if I do buy any more stories, the publisher is likely to give me a stern talking to. I don't want that, either. So, to be brutally frank, I'm just looking for a reason to send yours back to you. Don't give me one and you—like Julie Stevens—are ahead of the game by a long shot.

What do I consider a good reason for rejection? Well, right off the bat, if your manuscript is not typed, it goes back unread. If it is typed, but it's not double-spaced, it goes back unread. If it's typed and double-spaced but the point size is smaller than 10 (well, let's say eight for a really clear serif type), it goes back—you guessed it—unread.

Those are the easiest excuses you can give an editor. They're also the easiest to avoid. All you really need to do it is put yourself in my shoes for an instant. Not only do I have all these manuscripts to read for the magazine, but I also have a fulltime job as a literary agent which also involves reading manuscripts. Not to put too fine a point on it, when my eyes are open, they are reading.

I'm not going to make life harder on my eyes by asking them to read illegible scripts. Not to mention the fact that even if the finest short story ever written on this green Earth came to me single-spaced or hand-written and say, for the sake of argument, that I was in a really generous mood that day and read it anyway, and said to myself, "This is the finest story ever written on this green Earth," my next thought would have to be, "Too bad it can't be published if it's not typed." No typesetter will set type from a single-spaced or hand-written manuscript. They just won't do it—at least not for what magazines pay them. (I'm assuming here that if you're sending in single-spaced manuscripts it's because you don't have a computer and don't feel that someone as creative as you needs to retype it just because convention says you should. If you have a computer and can't push the double-space button—well, then . . .) In any case, those are by far the easiest rejection excuses to avoid. Get past that barrier, and you will get at least the first couple of lines of your story read. Congratulations! Like Julie, you've made the first cut.

Wait a second, you say. *What do you mean, the first couple of lines? This is the first cut?* Well, yes, I'm sad to say it is, and any editor who tells you that he or she reads every word of every story submitted is, to be perfectly honest, not being perfectly honest. We editors even have a catch-phrase for it: "You don't need to eat the whole fish to tell if it's bad." This comes under the writing-school subhead of The Hook. You've gotta get us with the first line, give us a sentence that forces us to read the next one, and so on and so on and so on till, gosh, we've read the whole thing.

Julie's hook is terrific: "On the night Kahuna was born, Manu Pueo, the owl from Hawaii's Thunder Mountains, swooped down from its perch on a nearby palm and frightened away the women attending the one who was becoming his mother." Being the jaded, been-there, read-that editor that I am, I thought, "Cool. A story that's not set in Imaginary Celtic Fairyland. Let's see where it goes." And just like that, she had me. I read the whole thing.

At this point Julie was two-thirds of the way to a sale. Why only two-thirds? Because even if we've eaten the whole fish and it wasn't bad, that doesn't mean it was actually good. Now we have to decide if we like the way it was prepared—did it enlighten us, amuse us, surprise us, engage us, show us something new? In Julie's case, the answer was yes. I was entertained, amused, surprised and enlightened by what she did with the material. She could easily have taken the path of least resistance and retold a Hawiian myth. But she didn't. She took the structure of a myth (and by the way, don't try this at home—it's not as easy as it looks to write a real story with plot, theme, characters, climax and denouement from an omniscient viewpoint with no dialogue) and turned it into something greater than itself. When we're done, we feel we know Kahuna—his ego, his culture, his faith and his fate. That the end works as beautifully as it does is another tribute to the author's talent, because when you sit back and analyze the story, the ending hinges on one of those coincidences that made us throw "The Gift of the Magi" halfway across the room. But the author is in such command of her material, and clearly has been from the story's first word, that it flows into the narrative in precisely the right way.

I wish I could give you some kind of magic key which would ensure that you were able to learn how to sell your stories merely from reading these words, but I'm afraid no such key exists. The only way to sell your stories is to write, but, just as importantly, read. And when you read, for instance, "Pacifica," don't read it simply to find out what happens—read for structure and technique. "Pacifica" is an easy story to read but a hard one to write—that's one reason I selected it for this book. If you can sit down and analyze how Julie Stevens pulled off the trick of turning a myth-structure into a full and complete short story, you'll have gained more insight into how to sell your stories than reading any ten of my essays. Enjoy.

SHAWNA McCARTHY is a literary agent with the firm of Scovil Chichak Galen, as well as being editor-in-chief of *Realms of Fantasy*. She's been in publishing for 18 years now, and was previously senior editor at Bantam Spectra Books as well as editor-in-chief of *Isaac Asimov's Science Fiction Magazine*, where she won the Hugo for Best Professional Editor.

Pacifica

J U L I E S T E V E N S

On the night Kahuna was born, Manu Pueo, the owl from Hawaii's Thunder Mountains, swooped down from its perch in a nearby palm and frightened away the women attending the one who was becoming his mother. That lady squatted in the moonless dark, sheltered by a small grove of coconut palms. She was aware of the danger, but she was unwilling to move and thereby risk the death of her baby.

Mele had witnessed her thirtieth harvest season and had long ago acknowledged, if not accepted, her position as Kelolo the Fisherman's barren first wife. From the first month in which she shed no woman's blood and thereby avoided kapu, she had known the child she carried was male, a son destined for greatness.

Frightened, abandoned by her midwives and racked by the pain of the child's coming, Kahuna's mother faced Manu Pueo alone.

A day and a half later, Mele walked out of the palm grove toward the village with her son at her breast. The women rushed to meet her, staring with horror and admiration at the striations left by the owl's talons across her thighs and belly. In sparse and heartfelt terms, for Mele was a fisherman's wife and not a storyteller, she related how the owl attacked her and how she had pleaded with it to spare her child. She told how the owl settled to the ground, folded its wings and backed away without harming her as she gave birth. Then she told how the owl spoke to her, said it was old and dying and needed a soul to inhabit;

finally, she told how she pitied the owl and held out her son to it and gave it permission to share her son's soul.

This was the strangest talk the women of the village had ever heard, but they agreed that Kelolo and his wife were specially blessed with mana and their son who held the owl's spirit, doubly so. The men of the village heard the cries of their women and came forward. They demanded that Mele tell them her story. She related it to them, and again to the high chief, and finally to the king himself, though she was forbidden to address the king directly and instead recited the events of the child's birth to a large boulder in the compound used by the king during his infrequent visits to the village, while he hid himself behind it and listened. The most powerful priest in the village was summoned for advice. The man consulted the omens, entreated the gods to show their will, and after much chanting and burning of sacrifices announced that a boy with the soul of an owl inside him must have great powers of prophecy and should be carefully trained in the use of his gift. The fisherman's son was not given a proper name, but called simply Kahuna, which could mean any priest or holy man; yet so far did the fame of his birth spread among the islands that unless a kahuna was referred to by another given name, it was assumed the owl-boy was meant.

Kahuna did not know just when he understood the extent of his mana. Certainly he was never without the knowledge that he was different. But he first remembered hearing of the owl that shared his soul just after his fourth harvest. That was when Kelolo came to take him from his mother's house. But instead of taking the boy to the men's lodge Kelolo shared with Kahuna's half-brothers, he led his son around the mud-laden Taro beds and down the beach to a hut belonging to Kuokoa, the most powerful kahuna in the village, and the man who would know what the gods had in store for the owl-boy.

Kahuna had always known he would be a priest; but now, as his father released him into the care of Kuokoa, Kahuna realized his training was to begin immediately. He wondered if his mother had had any say in the matter, for he was very young to be apprenticed. Although he saw her upon occasion after that, he never asked her, nor did she give him any hint.

Kahuna stayed with Kuokoa for twelve years. He tended the priest's fires, cooked his meals, and accompanied him on long journeys into the mountains to gather the materials a kahuna needs to make successful magic against malevolent spirits. Kahuna practiced faithfully until he could chant incantations against four hundred evils, more even than Kuokoa could remember without resorting to his memorysticks. Kuokoa told his charge that the nature of the owl spirit was the gift of prophecy. He sat in long vigils with Kahuna and carved many special charms by the light of a kikuinut lamp to help the boy corral the spirit and use its gift wisely.

Kahuna made his first prophecy during his tenth makahiki. Since makahiki was a festival in honor of Lono, who governed growing things and brought joy and peace, Kuokoa had prepared a fine chant to entertain the crowds. But the king demanded more. He had waited a long time to return to this poor village and he wanted to see something from the owl-boy. Kuokoa shook his head and made powerful magic. He did not think his pupil was ready but neither could he disobey a direct order from the king.

So, Kahuna prophesized. He leaned his head back and closed his eyes and said what first came into his thoughts. He said that the coming storm would bring a terrible destruction, worse than any in memory. There was a storm on the horizon, though it appeared no different than any other harvest storm. But the owl-boy's words were heeded and the festivities quickly ended. After the poi, salted fish, and pandanus flour were sealed into watertight containers and placed underground, the villagers gathered their possessions and moved into the shallow caves along the base of the inland mountain range to await the storm.

Yet when the storm came, it passed as any minor gale would. People glared at Kahuna from their cramped quarters and muttered under their breath. Even his own mother looked upon him with sadness rather than faith. He wondered if she thought the owl spirit had abandoned her son.

But close upon the first storm came another, and the chiefs ordered everyone back into the caverns. This time, the winds peaked in such fury as had seldom been seen in the islands; the waves covered the rocky beaches and reached across the palm groves to suck the roots from the taro beds. Boulders the size of a child were flung into the trees. When the storm was over, only one hut remained standing, and that was the one belonging to Kuokoa and Kahuna. From this did the people know that Kahuna and the owl were truly one.

Kuokoa had much to teach his apprentice. The elderly priest was consulted by almost everyone in the village for advice, for healing powders and potions, for intercession with the spirits. To his people, it appeared that Kuokoa knew everything, even those things they thought had been kept secret. Yet, while Kahuna was Kuokoa's willing pupil, he was puzzled by him, too, for it seemed that not all that the man taught was worthy of a kahuna. The intricately carved sticks the priest waved about as he performed his chants were memory guides which he used to recall the exact sequence of the chant, all the while appearing to be inspired by the gods themselves. Kuokoa listened carefully to what even the smallest child had to say, and by the quietness of his presence was often unnoticed by the villagers. In this way, he learned much that he would use again when a man or woman came to him for magic. But any man might observe and later couch his observations in such flights of language and clouds of smoke as to convince a lesser man that magic is in the air; that does not render illusion into reality, and Kahuna was greatly disturbed at how often Kuokoa resorted to these tricks. For himself, Kahuna refused to be a party to them. He held himself apart from the villagers, and when they came to him for prophecy, he gave it to them truly, scarcely changing the pattern he had begun as a boy at that tenth makahiki. Men asked whom they should marry, and he told them. Women asked where to plant their crops for the most fruitful harvest, and he told them. Chiefs came to him with their battle plans and never marched against an enemy but that Kahuna had selected the most auspicious date. The owl spirit filled him until it seemed that he could not talk without casting the future.

He continued to live with Kuokoa, but all was not well between them. Kahuna was self-righteous in his gift, and scornful of the devices Kuokoa used to compete. He lacked the patience to humor his teacher, and more and more it seemed to Kahuna that his village deserved a priest without tricks, a priest whom Manu Pueo had marked as his own. He spoke to Kuokoa of these things, for he did not want to conspire against the man without his knowledge. But Kuokoa counseled forbearance. Many times, he told Kahuna that for all of the owl's gift, Kahuna had not sufficiently developed his skill at prophecy. This, Kahuna knew to be nonsense. The proof of his skill lay in the bountiful harvests, the successful marriages, the victorious battles of the village.

e

Then, during Kuokoa's sixtieth harvest and Kahuna's twentieth, the elderly priest challenged his student to match chants with him, one for one until he or the apprentice lost memory. The owl inside Kahuna told him he would win, though mere observation would have told him as much. He slept on the mats beside Kuokoa and he heard the terrible coughing in the middle of the night which none of his potions could cure. He knew that Kuokoa relied more and more on his memorysticks not just for his chants, but for his magic, and often left out parts that were crucial to the success of his charms. The time had come for Kahuna to take his place as the most powerful kahuna in the village. Most of the people already knew his skill was greater than Kuokoa's, but now the old man gave Kahuna the chance to confirm it publicly. Kahuna was not completely comfortable with his decision to accept the challenge, but he assuaged his guilt by allowing Kuokoa the full measure of his tricks. He pretended that the memorysticks were mere charms and let Kuokoa carry them into the village where the contest was to be held. The people gathered around them as first Kuokoa invoked one god, and then Kahuna another. A day passed, a night, and part of another day. Kahuna was exhausted and exhilarated, filled to overflowing with the owl spirit, and when Kuokoa at last bowed his head in defeat, Kahuna drove his triumph home with the force of a full dozen more chants.

Afterward Kuokoa was very sick. He stayed in his hut and forbade Kahuna to enter, though Kahuna made all manner of enchantments outside it, beseeching the gods to let his teacher live. Still, he foresaw that Kuokoa would die soon. Moreover, Kahuna realized the old man never intended to win their priestly battle. But with the public duel, he left Kahuna behind as a master who had brought another master to defeat.

It happened as Kahuna knew it would, and a great funeral was held for Kuokoa. The priest's flesh was baked from his bones and the bones were given to Kahuna for hiding in some secret place where his enemies might never find him. Kahuna had chosen the place with care. It was a deep rift in the Thunder Mountains where steep canyon walls closed overhead to form a cavern so long that he had never explored it to its very end.

Kahuna fasted for three days and offered to the gods all the death prayers Kuokoa had taught him. Then he gathered Kuokoa's bones in a bundle of kapa cloth and left the village. High into the pleated mountains he walked, and, as he did so, he remembered all the times he had accompanied Kuokoa along these same leaf-shaded paths. It was during this final journey with his old friend that Kahuna's often-harsh evaluation of Kuokoa softened. Fraud or not, Kuokoa had taught him how to tame the owl's soul and use its gift for prophecy; Kahuna would always be grateful. If his mentor sometimes resorted to tricks, then it was because the old priest's mana was not strong—an accident of fate, and nothing to bring shame.

When Kahuna found the entrance to his hiding place, he pulled out a candle of oil kikuinut meats stuck on the end of a long stick, one of many he had carefully hidden, together with a fireplow, near these caverns. He made the fire to light his way and entered the darkness in search of the best resting place for the bones of Kuokoa.

The air inside the cave was thick and suffocating, though cold. He had not noticed this in his prior visits but neither had he ventured so deeply into the cavern. His candle sputtered and appeared about to die at any moment. He sheltered the flame with his hand and walked carefully among the stones that littered the floor. Intent upon protecting his light and his footing, he almost dropped the packet of bones. He should not have fasted, he thought; it made him weaker than he had intended. The one chosen to secret the body of a chief or a priest was hardly ever the same one who delivered the enchantments necessary to ensure a peaceful afterlife.

He finally halted on the edge of a small, dark body of water. There was a narrow path along one side of it, but Kahuna was tired and he thought it unlikely that anyone would search this far into the cave, if it were found at all. He tasted the water and was pleased to discover the sweetness of a spring-fed pond. Even more to his pleasure was the discovery of fish in the pond. He had chosen a good place for Kuokoa, a place where the gods themselves provided ample food and drink. He placed Kuokoa's bones on a small ledge overlooking the pond. Then he knelt beside the water to drink. He found he could catch the fish with his bare hands. They were small and unlike other freshwater fish he was used to eating. Oddest of all, the fish had no eyes. Scales were drawn tight and smooth across the head where the eyes should be. He caught several fish, cupping them gently in his hands as he inspected them. Not one had eyes, and, after much thought, Kahuna realized this was a particularly good sign that Kuokoa's bones were buried in a safe place. He wondered for a moment if eating such creatures would be right, but his hunger was great and he did not feel that any harm could result.

After he had eaten his fill, the young priest fell asleep on the stony ground beside the pond. But the owl inside him was restless and filled his sleep with dreams. He dreamt of floating islands that sailed from place to place, carrying people dressed more oddly than the strangest trader. He saw his people greet the new arrivals as gods, and saw at once that it was a terrible mistake. He watched as his people fell out of favor with the true gods and were afflicted with terrible diseases, such as no islander had ever experienced. This and more, the owl showed him until Kahuna awoke, shaken and screaming, in the darkness of the cave.

He sat for a long while, pondering the meaning of these events. When he tried to rise, dizziness overtook him, and he fell, retching, back to the cavern floor. When his stomach spasms ceased, he forced himself to his feet a second time and managed to remain upright. He had to leave; it would be an inauspicious sign if he were to be sick in Kuokoa's final resting place.

He left the cavern, stumbling through the darkness, breathing the harsh air. By the time he reached the entrance, he was still very ill, but he felt he understood something of his peculiar dream. He, who was blessed not only with the soul of an owl but with all its fortune and mana, and thus had become a prophet, had now found the place where his island kept its mana. Because Kahuna was a prophet with the owl's soul, he was shown not just his own future, nor the future of his village, but that of his entire world.

Kahuna's journey down the mountain was hampered by his physical weakness. He was becoming light-headed; none of the chants for protection from illness seemed to be working. Or in his tiredness, maybe he forgot parts that he thought were long ago committed to memory. He forced himself to keep his goal clear. He had to share his new-found knowledge with the king. Contained within his dreams was a warning that only he could deliver. And the cavern must be declared kapu and protected from desecration.

Just before he struck out across the small grassy plain that surrounded his village, he looked back at the Thunder Mountains. The yellow-green leaves of the Kikui trees against the hazy blue-gray of the mountains were a thing of beauty; they hid well the secret of the mountain cavern. After that, he fainted.

Kahuna awoke inside his own hut, but it was an uncertain awakening and he could not be sure if what he saw or heard was an illusion or reality. There was another kahuna, who chanted softly in one corner and was busily mixing potions in a carved bowl. He must have been very sick indeed if his people had sent all the way to Maui for this kahuna to attend him. It occurred to Kahuna that he might die. He searched himself and asked the owl spirit to tell him if this was so, but he could not find the answer. He was afraid he would die with no one knowing what he had learned in the cavern, so he began to tell the kahuna. The older man looked at Kahuna once or twice as though he heard his patient, but was uninterested in what Kahuna had to say. Kahuna tried to make the man understand. He told him of the floating islands filled with grizzled, light-skinned people who would one day come to their beautiful island. He warned the foreign kahuna that these were people, not gods, and that they would bring great destruction if the islanders were not careful. He told the man of weapons that spewed fire, and blades stronger than their best stone knives. He pushed away the potion the priest tried to force between his lips, and begged him to listen. But Kahuna could see the man thought the words were born in fever and gave them no value.

The Maui priest left and Kahuna could hear him chanting loudly outside his hut. Some time later, near morning Kahuna guessed, his mother came to him. She held many charms in her hand, all of them in the shape of owls. She looked so exhausted that he wondered if she had slept at all since his return. He could not be sure how long it had been since his journey into the Thunder Mountains. He tried to speak to her, but his throat burned with the effort and he made only coarse, grating noises.

While he stared at her through fever-glazed eyes Mele turned her charms over and over between her fingers. Then she began her own address to Manu Pueo. Kahuna listened, and wondered, and grew afraid.

She spoke of the time when she gave birth to him, but the story was not as he had always heard it. Instead of a glorious tale of a dying owl who inhabited a boy's soul, he heard of an old and vain wife struggling to hold the affections of a husband who even then was fonder of his newer wives who could give him many children. He heard of an owl who swept through the coconut grove where his mother labored, frightening away the attendants but itself leaving just as quickly.

He listened as his mother pleaded with the owl spirit to forgive her for marking herself and coming back to the village with a son and a story, both false. Mele sat crying beside him on the sleeping mat and asked the owl spirit to come to her son now as she had deceitfully told the world it had done, so many harvests ago.

There it was. Kahuna was no prophet made holy by the spirit of an owl inside him. He was a man as any other, and less fortunate than most. His life had been a lie, and his prophecy—what could be said about his prophecy? It never existed except in his illusions. He could not account for the strange dream he had had while in the cavern, but he knew now that it was no more real than anything else he had seen when he thought he shared his soul with the owl.

Once he knew the truth, he also saw how he had been misled into believing he was a prophet. That first prophecy during his tenth makahiki was an accident, a cruel accident, for it created a belief among the villagers that was never again put to a proper test. Kahuna realized that he had been called upon to direct people's lives, but not necessarily to prophesy. Who was to say he was wrong when he told a couple to marry, for who saw the alternative? If a chief marched into battle on Kahuna's word, and it did not go well, shouldn't it be assumed that the carnage would have been worse had Kahuna's advice not been heeded? He was a fool, Kahuna saw now. He had been one from the very beginning.

Kahuna recovered from his illness, but did not utter another word of prophecy, though he continued to make small magics such as Kuokoa taught him. He lived well enough. Some people thought the owl left him when it was believed he would die; others contended that Kahuna

373

was saving his strength for some great prophecy to come. But whatever they thought, they treated him well and allowed him his solitude.

He used that solitude to offer penance to the gods. Only occasionally did he contemplate how it might have been were he really a prophet and if he had had the power to truly cast the future.

Anatomy of a Sale:
The Fortunate Fall to Tor Books

PATRICK & TERESA NIELSEN HAYDEN

For all the talk of worldbuilding you hear at conventions, sf doesn't build worlds. Rather, it builds the similitude of them, with hints and fractional bits of data and odd sidelong references, so that while the readers are being introduced to the characters and setting and action, they're also imaginatively constructing the larger context in which the story takes place.

It's a huge expository burden: sf narrative must make the world, while telling a story set in that world, in the course of which story the world will be explicated, thereby creating the context wherein we understand the significance of the actions that make up the story. There is no single starting point; everything must go forward simultaneously. And this same prose must also flow naturally, in some recognizable version of the speaking human voice, and parcel out its strangeness so that the reader can assimilate one bit before swallowing another.

We call science fiction a literature of ideas, but if it is to coax those ideas into existence on the page, it must also be a literature of techniques. We have seldom seen a first-time novelist with a firmer grasp of this than Raphael Carter.

"Ashes to Ashes," the first chapter of *The Fortunate Fall*, begins with two unidentified voices talking about familiar, concrete smells: roses, grapefruit, horseshit. Then one voice says "Olfactory systems are go," and you discover that the two people who are talking are a thousand miles apart (one in Kazakhstan, one in Leningrad); that they're Keishi, a screener, and Maya, a camera (think film editor and cameraman), who are running a preliminary check on a direct mind-to-mind link; and that they both work for something called News One. Which—aha!—anchors you again: strange technology but a familiar situation, like a reporter shooting a little test videocam footage before the main event. (Blessedly, the characters don't talk about how this is like 20th Century TV news reporting.)

It helps that there is none of the awkward, forced-sounding futuristic slang so common in manuscripts we reject, no hazmat hardsoftpackage wetwilly scuzzware, just normal English turned to new meanings: "When she had finished, she would slide herself into my mind, like a rat into water." Where we do not stumble over the language, we are less likely to balk at the idea.

Having gotten us this far with the mind-to-mind link, Carter develops it with Maya's observation that after a half-hour as someone's screener you know them better than if you'd been friends for decades, and so cameras are constantly having their screeners conceive passionate, near-instantaneous loves and hates for them. It's believable; and because we believe in the emotional reaction to the technology, we believe in the technology itself.

The system check goes on. Maya is worried about Keishi's being her screener. They've never worked together before, and in Maya's ruminations about the perils of broadcasting live with an unfamiliar screener we pick up a lot more information about this world. Then Keishi says it's time for the broadcast to start, there's some last-minute nerves and fluster, and Maya starts talking to her audience.

We'll mention just two more things that help us over the threshold of belief here. The first is that we've followed these characters as they've prepared for this performance, and now we're with them as they perform; i.e., we don't have the automatic slight defensiveness of people who are being Told Something. If the book had simply started with the broadcast, assigning us only the role of its audience, we would not accept it the same way. The second is Maya's temporary shift of tense into second person singular, which is vivid, involving, and usefully distracting. By the time we've assimilated that second person—"*You* said it with me," "*we* strode forward up the hill"—we're well into the broadcast, with no time to argue. We're coming along for the ride.

Raphael Carter starts pushing the accelerator towards the floor. "This is what's left of Square-Mile-on-Chu," Maya says, near some crumbling ruins in an otherwise idyllic setting. As she talks, we become increasingly uneasy. These chimneys, she says, were typical Guardian *(Guardian?)* construction: slave-labor-intensive, to denote status. *(These Guardians were bad guys.)* She reminds her audience that there was once a time "when the word Guardian meant a good thing." *(Very bad guys indeed.)* Then Maya wades out into the cold muck of the lake and says, "It is a beautiful day in Kazakhstan, and you are standing calf-deep in the ash of human bodies."

Boom.

This was a death camp, a killing ground; and to this world that we have been absentmindedly compiling as we read, we suddenly have to add an entire Holocaust. We can't, of course, not right off; and it is in this moment of stunned confusion that Carter introduces the Unanimous Army.

At first we have only the sound of their marching feet, which Maya conjures out of the white noise of the river. It's a wonderful, imaginable detail, this sound of running water that turns to feet marching, and when Maya sculpts the hillside grass into the Army's soldiers we imagine, and see, that transformation as well. Carter is tactful here, neither pointing out that the white noise of a river sounds like a *great many* marching feet, nor calling the Army "innumerable as blades of grass," but we get the feel of huge numbers just the same.

And now that we've been completely set up for it, the Unanimous Army comes pouring over the hill. It is transcendently strange. It works. Read it and see for yourself.

Here's another reason we bought the book.

We really like the way Raphael Carter has constructed this world and its history. It has a very satisfactory breadth and complexity and variety, none of which seems contrived—except insofar as humans have contrived it within this history.

The careful preparation and build-up to the line, "It is a beautiful day in Kazakhstan, and you are standing calf-deep in the ash of human bodies," isn't there just for the aesthetic effect. It gives the moment the terrible moral weight it should properly have, and we can see that it has that weight for Maya and Keishi and their audience as well.

Here's a hot tip: You cannot write good science fiction—that is, you're unlikely to get past the slushpile—if the only thing you read is science fiction. You can't go making other worlds if you're not acquainted with this one. For instance, if you read some history you find out that human beings don't lightly forget cataclysms. This may seem too obvious to need saying. Nevertheless, we're forever seeing sf novels in which characters offhandedly refer to some megadeath war or plague or famine that happened in the middling-recent past . . . and then just as offhandedly move on to another topic.

It isn't that we don't sometimes appear to do this, in the real world, with our own recent history. We do. But our attitudes under the surface are complicated—perhaps, in one circumstance, offhand; in another, emotional; in still another, thoughtful or analytical. In the real world, our recent history—think World War II, or the space program, or "the sixties," or the Gulf War—has weight, gravity, *presence* for us, even if we work at distancing it or staying ignorant of it.

It's hard to replicate the sense of all that in a hypothesized future. It's even harder to do that while keeping a story moving forward. Part of how Carter does this, of course, is by holding back on exposition in order to dole it out later, a process only begun in Chapter 1. *(The Calinsh-china?)* The novel's pace of revelation is tantalizingly slow, and yet we always have that sense of being in strong, reliable hands. We never know as much as we want to—but we always know as much as we need.

The trick with science fiction is not to prove that something—a machine, a technology, a history, a new way of being—would be possible. It's to temporarily convince us that it already exists.

While it's interesting and instructive to go through a chunk of prose like this and look at how it works, readers shouldn't have to be consciously aware of all these little mechanisms operating under the surface the first time they read the book. (Unless they *enjoy* reading that way, which is Not Our Problem.) We don't read analytically like that either, the first time through.

But that doesn't mean it doesn't matter. We and all the rest of the readers know whether technique is there or not. Even readers who will never in their lives think about prose theory know that some writers just read more smoothly and clearly than others. The ground's solider underfoot. They may entirely lose track of the fact that they're reading a book, and be conscious only of the story as it unfolds.

As editors, how aware are we of prose technique? Easy: it practically shouts at us from the first moment we look at the manuscript. It's the basic fabric from which the book is made. Structural problems can sometimes be addressed by rewrites during the editing process, and surface glitches like spelling can be fixed in production, but if the fabric itself is of poor quality there's no recourse; it's going to be bad in every paragraph.

For instance, we could just as well have written this article about the second or third chapter from *The Fortunate Fall*, instead of the first. We'd have known from reading any chapter of it that we wanted to read it all. On the other hand, we sometimes hear from indignant writers who want to know how we can possibly judge a book without reading the whole thing. Sad truth is, with a lot of manuscripts three chapters and an outline are more than enough.

And one last word on this subject: technique is not the point. Or rather, technique for its own sake is not the point. Without it, you can't tell your story or get your ideas across; but it must always be in service to the story and ideas. It can't just sit there like a noun without a verb.

Why did we buy this novel? Because we loved it. Because we were fascinated by it. Because it made us want to wave copies of it in the air and yell "Here, read this!" Because in our editorial heart of hearts, there's a 9-year-old reader who likes big, adventurous stories about good people and interesting places, and a 12-year-old with an insatiable desire to know how the world works, and a 15-year-old who likes to see lots of slick maneuvers and snappy remarks and other cool stuff, and an 18-year-old who's grateful to the book for not being stupid and embarrassing . . . and so on. There are all the rest of our older selves, up through the somewhat stodgy middle-aged readers who can prize an author's masterful control of prose and just shaping of the story, because it means *we can simply lie back and enjoy the book.*

Because we have faith that at bottom, we're not all that different from the readers who buy our books. There's no sense in buying and publishing a manuscript you don't like, just because you think someone else ought to like this kind of stuff. After all, no reader ever buys a book because it strikes them as being the kind of thing somebody else might like.

And that's why we bought this first novel. Send us more like it.

PATRICK NIELSEN HAYDEN is senior editor of Tor Books' sf and fantasy line and the editor of the original sf anthology series Starlight. TERESA NIELSEN HAYDEN is a consulting editor for Tor Books and the author of the Hugo-nominated essay collection *Making Book*. They have been involved in the sf field for over two decades, and in New York publishing since 1984.

The Fortunate Fall

RAPHAEL CARTER

CHAPTER ONE
ASHES, ASHES

"Okay, what's this scent?"

"Roses," I said.

"And this one?"

"Citrus. Grapefruit."

"All right. What about this?"

"Cow shit."

"Close."

"Okay, horse shit."

"Bull's eye. Olfactory systems are go. Let's go hearing."

I was standing by the River Chu, in Kazakhstan, staring at a little hill from which three naked chimneys rose. I stood alone; but a thousand miles away, in Leningrad, a woman I had never met was testing my senses. When she had finished, she would slide herself into my mind, like a rat into water. As my thoughts went out live to the Net, she would screen them through hers, strengthening my foreground thoughts and sifting out impurities, so that—if she was any good—the signal that went out on News One would be pure and clear. And when she drew herself out of my mind again, five minutes later, she would know more about me than a friend of thirty years.

"I think it's an E flat," I said.

"Yes, but what instrument?"

"Brass."

"Be specific."

"Do I look like a conductor?"

"It's a trombone. You can tell by the glissando. Now what's this?"

I had never met this Keishi Mirabara. I had no idea what she looked like. But Keishi was a screener, so for her, our acquaintance of half an hour was already long. Hooking up mind to mind, the way they do, they can only scorn the glacial rituals the rest of us use to form friendships. By the end of the day, she might already hate me—not with some casual dislike, but with a deep, dissective hatred, such as is otherwise only attained after decades of marriage. It's bad stuff, their hatred.

Their love is worse: a surge of emotion that comes at you flood-fast, overwhelming your own feelings before you're even certain what they are. And the poor camera, who can reach out to another mind only with mute eyes and vague bludgeoning words . . . well, it's like being an amnesia victim, coming home a stranger to someone who's loved you all your life.

"All right, stop me when this stripe is the same color as the sky."

"Now—no, a little more—yes, there."

"You're coming through faded, then. I'm going to split your field of vision. What you're seeing will be on your left, and what's coming through here will be on your right. Tell me when the colors are the same. Ready?"

"Ready," I said. I gave it only half attention. I had done this all before.

Keishi had come in to screen for me only that evening, when my last screener, Anton Tamarich, disappeared on the day of a broadcast. It didn't surprise me—screeners go burnout all the time—but it left me stuck going live with a screener I'd never worked with before. It's the beginning of any of a dozen camera nightmares. You're working with a new screener who falls asleep at the switch just when you remember something you heard once about how to make brain viruses, and a Weaver possesses the man you're interviewing and kills you on the spot. Or some especially compromising sexual fantasy flits through your head and out into the Net and is the scandal of the week. The untried screener is the camera's equivalent of having your fly open.

It was scary enough that—though I'd never thought I'd say it—I missed Anton. I hadn't liked him, but I'd liked working with him. He was an informer for the Post police, and he hated me. I knew where I stood.

"Say the words that come into your head."

"Excrescence. Trapezoid. Spark. Blanket. Bolus. Rust."

"Verbal, go. Okay, Maya, I'm ready for link-up. Say when."

I walked halfway up the hill, arranged myself facing the river, and started to prepare myself for contact. After all these years of having strangers in my head, it's still not easy. I scratched my nose, adjusted the camera moistware in the temporal socket at the side of my head, and made sure for the tenth time that I really did not have to go to the bathroom.

"Relax, will you?" Keishi whispered in my ear, from Leningrad. " 'So Your Camera Has To Pee' is chapter two in the Basic Screening textbook, and heck, girl, I'm up to chapter four already."

At that moment gallows humor was not what I needed. Fear shifted in the coils of my intestines, like a restless snake. I would forget my lines. I would trip on a buried cobblestone and half the Russian Historical Nation would feel me break my nose. I fixed my eyes on the ground and began to hyperventilate, fighting for control.

And Keishi, knowing that anything she said would make it worse, did the only thing she could do to help. She plugged in her screening chip and patched into my mind.

There's a sense of presence when the screener comes on line, a faint heat, a pullulation. Keishi's feedback was clear and warm and reassuring, the strongest I've ever felt—as though someone had wrapped a blanket around my head. ("That's me," Keishi agreed. "An electric babushka.")

Maybe this would work out after all, I decided, knowing she heard the thought.

"Ten more seconds," she warned me. "Five. Four. Three . . . and you're *live* girl." I felt the "up" drug flood my visual cortex, making me strain my eyes to separate the river from the rolling hill behind it. Keishi fed the hours of interviews and research that Anton and I had done into my memory, so that the five-minute Netcast could imply a whole week's worth. And you came online, a shadow audience that always stood behind me no matter how I turned my head.

"This is what's left of Square-Mile-on-Chu," I said aloud, panning slowly around from the river. You said it with me. In a single body, with the same volition, we strode forward up the hill. "Three crumbling chimneys and some scattered stones, half sunk into the ground." I had reached the middle chimney now; I walked around it, running my hand over the cobblestones to transmit their tiled smoothness. "Typical Guardian construction: cobblestone instead of brick because of the thousands of hours of slave labor it took to gather the stones, carry them up here, and fit them together. The more labor-intensive, the greater the status."

I panned around to view the river again, then carefully leaned against the chimney, feeling it cool and lumpy against my back. "It's as idyllic a scene as you'll find anywhere in Karakhstan. You can spend hours in this place. Nature bounces back, you think, whatever humans do. The hills are leaved with grass, and laced with branches, growing the same as ever. The birds have long forgotten what happened here, if indeed they ever noticed, and are building their nests now. And the river flows on, just as it did when the word Guardian meant a good thing."

I started to walk down the hill, slowly, letting the sun warm my back that the stones had made cold. It was an aggressively beautiful spring day, tyrannically perfect: the kind of day that spurs the suicide to action by its mocking contrast to her own despair. *Lull them, Keishi,* I subvocalized. *Make them* feel *it*.

"I'm lulling, I'm lulling," was her reply, as laconic as the mood I wished to set and as the day itself.

Walking slowly in the mild breeze, I approached the lake, reached it, and did not stop. Without removing my shoes or rolling up my cuffs or bracing myself against the touch of the water, I walked off into the muck. Skirls of shock and disgust mingled with the cold—your shock. Feedback to the limbic system, say the manuals; what it means is that what you feel, I feel. And vice versa: I took the feeling and intensified it, hurling it back out at you.

"It is a beautiful day in Kazakhstan," I said, "and you are calf-deep in the ash of human bodies." A second long wave of mute horror as the ash and mud cemented in around my legs, entrapping them.

"The Unanimous Army came through here in the fall of 2246," I said when the audience had quieted. Calling on my imagination chip, I drew a sound of marching out of the white noise of the river. Then I looked up at the shadowed hillside and began to sculpt its waving grasses into men. "Imagine a solid column of humanity, twenty abreast, and so long that if you wanted to cross their path you'd have to camp here until dawn tomorrow. They have no uniforms, but wear whatever they happened to have on when they were absorbed: overalls, cocktail dresses—some are naked beneath makeshift coats. But all have the same round black chip, the size of a ruble coin, in their left temples. From time to time a memory unit passes, like the nameless man we met last week"—and here Keishi lifted a curtain from the memory—"people whose minds the Army erased and filled with its data, so the memories of the others could remain inviolate. The memory units can no longer even walk, so they are carried along—but upright, to confuse snipers.

At this distance they are lost in the crowd, and you will never know them."

By now the Army was almost as clear as reality, thanks to the imagination chip in my right temporal socket. Keishi flashed the word "recreation" at the bottom of my field of vision, so credulous channel-flippers wouldn't call the station thinking that the Army had returned.

"The first quarter-mile of the Army consists of people who are weak or dying or otherwise of little use. Their only purpose is to march blindly into everything and see if it will kill them. Now that they've marched through the Square Mile without harm, Sensors start to break away from the column: Eyes, Ears, Noses, Fingertips, each with its respective sense enhanced and all the others numbed. They swarm over the Square Mile in thousands, sniffing and prodding and tasting. They take nothing, but now and again they smear something with a fragrant paint they carry with them, or with urine or blood.

"When the Sensors return to the march, the column slows and spreads out to the width of the Square Mile. And when it has passed, hours later, everything in the camp—the barbed wire, the burnt wood, even the concrete from the foundations—is gone, digested into that great worm of meat that once was, and will soon again be, human.

"By November, every man, woman, and child over five in Karakhstan had been taken up into the One Mind and was marching on Occupied Russia. And in 2248, when the Army software detected victory and suddenly erased itself from all its component minds, more than half the people in the world found themselves at least a thousand miles from home. It was a time of global confusion, during which millions starved or were murdered. Not many people were concerned with seeing to it that places like this were remembered."

"But is that the whole explanation?" (*Okay, let's wind it up,* I subvoked.) "Or is there a deeper reason? The Holocaust and Terror-Famine both haunted the consciences of generations, yet the Calinshchina is barely remembered—why? We'll have some answers for you next week, in the third and last part of our series."

And then it's back to fads and scandals for the both of us, I subvoked to Keishi, who chuckled politely in reply. I closed by eyes, calling up my quite beautiful and utterly fictitious Net-portrait, and signed off: "Maya Tatyanichna Andreyeva. Of News One hearth, a Camera."

No sooner had the audience fallen away than Keishi said: "I can't believe you gave that whole speech standing in the water. I filtered out most of the cold and wetness, but even so, it wasn't easy to keep their minds on history while water was seeping into their underwear."

"If I'd walked out of the water and stood around dripping," I said, sitting down on the grass to take off my shoes, "it would have been even more distracting."

"You could have saved your swimming lesson for the very end," she said. "You could—" but I had pulled the Net chip out of my head, cutting her off. The chip was long and white, with many metal legs; cupped in my hand, it looked like some pale, crawling thing that you'd find living under a rock. Vermin. I slipped it into a pocket and began to scrape the ash off of my shoes.

✳ ✳ ✳
Anatomy of a Sale:
An Exchange of Hostages
to AvoNova

E L U K I   B E S   S H A H A R

▼

It's a typical day at the office. Yesterday's mail is still in the "In" box; another 25 unsolicited manuscripts arrive before the first cup of coffee's had time to cool. By the time one o'clock rolls around, you've fielded calls from three different agents who want to know why you haven't read their client's manuscript *now*, asked the art department where the sketches you were supposed to see for the September sf lead title are—turns out they've been lost, and you've still got to okay photocopied six copies of a manuscript to send out for quotes, express-mailed a set of proof pages to an author in Alaska who you haven't been able to reach by phone for the last two weeks (is he still alive?), and spent an hour doing a final check of a copyedited manuscript that's come back from *its* author looking like an advanced cryptography coursebook. Your afternoon is equally full, and somewhere in there you've got to make the time to go through that rapidly-increasing pile of agented and unagented manuscripts.

Welcome to the wonderful world of publishing. My name is eluki bes shahar, and for the past year I've been the assistant first to John Douglas, then Jennifer Brehl in the sf and fantasy department at Avon Books. Before that, I was (and still am) a writer; as Rosemary Edghill I've published more than two dozen books and short stories from sf to romance. I know what I like; I know what Avon likes; and I know what sells. Sometimes, when I'm lucky, all three are the same thing.

Before I started in Avon editorial, I knew the submission process from the writer's side. I could swap writer's horror stories with the best of them—manuscripts obviously not read, manuscripts held for months and even years, manuscripts that simply vanished. It was only after I got behind the Avon desk that I realized editors have their horror stories, too—the 900-page single-spaced manuscript printed out on a 9-pin printer with a weak ribbon; the beautifully laser-printed submission— double-sided in 8 pt. Times Roman with half-inch margins; and, most heartbreaking of all, the perfectly professional-looking manuscript that somehow never quite manages to "come alive."

It's a fact of life in the business of genre fiction: hook your reader with the first five pages or risk losing him entirely. The reader who picks up your book in a mall bookstore may be willing to read 50 pages to see if it "gets better"—an overworked editor looking at 50 to 70 new submissions each week can't afford to.

Does this mean you have to have a slam-bang start? Not really; some of the "near-misses" I've reluctantly rejected have contained more action in the first ten pages than all three *Star Wars* movies put together. It's hard to define in objective terms just what it is about a particular manuscript that makes an editor—and later, a reader—keep reading. I call it *magic*—a quality of confidence, of assurance that the writer knows this territory very well and is ready and willing to conduct the reader on a tour of it. Every reader is a guest in a world that the writer creates, and writers with *magic* manage to convey—along with the mechanics of plot and characterization—their delight that the reader has come to visit and their eagerness to show him a good time.

Of course craft and presentation count in every submission, but if you aren't eager to tell your story, you don't have a novel; you've got a typing exercise, and you might as well tuck it back in the drawer and step up to the plate with a different bat. Three things a working sf editor doesn't have time to do are suggest someplace else that might like your manuscript better, write you a long, detailed rejection letter pointing out areas that need work, and finish a manuscript that she doesn't think she's going to be able to buy.

It was on a day much like the one I've described at the beginning of this article that I picked up the top manuscript on my To Be Read pile and read:

Fleet Orientation Station Medical was a bleak and lifeless piece of planetesimal, and Andrej eyed its barren ocher craters sourly as his fasterthan skimmed through the yellow upper layers of its dirty atmosphere. . . .

I'd read ten pages before I reluctantly pulled myself out of the manuscript to take a closer look at the first page. Susan Matthews. No agent, or the manuscript would have come from her; no mention of previous credits. Yet, as I returned to *An Exchange of Hostages*, I realized that this was, indeed, a "magic" manuscript; one good enough to compete for—and win—my attention on an editorial workday filled with urgent distractions. I only hoped the writer could go the distance—the manuscript ran over 150,000 words; like the Kentucky Derby, a killing length for a beginner. But the start was strong, and leafing through the rest to make sure everything was in order, I realized Susan had made a number of excellent storytelling choices.

Her story was set against the sprawling background of Jurisdiction Space—our old friend, the Evil Galactic Empire. But in Susan's hands, the moral decay that had set in as the Jurisdiction's borders expanded made her galactic civilization not a monolithic backdrop for a swashbuckling adventure, but another character in the story she was telling—a character with a complex, fully-realized past and an uncertain future.

And instead of giving us an ensemble of smugglers, rogues, and other disenfranchised outsiders to scamper around its edges, Susan chose to show us the effects of Jurisdiction rule from the center of its power, through the intensely-personal story of one man, Andrej Koscuisko, a young aristocrat who has run out of options, out of time, and—as *An Exchange of Hostages* unfolds—out of defenses against an experience that is destroying both his sanity and his mind: his training as Fleet Inquisitor, holder of the feared and powerful Writ to Inquire—a gifted neurosurgeon trained by the Imperial Starfleet to torture and kill.

When I finished reading *An Exchange of Hostages* that weekend, what I saw in the manuscript was an author whose appealing style was being used to tell a story that took traditional ideas and presented them with a refreshing originality. Since she knew her fictional world was a type that would have some familiarity for the average sf reader, Susan took major chances and filled that world with complex and carefully-drawn characters facing real and difficult choices. With all these elements going

---

ELUKI BES SHAHAR is the author of books in several genres, including *Turkish Delight* (romance), *Hellflower* (sf), and *The Book of Moons* (mystery). Her latest project is *Children of the Atom*, an X-Men novel for Byron Preiss Multimedia. In 1995 she took a job at Avon Books in the science fiction department, and does freelance editing and manuscript evaluation.

for it, I knew I had a winner, and Avon agreed.

In the spring of 1997—two years to the month since I first received the manuscript—Avon Books will publish *An Exchange of Hostages* by Susan R. Matthews.

I hope you enjoy it as much as I did.

An Exchange of Hostages
SUSAN R. MATTHEWS

CHAPTER ONE

Fleet Orientation Station Medical was a bleak and lifeless piece of planetesimal, and Andrej eyed its barren ocher craters sourly as his fasterthan skimmed through the yellow upper layers of its dirty atmosphere. It had been harvest time, when he'd left his school on Mayon, and he could still almost smell the sharp bright scent of the trees in full autumnal bloom. And it was early planting, in the family's grain-fields on Azanry, but there was no grain nor any other growing things to be seen on the surface as the fasterthan made its final approach to the landing site. The gravity had already been adjusted to compensate for the local standard—Jurisdiction Standard, most closely approximating that of the systems-of-origin of the greatest number of the hominid species under Jurisdiction. He felt a little sick to his stomach, even past the stress that had kept him company since his final, ferocious—unavailing—argument with his father. It had taken him days to adjust to Jurisdiction Standard gravs, at school. Azanry was a denser world than most, and the alien Standard gravity made him nauseous, as if his stomach was moving at a different speed than the rest of his body—his vitals true to the land of his Blood and birth even when his body was far, far away. And he didn't want to be here in the first place.

Obedient to the Blood and to his birth he had come here, after breaking almost every taboo in the Book in his ultimately fruitless attempts to get his father's attention. Obedient to his birth and to the Blood he would do as his father had ordered, because there was no other way, not even when it went against every tender feeling—every instinct of justice and decency—that had set him in the road to a healer's skills in the first place. The fasterthan was slowing perceptibly, now, and he could count the dull grey featureless roofs below him as if the Center were a monstrous millipede, and every segment yet another wriggling joint. Rogubarachno was built of stone, not stalloy, and this seemed so much less hospitable for that—even if he knew what form the greeting he would get would take. He would be landing, soon. He would be met by orientation staff and fitted into uniform, would take his oath to Jurisdiction, and would set himself to learn what would be needful. He would do well; it was expected. It was required. It was demanded by the centuries and the Blood, by the words of the Book as his priestly uncle had read the service of going out from home. "Your father has stretched out his hand and raised you from the dust, therefore remember that what you will and what you wish are as dust beneath your father's foot . . ."

And when he left this place again he would be Ship's Surgeon, on board of the Jurisdiction Fleet Ship Scylla. But he did not want to be Inquisitor.

There was the smell of too much tinso in the air, and the noise levels were rather in excess of established norms. Tutor Chonis—waiting in the small staging-room, not very patiently, for his Student to arrive— suppressed an impatient twitch, studying the status-display. Another seven, and he'd be face to face with this term's problem, and they could get started. No, he reminded himself, clasping his hands behind his back to control his impulse to pace. Not this term's problem; the other of this term's two problems. Mergau Noycannir he had already met, and seen settled into quarters. More of a concession than he had ever imagined himself making, for a Student whose only excuse for being here was the Third Judge's rather scandalous reliance upon the First Secretary for support and protection. Together with consequent concessions to Secretary Verlaine's demands. At least this Koscuisko fellow had the required medical training—and quite an impressive precis, actually, from record.

And if he was just a little slow in arriving for his orientation, who was to blame him, considering what he was coming here for? The noise in the receiving area increased to a thunder of explosive power before the hushers finally engaged. They needed more maintenance than they'd been getting—all the decent engineers had been sent out to Fleet. Why brood about things that could not be changed? The Fleet had always had precedence.

Since he was not an engineer he had been unable to decipher much from the display arrayed against the wall, adjacent to the inner window. It was a smaller craft than one of the freights familiar from the frequent supply runs the Center's relative isolation necessitated; that much he could tell. Now that the display had cleared and the window's protective iris had slid away he could see the actual craft, for the first time, laboring into the maintenance-space on a slow scraping pulse of the docking jets. Raising his eyebrows—why was he surprised at all?— Chonis studied the craft. A passenger freight, and only one pod loaded into its cargo compartment, instead of the ten to twenty a passenger freight would usually hold. One pod. *What arrogance*, Chonis thought. Anybody with enough money to commission a fasterthan as a personal courier ship had too much money, and that was all there was to it. He didn't rate a personal courier, and he was among the most senior officers in all of Fleet Medical by virtue of his unique responsibilities. The Administrator didn't rate a personal courier. Fleet Captain Irshah Parmin—Student Koscuisko's future commander—didn't rate a personal courier, although a personal fighter could be pressed into service.

But the First Secretary had a personal courier, even if Student Noycannir had not arrived in it. Perhaps the two of them would turn out to be well matched, after all.

With so little cargo to unload the passenger pod would be ready to unseal within moments. Chonis turned the window off, standing in the newly darkened room for a moment while the iris spun its black whorl toward the center of the visual field beyond. Still, he had need of haste, and could not tarry. Just because Koscuisko had waited until the last possible moment to arrive . . . or possibly because Koscuisko had put off his arrival as long as could be done without charges of absence without leave . . . Chonis intended to make a point of punctuality. He was responsible for Koscuisko's development as an officer. He intended his charge to be a credit to him. He would be needing a brilliant student, to balance out the failure that Student Noycannir was all but predestined to become.

When the pod had come to rest and the atmosphere-triggered sealer membrane had cleared from the outer skin, the passenger loading gate began to slide open with a delicate sussuration, and Andrej could look through the widening gap at the station beyond. There seemed to be a man waiting for him there, revealed from waist-height to a full figure as the loading gate continued to separate along its diagonal track. A man in uniform, light grey with yellow piping, whose formal tunic with its rows of braid along the collar mocked the form and function of the surgical smock that Andrej had learned to associate with benign—if radical—intervention, ruled by a passion to help and to heal. It was the uniform of Fleet Orientation Center Medical, and the braid-rank meant that the man wearing it was a Tutor.

Andrej had studied his preliminary briefings during his transit, as much to take his mind off of his misgivings as anything else. He knew what was expected, and he could no more hope to escape from this place than talk Amberic Rhinlit into clearing him from gross lab without cleaning his work area. The way was clear and the connecting walk had engaged—bare and utilitarian, covered in a dark grey felting to prevent slippage. The boarding-treads at the embarkation site reserved for his family in port Orhalav had been carpeted in hand-knotted runners, fringed and padded, and the contrast with this was curiously enough the most depressing thing Andrej could imagine, at the moment. Action was the best response, to such sudden fits of self-pity; taking up his documents case, he hurried across the walk, stopping a polite distance from the Tutor to make his salute—a formal inclination of the upper body, much as one bowed to one's Mother—and frame his first words with care.

"I am Andrej Koscuisko."

The Tutor was eyeing him with what seemed to be a mixture of disapproval and impatience. Why did he feel like a first-year student, again, signing on to assessment net for the very first time? The perfection of the shine on the Tutor's regulation boots was intimidating.

"That is to say, Student Koscuisko, arriving for training. It is kind of you to meet me, Tutor."

There was no help for it, and he had realized how narrowly he'd shaven his report time. He would just have to suffer the consequences of having made so less than perfect a first impression as he clearly had.

"I suppose you are," the Tutor responded.

Are what? The Student Koscuisko? Confused, Andrej set down his documents case, waiting for an explanation. He didn't get one. Instead, the Tutor snapped his fingers, and another uniformed man—rather differently uniformed, and fascinating in the implications of the uniform he wore—came forward. Bowing deeply to the Tutor and to Andrej at once, the man picked up Andrej's documents case; the Tutor, turning around without another word, started walking toward a pressure-door some distance away.

What was he to do? Andrej wondered.

Follow the Tutor, the waiting stance of the other man implied. So Andrej went after the Tutor, with the other man respectfully behind— where Andrej couldn't look at him, which was a shame. The man's uniform was that of a Bond-Involuntary. A Security slave. Andrej had never met a slave, before. Slavery was illegal under Jurisdiction, except for Fleet—and the usual allowances for religious practice, of course.

Halfway across the dull metal apron of the passenger boarding dock the Tutor started to talk again. By that time Andrej had caught up, remembering—reminded by the bond-involuntary's behavior—that rank considerations required him to stay to the left and somewhat back from more senior officers.

"My name is Tutor Chonis, and since you are to be my responsibility you are permitted the use of my personal name—which is Tutor. You will speak when you are spoken to when in the presence of your Tutor. You have only a few months in which to learn everything that Fleet and your duty require of you."

It all came back to him quite easily—he had been raised on rank protocol, after all, bred and borne and nursed and weaned on privilege and propriety. He'd enjoyed his years at school, away from home, away from the excesses of formality. He'd enjoyed them too much to hope that his freedom during those years could last, whether he went to Fleet or simply home to Azanry.

"I understand, Tutor Chonis."

They were at the pressure door, going through. Another bond-involuntary was in the corridor beyond, standing quickly to attention with his back against the wall as they passed. The Tutor ignored him, and Andrej knew by that token that he should not return the offered courtesy.

"This troop is called Joslire Curran," the Tutor said, with a casual glance behind them to indicate the bond-involuntary who was carrying Andrej's documents-case. "He will be responsible for your uniform, your meals, and your exercise. You are to become accustomed to his kind while you are here. Upon completing your instruction your Security will be entirely composed of bond-involuntaries like Joslire."

If "Josline Curran" had any reaction to hearing himself so baldly categorized, Andrej did not detect it. Maybe Curran was accustomed to such treatment? Joslire Curran. That would mean the Curran Detention Facility, in Verchute sector. The Curran Prison was where Joslire had been condemned to death. Distracted by the subject, Andrej did not answer—what was there to say?—only continuing to follow the Tutor, his Tutor, down the hallway. The corridor looked grey and unfinished to the eye, functional and not one comforting fraction more than purely—coldly—brutally functional. It was hard to suppress a shiver, in this place, it looked cold, whether it was or not. And he was expected to live here, to work here, for the next eight years of his life—if not literally at Fleet Orientation Station Medical, then still in this disheartening environment. The preliminary briefing had emphasized that although the station was larger as a physical plant than a cruiserkiller, the internal architecture had been carefully constructed to provide an analog to the ship's environment. So that the Student would have a chance to grow accustomed to the isolation, the restrictions. So that the Student would feel at home when the time came to report to a cruiserkiller for duty.

The corridor widened, the walks bowing out in a gentle curve before returning back to their previous narrow severity a few eighths of a measure further on. There were banks of doors on either side of them, lining the curvature of the walls—a lift nexus. The Tutor slowed to a stop near one of the further lifts and signaled for a car.

"Now I will leave you to get settled."

It was the first good look Andrej had had at Tutor Chonis; category four hominid, of a height with Andrej, his deeply lined forehead and the generous strand of brilliantly silver hair amidst the light brown of the Tutor's moustache and beard indicating a respectable age. But the Tutor's unblinking brown eyes were searching, and did not seem to have been much pleased by their discoveries, at least insofar as Andrej was concerned. That was annoying: surely being this close to late, and rumpled from the uneasy journey, were not faults grave enough for such sour looks?

Chonis seemed to come to a decision about something. Sighing, he puffed his cheeks with air, as if expelling an unpleasant flavor from his mouth.

"You are to dine with me tonight, before the Term opens tomorrow. Curran will select the appropriate uniform. Tutor's Mess, at sixteen, and be prepared to discuss your background and your interest in the field of Judicial administration. You'll be meeting my other Student, since you will be working together with her quite a bit on the theoretical side. Understood?"

There seemed to be no room for any misunderstanding. Andrej answered with a bow—salute, here, but submission as well. As it was at home. As it was with his father. When he straightened up, however, Tutor Chonis was still regarding him with expectation, indicating that a more obvious answer was in fact required of him.

"I understand, Tutor Chonis." Not as if he should be surprised by that. Discipline depended upon the utter absence of ambiguity: as it has been at home; as it was here. Disobedient children were expected to respect the figurative rod of correction with a submissive kiss. Tardy young officers were expected to acknowledge the simplest of instructions as if they were so thick-headed that one needed to be reassured that they understood how to breathe.

"At sixteen. In the Tutor's Mess."

This seemed to soften the Tutor in some way, finally. The frown between his eyebrows relaxed fractionally, and Andrej wondered whether the Tutor might actually be smiling.

"Don't be late," Tutor Chonis said. "They're watching you, every minute, here, whether you know it or not. They're watching all of us."

The lift's doors opened; the car stood waiting. Tutor Chonis nodded a dismissal. Andrej bowed once more—better too polite than not polite enough—and went in, as the Tutor seemed to indicate that he should. He heard Curran behind him, and the doors closing; Curran must have coded in their level—but he didn't really want to turn around, not just yet. He had survived his entry, preliminary as it was, into this unnatural environment. He needed a few moments to collect himself before he faced the next step.

The Road to a First Novel

J . V .   J O N E S   &   B E T S Y   M I T C H E L L

The Editor: Betsy Mitchell
In July 1993, Warner Books hired me to revitalize its science fiction and fantasy line, where sales had been dwindling. There were almost no manuscripts in inventory—unlike at my previous publisher, where we were bought up for a year and a half ahead.

Although most large publishing houses no longer accept slush manuscripts—those submitted directly by writers, not via an agent—I was in desperate need of novels to build my line. My assistant and I plunged into a pile of manuscripts addressed to the previous editor. Most were not what we were looking for. However, the cover letter for something called *Immortal Longings* from a British writer named J.V. Jones caught our interest. It began:

> I have just completed my first novel and am seeking publication of my work. My book is aimed primarily at the substantial "speculative fiction" market, and I am aware that Warner has had considerable success in this area.
>
> My novel takes place in a medieval setting and has a Chaucerian array of characters: a scheming chancellor, an avaricious madam, a gluttonous archbishop and a queen too long barren. . . .

The Author: J.V. Jones
I wrote my cover letter with one basic criterion: Keep it short. I did not want to bore anyone with the entire plot line, or my personal résumé; instead I chose to present a brief description conveying the *flavor* of the novel, followed by a few basic facts about myself. I knew that I would

get one shot at catching Betsy Mitchell's attention, and I realized that above all, my letter would be judged on its professionalism: spelling, grammar, and the ability to get to the point.

The Editor

The well-written (and blessedly brief) cover letter drew us on. Because of the numerous duties competing for any editor's time, an editorial assistant is always first reader on slush pile manuscripts, and my assistant delved into *Immortal Longings*. In a few days it graduated to my desk, accompanied by an enthusiastic report.

Indeed, the manuscript had the spark of something new. It was written in a vigorous, cinematic style that put the reader vividly into the setting. The enormous cast of characters, even those in small background roles, was distinctively created. But the novel, even at 150,000 words, was nowhere near a finished story! Ms. Jones's cover letter had left out the important fact that *Immortal Longings* was only the first third of a trilogy.

Launching a new author with a three-book series is tricky. If anything at all goes wrong with publication of the first book—the cover artist does a mediocre job, or the novel appears in the same month as something similar by a much bigger name or one of the major bookstore chains simply doesn't order it for whatever reason—then the second and third books stand even less of a chance, since their advance orders will depend on the sales of Book 1. Still, Ms. Jones showed strong potential, and I was loathe to dismiss *Immortal Longings*. I requested an outline of the complete series.

The Author

From the start, I knew it would be difficult to sell an editor the idea of a trilogy from an unpublished writer. With that in mind, I decided to lessen my odds by not mentioning it in my cover letter. It was a risk, but I was banking on the idea that either Ms. Mitchell would like my work well enough to pursue it further, or, finding it wholly unsuitable, not read it past the first 20 pages and never discover that the novel was the first of three.

When Ms. Mitchell called and asked for the complete outline of the series, naturally I was thrilled. However, up until that point, I had only the bare bones of the plot committed to paper. I worked on the outline for several days, changing, revising and expanding, and then faxed it to Warner to see what she thought. As with the original query letter, I tried to ensure that the document had a clean, businesslike tone, but this time I added something extra: a few sentences stating my willingness to be flexible and work with Ms. Mitchell to make the series stronger.

The Editor

Julie Jones's outline posed almost more problems than it solved. The story promised plenty of action, romance and magic, but after three long books, several major plot lines were left unresolved, and another important plot line ended with the death of a major sympathetic character, leaving his lifelong mission unfinished. Ms. Jones was suffering from what I privately call "British disease"—the tendency for many British authors to write with a dark, depressing slant. American audiences want uplifting, happy endings. Would she be willing to revise not just her outline, but much of the emotional feel of her trilogy, still with no promise of a contract? I sent my suggestions in a three-page, single-spaced letter.

The Author

Betsy is right about us Brits—we hate a happy ending. One high school semester my official reading list was *Hamlet, Tess of the d'Urbervilles* and *Brideshead Revisited*. Not a happy ending among them! Depressing tendencies of the English aside, as soon as I read her fax I saw she had raised several important points: Not only did the series need a more upbeat ending, but it also needed a greater sense of closure. In the original outline I left the fate of a major character dangling and some subplots unresolved. Betsy urged me to rework the outline, paying special attention to the buildup of the story line, strengthening the role of the leading character and, as she put it, "answering all the questions." Sound advice has a clear ring to it, and my ears responded to the call.

From my point of view, this was a good chance to work with a professional editor—someone with the practical experience needed to know what it takes to capture and keep a reader's interest. I didn't look on the situation as having to revise the outline without a contract, but rather an opportunity to receive the benefit of Betsy's editorial expertise for free.

There followed a series of faxes, where we not only worked together to fine-tune the outline, but went into detail discussing potential changes to Book 1. My priorities during this exchange were first, to demonstrate my ability to both take, and work from, constructive criticism; and second, to appear professional at all times. If this was a test, then I was determined not to lose points for bad presentation or inflexibility.

The Editor

The time had come! Julie Jones had proven herself willing to revise her original concept and very capable of doing so, as her imaginative responses to my suggestions clearly showed. I made her an offer for the trilogy, discussing all aspects of the contract just as I would with an agent, and the paperwork was drawn up. The usual periods of first-deal billing and cooing ensued. Then a long letter of comment regarding Julie's manuscript went off to England. But now she could start her revision with the promise of an on-signing payment close at hand.

The Author

By the time I received Betsy's rewrite suggestions, I was raring to go. Her throughts were laid out in a precise, page-by-page format that I found easy to work from. A pattern quickly emerged from Betsy's numerous recommendations and proposals: Lose the fat. Anything that was extraneous or self-indulgent had to go. It was a learning experience for me; not only did I emerge better equipped to look at my work more objectively, but also with a valuable insight into the editorial process.

What I found most rewarding about the rewrite was the way Betsy's suggestions prompted me to come up with some wonderful new material for the book. We added a prophecy that immediately became central to the whole story line, provided a tragic background for a central character and fleshed out areas that required more explanation. By the time the rewrite was finished, Book 1 had emerged as a stronger piece of fiction.

During this time, if I ever got a little burnt out with working all day and then coming home to write all night, I just reminded myself how lucky I was to actually have a publishing deal. Before I sent my manuscript to Warner, I sent it to two publishing houses and a handful of agents, all of whom politely rejected my work. If anything, it was the fear of being on the receiving end of more of these bleak, discouraging letters that kept me going. Yes, Warner was asking a lot of me, but at least they were *asking*!

The hardest thing about the rewrite was having to cut scenes that *I* really liked, but that Betsy judged unnecessary to the plot. My one sex scene, which I had lovingly giggled over many a time, had to be cut. This was quite a blow to me and I had to learn how to bite both my tongue *and* the bullet at the same time.

The Editor

Because Warner's publishing schedule is drawn up a solid year in advance, even before the author returned her signed contract to Warner, it was already time to write cover copy for the novel! The first-draft manuscript went to Mark Arnold, a copywriter with years of experience in science fiction and fantasy. Julie's story captivated him—but also gave him much cause for comment. In a rather long letter to me, he communicated his concerns about various plot points. And since several of them raised topics that I had not discussed with the author, I passed the letter on to her.

The Author

I was by the fax machine when this one came in. Half an hour later it was still coming. To say that it was long is like saying that the bubonic plague killed a few people! I was due to go out that night, but stayed in instead. Mark Arnold proved to be stimulating company.

Basically, his fax challenged me to take a fresh look at my plot, with a view to tightening my grip on it. He pointed out that it would be a shame to leave certain characters along the wayside in Book 1, and suggested ways I could reintroduce them in later volumes to benefit the series as a whole. He went on to give lots of helpful advice about settings and form, and pointed out several areas that would benefit from further consideration.

I was grateful for his counsel, and promptly revised the series outline, keeping his comments about plot in mind. Once again I was in the fortunate position of receiving expert advice, and I readily agreed to an expanded rewrite of Book 1. The extra work wasn't important; making the manuscript the best that it could be was what counted.

The Editor

Many authors might have balked at receiving so many comments from an "unofficial" source. The wise author will recognize helpful advice wherever it comes from. If Julie had refused to incorporate Mark Arnold's suggestions into her revised manuscript, I would have wondered how serious she was about her writing career.

On the other hand, she did stick up for herself when she felt strongly enough that something shouldn't be changed. I tried to push her into concluding one too many subplots with a happy ending. Julie pointed out that her characters were busy enough already; how could I expect them to clear up *all* the problems of her fantasy world simultaneously? This answer I respected; editors recognize good reasoning when we hear it, too.

By the way, it doesn't behoove an editor to ignore sound observations simply because he or she didn't think think of them. Editing is an imperfect and subjective art. If we expect 50,000 or so people to buy a book that we put out, certainly more than one pair of eyes can be useful in editing it!

Now we had just one final challenge: to find a strong title. *Immortal Longings* sounded to me like a romance, not an epic fantasy. If possible, a title should be memorable and communicate the type of story that it names. We needed something that promised a mysterious prophecy at work in a magical world. Even Julie's original title would have to be edited.

The Author

I liked my title a lot. I took it from *Anthony and Cleopatra*, the first Shakespeare play I ever read, and I remember it with a sort of fuzzy, pubescent fondness. Of all the changes that Betsy proposed, this was the most difficult to accept. For years I had carried my title around in my head, keeping it safe until I was ready to write my first book. I suppose that was the problem: No matter what I wrote—be it mystery, high-tech thriller or a car-maintenance manual—it was going to be called *Immortal Longings*.

Betsy rightly pointed out that this sounded like a "romantic bodice-ripper," not a fantasy novel, and so, with my newly acquired oral skill of biting tongue and bullet simultaneously, combined with enough sense to realize that Betsy knows the best way to target her market, I agreed to her suggestion of *The Baker's Boy*. We settled on The Book of Words as the overall trilogy title.

Traveler's Advice

Says J.V. Jones: "My advice to first-time writers is to be prepared to work *with* an editor. Never love your manuscript so much that you're unwilling to make changes. And always put your best foot forward. A little luck goes a long way, but a professional attitude will take you further."

Says Betsy Mitchell: "Julie was lucky in that her manuscript was on my desk when I needed to buy—and there will always be editors in that situation. But *don't* rely on luck: Read *Publishers Weekly* and *Writer's Digest* for news of book lines being started; editors changing houses; special projects needed. Subscribe to newsletters that specialize in your area of the field. When the big chance arises, act like the professional writer you'd like to be. If Julie hadn't proved willing to make the many, many changes her manuscript needed, it would have stayed unsold."

J.V. JONES's first two Book of Words novels, *The Baker's Boy* and *A Man Betrayed*, were released by Warner Aspect in 1996. British rights have been sold to Orbit Books. BETSY MITCHELL is editor-in-chief of Warner Books' science fiction/fantasy/horror line, Aspect. She previously worked at Baen Books and Bantam Spectra, where she edited such bestsellers as William Gibson's *Virtual Light* and Timothy Zahn's Star Wars trilogy. She received a World Fantasy Award in 1994 for co-editing the original anthology *Full Spectrum 4.*

✳ ✳ ✳
First Sales

I n this section, you'll meet four authors who recently published their first novels. They hail from Florida, Ohio, California and even Manchester, England. Their novels have equally diverse settings—a nanotechnology-warped Cincinnati, a post-apocalypse America, a surreal future California and a drug-induced virtual reality in Manchester. Their characters, writing habits and paths to publications also differ.

In fact, these writers have very few things in common, except they all started out (like everyone else) making mistakes, fighting frustration and pressing on despite the odds. They made it.

So can you.

Kathleen Ann Goonan
Queen City Jazz

"When I started writing *Queen City Jazz*," says Kathleen Ann Goonan, "I thought it was going to be another short story, because that's what I had been writing." Instead, she says, the story turned into a novella and the novella slowly became a full-blown novel.

Goonan's protagonist is a young Shaker woman who leaves her family and travels to nearby Cincinnati to save her lover's life. Once in the city, however, she quickly becomes involved in a battle against the "nan" which has turned Cincinnati into a surreal setting filled with long-dead jazz stars and giant bees. In order to survive, she must infiltrate the bee's hive and alter the nan's program, a task she finds may destroy her anyway.

"It was sort of the nexus of everything I was thinking about at the time, and it all came together as I was out running one day. I was running quite a bit and I found that as I ran, I would use that time to help clarify things in my stories that were problematic. So that day I saw this building with a huge flower on the top, and that suggested giant bees to me. And I'd been reading Drexler's work on nanotechnology, so all that suddenly fell together."

Still, it would be some while before the idea became the novel. "When I was through with the novella, I realized that it wasn't finished. I actually threw that particular version away several times before I finally got really started on it." That first section did accomplish one thing, however—it got her an agent. Virginia Kidd took Goonan on as a client based on the strength of that first section and the fact that Goonan had published several short stories.

Although Goonan knew much about nanotechnology, she had to research the other elements in the book. "I ended up reading a lot about bees and flowers; how bees communicate, how they see the world, how they polarize the sun with their vision—all of these things. I did extensive research on Shakers and the Shaker community around Dayton and Lebanon, Ohio. And I researched Cincinnati and jazz, of course." Goonan has what she describes as a "platonic" method of researching, usually gathering information as she goes along. "As I write, I also am reading and trying to learn more about what is going into what I'm working on. I feel like it's my job to make the story I'm writing more real. The research and the reading that I do kind of stimulate these different elements that have been kicking around and help them to coalesce."

Goonan describes her background as that of a "typical writer," spending her teenage years filling up "big stacks of notebooks" with poetry but rarely sending any of it out. "I received an English degree in college and I decided I needed a profession while I was learning how to write. So I got a Montessori certification and started a Montessori school in Knoxville, Tennessee, with a partner," she says. The school grew quickly, however, and began taking up 50 or 60 hours of her time per week. "I really loved it. For a while, I started thinking that writing was too distant a goal. But it was always in the back of my mind, so when I was 33, I suddenly started writing again and this time I was writing prose. I wrote a novel in a year. I never sold it and I don't even send it out anymore, but I wrote it. I would get up early and write and come home at lunch and write and I would write on the weekends. And after that was over, I started writing short stories and sending them out to the science fiction magazines."

Goonan says she started writing science fiction because she majored in philosophy at Virginia Tech. "I mostly studied classical literature for my English degree," she says, "But I also got enough hours to get a major in philosophy. And philosophy is kind of the discipline of putting yourself outside of what's going on and trying to look at it in a way that's almost alien. What I like about science fiction is the ability to create worlds which you think about as critically as a philosopher thinks about this world." Every philosopher has his own way of looking at this world, Goonan says, but each one has a different theory about how everything in this world works. "I think that led to my interest in science fiction. When I started writing, I wrote from that kind of basis—as a philosopher, examining one strange thing about life or another."

Goonan used to belong to a writer's group in Washington, D.C., but couldn't find any writers in her area when she moved to her current Florida home. Nevertheless, she feels writer's groups are invaluable and still sends her short stories to her D.C. group for long-distance critique. "You can't just sit and write by yourself and send things off to an editor and get all your feedback from them," Goonan says. "At some point, it's a very important step to be in a writer's group and have that feedback. It's painful at first, and you think, 'Well, they just don't understand what I'm doing.' And that's probably true, but it's because you need to improve your writing skills so that what you hear coming back from them is what you intended. It's like a mirror. You don't know if you're accomplishing what you set out to accomplish, and editors don't have time to give you that information. That was the biggest revelation to me. I had this picture of a writer sitting completely isolated and writing and sending stuff out. It may happen that way for some people, but I think to become part of a community of writers is a really important step."

Goonan now writes fulltime and has finished two more novels— *The Bones of Time*, set in near-future Hawaii, and *Mississippi Blues*, the sequel to *Queen City Jazz*. *Crescent City Rhapsody* will be the third book in that trilogy.

Goonan says the only reason she can write fulltime is because her husband has supported her since she left her business. "He said, 'You've always wanted to be a writer and you're really not writing. You're working really hard in your spare time, so why don't you just quit and try writing full time?" And so she did, but not without a few regrets. "I wish I would have known how long it would take to actually make money doing this. I didn't really have a clear idea of what it would take. If I had known, then I would have kept my business and rearranged it somewhat, so that I would have more time to write and still be able to make money while I was doing it." But Goonan persevered. "I felt that I could be successful, and I think that one of the elements of almost everyone who becomes a writer is that they believe they will be successful. That's one of the things you really need, whether or not it's realistic. To go out and try to do this and be rejected hundreds of times, you have to have the kind of mind set that is able to withstand that."

Jonathan Lethem

Gun, With Occasional Music

"I'm not certain everything I write is science fiction," says Jonathan Lethem, author of *Gun, With Occasional Music*. "I know that everything I write has other influences mixed in and that comes from my mixed reading habits growing up. When I was discovering fiction for adults, I was voraciously reading tons and tons of sf, tons and tons of hardboiled mysteries and all sorts of literary fiction all at the same time. I never made hard distinctions between these categories; for me, it was all stuff I liked. The only thing I was certain of was that the stuff I liked best and that excited me the most, was the weirdest."

His affinity for the literature of the strange has had a definite impact on his work. *Gun, With Occasional Music*, for example, is set in a world filled with bio-engineered talking kangaroos, hyper-intelligent children known as "babyheads" and legal drugs such as Forgetall. Lethem's hero is a hardboiled private eye who must solve a murder mystery before his karma runs out and he's literally "put on ice"—in cryogenic suspension.

Nominated for a Nebula Award in 1994, *Gun* received much critical acclaim in the speculative fiction field. "In a funny way," Lethem says, "it was a book that I wrote because there was a lot of talk in sf at that point about hardboiled detective fiction. William Gibson had just been a huge success with *Neuromancer* and people were talking about what Gibson might have imported from Raymond Chandler. I felt there was a deep intrinsic quality in the classic hardboiled voice that hadn't been imported yet, or had been imported in very goofball, satirical ways." Lethem says he became excited with the idea of applying the classic detective voice to a science fiction scenario. "Chandler's detective is already a man out of time. He's a tarnished knight from an earlier era walking around in what's essentially a dystopian future. The contemporary California that Chandler was writing about struck him as an amoral society, so his detective was a throwback. I took something that was under the surface of Chandler's works and made it extremely literal. Almost comically literal. I took a Chandleresque detective and put him in and out-and-out Orwellian dystopia. And that's what I do in general. Many of my ideas have to do with taking things that are already lurking under the surface of things and making them comically literal."

Lethem hesitates to call his work science fiction, however, because it is not based much in real science. "I tend to think that if I were writing in another language and being translated into English, my work might be regarded as magic realism. It certainly isn't very scientific in the classic sf sense. I draw my metaphors, my bizarre imagery and my pool of iconography and motifs very much from American sf and from living in a technological society. I am writing more in reaction to other science fiction than I am writing in reaction to scientific developments in the real world. I bought the ticket for a while that I was supposed to keep up with contemporary science and supposed to write things that in some way made a nod to scientific accuracy. But as my real interest in writing emerged and clarified, that became a sillier and sillier mismatch for me. It didn't really have anything to do with what I wanted to do."

Lethem does research, but it is not usually in the sense one thinks of as research. "I deliberately provoke responses in myself with film and fiction influences. I reread novels and I review movies, sometimes obsessively, to catch narrative flavors that I'm looking to reproduce. Apart from few token investigations into bits and pieces of nonfiction information that I need, almost all of my research is reading other novelists and viewing films. For example, I have a book in progress right now that's a response in many ways to John Ford, the American filmmaker, and his Westerns. Specifically *The Searchers* and *The Man Who Shot Liberty Valance*. I'm two thirds of the way through this book and I've already watched *The Searchers* seven or eight times, and I wouldn't be surprised if I'll have seen it 12 or 15 times in a two-year period before I'm finished."

Lethem says he is very conscious of his influences, even if the reader is not. His second book, *Amnesia Moon*, he says was influenced by Philip K. Dick, Steve Erikson, Jack Kerouac, R. Crumb and J.G. Ballard. Other reviewers have compared Lethem's work to that of Harlan Ellison and Jim Thompson, which Lethem finds complimentary, but somewhat inaccurate. "It may not be inaccurate from a reader's perspective, but those are not people I was holding consciously in mind or that I see traces of in the book myself, in terms of my own influences." But Lethem does agree with another reviewer, who says *Amnesia Moon* smacks of Dr. Seuss and says Seuss is even more of an influence on his third book, *As She Climbed Across the Table*.

Beside a few side jobs—teaching a writing class once a week and "doing a cyber-journalism gig" for *HotWired* (an online version of *Wired* magazine)—Lethem writes fulltime. "I try to look at it as very much a regular job, and I get up early every morning and get right to it. It always seems to me that the best energy is available first thing in the morning. It's not impossible to write later in the day, but it often seems to me there's this natural progression where other events begin to trickle in. The phone begins to ring, the mail comes and your mind begins to connect to the shallower stratum of activity. Most often I'm writing real first draft material in the morning and doing other author-related activities in the afternoon. And, of course, the phone often becomes a big part of my work day, and I'm starting to talk to people and by the end of the day I'm impatient to see some people and have a life. Every day is a sort of progression from the solitary, Zen-like workspace into the world of people."

Part of that world of people includes Lethem's writer's group. "The main purpose of the writers group is that it's just one of the things I do that cuts the isolation of the writer's profession. We're a social gathering, we're a sewing circle, and that part of our function is more important to me ultimately than the feedback on my manuscripts. I could revise my work on my own and generally get the results that I wanted, but it's very important to find ways to see other people, especially when you're writing fulltime and you're not in any other kind of workplace environment." Lethem says he attends sf conventions for the same reason.

Lethem says that, looking back, he wishes he had valued his earlier writing days a bit more. "It took me a long time to break in and all the time I was obsessed with breaking in. After I did, I realized that I was looking back nostalgically at the relation I had to my writing when there wasn't any audience and there wasn't any editor, when it was just me and my burning ambition and the blank page. There was something pure and wonderful about that time, and it will never be exactly like that again. It doesn't mean that I would ever want to give up the rewards that have come from finding an audience, but I wish I'd known to value that effort and that time for itself."

As a successful writer and a writing teacher, Lethem advises beginners to finish what they start and then move on. "I think you learn much more and you grow much more by writing another story than you do by revising the same one again and again and again. Sometimes I see young writers trying to perfect a given piece or being wedded to a first novel and tenaciously revising it. Close the door on that project, put it out on the market and start another one. It's a little bit magical, but there are leaps you make just by moving on to the next project that you can never make no matter how hard you rework the one before."

Jeff Noon
Vurt

"It was like a release of energy from my head," says Jeff Noon, award-winning author of *Vurt*. "An explosion onto the screen. That's how *Vurt* came about, really." *Vurt* was an explosion in the field of speculative fiction, as well, earning Noon both the John W. Campbell Award for Best New Writer and the Arthur C. Clarke Award for Best Science Fiction Novel of 1994.

Vurt is the story of Scribble, a young Manchester man desperately trying to get his sister back from a virtual reality/alternate dimension called "the Vurt." The Vurt is accessed by feathers laced with nanotechnology programs, and Scribble's sister was lost when she and Scribble experimented with an illegal yellow feather. Now he must find another similar feather in order to get her back.

"It's actually a very simple story, if you look at it in its basics," Noon says. "It's got a lot to do with the Orpheus myth. It's a quest; it's a romance; it's a love story. It's all of that and it's also very weird on top of that. But underneath, at the core, you've got this very powerful, very old story which has been around since the Greeks started writing their plays."

It's no surprise that Noon's work is influenced by plays; he is a playwright himself. In 1984, he graduated college with a Bachelor's degree in painting and drama. "I decided to concentrate on one thing, and I chose playwriting because I was excited by it and I found it quite difficult. Music and painting seem to come easy to me, but writing I really found a challenge." Noon says he gave himself a year or two to see what developed from his playwriting, involving himself with the fringe theater scene in Manchester. While he was doing this, he entered his play, *Woundings*, in a contest sponsored by the Royal Exchange Theatre, Manchester's largest theatre. It won, earning Noon the position of writer-in-residence at the Royal Exchange. "I survived on the money from that for about three years, during which time I started to write a second play and various other projects. And I didn't have any success at all. Nobody wanted it, and I started to feel despondent. I carried on and I kept writing, but I didn't have any success. So I ran out of money and I was on an unemployment benefit for a number of years, still writing, still trying to get people interested in putting the plays on."

With the money running out, Noon took a job at Waterstone's Book Shop in Manchester and found himself working with a friend from his fringe theater days. "We spent five years in the shop, plotting our escape and never quite managing it," Noon jokes. "And then one day, he came up to me and said, 'I'm going to start my own publishing company. Write me a novel.' I really hadn't thought about writing a novel before, but I went home that night and started writing." For Noon, it was a new experience in writing. "I used to plan my plays very, very carefully, but this time I didn't do anything. I just turned the computer on and wrote. And the first page of *Vurt* came out more or less as it is now." He enjoyed the process and let the story develop on its own as it went along. "I changed bits here and there to make sure it made some kind of sense, but I really wasn't too worried about that. I was just excited by the ideas and the style of the writing. It seemed like all the mad ideas that I hadn't been able to use in plays suddenly started coming out. The main idea I had in my head was to do something about virtual reality. By that time, virtual reality had more or less been done anyway. But I thought, 'I don't think it's been quite drained yet of ideas, so I'll have a go.' I made up the word 'vurt' because it was short for 'virtual reality.' I thought I would come up with a great name for it later on, but I didn't and it stuck."

Just as he didn't plan the writing of the book, he didn't really expect it to sell, either. "I'd been working in a book shop for five years, so I'd seen thousands and thousands of books come and vanish. So I had no illusions and I wasn't bothered if nobody bought it. If nobody reads it, fair enough, but it's there; I've done it and I can be proud of that. It's not that way with plays. Plays are blueprints; they don't exist until they've been put on."

WRITE SCIENCE FICTION THAT'S OUT OF THIS WORLD

with help from these Writer's Digest Books!

The NEW Science Fiction Writing Series gives you the knowledge you need to make your fiction read like fact!

Aliens and Alien Societies
by Stanley Schmidt

Gain a better understanding of extraterrestrial life to develop viable creatures and cultures using this fascinating reference. You'll have science on your side as you uncover the secrets of biochemistry, engineering and space travel. Plus, you'll learn to portray aliens as individuals, true to their species. #10469/$17.99/240 pages

World-Building
by Stephen L. Gillett

Write fiction that transports readers from this world to another...of your making. You'll mix elements and build planets with chemically credible and geologically accurate characteristics as you uncover a myriad of topics including facts on gravity, atmospheric science, star types and much more! #10470/$16.99/224 pages/14 b&w illus.

The Craft of Writing Science Fiction That Sells
by Ben Bova

Fascinate audiences (and attract editors) with imaginative, "unearthly" science fiction. Bova shows you how to create your own universe using the major elements of strong science fiction storytelling. Then he gives you dozens of marketing hints to help your sales soar! #10395/$16.99/224 pages

Turn Over for More Great Books!

☐ **Yes!** I want to write science fiction that's out of this world! Please send me the following books:

Book # _____ Price $_____

Book # _____ Price $_____

Book # _____ Price $_____

Book # _____ Price $_____

Subtotal $_____

*Add $3.50 postage and handling for one book; $1.00 for each additional book.

Postage and handling $_____

Payment must accompany order. Ohioans add 6% sales tax.

Total $_____

VISA/MasterCard orders call TOLL-FREE 1-800-289-0963

☐ Payment enclosed $_____ (or)

Charge my: ☐ Visa ☐ MasterCard Exp._____

Account # _____

Signature _____

Name _____

Address _____

City_____ State _____ Zip _____

Phone Number _____
(will be used only if we must contact you regarding this order.)

30-Day Money Back Guarantee on every book you buy!

☐ **FREE CATALOG.** Ask your bookstore about other fine Writer's Digest Books, or mail this card today for a complete catalog.

Mail to:

Writer's Digest Books
1507 Dana Avenue
Cincinnati, OH 45207

6894

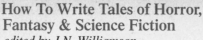

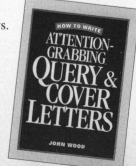
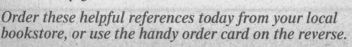

Noon says it wasn't a conscious choice to write science fiction, and he really never read much sf growing up. He discovered J.G. Ballard's *The Atrocity Exhibition* when he was 20, and quickly became "totally obsessed" by Ballard for years, reading everything that author had written. "The interesting thing about him is that he's been working for years, writing novels about Britain," Noon says. "But nobody reviewed them, none of the big papers touched them, didn't even know he existed. And then as soon as he wrote a realistic book about his childhood, *Empire of the Sun*, everyone discovered him. He's been writing these novels—brilliant books—for years! That's what happens to science fiction writers, you see. They get hidden."

Writing, Noon says, is a solitary occupation. "I think that my view on it is that writing is a lonely thing. And this can get you down. At the moment, it gets me down, because I've been two and a half years in my room, writing, and I want to get out again and work with people."

Noon's writing day typically begins at eleven in the morning and finishes about three in the afternoon, with occasional sessions at night. "Because I wrote *Vurt* while I was working at the bookshop, I wrote it completely at night. So if I'm writing at night, I'll start again around eleven, and finish at two or three in the morning. I do my best work at night."

When he is writing, Noon says he must have his guard up against the "bad voice" of criticism. "There are two voices talking to you when you're a writer. One voice is the perfect reader. This reader is intelligent; he gets everything—every single idea, every single image, the lot. And he's saying to me, 'God, Jeff, this is great, I love this. Brilliant sentence! Yes!' Any other time, you've got this voice that's in the other ear saying, 'Oh, God, that is so boring. Why are you bothering? Why don't you get a real job?' So it's like this constant battle, and one day one voice is more powerful and the next day the other's more powerful. There's no way you can predict which it is. I think that when you get the bad voice, you just have to write a few sentences and wait. Just write crap and go back. You can always go back and change crap. As long as something's down on the paper, you can do something with it. But if you're just staring at the blank screen, nothing's going to happen."

One of the ways he combats the bad voice is to stay excited about what he is writing. "A novel is 300 pages of manuscript, and that's a hell of a lot. That was the main fear I had, that it was going to be too long, that I was going to run out of energy. I think what you have to do is become excited by it. You have to actually want to write the next sentence because you can't stop writing. The way I do it is very scatter-shot; I'm just firing words down at the page and seeing what happens. If you do something like that, I think it's quite easy to keep the excitement going because you're not really sure what's going to come out next. Sometimes you write really embarrassing sentences, but they excite you because they're weird and strange.

"The other thing I'm doing is that I'm constantly thinking all the time, coming up with new ideas. Because when you reach page 100, say, of the manuscript, you're starting to think about what's going to happen on page 150, and then 200. And by the time you reach 200, you're thinking 'Ah, now I've got to start thinking of an ending and it's got to be really good.' Once you come up with a great ending, you can move towards it. You've got to set yourself goals. By page 50, this has got to happen. And it's got to be something good, that you really want to get to, that you really want to enjoy writing."

Noon says he tries to keep one thing in mind while he writes. "What I'm trying to do, basically, is amaze myself with what I'm coming up with. If I do that, then there's a chance that the somebody else somewhere will be amazed as well. So the reaction I'm looking for most of all is 'How the hell did he come up with that?' "

Ron Sarti

The Chronicles of Scar

While "quitting their day job" is probably the last thing first novelist Ron Sarti would advise aspiring writers to do in pursuit of their craft, it worked for him.

But then Sarti, who sold his first novel, *The Chronicles of Scar*, after a ten-year hiatus from writing fiction, is not your typical slush to sale story. "Writing is a very *uncertain* livelihood," he says wryly. "It's what I had always thought I wanted to do. I can remember writing stories and journal entries when I was seven years old and knew even then that I'd like to be a fiction writer."

However, after several discouraging sorties into the field of short fiction publishing years ago ("After receiving little or no response to my work, I retreated, bleeding, from the field.") Sarti was prompted to put down his pen and discover more "acceptable" career pursuits. He found them and has enjoyed reasonable success for the past two decades.

If it weren't for a nagging voice inside Sarti, that might have been the end of it. "Every couple of years or so the little voice would urge, 'Try . . . Try!' " says Sarti. Yet more time went by, the voice still unheeded. "Until a few years ago—I think I was 45 at the time—the voice said something else: 'Last chance . . . Last chance!' It scared me to death."

Dusting off the beginnings of a manuscript that he had put away more than a decade before, Sarti took the plunge. He quit his administrative job at an area university and began writing fulltime. "I talked to my wife," Sarti says with a smile. "She had a good job and the mortgage was paid."

Several months and 180,000 words later, *The Chronicles of Scar* was born. "I immediately sent out a proposal with three sample chapters and waited," recalls Sarti. "I continued to write, though. I had many more ideas to explore within the world I had created." After all, you can hardly expect a chronicle to be contained in one slim volume.

About five months later, Sarti received some encouraging words from the publisher. "At first there was some concern over the length. Thoughts that it might be too long and complicated, but it was an overall good response. So I chopped it down, revised, compressed and, I hope, enriched the book."

Another few months went by, Sarti received another promising letter, but still no sale. "They were still interested, but they had a full schedule and wanted to hang onto the manuscript for a while." Not wanting to be caught in this sort of publishing purgatory, an anxious Sarti thought he'd better seek professional help. He found himself an agent. "I had taken it as far as I could on my own. I thought an agent might be able to speed up the process."

Sarti secured the service of Donald Maass, an agent he had learned of at a local science fiction convention. Within two months, his manuscript was sold—albeit to a different publisher, AvoNova, the science fiction/fantasy imprint of Avon Books. "Don just snatched up the manuscript and peddled it around to some of his industry contacts. He opened doors that I didn't even know existed."

Sarti describes his first novel, *The Chronicles of Scar*, as speculative fiction. "Technically, it's science fiction. Nothing that happens within the story is scientifically impossible—improbable science perhaps, like the science in *Jurassic Park*, but theoretically possible. However, it's being marketed as a fantasy, because it reads like an epic fantasy. There are no elves or dwarves, but neither are there ray guns or rocket ships." Set 600 years in the future in the feudal post-apocalyptic American Midwest, it relates the story of a young boy's rise from "gutter rat" to royalty. "It is essentially a novel of coming of age in a future setting with solid characters and a touch of humor," says Sarti.

The idea for the novel is something Sarti had carried with him for a long time. Its very first incarnation appeared in a college writing class—a short story about a boy on the streets in pseudo-medieval society and a case of mistaken identity. "As time went by, it just kind of evolved," says Sarti. "Time goes on and ideas come together in the creative process. I didn't always know where it was going, and some of the things that happened surprised me." Before he knew it, Sarti had the outline for a novel. "Even after I was unable to find the time to continue to write," says Sarti, "the story stayed with me and was waiting when I went back to it ten years later."

Of his decision to write fulltime, Sarti is fatalistic. "It was just something I had to do," he says. "I was afraid of getting old and looking back over the years and thinking I didn't really give my writing a chance. If I tried and failed, I could live with that. But to not even try . . ."

Though successful, the route Sarti took, even by his own estimation, is extreme. "You have to be very careful if you're going to decide to do this fulltime. You have to have a secure income. You should be out of debt and have money in the bank. Perhaps most essentially, though, you need the support of your family.

"Even if you sell your manuscript most publishing novelists don't make enough to pay the bills. You're not going to get rich by publishing. That's lightning striking. For most of us it will take years in the making just to have an adequate salary."

Rather, Sarti suggests that it might be better to take a more conservative approach—put an hour or two aside to write at least four or five nights a week. If you are diligent, you should have the better part of a manuscript at the end of a year or so. Is it a slow process? Yes. But much more advisable than quitting your job and leaping into it full blown.

"Do an honest assessment of your skills," says Sarti. "Are you in love with writing or just the idea of being a writer? Also, can you work alone, and are you self-disciplined? A writer can always find an excuse for not writing. But you have to overcome the excuses. Write, rewrite and revise. *The Chronicles of Scar* went through at least 20 drafts because I had to learn my craft. Thank goodness for word processors."

But most importantly, Sarti says, "Don't get discouraged. Don't give up. After talent, perseverance is most important. In combination, they can't be denied."

SECTION VII

RESOURCES

Online Resources

Almost everything the speculative fiction writer needs is online—reference and research material, publishers, agents, writer's groups and more. You can search the **World Wide Web**; you can **FTP**; you can **e-mail** and **chat** and post to **special interest group (SIG)** bulletin boards. And you can do it all 24 hours every day!

"Surfing the Net" can cut your research time in half, but beware—you are in dangerous waters. Without a measure of self-discipline, you can quickly find yourself online all the time, with little interest in pursuing your own writing. Spend time with people already on the Net and you'll hear them talk about staying up until the wee hours of the morning exploring the Web or playing "Doom" with their pal in Madagascar. It may sound ridiculous to you now, but wait until you're out there. The Net can be addictive.

Finding the balance between cutting your research time and wasting your writing time isn't easy, but it helps if you know a few starting points. To that end, we've put together the following overview of popular Internet resources. It is not intended to be complete, nor could it be, given the incredibly dynamic nature of the medium. The Net is in a constant state of flux—as witnessed in the rapid growth of the World Wide Web.

The World Wide Web

Two years ago, hardly anyone had even heard of the Web. Today, it's a household word with millions of people accessing it around the globe. The reason the Web has become so popular is that it basically does for the Internet what Windows and the Macintosh do for personal computers: It allows users to forgo the keyboard and use the mouse instead. Just as Windows creates an environment filled with graphic icons on which users can "point and click" to run programs (instead of typing out commands), so the Web uses **hypertext** to access information on the Net. In other words, the Web allows users to get immediate information on highlighted words or ideas by merely pointing and clicking on them.

If, for example, this were a hypertext document on your screen, you could select any of the **boldface** terms and that term's definition would appear. Since this isn't hypertext, you have to go to the "Tackling the Terminology" sidebar or the glossary.

While this seems a rather mild concept, think of it when applied to a global network such as the Internet. Visit a **webpage** for nanotechnology and you might see a digital photo of the IBM logo next to text about contemporary nanotech research. Click on that photo, and it may give you the story behind it—how IBM was able to write its logo in letters no bigger than a few molecules. Or it may take you to the IBM nanotechnology team's webpage, to find out about their latest breakthrough. It doesn't matter that the IBM team is in Seattle and you're in Florida; you can access that information almost instantly.

Finding this information is relatively easy. However you choose to access the Web, either through an **Internet Service Provider** (such as AT&T Worldnet or NetCom), an **Online Service Provider** (America Online, CompuServe, etc.) or some other way, you'll be using a Web **browser**. Two of the most popular browsers are Netscape Navigator and Microsoft Internet Explorer and both of them enable you to access **search engines**—a program that allows you to type in a word or a set of words which the engine then tries to find a match for on the Web. To use our earlier example, if you type in "nanotechnology," the search engine might return a list of 50 or so "hits," or web pages in which it found some mention of nanotechnology. Of those 50, however, only five or six may be of use.

Why the huge waste-to-use ratio? Put simply, there's a lot of noise on the Net. It's simple to create a webpage and many people do it just for kicks. It's these people who create most of the noise by mentioning your topic (in this case, "nanotechnology") in their list of interests or such.

To cut down on the amount of useless hits you get, try entering more than one keyword. If you're looking for just the medical uses of nanotechnology, type in "medical" and "nanotechnology." You'll still get some noise, but if you're lucky, it won't be that much.

There are webpages for libraries, universities, NASA, publishers, magazines and much more. Here are a few webpages of interest, to get you started. Remember, this is just a small taste of what's out there; we couldn't possibly list every website of interest. (Note: Web addresses, unlike e-mail addresses, must be typed in exactly as you see them, with the capital letters, tildes, etc.)

http://www.greyware.com/sfwa/ The webpage for the Science Fiction & Fantasy Writers of America. All you ever wanted to know about SFWA, including the most recent Nebula Award winners, membership policies and news.

http://www.horror.org/HWA/ The Horror Writers of America web page. Similar to the SFWA page, this has information about HWA, it's members and other horror industry-related news.

http://www.nasa.gov/hgpao/roadmap.htm This page is a "road map" to the NASA webpage. It includes a welcome from NASA Administrator Daniel Goldin, "Today @ NASA," links to other NASA pages and other data.

http://www.nanothinc.com/ The Nanothinc webpage. Nanothinc is "an Internet-based publisher/developer/distributor" dedicated to organizing "a well-defined community of scientists, researchers, educators, consumers, buyers and sellers in order to empower a wide range of informed, value-added transactions" of nanotechnology-based products and services. Annoyingly slow to access, but provides a lot of information on the topic.

http://www.contrib.andrew.cmu.edu/~shawn/occult A very informative, A-to-Z listing of occult topics.

http://mud.bsd.uchicago.edu/~mohanraj/balist.html "Alternative Sexualities in Fantasy & SF Book List" Visually uninteresting, but very good information here.

http://www.omnimag.com *Omni Online* magazine. Like the now-defunct newsstand version, this page has fiction, science articles, science updates and more.

http://www.greyware.com/authors/LWE/realm.htm The webpage for *Deathrealm* magazine. Find out what's in the next issue, read the editor's comments, and send e-mail to the magazine from this page.

http://www.wickedmystic.com/ *Wicked Mystic* magazine's webpage. Information on the magazine, submission guidelines, author photos and bios and some of the best animation and graphics anywhere. This is one cool webpage.

http://w3.gwis.com/~prlg The DarkEcho webpage. This online newsletter is primarily directed at horror writers, but has information and market news of interest to fantasy and sf writers, as well.

http://www.wizards.com Wizards of the Coast webpage. Information on their *Magic: The Gathering* games and books, plus other products.

http://users.aol.com/marketlist This online database of sf/f/h markets is updated monthly.

You can also use the Web as a promotional tool. Several authors have created and maintain their own webpage, so that their fans can keep up on where their next short story will be published and when the next novel is coming out. Author pages often have some background information on the author, notes to the author's fans, information about the author's fan club, dates of book signings and convention appearances and other such data. If you want to get some ideas for your own webpage, check out these authors' pages:

http://jvj.com (J.V. Jones)
http://www.en.com/users/mcq (Maureen F. McHugh)
http://www.winternet.com/~joelr (Joel Rosenberg)

The World Wide Web continues to change and by the time you read this there will certainly be new additions to, and uses for, this popular Internet resource. Check it out.

The Web is by no means the first nor the final way of finding information on the Net. It's popularity has partially eclipsed some of the older resources, but those resources still remain valid and are especially useful to you if you have an older, non-Windows or non-Macintosh machine. Let's take a brief look at other uses for the Internet.

Online Service Providers (OSP)

Even if you don't use an OSP, you probably know some names: America Online, CompuServe, Delphi, GEnie, the Microsoft Network, Prodigy, etc. Unlike ISPs, which provide only a connection to the Internet, OSPs also provide content. Typically, an OSP will offer bulletin boards, chat rooms (the Net's version of a conference call), home shopping, news and weather updates, online games, reference services, Web access and more.

The biggest OSP boons for the writer are the bulletin boards and chat rooms. Bulletin boards allow you to read and respond to other people's messages at your leisure. Chat rooms allow you to hold online meetings with other users of the same OSP. Many writers use chat rooms for weekly writer's group meetings. Delphi and GEnie are especially popular among the big name writers for this type of activity, but the other OSPs have sf and fantasy chats, too.

Beyond bulletin boards and chats, another major OSP bonus is e-mail. You don't have belong to an OSP to get an e-mail account, but OSP accounts are usually faster and more reliable than other accounts.

Electronic Mail

Electronic mail, or "e-mail," is probably the most common use of the Internet. Even more people use e-mail than the Web. Parents communicate with their kids in college, sisters communicate with brothers on the other side of the world, business people exchange information with their clients and outlying offices.

From a writer's perspective, e-mail can be useful in many ways. You can exchange your work with other writers for critique, contact experts with research questions, submit queries to magazines and book publishers (if they prefer it) and tap into some of the other resources listed later.

E-mail addresses have become as common as phone and fax numbers. It's a happy medium between a phone call and a letter; you can choose and edit what you say (and talk as long as you want) and still get it there as fast as—and cheaper than—a phone call. Especially if whom you're e-mailing lives in Guam.

FTP

File Transfer Protocol, or FTP, is a way you can retrieve files from other computers on the Net. You can use FTP with just an e-mail account to download software, graphics, sound files, video clips and just about everything else. Some OSPs have made FTP easier by putting the most popular sites on a hypertext "hot list" so you can just point and click. Other OSPs and ISPs allow you to access FTP clients, which act almost as a browser for popular FTP sites.

Normally, however, you must send a message to the FTP site from your e-mail account, requesting the file you wish to download. The host computer then e-mails the file to you. This can take anywhere from a minute to a day or two, and the file arrives compressed into a smaller file. Like adding water to dehydrated milk, you must uncompress the file before you can use it. Usually, the instructions for uncompressing the file come with the compressed file.

Mailing Lists

While mailing lists have fallen somewhat out of favor, they still can be a valuable tool for the writer. In essence, a mailing list is like the letters to the editor page of your favorite magazine. You subscribe to the list and the host computer, or "listserver," begins sending you all the mail that other members of the list generate. It also sends your messages to all the other members. For example, joining a fantasy writer's list will involve you in an on-going e-mail discussion of fantasy writing. Ostensibly, the only mail you get from that listserver will be mail from people interested in fantasy writing.

We say "ostensibly" because one of the main drawbacks of mailing lists is noise. Arguments begin, discussions get off topic, list members start having personal discussions on the list instead of in private e-mail and without careful management by the host, the list can snowball into a daily mountain of useless information. Many users have unsubscribed from lists because they began receiving hundreds of useless messages *per day*.

When they work, mailing lists are wonderful ways to keep abreast of the latest news on a topic, exchange ideas and even get quick feedback on your work.

Usenet Newsgroups

Newsgroups aren't really news, and why they're called newsgroups is one of the Net's many mysteries. Newsgroups *are* somewhat the reverse of mailing lists, in that you must go to them, rather than their delivering the messages right to you.

Newsgroups are like the bulletin boards of the OSPs, except with a larger contributor base. Thousands of people might read and contribute to a newsgroup, depending on the topic.

Broken down by subject, newsgroups can range from the silly and frivolous (**alt.startrek.wesley-crusher.die.die.die**) to the useful and interesting (**alt.science.nanotech.tech**). You can access newsgroups from almost any type of account, depending on your software.

Practice Safe Surfing

As we noted earlier, these are dangerous waters. No doubt you've already heard about computer viruses. Remember that anything you download from another computer could be infected, so get a good virus checking program and use it constantly.

Also, take care when downloading the more "alternative" things you might find on the Net. Unfortunately, it is becoming all too common for average citizens to have their personal computers seized by the police in the name of "community values."

Although these cautions may seem out of place in an article on online research, remember that you'll do little writing and no online research with a crashed or confiscated computer.

Go Forth and Surf

With caution and self-discipline, the Internet can be a valuable and fun tool for research and promotion. Great friendships have formed over the Net, some of them resulting in marriage. Business contacts have been made. Careers have been boosted.

The possibilities are as vast as the Net itself. Come on in, the water's fine!

TACKLING THE TERMINOLOGY

E-mail—Electronic mail. Mail generated on a computer and delivered over a computer network to a specific individual or group of individuals. To sent or receive e-mail, a user must have an account, which provides an e-mail address and electronic mailbox. Such accounts can be set up through online service providers.

Hypertext—Words or groups of words in an electronic document that are linked to other text, such as a definition or a related document. Hypertext can also be linked to illustrations.

Internet—A worldwide network of computers that offers access to a wide variety of electronic resources.

Internet Service Provider (ISP)—Computer network accessed via modem. These services provide users with direct access to the Internet, but do not create or maintain content, as do the online service providers. ISP users have e-mail and access to the World Wide Web and other online resources.

Message board—An area of an online service provider where users can read and respond to messages left by other users.

Modem—MOdulator/DEModulator. A computer device used to send data from one computer to another via a telephone line.

Newsgroups—Message boards defined by topic and accessible via the Internet. Newsgroups are not part of a service provider, but can be accessed from one.

Online Service Provider (OSP)—Computer network accessed via modem. These services provide users with various resources, such as e-mail, news, weather, special interest groups and home shopping. Examples of such providers include America Online and CompuServe.

Special Interest Group (SIG)—A collection of message boards all geared to a related topic. A science fiction SIG might include message boards for sf book reviews, general discussion, Star Trek discussion, etc.

World Wide Web (WWW)—An Internet resource that utilizes hypertext to access information. It also supports formatted text, illustrations and sounds, depending on the user's computer capabilities.

—Richard Muskopf

✳ ✳ ✳

Organizations

▼ f you're finding it a little lonely out there behind your keyboard, maybe
these fiction writer's groups will help. All are devoted in one way or
another to science fiction, fantasy and/or horror. Each offers varying
levels of service and support for members, ranging from information on
markets and conventions to sponsoring awards and handling grievance
procedures. Most important, they offer the opportunity for contact with
your peers. Annual membership costs vary by organization and membership level, but are generally in the $25-$75 range.

Organizations are listed here alphabetically.

GARDEN STATE HORROR WRITERS

ADDRESS: P.O. Box 178, Beverly NJ 08010

CONTACT: Dina Leacock, President

PROFILE: Garden State Horror Writers is a multigenre association whose
aim is to produce publishable material from its members. Scope is not
limited to the East Coast. Members are entitled to attend workshops
and lectures sponsored by the organization, a critiquing service—in-
house or by mail—and a monthly newsletter called *Graveline*. There
are two level of memberships: Regular ($30/year) and Associate ($20/
year). Associate members receive no voting rights on organization
issues. Local members meet the second Saturday of each month at the
Manalapan Library on Symmes Road in Manalapan, NJ.

THE GENRE WRITER'S ASSOCIATION (FORMERLY SMALL PRESS GENRE ASSOCIATION)

ADDRESS: Dark Regions Press, P.O. Box 6301, Concord CA 94524

CONTACT: Joe Morey or Bobbi Sinha-Morey

PROFILE: The Genre Writer's Association has replaced the Small Press

Genre Association, but has kept the same membership. The organization's primary focus remains science fiction, fantasy and horror, but its scope has expanded to include writers and artists who work in the mystery and western genres as well. Membership is open to anyone working in these areas in the pro/semi-pro/small press.

Dues are $25 per year for members from the U.S. and Canada, and $30 (U.S.) for members located in other countries. Membership is between $200 and $300. The group publishes a biannual tabloid called *The Genre Writer's News* which publishes fiction, market news, interviews and articles on writing genre fiction; and a biannual "Market News Supplement." Sample copy available for $3. In alternate months members will receive *Horror: The News Magazine of the Horror & Fantasy Field* (see listing in **Nofiction Magazines/Publications of Interest** section). The group also sometimes sponsors contests or awards.

HORROR WRITERS OF AMERICA (HWA)

ADDRESS: P.O. Box 423, Oak Forest IL 60452
E-MAIL: hwa@horror.org
WEBSITE: http://www.horror.org/HWA/
CONTACT: Robert Weinberg, Vice President
PROFILE: HWA is dedicated to writers of dark fantasy and horror. Active members must have sold at least three short stories or one novel to a commercial publisher; associate membership is available for writers with an interest in the field. Membership benefits include access to HWA's resource library, members-only anthologies, grievance committee, etc. HWA also publishes a bimonthly newsletter and presents the Bram Stoker Award for outstanding work in the horror/dark fantasy field (see listing in **Contest** section). Membership fees are $55 per year.

NATIONAL FANTASY FAN FEDERATION (N3F)

ADDRESS: 1920 Division St., Murphysboro IL 62966-2320
CONTACT: William T. Center
PROFILE: This is primarily a correspondence organization for fans of all aspects of fantasy and science fiction. Features numerous bureaus with different interests and focuses: a writer's exchange, reviews, critiques,

amateur press alliance, costuming, comics, etc. N3F sponsors a short story contest annually (see listing in **Contest** section). Publishes *The National Fantasy Fan*, the club 'zine, and *Tightbeam*, the letterzine, each coming out in alternate months. Dues are $18 per year. Write for more information.

SCIENCE-FICTION AND FANTASY WRITERS OF AMERICA, INC. (SFWA)

ADDRESS: 5 Winding Brook Drive, #1B, Guilderland NY 12084
PHONE: (518)869-5361
CONTACT: Peter D. Pautz, Executive Secretary
PROFILE: This is the professional organization for writers of science fiction and fantasy. Two levels of membership—active and affiliate. One novel or three short story sales are required for active membership; one story sale qualifies a writer for affiliate membership. They publish *SFWA Forum* ("Insider's" newsletter for active members only) and *Bulletin* (for all members, or by subscription). SFWA has a grievance committee and other services and presents Nebula Awards for outstanding science fiction and fantasy. There are over 1,200 members. Membership fees vary.

SCIENCE FICTION POETRY ASSOCIATION (SFPA)

ADDRESS: 6075 Bellevue Dr., North Olmsted OH 44070
CONTACT: John Nichols, Secretary/Treasurer
PROFILE: The Science Fiction Poetry Association is a group of more than 200 poets interested in all aspects of poetry in sf, fantasy, horror and related genres. They publish a bimonthly newsletter, sponsor awards, and publish an anthology of award-winning work (see listing for *Star* Line: Newsletter of the SFPA* in the **Nonfiction Magazines/Publications of Interest** section).

SCIENCE FICTION RESEARCH ASSOCIATION (SFRA)

ADDRESS: 6354 Brooks Blvd., Mentor OH 44060
PHONE: (216)257-3646
E-MAIL: joesanders@aol.com
CONTACT: Joe Sanders, President

PROFILE: Founded in 1970, the SFRA was organized to improve classroom teaching, encourage and assist scholarship, and evaluate and publicize new books and magazines dealing with fantastic literature and film. Among the membership are people from many countries—authors, editors, publishers, librarians, students, teachers and other interested readers. Academic affiliation is not a requirement.

Memberships are available at a variety of levels: individual, joint, student, institution and emeritus. Membership benefits include subscriptions to two journals, *Extrapolation* and *Science Fiction Studies* (both listed in the **Nonfiction Magazines/Publications of Interest** section), and the *SFRA Review*, a newsletter, as well as participation in organization-sponsored activities, such as an annual SFRA conference. Fee: Individual membership $60 (U.S.), $65 (Canada), $70 (overseas); Joint $70 (U.S.), $75 (Canada), $80 (overseas); Student $50 (U.S.), $55, (Canada), $60 (overseas); Institution $80 (U.S.), $80 (Canada), $80 (overseas); Emeritus $30 (U.S.), $35 (Canada), $40 (overseas).

SCIENCE FICTION WRITERS OF EARTH

ADDRESS: P.O. Box 121193, Fort Worth TX 76121
PHONE: (817)451-8674
CONTACT: Gilbert Gordon Reis
PROFILE: The Science Fiction Writers of Earth was established to promote the art of the short story in science fiction and fantasy writing. The only criteria for membership consideration is a short story submission to the organization's annual contest. (See listing in the **Contest** section.) $5 covers membership and first story entry fee. The organization welcomes international participation from English-speaking countries (England, Australia and Canada all participated in 1996).

SF CANDA

ADDRESS: Wordworks Society, 11759 Groat Rd, 2nd Floor, Edmonton, Alberta T5M 3K6 Canada
CONTACT: Diane L. Walton, Secretary-Treasurer
PROFILE: SF Canada is open to any Canadian writer (citizen or landed immigrant) who has had at least one piece of speculative fiction professionally published. Other Canadians with a substantial professional

interest in speculative writing will be considered for membership on an individual case basis. SF Canada's goals are: to foster a sense of community among Canadian sf writers; to improve communication between Canadian sf writers; to lobby on behalf of sf writers in Canada; to foster the growth of quality writing in Canadian sf; to encourage the bilingual translation of Canadian sf; and to promote positive social action. Membership fees are $25 (Canadian) per year.

SF Canada also publishes a bimonthly newsletter entitled *Communiqué*, which is available for subscription to nonmembers. Its companion piece, *Top Secret*, is sent only to SF Canada members.

✳ ✳ ✳
Conventions

PATRICK SOUHAN

T he first World Science Fiction Convention was held in 1939. About 300 people attended. For the time, that total was considered astronomical. Last year, more than 15,000 fans and professionals from the fields of science fiction and fantasy consorted at Dragon*Con in Atlanta, the site of the North American Science Fiction Convention, to celebrate a vital and vibrant sf culture. After almost 60 years, the scene is going stronger than ever.

From the beginning, conventions (often called "cons") were conceived as a social weekend for the professionals that compose the field—the authors, artists and editors—to hobnob with the fans during various programs throughout the day and other social functions after hours.

Over the years the culture has changed, but the driving idea has remained the same. Heinlein, Asimov and Clarke, today considered the old masters of the science fiction field, were the guests at those first conventions, and the people who read them in the old pulp magazines were the fans who attended. Today the genre has broadened and branched out in so many different directions—from cyberpunk to magic realism; contemporary fantasy to sociological science fiction—that there is no typical fan. Many conventions, especially the larger ones, try to address this diversity and feature a little bit for everyone in the programming. But some conventions are specifically geared to a particular subgenre or even author (e.g., Discworld Con is devoted exclusively to British author Terry Pratchett and his Discworld Universe).

Most conventions follow a particular format. Almost all feature a guest or guests of honor, usually an established sf or fantasy writer. Much of the programming will then revolve around that author's work. Other guests will usually include artists, editors and even fans. Throughout the convention there will also be numerous standing exhibits, art shows, dealers' rooms, books, mags, film, video—the whole galaxy of science fiction and fantasy culture.

Lectures, workshops and panel discussions constitute the bulk of the programming and can often be most informative and beneficial to aspiring writers. In these programs, science fiction professionals answer questions, share their experiences or speak on issues that impact the field as whole.

There's no need to worry about approaching the assorted professionals in attendance. "It's a very open forum," says Patrick Nielsen Hayden, avid convention-goer and senior editor at Tor Books. "In general, the atmosphere is very laid back. Most everyone is approachable. Just be pleasant and low-key—that will serve you far better than being obnoxious and pushy."

As a whole, the science fiction community is very fan-friendly. "It's not like so many other fields where there's this 'groundlings-hoping-to-catch-a-glimpse-of-the-celebrity-on-the-stage' mentality," says Nielsen Hayden. Fans and authors relax and interact in a social setting. By necessity, most of the established professionals were once fans, too (and they still are).

However, just because the ambience is so familiar and convivial, don't expect to push manuscripts off on unsuspecting editors, agents or writers—no matter how brilliant you suspect your work to be or how eager you are for professional criticism. This is a cardinal sin. "I do like to meet writers, published and unpublished, but I don't necessarily want to see their manuscripts," says Nielsen Hayden. "I have enough things to remember to take back with me without having to worry about additional manuscripts."

If an editor asks to see your manuscript, it's a whole new ball game. But don't count on that happening. More likely than not, dozens of would-be writers, manuscripts in hand, will clamor for the attention of one of the editors or agents present. Instead, impress the experts by acting professional and showing them courtesy.

But don't necessarily leave that manuscript at home. As mentioned earlier, many conventions feature some sort of workshop programming. The workshop is conducted by one or more well-known sf or fantasy authors, and may include critiques, lectures or panel discussions. It is always best to check with the programming board of the given convention to learn the specifics of a workshop.

Writers that have perhaps one or two books under their belts often use conventions to promote a new book or to solidify their position in the marketplace. Some currently well-established writers such as Robert Lynn Asprin, Marion Zimmer Bradley, Katherine Kurtz and Glen Cook, were frequent travelers on the convention circuit at some point during their careers.

While conventions might not be a market for your unpublished novel, they can still serve as important tools for aspiring authors looking for an edge. New writers can get a feel for the culture of the science fiction community. They can get an idea of what's hot and what's not; where things are going and what's happening in the field. Who's publishing what or who. They can even make contact with specific editors, authors and agents. And just talking with fellow fans can be informative. Swap experiences and exchange market information. Every little bit helps. Network. Establish contacts. Gain a deeper knowledge of the field. Attend programs, panels and lectures. But most of all relax and have a good time. That's what conventions are for.

For More Information

Through the 1960s, there were probably only a couple dozen general science fiction conventions. But then with the giant leaps being made by NASA in space exploration and the success of *Star Trek*, interest in science fiction conventions and the field as a whole took off. Today, almost every major city or region hosts a science fiction and fantasy convention. Hardly a weekend (most conventions are held Friday-Sunday) goes by without at least two or three conventions vying for the attention of fans. Keeping track of all of them is not simple.

A number of sources provide information about upcoming conventions. The foremost is *Science Fiction Convention Register*, a magazine tracking more than 600 conventions across the United States and abroad. "I was missing too many conventions," says Erwin S. Strauss, publisher of the *Register* and long-time science fiction fan. "I figured if I put out a list everybody would make sure I heard about their conventions." See listing on page 468 for more about the *Science Fiction Convention Register*.

Many nonfiction and some short fiction sf publications also carry convention listings. *Locus* and *Science Fiction Chronicle* are two of the best sources; a couple times a year each will feature an expanded convention coverage. Short fiction magazines like *Asimov's*, *Analog* and *Science Fiction Age* may also be helpful.

Writer's groups and other science fiction organizations can also provide convention information. You can often find listings in the organizational newsletter or by contacting the group directly. See the **Organizations** section.

Most of these listings should be able to give you everything you need to know: dates, locations, guests that will be in attendance, associated costs. Within each listing there should also be a specific contact name or address you can write to request more information.

Major National and International Conventions

Each year, thousands of attendees flock to large regional conventions in Chicago (WindyCon), Philadelphia (PhilCon), Los Angeles (L.A.Con) and other major cities. But the largest and most significant of the science fiction and fantasy conventions are the annual World Science Fiction Convention (WorldCon) and the World Fantasy Convention. These are the gala events of the science fiction and fantasy fields. They draw the brightest stars of the science fiction universe, and some of the sf community's most prestigious awards are presented. The location of these conventions vary from year to year, but the following listings should keep you updated:

1997

March 28-31 • **INTERVENTION/48TH BRITISH NATIONAL SF CONVENTION**

Adelphi Hotel, Liverpool, UK. **Guests of Honor:** Brian Aldiss, Octavia E. Butler, David Langford. **Fee:** 20£ attending; 10£ supporting. **Contact:** Wincon, 12 Crowsbury Close, Emsworth Hants PO10 7TS UK (checks payable to Wincon). **E-mail:** intervention@pompey.demon.co.uk

September 3-7 • **LONESTARCON/55TH WORLD SF CONVENTION**

Convention Center, Marriott Rivercenter and Riverwalk Hotels, San Antonio TX. **Guests of Honor:** Algis Budrys, Michael Moorcock. **Fee:** $95 attending; $25 supporting. **Contact:** LoneStarCon 2, P.O. Box 27277, Austin TX 78755-2277. **E-mail:** lsc2@io.com

October 30-November 2 • **23RD WORLD FANTASY CONVENTION**

International Hotel, London Docklands, UK. **Guests of Honor:** Joan Aiken, Bob Eggleton. **MC:** Robert Holdstock. **Fee:** $120 attending; $50 supporting. **Contact:** World Fantasy Convention, Box 31, Whitby, North Yorks YO22 4YL UK

1998

August 5-9 • BUCCONEER/56TH WORLD SF CONVENTION

Convention Center, downtown hotels, Baltimore MD. **Guests of Honor:** C.J. Cherryh, Stanley Schmidt. **Toast Master:** Charles Sheffield. **Fee:** $80 attending; $30 supporting. **Contact:** Bucconeer, Box 3124, Annapolis Junction MD 20701. **E-mail:** baltimore98@access.digex.net **Website:** http://www.access.digex.net/~balt98

Workshops

Writing workshops are not for everybody, but the writers who have participated in them say they offer a unique and invaluable experience. Unlike conventions in which the main focus is on meeting others in the field, the focus of workshops is primarily on the work at hand—the writing. Workshops are long, intensive writing and critiquing sessions. The work is hard and the tuition is high, but many writers say the rewards—better writing skills, an improved manuscript, the opportunity to work with some of the best writers and editors in the field, increased chances for publication and professional contacts—are often worth the effort and expense.

In the science fiction field, there are only a few very structured workshops devoted to the genre. These typically last two to six weeks, with each week's session led by a different established author. It's not easy to get into these programs—the cost can be high and writers must be selected for participation. Typically, they are asked to submit a body of work (some short stories or novel chapters) for approval. Since room in these workshops is limited, the directors select writers to participate based on the promise of their material and the seriousness of their intent.

Writers work on either the material they submitted or on other works in progress, depending on the writer's and the instructor's preferences. Each week is led by a different instructor, so writers get the benefit of working with a different established science fiction pro each week. Often writers critique each other's work in the morning and read work and write in the afternoons and evenings. On weekends there may be free time (usually taken up by more writing) and special guest speakers, events or panels.

Tuition can be more than $1,000 (including the cost of accommodations), but most have some scholarships available. Workshops are often taught at a local college campus, and participants stay in a nearby dorm.

In addition, there are often shorter and less-intensive writing workshops offered at sf conventions. Check convention listings and write the current secretary or director to get the details. These workshops usually run the same time as the convention and, therefore, cost much less and generally run a few days to a week. Still, writers are expected to be prepared to work on their writing. Instructors are established authors or editors who may be speaking at the convention as well.

Most of the commercial online services also offer general fiction and science fiction workshops. See **Online Resources** on page 417 for more information. There are also a few retreat-type writing weekends offered irregularly by groups of established authors. Information about these is primarily by word of mouth. The best way to learn about these is to listen for information at conventions and watch for announcements in trade magazines, newsletters or on electronic bulletin boards. Some general writing conventions have conducted science fiction writing workshops as well. To find out more about these conventions, see the **Conferences and Workshops** section of *Novel & Short Story Writer's Market* (Writer's Digest Books).

A list of the major science fiction workshops follows. Each listing includes a profile of the workshop—how it operates, what is expected from writers attending, recent instructors and accommodation information. Keep in mind some or all of the instructors change each year. We've followed the profile with information on how to contact the workshop, including what to submit and deadlines for submission. Lastly, we've listed the fees for 1996. Tuition and accommodation costs will vary each year, so write for updated cost information and guidelines before you submit.

CLARION

CONTACT: Mary Sheridan, Administrative Coordinator

PROFILE: Clarion is the oldest, most established intensive science fiction workshop. It was started in Clarion, Pennsylvania, in 1967 and moved to Michigan State University in 1972. Each workshop lasts six weeks, starting in June and running into July. This workshop has featured several hundred of the top science fiction authors and editors as workshop instructors, including such writers as Damon Knight, Kate Wilhelm, Samuel R. Delany, Tim Powers, Octavia Butler, Joe Haldeman, Nancy Kress, Kim Stanley Robinson and Connie Willis. Application manuscripts are evaluated by a panel of past and present writers in residence. There is only room for 15-20 participants, so the competition to get in is keen. In fact, the review committee ranks applications into three groups—accepted, alternate and keep trying.

Once accepted, writers begin an intensive six-week-long workshop. During the first week, they may work on the material they submitted or on new material depending on their and the instructor's wishes. Generally, each week the writers work with a different instructor in a classroom situation. Participants develop new work throughout the workshop which is submitted, copied, handed to others in the class and critiqued. This may be a structured process, or the instructor may plan special lectures or assignments. Typically, the organizers say, participants end up working on their writing eight or more hours each day.

Weekends sometimes feature guest lecturers or panels. Participants stay in a graduate hall (private rooms) on the Michigan State University campus. College credit is available.

HOW TO CONTACT: Writers must submit an application with an application fee of $25 and two manuscripts, usually short stories, but part of a novel may be acceptable—in total the submission should be 15-25 pages long. The application/submission deadline is April 1. Send SASE first for details and an application.

COSTS: In addition to the $25 application fee, costs, based on 1996 figures, are $800 for tuition, a $100 nonrefundable acceptance fee, and about $800 for housing. Some scholarships are available.

ADDRESS: Lyman Briggs School, Michigan State University, East Lansing MI 48825-1107

PHONE: (517)355-9598

CLARION WEST

CONTACT: David Myers, Administrator

PROFILE: Clarion West, while not affiliated with Clarion, is modeled after the original workshop. "The idea behind this workshop is for students to completely immerse themselves in writing for six weeks," says David Myers, one of the administrators of the program. The workshops are sponsored by a nonprofit group and run by volunteers, often alumni of the program and Seattle-area science fiction writers.

Like Clarion, the workshops run for six weeks. The workshop is held around the third week of June through the end of July. Classes are taught by a different group of instructors each year, all established authors in the field. Recent instructors have included Nancy Kress, Lisa Goldstein, Elizabeth Hand, Michael Swanwick, Beth Meacham, Tappan King and Joe Haldeman.

Applications and submissions are subject to the review process and there 20 slots available each year. Workshops are held on the South Central Community College campus in Seattle, and participants stay in the dorms there. Usually, says Myers, the participants meet for three or four hours in the morning to critique work and then read others' works and work on their own writing in the afternoon and evening. Weekends are left unstructured, he says, but most writers end up using the time to write. College credit is available.

HOW TO CONTACT: Send SASE for the appropriate forms first. Applications should include 20-30 pages of original work (either short stories or a novel excerpt), typed and double-spaced, and a $25 application fee. Include a cover letter outlining your reasons for wanting to attend the workshop, and, if you are applying for a scholarship, send scholarship application forms at that time.

COSTS: In addition to the $25 application fee, the tuition is $1,300, not including dorm costs. Some scholarships are available. The application and submission deadline is April 1.

ADDRESS: 340 Fifteenth Ave. E., Suite 350, Seattle WA 98112
PHONE: (206)322-9083

ODYSSEY

CONTACT: Jeanne Cavelos, Director
PROFILE: Odyssey is a newer summer writing workshop for writers of fantasy, science fiction and horror to be held annually on the campus of New Hampshire College in Manchester, New Hampshire. Running for six weeks, from mid-June to late-July, the workshop combines intensive learning and writing experience with in-depth feedback on students' manuscripts. Odyssey is for developing writers who want to put aside all their other concerns for six weeks and focus solely on their writing, says workshop creator Jeanne Cavelos, former senior editor at Dell Publishing and winner of the World Fantasy Award. Odyssey will provide a supportive, yet challenging, energizing envi-

ronment for authors.

Class meets for three hours in the morning, five days a weeks. Students use the afternoons and evenings to write and read each other's work. While Cavelos is the primary instructor, guest lecturers teach once a week to add their own unique perspectives. Past lecturers have included: Jane Yolen, Hal Clement, Elizabeth Hand and Ellen Kushner.

Because enrollment is limited to 20 students, applications are subject to a review process. Students are housed at the nearby Inn at Amoskeag Falls. A free shuttle provides transportation between the inn and the campus. College credit is available.

HOW TO CONTACT: Send SASE for further information and an application. Writers must submit a $20 application fee with the application and a writing sample of approximately 10 pages. Application deadline is April 1 annually.

COSTS: Tuition is $980, housing is $270 for a double room, $701 for a single room. Food can be purchased through a debit card.

ADDRESS: 20 Levesque Lane, Mont Vernon NH 03057

PHONE/FAX: (603)673-6234

SCIENCE FICTION AND FANTASY WORKSHOP

CONTACT: Kathleen D. Woodbury, Director

PROFILE: The Science Fiction and Fantasy Workshop is actually an organization with 400 members. It was created, says Director Kathleen Woodbury, for sf and fantasy writers who are unable to attend one of the big, intensive workshops, but who would like the hands-on workshop experience. "Basically, we're a workshop by mail," she says.

Members may be "active" or "inactive," but active members are put on the membership roster. That roster is made available to all members. Members are also provided with a list of the various critique groups and the names of contact people for each group. There are several groups, each with a specific topic or subject of interest. For example, if a writer would like to join a group that is critiquing short short science fiction stories, he or she would write the contact person for that critique group. The contact would then make available the roster of people involved in that group, and the writer would contact at least three people on this list to exchange and critique manuscripts.

"This way," explains Woodbury, "the member gets six learning experiences—three critiques of their work and the experience of critiquing the work of three other people."

Members communicate (and announce new critique groups forming) through the organization's newsletter. The SFFW also produces a number of helpful publications available through subscriptions. *Promises, Promises* is a booklet produced irregularly containing one short story and critiques of that story by three professional writers. A subscription for five issues costs $5. *Outlines, Synopsis and Proposals That Sold* is a quarterly publication featuring book proposal packages from books that have been sold. Books come from both established authors, such as Mike Resnick or Judith Tarr, and from first-time authors. The cost is $9 for a one-year subscription.

HOW TO CONTACT: Write for details. You may subscribe to the monthly newsletter, *SF and Fantasy Workshop*, for $15 per year without becoming a member.

COSTS: The cost of membership is a one-time $5 fee that is used to cover the cost of the roster and new member packet plus $15 for the newsletter. After this, membership is automatically renewed when members resubscribe to the newsletter.

ADDRESS: 1193 South 1900 East, Salt Lake City UT 84108

PHONE: (801)582-2090

THE WRITERS WORKSHOP IN SCIENCE FICTION

CONTACT: James Gunn, Director

PROFILE: The Writers Workshop in Science Fiction is sponsored by the University of Kansas's J. Wayne and Elsie M. Gunn Center for the Study of Science Fiction and is held in conjunction with the Center's summer Intensive English Institute on the Teaching of Science Fiction program.

The workshop is held before the program and lasts two weeks. In 1995 the dates were July 1 through July 14, but these vary each year. Like the longer workshops, admission into this workshop is by application and review of a writing submission. The workshop is led by James Gunn from the Center and usually features a guest writer and editor who participate in the last few days of the conference. In 1994 the guests were Frederik Pohl and an sf editor from Pocket Books.

Participation is limited to 12 writers. As with other intensive work-shops, the participants work on the material they have submitted with their applications and on other works in progress (they critique three short stories or a novel excerpt). Work is critiqued in a classroom setting, and writers spend part of the day reading others' work and writing.

HOW TO CONTACT: Send a manuscript "of professional appearance," 1 short story or a novel chapter and a letter of application (check with Gunn for details). The deadline for application/ submission is June 1.

COSTS: Tuition is $400; accommodations are in the dorms. In 1995 the dorm cost was $12 a night for double occupancy and $20 a night for single occupancy.

ADDRESS: English Department, University of Kansas, Lawrence KS 66045

✳ ✳ ✳
Contests

The contests and awards listed in this section offer science fiction and fantasy writers an array of opportunities. Some are very prestigious and can lead to national and international recognition and increased sales for an author's work. Others give new writers publication experience and exposure. Some even offer cash awards from $25 to $10,000.

For new writers in particular, contests and awards cannot only lead to first publication, but they can also help you to get feedback on your work and make important contacts in the field. Recognition from your peers may give you a step up on the publishing competition by bringing your work to editors' attention.

While we have listed several of the larger and more well-known contests, this is not a complete list. Many contest programs are operated by those who put on conventions. For more on these, contact the current convention director. Information on these is available in science fiction trade magazines such as *Locus* and *Science Fiction Chronicle*.

To help you target those contests appropriate to your work, at the start of each listing, we've indicated what the award is for—short stories, novels, novellas, novelettes—and whether it is for works of science fiction, fantasy or both. We've also included whether it is open to published or unpublished work and how often the award is given.

A brief description follows that may include the philosophy or purpose behind the award. It also includes the sponsors of the award and what the prize or award is. If there is more than one level of award, such as first, second and third prizes, that information appears in the description as well. We've listed the judges, if they are known, and how work is nominated or selected.

In "How to Enter," we've told you submission requirements and how you may find out more information. Entry fees, if any, are listed here and, most importantly, the entry deadline.

If you can submit your own work to a contest or awards program, be sure to follow the guidelines carefully. Send a SASE for additional contest

There are seven **Writer's Digest School** courses to help you write better and sell more:

Novel Writing Workshop. A professional novelist helps you iron out your plot, develop your main characters, write the background for your novel, and complete the opening scene and a summary of your novel's complete story. You'll even identify potential publishers and write a query letter.

Nonfiction Book Workshop. You'll work with your mentor to create a book proposal that you can send directly to a publisher. You'll develop and refine your book idea, write a chapter-by-chapter outline of your subject, line up your sources of information, write sample chapters, and complete your query letter.

Writing & Selling Short Stories. Learn the basics of writing/selling short stories: plotting, characterization, dialogue, theme, conflict, and other elements of a marketable short story. Course includes writing assignments and one complete short story.

Writing & Selling Nonfiction Articles. Master the fundamentals of writing/selling nonfiction articles: finding article ideas, conducting interviews, writing effective query letters and attention-getting leads, targeting your articles to the right publication. Course includes writing assignments and one complete article manuscript (and its revision).

Writing Your Personal or Family History. With the help of a professional writer you'll chronicle your life or your family's. Learn the important steps to documenting your history including researching and organizing your material, continuity, pacing and more!

Writer's Digest Criticism Service. Have your work evaluated by a professional writer before you submit it for pay. Whether you write books, articles, short stories or poetry, you'll get an objective review plus the specific writing and marketing advice that only a professional can provide.

Secrets of Selling Your Manuscripts. Discover all the best-kept secrets for mailing out strategic, targeted manuscript submissions. Learn how to "slant" your writing so you can publish the same material over and over, which publishing houses are your best bet, and much more.

Mail this card today for **FREE** information!

guidelines when available. A submission that does not follow the rules may be disqualified. If your work must be nominated, find out if your publisher can do it and let him or her know about your interest.

THE ISAAC ASIMOV AWARD

AWARD FOR: Best Science Fiction Short Story
OPEN TO: Unpublished submissions by college undergraduates
FREQUENCY: Annually
COMMENTS: The Isaac Asimov Award for Undergraduate Excellence in Science Fiction and Fantasy Writing is cosponsored by the International Association for the Fantastic in the Arts and *Asimov's* science fiction magazine. "The award honors the legacy of one of science fiction's most distinguished authors through an award aimed at undergraduate writers." Winners receive $500 and are considered for publication in the magazine. Entries are judged by *Asimov's* editors. Submit an unpublished short story. Participants must be undergraduate college students. There is no entry fee. Contest guidelines are available for SASE. The deadline in December 1.
CONTACT: Rick Wilber, Award Administrator, USF 3177, 4202 E. Fowler, Tampa FL 33620-3177.
PHONE: (813)974-6792

AURORA AWARDS

AWARD FOR: Best Canadian Science Fiction or Fantasy Novel, Short Stories and awards in other categories in both English and French
OPEN TO: Published submissions by Canadians (residents or citizens living abroad)
FREQUENCY: Annually
COMMENTS: These awards are sponsored by different organizations in Canada each year. Awards are made in several categories including novels and shorter work and are presented for the best in English and the best in French. Novels must have been published within the last two years and written by Canadian authors living in Canada or abroad. Other awards are for work published within the last year. The voting for the awards is a two-step process. Anyone living in Canada and Canadian citizens living abroad may submit or nominate

work. The Merril Collection in Toronto helps with compiling a list of eligible works. Voting ballots containing the top five (or in the case of a tie, the top six or seven) nominees are made available across the country at bookstores and through fanzines and writers' magazines. The ballot costs $4. The award is an aluminum figure representing the Northern Lights (Aurora Borealis) with a stylized "SF" and a maple leaf symbol. Location of the award ceremony varies (it is given at a convention and sponsors try to alternate between east and west coasts). Deadlines also vary. Write for further information.

CONTACT: Dennis Mullin, Administrator, 69 Donald St., Unit 6, Kitchner, Ontario N2B 3G6 Canada

BEST OF SOFT SCIENCE FICTION CONTEST

AWARD FOR: Best Science Fiction Short Stories (first, second and third prize)

OPEN TO: Published submissions (see below)

FREQUENCY: Annually

COMMENTS: This award is sponsored by the Soft SF Writers Association and was created to "encourage the publication of science fiction styles in which values, emotional content and artistic effort are emphasized rather than plot and deterministic science." Stories must have elements of science fiction, but cross-genre stories are acceptable. Short stories must either be submitted for publication or have been published between January 1 and December 15. Entries are judged by members of the Soft SF Writers Association. First prize is $100, second is $50 and third is $25. Submit short story up to 7,000 words. There is no entry fee. Guidelines are available for SASE. Stories may be submitted between October 1 and December 15.

CONTACT: Lela E. Buis, Contest Director, Soft SF Writers Association, 1277 Joan Dr., Merritt Island FL 32952.

BRAM STOKER AWARD

AWARD FOR: Best Horror Novel

OPEN TO: Published works

FREQUENCY: Annually

COMMENTS: The Bram Stoker Award for Superior Achievement in horror fiction and nonfiction is sponsored by the Horror Writer's Association (HWA). Published works are recommended and voted on by active members of the HWA. Categories include Best Novel, First Novel, Short Story, Novelette, Nonfiction and a Lifetime Achievement Award. Winners receive "fame, glory and a nifty trophy of a haunted house." Deadline for the award is January 1.

E-MAIL: hwa@horror.org

WEBSITE: http://www.horror.org/hwa/

JOHN W. CAMPBELL MEMORIAL AWARD

AWARD FOR: Best Science Fiction Novel of the Year

OPEN TO: Published submissions

FREQUENCY: Annually

COMMENTS: This award is sponsored by the Center for the Study of Science Fiction. Award is a certificate, and the winner's name is engraved on a trophy. Novels must have been published in the previous year. Send SASE for the list of jurors. Winner is brought to the campus for the Campbell Conference. Usually publishers enter the published novel, but authors may do so when their publisher does not. There is no entry fee. The deadline is May 1.

CONTACT: Professor James Gunn, Director, Center for the Study of Science Fiction, English Department, University of Kansas, Lawrence KS 66045.

PHONE: (913)864-3380

ARTHUR C. CLARKE AWARD

AWARD FOR: Best Science Fiction Novel (published in the United Kingdom)

OPEN TO: Published submissions

FREQUENCY: Annually

COMMENTS: This award was created in 1986 by Arthur C. Clarke to honor the best science fiction books published in the United Kingdom within the previous year. The award is an engraved bookend and £1,000. The winner is chosen by a jury representing the British Science Fiction Association, the Science Fiction Foundation and the International Science Policy Foundation, who jointly administer the award.

Books receiving their first British publication in the year prior to the award are eligible. Write for additional details and deadlines.

CONTACT: Paul Kincaid, Award Administrator, 60 Bournemouth Rd., Folkestone, Kent CT19 5AZ UK

PHILIP K. DICK AWARD

AWARD FOR: Distinguished Paperback Original (first and second prize)
OPEN TO: Published submissions
FREQUENCY: Annually
COMMENTS: The Philip K. Dick Award was created by Thomas M. Disch and others to honor the memory of the writer and to honor "a distinguished book published for the first time in the U.S. as a paperback original." The book nominated must be published in the previous year and must be a paperback—either trade or mass market. Books may be novels, short story collections or even anthologies. The award is sponsored by the Philadelphia Science Fiction Society and is given at NorwestCon held in Seattle in late March/early April each year. The award is a certificate and cash (amount varies with funding). A panel of five judges are nominated by the administrators each year, but these are usually taken on recommendation of the previous year's judges. Judges are writers or scholars only (not those involved in other areas of publishing). Both first and second prizes are awarded. Writers and publishers may submit published books to the judges for consideration. The list of judges is announced in sf trade journals such as *Locus* and *Science Fiction Chronicle*.

CONTACT: David G. Hartwell, Administrator, 153 Deerfield Lane N., Pleasantville NY 10570

L. RON HUBBARD'S WRITERS OF THE FUTURE CONTEST

AWARD FOR: Best Science Fiction or Fantasy Short Stories or Novelettes
OPEN TO: Unpublished submissions by new writers
FREQUENCY: Quarterly plus one annual grand prize award
COMMENTS: This award is presented to "find, reward and publicize new speculative fiction writers, so that they may more easily attain professional writing careers." The competition is for new or amateur writers of either science fiction or fantasy and is open to unpublished short

stories and novelettes. Annual grand prize is $4,000. Other awards are presented quarterly. These include $1,000 for first prize, $750 for second prize and $500 for third prize. Submissions are judged by an "outstanding professional panel."

ENTRY FEE: There is no entry fee. Guidelines are available for SASE. Bridge Publications publishes an annual anthology featuring winning stories.

CONTACT: Claude Sandoz, Contest Administrator, P.O. Box 1630, Los Angeles CA 90078

THE HUGO AWARD

AWARD FOR: Best Science Fiction or Fantasy Short Story, Novel and other categories

OPEN TO: Published submissions

FREQUENCY: Annually

COMMENTS: A Hugo Award is one of the most prestigious honors offered in the science fiction field. The award is voted on by ballot by members of the World Science Fiction Convention for material published in the previous year. The award is a metal spaceship, 15 inches tall, and the winning novel or short story almost always results in reprint of the original material and, therefore, increased payment. Work is nominated by members of the World Science Fiction Convention.

CONTACT: This address changes each year; check *Locus, Science Fiction Chronicle,* or the *Science Fiction Convention Register* for current address.

MYTHOPOEIC FANTASY AWARD

AWARD FOR: Best Fantasy Novel (one for adults, one for children)

OPEN TO: Published submissions

FREQUENCY: Annually

COMMENTS: This award is sponsored by The Mythopoeic Society and members judge the entries. The award for a fantasy novel published in the previous year is a statue of a lion. Awards are given for both adult and children's novels.

Books must be nominated by Society members, but writers who are members may nominate their own work. Guidelines are available for SASE. The deadline is February.

CONTACT: David Bratman, Chair, Awards Committee, P.O. Box 6707, Altadena CA 91003

NEBULA AWARDS

AWARD FOR: Best Science Fiction or Fantasy Short Story, Novel and other categories

OPEN TO: Published submissions

FREQUENCY: Annually

COMMENTS: This award is sponsored by the international organization for sf/fantasy writers, the Science-fiction and Fantasy Writers of America, Inc (SFWA). Short stories, novels, novelettes, novellas and other published works are nominated by SFWA members throughout the year. A Nebula is one of the most respected awards in the industry. The award is for works published in the previous year. Writers cannot nominate their own work; work must be nominated by an active SF-FWA member. The deadline is December 31.

CONTACT: Peter Dennis Pautz, Executive Secretary, 5 Winding Brook Dr., #1B, Guilderland NY 12084.

PHONE: (518)869-5361

N3F AMATEUR SHORT STORY CONTEST

AWARD FOR: Outstanding Science Fiction, Fantasy or Horror Short Story

OPEN TO: Unpublished submissions

FREQUENCY: Annually

COMMENTS: This contest is sponsored by the National Fantasy Fan Federation (N3F). Fiction must be an original unpublished work. Open to both members and nonmembers of the federation. Contest is judged by a professional author in the fantasy and science fiction field. First Place: $50; Second Place: $30; Third Place: $20. N3F actively encourages and pursues professional sales for winning entries. Word Length: to 7,000. Entry fee: $2 for N3F or BSFA members; $4 for nonmenbers. Contest receives 150 entries. Guidelines are available for SASE. Deadline: Dec. 1.

CONTACT: Donald Franson, 6543 Babcock Ave., North Hollywood CA 91606-2308

SCIENCE FICTION WRITERS OF EARTH SHORT STORY CONTEST

SPONSOR: Science Fiction Writers of Earth (SFWoE)

AWARD FOR: Best Science Fiction or Fantasy Short Stories (first, second and third prize)

OPEN TO: Unpublished submissions by amateur writers

FREQUENCY: Annually

COMMENTS: This award, administered by Gilbert Gordon Reis for the Science Fiction Writers of Earth (SFWoE), is designed to "promote the art of science fiction and fantasy short story writing." The final judge is established author, Edward Bryant. The award is $200 for first prize, $100 for second, $50 for third. Submit an unpublished science fiction or fantasy story between 2,000 and 7,500 words. Guidelines are available for SASE. Entry fee is $5 for the first entry, $2 for additional entries. The deadline is October 30.

CONTACT: Gilbert Gordon Reis, SFWoE Administrator, P.O. Box 121293, Fort Worth TX 76121.

PHONE: (817)451-8674

THEODORE STURGEON MEMORIAL AWARD

SPONSOR: Center for the Study of Science Fiction

AWARD FOR: Best Science Fiction Short Story of the Year

OPEN TO: Published submissions

FREQUENCY: Annually

COMMENT: This award is sponsored by the Center for the Study of Science Fiction. Award is a certificate, and the winner's name is engraved on a trophy. Short stories must have been published in the previous year. Send SASE for the list of jurors. Winner is brought to the campus for the Campbell Conference. Usually editors or publishers enter the published short story, but authors may do so when their publisher does not. There is no entry fee. The deadline is May 1.

CONTACT: Professor James Gunn, Director, English Department, University of Kansas, Lawrence, KS 66045.

PHONE: (913)864-3380

JAMES TIPTREE, JR. MEMORIAL AWARD

AWARD FOR: Best Gender-Expanding SF or Fantasy

OPEN TO: Published submissions

FREQUENCY: Annually

COMMENTS: This is a fairly new award, established in 1992, designed to honor the best sf or fantasy work published in the previous year that has included "gender-expanding or exploring" themes or characters. The award is $1,000 and a trophy. Work is judged by a group of independent judges, mostly established authors. The judges select a winner and publish a list of recommended works from the previous year. The award is often presented at WisCon, usually in May. Works may be recommended to the judges by people in the science fiction community. Write for additional details and information about deadlines.

CONTACT: Karen Joy Fowler, 457 Russell Blvd., Davis CA 95616

WORLD FANTASY AWARDS

AWARD FOR: Best Fantasy Short Stories, Novels and other categories

OPEN TO: Published submissions

FREQUENCY: Annually

COMMENTS: These awards are presented at the World Fantasy Convention each year. Fantasy novels, novellas, short stories, collections and anthologies are nominated for the award. The nomination process is twofold. Members of both the previous and current convention may nominate material published in the previous year. Two places on the nomination ballot are reserved for these "popular ballot" nominees. A panel of five judges (selected by the award administrators) then nominate the rest and make up the final ballot. The World Fantasy Convention is always held on Halloween weekend; locations vary each year. Members of the previous and current World Fantasy Convention can nominate works. For a list of judges, see announcements in sf trade publications such as *Locus* and *Science Fiction Chronicle*.

CONTACT: Peter Dennis Pautz, President, 5 Winding Brook Dr., #1B, Guilderland NY 12084.

PHONE: (518)869-5361

Nonfiction Magazines/
Publications of Interest

This section is made up of magazines that print primarily nonfiction from both the United States and overseas. Included are critical journals, trade publications, newsletters, media-related magazines and publications that list market information. These magazines can be invaluable resources for aspiring writers who want to learn more about the field, as well as for scholars interested in the literary aspects of sf. The international listings can offer a glimpse into sf elsewhere in the world. In addition, many of these publications actively seek writers for their nonfiction articles.

First you'll find the address to which you should direct inquiries about submissions and subscriptions. You'll also find some basic descriptive information that will give you an idea of the magazine's size and importance. At the top of the listing are categories of nonfiction published in the magazine. These give a general indication of what you'll find within—whether it's mostly articles, listings, reviews or a mix thereof.

A paragraph or two is then devoted to describing the magazine's editorial philosophy and reason for existence. We've quoted the editors where possible to give you a good impression of the publication. Also listed here are prominent authors who have appeared in the magazine.

The "How to Contact" section will tell you if the publication is seeking submissions and for what kinds of nonfiction. Included here are payment and reporting times. Subscription information follows.

AMBERZINE

Established: 1992 • Circulation: 1,000 • Frequency: Irregularly • Size: 6 × 9 • Pages: 160

Contact: Erick Wujcik, Editor

CATEGORIES
Essays/Articles, Role-Playing Science Fiction and Fantasy

According to editor Erick Wujcik, "*Amberzine* is a highly polished, professional journal that specializes in covering Roger Zelazny's Amber Universe. Does not publish Amber fiction per se. Fiction submissions must be based on the Amber diceless role-playing game. "Our highest priority is nonfiction about Amber, Roger Zelazny and related topics." They receive around 6 unsolicited manuscripts per month and publish 3-6 in each issue. "Always looking for artists for Amber cartoons, comix and illustrations."

HOW TO CONTACT: Send query by mail. Simultaneous submissions, electronic (disk) submissions and reprints are acceptable. They report back in 3-6 months. Manuscripts are published 9 months after acceptance on average. A sample copy is available for $10.
PAYMENT: Payment varies—approximately $5/page minimum.
TERMS: Acquires one-time serial rights.
ADDRESS: Phage Press, P.O. Box 310519, Detroit MI 48231-0519
PHONE: (313)533-3122

CCSTSG Enterprises

Established: 1990 • Circulation: 300 • Frequency: Monthly • Pages: 12-16 • Size: 8½ × 11

Contact: Jeffrey H. Mills, Publisher/Editor

CATEGORIES
Articles/Essays, Industry Reports, Interviews, Reviews

CCSTSG Enterprises is a monthly compendium of news, views and critical analysis, with loving, insightful and irreverent looks at the Star Trek phenomenon. "Be provocative. Put forth a thesis no one has presented before. Then write it well. We publish principally Star Trek-related critique, humor pieces and reviews; scholarly approaches welcome."

HOW TO CONTACT: Does not accept unsolicited manuscripts. Query first. Accepts electronic queries. Considers simultaneous submissions and reprints. Submissions on computer disk should be formatted for Mac or IBM word processing (any). Preferred word length: 750-2,000. Reports on queries in 1 week. Sometimes comments on rejected manuscripts. Writer's guidelines available for SASE. Sample copy available for $2. Subscription cost is $16 for 12 issues.

PAYMENT: Pays 2 contributor's copies.

TERMS: Purchases one-time rights. Manuscript published 1-6 months after acceptance.

ADDRESS: 7 Quarry St., Ellington CT 06029

PHONE: (860)875-6522

E-MAIL: notherbert@aol.com

PHOTO: MINDAS

CINEFANTASTIQUE

Established: 1970 • Circulation: 50,000 • Frequency: Monthly • Pages: 64 • Size: 8½ × 11

Contact: Frederick S. Clarke

CATEGORIES
Articles/Essays, Industry Reports, Interviews, Overseas Reports, Reviews (TV, Film, Video).

Looking for fantastic TV, film and video coverage. "Pick up a copy on the newsstand to see what we use."

HOW TO CONTACT: Unsolicited manuscripts welcome but prefer writers to query first. Accepts faxed queries. Submissions on computer disk should be formatted for Mac Quark Express or saved to ASCII text.

Receives approximately 20 unsolicited manuscripts each month. Preferred word length: 500-10,000. Reports on queries (only if interested) in 2 weeks. Sometimes comments on rejected manuscripts. Sample copy available for $5. Subscription cost is $18 for 4 issues.

PAYMENT: Pays 7¢/word and 3 contributor's copies. Additional copies available at 50%. Pays upon publication.

TERMS: Purchases all magazine rights. Manuscript published 4 months after acceptance.

ADDRESS: P.O. Box 270, Oak Park IL 60303

PHONE: (708)366-5566

FAX: (708)366-1441

CONNOTATIONS

Established: 1990 • Circulation: 13,000 • Frequency: 3-4 times/year • Size: 7½ × 10 • Pages: 48

Contact: Margaret Grady, Editor

> CATEGORIES
> Articles/Essays, Convention/Workshop Listings, Dark Fantasy, Fiction/Nonfiction, Humorous Science Fiction, Industry Reports, Interviews, Reviews, Sociological Science Fiction, Traditional Fantasy, TV & Film Updates

ConNotations is a professional-looking publication created entirely by volunteer effort in association with the Central Arizona Speculative Fiction Society. It consists of a useful and interesting mix of fiction and, predominantly, nonfiction. They print 1-2 short stories in each issue, but do not pay authors. Stories should be from 800 to 3,500 words and are printed 1-4 months after acceptance.

The bulk of the magazine is made up of reports on the sf industry, with a focus on Arizona. They also publish around 30 book reviews, as well as commentaries on the latest TV and film releases. There are also extensive convention listings and reports. The magazine is free, but the editors request $5 for every 4 issues to cover postage and handling. You can also find this publication at the freebie tables at various conventions.

HOW TO CONTACT: Submit fiction manuscripts to the address above and include SASE. Query for nonfiction submissions. They accept simultaneous submissions and reprints.

ADDRESS: Central Arizona Speculative Fiction Society, P.O. Box 62613, Phoenix, AZ 85082-2613

E-MAIL: connote@casfs.org

WEBSITE: http://www.casfs.org/connote/

d8 MAGAZINE

Established: 1995 • Circulation: 7,500 • Frequency: Quarterly • Pages: 72 • Size: 8½ × 11

Contact: Holly Riggenbach

> CATEGORIES
> Advice Columns, Articles/Essays, Industry Reports, Interviews, Reviews, Shared World (Fantasy)

"*d8* is a magazine which deals with the roleplayer, what we're interested in, what we do and what we want to know. We're literate and computer literate; we are interested in history and in the future. We publish articles that aid the gamer around the kitchen table, online or out at an event. *d8* is a magazine about the culture of roleplaying. One of *d8*'s main purpose is to give new, talented writers in the roleplaying field the exposure they deserve. We are interested in articles which look at the roleplaying industry, roleplaying itself and areas of cross interest to gamers. We won't shy away from controversy. We want writers who will explore new territory and write about aspects of roleplaying which have gone unnoticed. Please write all gaming articles for generic game systems and please footnote all sources." Fiction submissions must be set in *d8*'s fantasy world "Ahremon."

HOW TO CONTACT: Unsolicited manuscripts welcome. Query first or send full manuscript. Accepts faxed and electronic queries. Considers reprints. Submissions on computer disk should be formatted as text only (Mac or PC). Receives approximately 20 unsolicited manuscripts each month. Preferred word length: 2,500. Reports on queries in 1 week, on manuscripts in 3 weeks. Sometimes comments on rejected manuscripts. Writer's guidelines available for SASE. Sample copy available for $4.95. Subscription cost is $14 for 4 issues.

PAYMENT: Pays 5 contributor's copies. Author's bio (short) published on webpage.

TERMS: Purchases first worldwide rights. Manuscript published 1 year after acceptance.

ADDRESS: 1129 Seagull Lane, Cherry Hill NJ 08003

PHONE/FAX: (609)795-1370

E-MAIL: d8editor@aol.com

WEBSITE: http://www.voicenet.com/~d8mag

EXTRAPOLATION

Established: 1959 • Circulation: 1,000 • Frequency: Quarterly • Size: Digest • Pages: 90

Contact: Donald M. Hassler, Editor

CATEGORIES
Book Reviews, Literary Criticism

Editor Hassler describes *Extrapolation* as "the first journal devoted to the study of sf. We publish scholarly, critical bibliographic essays on sf and fantasy. We only review scholarly and critical books."

They have published Frederik Pohl and Jack Williamson writing about the genre. Manuscripts are published 18 months after acceptance.

HOW TO CONTACT: Submit your essay with SASE. They will sometimes comment on or critique manuscripts and take 3 months to respond to submissions. They do not accept simultaneous submissions. A single copy is available for $5, and an annual subscription is $18.

PAYMENT: Nonpaying market. Scholarly journal.

ADDRESS: Kent State University, Kent OH 44242

E-MAIL: dhassler@kentun.kent.edu

PHOTO: LORI EANES
DESIGN: MARK FRISCHMAN

FACTSHEET FIVE

Established: 1982 • Frequency: Bimonthly • Size: 8½×11

Contact: R. Seth Friedman, Publisher

CATEGORIES
Book Reviews, Magazine Reviews

As "the definitive guide to the 'zine revolution," *Factsheet Five* reviews over 1,000 small press publications each issue, with a section devoted exclusively to sf fanzines and semiprofessional magazines. The magazine was started by Mike Gunderloy who has written extensively about the small press. His book, *The World of 'Zines: A Guide to the Independent Magazine Revolution*, is a must for anyone interested in the 'zine phenomenon.

A single copy is available for $6. Subscriptions are $20 for individuals and $40 for institutions. *Factsheet Five* is also available electronically as a free online service.

ADDRESS: P.O. Box 170099, San Francisco CA 94117-0099
E-MAIL: jerod23@well.sf.ca.us

FAN NEWS

Established: 1992 • Circulation: 1,500 • Frequency: Monthly • Pages: 24 • Size: 8½×11

Contact: Martin A. Smith, III

> **CATEGORIES**
> Advice Columns, Articles/Essays, Convention/Workshop Listings, Industry
> Reports, Interviews, Overseas Reports, Reviews

"*Fan News* explores the entire galaxy of fandom. We're going onto the world wide web any minute. We are interested in the wide range of sf, fantasy and horror fandoms. Tell us what's happening in your area of the country (or the world)."

HOW TO CONTACT: Unsolicited manuscripts welcome. Send full manuscript. Considers simultaneous submissions and reprints. Submissions on computer disk should be formatted on 3½″ disk as Wordperfect 5.1/5.2. Receives approximately 6 unsolicited manuscripts each month. Preferred word length: open. Reports on queries in 6 weeks. Sometimes comments on rejected manuscripts. Writer's guidelines available for SASE. Sample copy available for $1. Subscription cost is $12 for 12 issues..

PAYMENT: Pays $5-10/article.

TERMS: Rights purchased vary with article. Manuscript published 3 months after acceptance.

ADDRESS: P.O. Box 14947, Jacksonville FL 32238

E-MAIL: fannews2m@aol.com

FILE 770

Established: 1978 • Circulation: 450 • Frequency: Bimonthly • Pages: 22 • Size: 8½ × 11

Contact: Mike Glyer

> **CATEGORIES**
> Articles/Essays, Convention/Workshop Listings, Obituaries, Overseas
> Reports, News

"This is a newsletter about science fiction fandom, conventions and clubs. It has won three Hugo Awards from the World SF Convention as Best Fanzine of 1984, 1986 and 1989."

HOW TO CONTACT: Does not accept unsolicited manuscripts. Query first. No simultaneous submissions or reprints. Never comments on rejected manuscripts. Sample copy available for $2. Subscription cost is $15 for 10 issues.

TERMS: Manuscript published 2 months after acceptance.

ADDRESS: P.O. Box 1056, Sierra Madre CA 91025

PHONE: (818)355-3090

E-MAIL ADDRESS: 72557/1334@compuserve.com

GILA QUEEN'S GUIDE TO MARKETS

Published: Monthly • Size: 8½ × 11

Contact: Kathryn Ptacek, Editor

CATEGORIES
Articles/Essays, Convention/Workshop Listings, Industry Reports, Magazine Reviews, Market Listings, Overseas Reports, Workshop Listings

---

This publication includes complete guidelines for fiction markets, with the April issue featuring sf/fantasy/horror. Every issue covers the markets in minute detail: address changes, dead markets, conferences, contests, moving editors, anthologies and publishing news in general. They also publish articles on writing topics and review software and books of interest to writers. Single copies are available for $5, and subscriptions are $30 per year for the U.S., $34 per year for Canada, and $44 per year overseas. The *Yearly Index of Markets* is available for $4 plus SASE. *Dead Market Listings* (from 1988 to the present) are available for $5.

ADDRESS: P.O. Box 97, Newton NJ 07860-0097

HORROR: THE NEWS MAGAZINE OF THE HORROR AND DARK FANTASY FIELD

Established: 1994 • Circulation: 3,000 • Frequency: Bimonthly • Size: 8½ × 11 • Pages: 44-64

Contact: Joe Morey, Editor and Publisher

> **CATEGORIES**
> Articles/Essays, Book Reviews, Film Reviews, Industry Reports, Interviews, Market Listings

Horror is a cross between *Locus* and *Mystery Scene*—it's a reference for professionals. Joe Morey also runs Dark Regions Press, a small press that publishes sf/fantasy/horror in limited edition trade paperbacks and hardcover books. A single copy costs $5, and subscriptions are $19.95 for 6 issues and $36 for 12. *Horror* is looking for writers for interviews, news items and essays on trends or horror-related subjects. Payment is by arrangement.

ADDRESS: Park Regions Press, P.O. Box 6301, Concord CA 94524

LOCUS, THE NEWSPAPER OF THE SCIENCE FICTION FIELD

Frequency: Monthly • Size: 8½ × 11

Contact: Charles N. Brown, Editor and Publisher

> **CATEGORIES**
> Articles/Essays, Book Reviews, Convention/Workshop Listings, Industry Reports, Interviews, Magazine Reviews, Market Listings, Overseas Reports

Locus is the professional newszine for science fiction, fantasy and horror. It includes information about all aspects of the field, including publishing news, awards, bookstores and conventions. Four times a year, *Locus* lists all forthcoming books from both American and British publishers and provides complete convention listings. They have extensive book and magazine reviews. Subscriptions cost $43 per year (second class mail) or $53 (first class) for the U.S.; $48 (second class) or $53 (first class) for Canada; $48 per year (sea mail) for overseas.

ADDRESS: P.O. Box 13305, Oakland CA 94661
PHONE: (510)339-9196
FAX: (510)339-8144

THE NEW YORK REVIEW OF SCIENCE FICTION

Established: 1988 • Circulation: 1,000 • Frequency: Monthly • Size: 8½ × 11 • Pages: 24

Contact: David G. Hartwell

CATEGORIES
Book Reviews, Essays

The *New York Review of Science Fiction* contains 7-10 novel or anthology reviews, as well as essays, occasional "think" pieces and reading lists. They have recently published articles by the likes of Brian Aldiss, Terry Bisson, Rachel Pollack, Michael Bishop, Samuel R. Delany and Gene Wolfe.

David G. Hartwell, features and reviews editor of this publication, says, "Most other review publications in the field only offer brief, market-oriented reviews (which largely consist of plot synopses). We are interested in longer, more thoughtful examinations of a given work and how it fits within the larger context of the field. We also strive for the best-written reviews possible." The writer's guidelines continue, "We seek popular essays, parodies, studies and thought pieces on topics related to science fiction, fantasy and horror literature." A single copy is available for $3.50. An annual subscription costs $31 for the U.S., $36 for Canada and $44 for overseas.

HOW TO CONTACT: David G. Hartwell is seeking reviews and essays. They accept disk submissions and will sometimes reprint "if a work has been published in a market that's far outside the sf/fantasy field." They will not accept simultaneous submissions and will reply in 1-2 months. "Write for guidelines."

PAYMENT: Pays $10 for reviews, $25 for essays.

TERMS: Purchases first North American serial rights and nonexclusive anthology rights.

ADDRESS: Dragon Press, Publisher, P.O. Box 78, Pleasantville NY 10570

PHONE: (914)769-5545

THE NIGHTMARE EXPRESS

Established: 1986 • Circulation: 150 • Frequency: Bimonthly • Size: 8 × 11 • Pages: 12

Contact: Donald Miller

CATEGORIES
Advice Columns, Articles/Essays, Convention/Workshop Listings, Industry Reports, Interviews, Market Listings, Reviews

"*The Nightmare Express* would like to see strong advice columns aimed at getting published and unpublished writers given more access to becoming published." Also features articles on how to market your horror fiction.

HOW TO CONTACT: Unsolicited manuscripts welcome. Send full manuscript. Considers simultaneous submissions and reprints. Receives at least 30-50 unsolicited manuscripts each month. Preferred word length: to 2,000. Reports on manuscripts in 6 weeks. Sometimes comments on rejected manuscripts. Writer's guidelines available for SASE. Sample copy available for $2.

PAYMENT: Pays ¼¢/word and one contributor's copy. Additional copies available at 50% discount. Pays upon acceptance.

TERMS: Purchases first North American serial rights. Manuscript published 4 months after acceptance.

ADDRESS: 11 W. Winona St., St. Paul MN 89170

PHONE: (612)227-6958

RENAISSANCE

Established: 1996 • Circulation: 6,000 • Frequency: Quarterly • Size: 8½ × 11 • Pages: 52

Contact: Kim Guarnaccia

> **CATEGORIES**
> Articles/Essays, Convention/Workshop Listings, Industry Reports, Interviews, Overseas Reports, Reviews

Renaissance covers all aspects of the Renaissance Period—historical or contemporary (current fairs and festivals). Topics covered include re-enactments, costuming, feasts and banquets, etc. Also includes interviews with with vendors and artisans, and Renaissance book, movie and role-playing game reviews.

HOW TO CONTACT: Unsolicited manuscripts welcome, but prefers writers to query first for guidelines before submitting. Accepts faxed and electronic queries. Considers reprints. Receives at least 4 unsolicited manuscripts each month. Preferred word length: to 3,000. Reports on queries in 1 week, on manuscripts in 2-6 weeks. Always comments on rejected manuscripts. Writer's guidelines available for SASE. Sample copy available for $3.95 Subscription cost is $14 for 4 issues; $25 for 8 issues.

PAYMENT: Pays 3¢/word (published) and 1-3 contributor's copies. Additional copies available at 50% discount. Pays upon publication.

TERMS: Purchases first North American serial rights. Manuscript published 12-18 months after acceptance.

ADDRESS: Phantom Press, 5A Green Meadow Dr., Nantucket MA 02554

PHONE: (508)325-0411

FAX: (508)325-0056

E-MAIL: 76603.2224@compuserve.com

ART: MARK RICH

SCAVENGER'S NEWSLETTER

Established: 1984 • Circulation: 850 • Frequency: Monthly

Contact: Janet Fox, Editor

> CATEGORIES
> Articles/Essays, Flash Fiction, Market Listings, Poetry, Reviews

January 1994 marked the tenth anniversary of *Scavenger's Newsletter*, a monthly markets newsletter, created, edited and published by Janet Fox. Devoted to the small press, the publication focuses on small magazine markets for science fiction, fantasy, horror and mystery. For years Fox edited a small markets newsletter for the Small Press Writers and Artists Organization (SPWAO), a group formed to promote the interests of writers and artists working in that realm. (SPWAO has gone through a number of changes. It is currently The Genre Writer's Association. See listing on page 425.) Because the number of markets continued to grow and because there seemed to be widespread interest, she decided to make the information available to a wider audience in the form of *Scavenger's Newsletter*.

"I had no idea when I started that things would go nuts in the small press," says Fox. "My first print run was for 25 copies on one sheet of legal-sized paper folded over into a pamphlet. Now I have a print run of 1,000 with 850 subscribers. We've grown to 28 pages."

She attributes the growth to the tremendous changes in the small press over the last ten years. "The cost to publish a small magazine has gone way down, and with the computer so much more is possible." It used to be, she says, there were only a few people publishing small magazines, typing them out and copying them on a ditto or mimeograph machine. These were mostly what people in the small press arena call "personal 'zines," those featuring the work of one or a small handful of writers and distributed to contributors and a few family members and friends. With computers, says Fox, people are able to create more sophisticated-looking publications, and with that, they seem more willing to include the work of other writers and to share them with a larger audience.

When Fox started her newsletter, she knew of five or six science fiction or fantasy publications. The number of these publications has grown, yet about 80 percent of the markets she lists are for horror. "I think it's because there are very few large, mainstream markets for horror short stories, while smaller science fiction magazines have to go head-to-head with several commercial magazines such as *Asimov's* and *Analog.*"

It's difficult to find many hard science fiction stories published in small magazines, says Fox, because the larger publications are eager to publish this work. Instead, small science fiction magazines tend to publish a lot of "speculative fiction," an umbrella term used to cover literary science fiction and any fiction that might be considered weird, fantastic, experimental or "new wave."

By "new wave" Fox says she is referring to a certain literary approach and style in science fiction characterized by the work of Samuel R. Delany, Michael Moorcock and Phillip J. Farmer. While commercial science fiction publications are using less of this type of work now because it is not commercial enough (although examples of this type can be found in each of them), the small press has become a big outlet for literary and experimental science fiction.

Fox had been writing and publishing for 20 years before she started *Scavenger's Newsletter.* "I'm most interested in fantasy, but I've had more luck publishing horror." Although she's published widely in the small press, she also has had stories in *Twilight Zone* and Marion Zimmer Bradley's anthology, *Sword & Sorcery.* She was the author of books two through six of the "Scorpio" series, a science fantasy about a magical time machine, which she wrote under the name Alex McDonald for the book packager, Byron Preiss. The series was later bought by Ace.

She is also a member of the Science Fiction Poetry Association (see listing on page 427). While there has been a growth in science fiction-themed poetry in the last few years, Fox says most of the magazines that feature it cover all forms of "speculative" poetry including surreal, gothic and horror-related poetry.

Comics, personal 'zines and fanzines based on television, movie and book characters are plentiful in the small press, but Fox sticks to just one type of market. In *Scavenger's Newsletter*, she includes only fiction publications. "I feel strongly this is about original fiction, not [television-and movie-inspired] clones or comics. And I simply don't have the space." From time to time, Fox lists media market letters in exchange for a mention of *Scavenger's* in their publications.

Scavenger's Newsletter is chock-full of markets and, even at 28 pages, it looks like Fox is running out of room. Still printed on legal-sized paper folded and stapled, the typeface, cover and interior art have improved steadily over the years as Fox has upgraded her production equipment. The core of the newsletter is the "Scroungings" section, which contains up to 40 market listings, most of which include personal notes from the editors in addition to information on how to submit, payment and needs. Fox separates out listings from the United Kingdom in "UK Update," by Steve Sneyd, and includes shorter listings, notes on various publications, and brief comments on markets by writers in "Slim Pickins."

Fox also includes a number of articles on issues in the small press, which are written by contributors; a "Flea Market" area listing magazine copies and subscriptions for sale; "The Dip List," listings of publications that will review writers' work; and "The Skeptic Tank," which includes magazine reviews by contributor Jim Lee. "Junkmail" is a lively letters-to-the-editor page, and, with Fox's policy of allowing rebuttal, it's home to a number of ongoing "discussions." This is a lot of material to pack into a small space, but Fox manages with a surprisingly easy-to-read, two-column format.

"When I started, I thought *Scavenger's* would be a place we could rat on editors, especially about rudeness and problems with response times. This is still an aspect and I've found a lot of editors read the newsletter to get feedback on how they are doing." In addition to the "Slim Pickins" section and the "Junk Mail," she helps in this respect by including a chart, "Random Numbers" that lists various magazines' longest, shortest and average response times based on information provided by writers.

Fox also publishes *Scavenger's Scrapbook*, a biannual (January and July) compilation of capsulized reviews from past editions of the newsletter. Although she includes only one to two poems and a small number of "flash fiction" stories (short short fiction to 1,200 words) in *Scavenger's Newsletter*, she does publish an anthology of winners from her Killer Frog Contest, a contest for short, humorous or overdone horror fiction.

Submissions to the contest must be postmarked between April 1 and July 1 of each year, and winners receive $25 and the "coveted froggie statuette," as well as a copy of the anthology.

The biggest problem in the small press, says Fox, is the lack of stability. Publications go in and out of business at such a dizzying rate, she says, that it's hard to keep up, even with a monthly publication. Yet some publications have staying power, and "you can practically watch their continuing story in the newsletter over the years," she says.

Of those that publish science fiction and fantasy, she says *Space and Time* and *Absolute Magnitude* are two worth watching.

For any writer interested in publishing in the small press, Fox says there are plenty of opportunities. "But writers need to understand the small press situation. Magazines may be here today, gone tomorrow. It's not unusual to have a piece accepted, but never see it in print. The good news is you can get in on the ground floor when a magazine is first starting, and overall there's more opportunity for new writers to see print for the first time."

HOW TO CONTACT: Fox accepts nonfiction articles on issues in the small press, flash fiction to 1,200 words and 1-2 poems each issue. A single copy of *Scavenger's Newsletter* is available for $2. Subscriptions are $7.75 for 6 months $15.50 for 1 year in the U.S. Canadian subscriptions are available for $9.25 for 6 months, $18.50 for 1 year (U.S. funds). Overseas subscriptions are $12.25 for 6 months, $24.50 for 1 year (U.S. funds).

PAYMENT: Pays flat fee of $4 (fiction and nonfiction) and $2 (poetry).

TERMS: Purchases one-time rights.

ADDRESS: 519 Ellinwood, Osage City KS 66523

PHONE: (913)528-3538

ART: ED EMSHWILLER
© 1996 CAROLYN EMSHWILLER

SCiENCE FiCTiON ChRONiCLE

Established: 1979 • Circulation: 6,000 • Frequency: Monthly • Size: 8 × 11 • Pages: 52

Contact: Andrew I. Porter, Editor and Publisher

CATEGORIES
Articles/Essays, Convention/Workshop Listings, Film News, Industry Reports, Interviews, Market Listings, Overseas Reports, Reviews

Science Fiction Chronicle is a news magazine for professional writers, editors and readers of sf, fantasy and horror. They review around 50 books each issue. A sample copy is available for $2. Annual subscription costs: for the U.S., $35 for 1 year, $65 for 2 years; for Canada, $42 for 1 year, $79 for 2 years; for overseas, $49 for 1 year, $95 for 2 years.

If you want a book reviewed, send the galleys to Don D'Ammassa, book review editor, at 323 Dodge St., E. Providence, RI 02914. Final copies of all books must go to this address and to the *SFC* address above.

PAYMENT: Pays 3½¢/word for nonfiction.
ADDRESS: P.O. Box 022730, Brooklyn NY 11202-0056
E-MAIL: a.porter2@genie.com

ThE SCiENCE FiCTiON CONVENTiON REGiSTER

Established: 1974 • Circulation: 300 • Frequency: 3 times/year • Size: 8 × 11 • Pages: 38

Contact: Erwin S. Strauss

CATEGORIES
Convention Listings

The Science Fiction Convention Register is a list of upcoming sf, fantasy and related conventions (about 800 each issue, most in the upcoming 12-month period) indexed by name, location and participants. Sample copy available for $4. Subscription cost is $12 for 3 issues; $24 for 6 issues.

ADDRESS: 101 S. Whiting St., Suite 700, Alexandra VA 22304

SCIENCE FICTION EYE

Established: 1987 • Circulation: 8,000 • Frequency: Semiannually • Size: 8 × 10½ • Pages: 120

Contact: Stephen P. Brown, Editor and Publisher

CATEGORIES
Articles/Essays, Book Reviews, Interviews, Literary Criticism, Science Articles

Science Fiction Eye is a mix of reviews, commentary, criticism, debate, interviews and essays. Editor Brown says, "*Science Fiction Eye* contains unusual and elaborate graphics and is a forum for science fiction writers and readers to engage in a lively discussion about a broad range of topics, literary or otherwise." *Science Fiction Eye* has published articles by or interviews with Bruce Sterling, John Shirley, Jack Womack, Kim Stanley Robinson, William Gibson, Terry Bisson and Thomas Disch.

HOW TO CONTACT: Query Brown on ideas for essays of 500-10,000 words in length on aspects of contemporary science fiction and today's science and culture. He will reply within a month. Single copies are available for $5. Three issues cost $12.50 in the U.S. and $20 overseas. Six issues are $25 in the U.S. and $40 overseas.

PAYMENT: Pays in contributor's copies.
TERMS: Purchases one-time North American serial rights.
ADDRESS: P.O. Box 18539, Asheville NC 28814
E-MAIL: eyebrown@interpath.com

SCIENCE FICTION ROMANCE

Established: 1994 • Circulation: 200 • Frequency: Monthly • Pages: 4 •
Size: 8½×11

Contact: Jennifer Dunne, Editor

CATEGORIES
Advice Columns, Articles/Essays, Convention/Workshop Listings, Industry Reports, Interviews, Market Listings, Reviews

"We focus on the emerging sub-genre of science fiction romance. While we will consider material relevant to either sf or romance, preference is given to material dealing with both aspects. Also, straight romance material is given preference over straight sf material. Limited hard copy editions of the newsletter are printed each month. Most subscriptions are through e-mail distribution. The current and back issues are also available via the web."

HOW TO CONTACT: Unsolicited manuscripts welcome. Send article with cover letter. Accepts electronic queries. Considers reprints. Submissions on computer disk should be as formatted ASCII text. Receives approximately 2 unsolicited manuscripts each month. Preferred word length: 500-1,000. Reports on queries and manuscripts in 1 month. Sometimes comments on rejected manuscripts. Writer's guidelines available for SASE. Sample copy available for 50¢ hard copy, free electronically. Subscription cost is $3 for 6 issues.
PAYMENT: Pays 1 contributor's copy. Additional copies available at cost. Advertisement space given in exchange for interviews.

TERMS: Purchases one-time rights, print and electronic, plus archived electronic issues. Manuscript published 1 month after acceptance.
ADDRESS: P.O. Box 496, Endicott NY 13761-0496
E-MAIL: yeep@aol.com

SCİENCE FİCTİON STUDİES

Established: 1973 • Circulation: 1,000 • Frequency: 3 times/year • Size: 6×9 • Pages: 128-160

Contact: Dr. Arthur B. Evans, Publisher

CATEGORIES
Articles/Essays, Book Reviews, Literary Criticism

Publisher Evans says, "*SFS* is the most respected international academic journal devoted to sf. It is a refereed journal. It contains articles on sf, review-articles (long reviews) on sf criticism, and book reviews on sf criticism." They have published articles by the likes of Brian Aldiss and Stanislaw Lem.

HOW TO CONTACT: *SFS* accepts critical articles of around 8,000 words. The editors receive 5-10 each month and will usually send back the critiqued manuscript in 2 months. Essays appear in the journal 6 months to 1 year after acceptance. Send 4 copies of the manuscript when submitting. Annual rates in the U.S. are $15 ($22 for institutions), in Canada are Can$17 (Can$25 for institutions), and for overseas are $18 (U.S.) ($26 for institutions) plus $7.50 for airmail.
PAYMENT: Nonpaying market (scholarly journal).
ADDRESS: East College, DePauw University, Greencastle IN 46135
PHONE: (317)658-4758
E-MAIL: aevans@depauw.edu

SCi-Fi UNiVERSE

Established: 1994 • Circulation: 115,000 • Frequency: 9 times/year • Pages: 80-96 • Size: 8½ × 11

Contact: Mark Altman

> CATEGORIES
> Advice Columns, Articles/Essays, Convention/Workshop Listings, Industry Reports, Interviews, On-The-Sets, Overseas Reports, Reviews

"*Sci-fi Universe* is the magazine for science fiction fans with life-em-phasizing, intelligent, sophisticated and witty entertainment reporting. Acclaimed by *Wired* magazine as the best of the new sf magazines. Submit articles on spec; tough to get assignment without something very juicy."

HOW TO CONTACT: Unsolicited manuscripts welcome. Send full manuscript. Receives approximately 30 unsolicited manuscripts each month. Preferred word length: 1,500-3,000. Reports on queries in 8-10 weeks. Sometimes comments on rejected manuscripts. Writer's guidelines available for SASE. Sample copy available for $4.99. Subscription copy is $21 for 9 issues

PAYMENT: Pay ranges from $50-1,000 based on size of article, see writer's guidelines. Pays upon publication.

TERMS: Purchases first worldwide rights. Manuscript published 5-10 months after acceptance.

ADDRESS: 8484 Wilshire Blvd., #900, Beverly Hills CA 90211

PHONE: (213)651-5400

FAX: (213)651-2741

ART: STACY DRUM

THE SCREAM FACTORY

Established: 1988 • Circulation: 3,000 • Frequency: Quarterly • Pages: 136 • Size: 8½ × 11

Contact: Bob Morrish

CATEGORIES
Articles/Essays, Industry Reports, Overseas Reports, Reviews

"*The Scream Factory* is the nonfiction magazine of the horror genre. The magazine's emphasis is on coverage of fiction (both novels and short stories), but *TSF* also covers films, television, comics and other forms of popular culture. In conjunction with articles, interviews, etc., we like to see accompanying lists and sidebar features. What we don't want to see: fiction; articles about recent low-budget films; book reviews that merely summarize the plot; book reviews of popular books that you can read about in your typical newspaper."

HOW TO CONTACT: Unsolicited manuscripts welcome, but prefers writers to query first. Accepts faxed and electronic queries. Considers simultaneous submissions. Submissions on computer disk should be formatted as ASCII text or any popular word processor format (Mac or IBM). Receives approximately 5 unsolicited manuscripts each month. 10% of accepted manuscripts are submitted through agents. Preferred word length: 3,000-8,000. Reports on queries in 2-3 weeks, on manuscripts in 3-4 weeks. Always comments on rejected manuscripts. Writer's guidelines available for SASE. Sample copy available for $7. Subscription cost is $23 for 4 issues.

PAYMENT: Pays ½¢/word. Pays upon publication.

TERMS: Purchases first North American serial rights. Manuscript published 3-9 months after acceptance.

ADDRESS: 16473 Redwood Lodge Rd., Los Gatos CA 95030
PHONE: (408)353-4450
FAX: (408)353-2786
E-MAIL: bmorrish@netgate.com

STAR*LINE: MAGAZINE OF THE SCIENCE FICTION POETRY ASSOCIATION

Established: 1978 • Circulation: 200 • Frequency: Bimonthly • Size: Digest • Pages: 20

Contact: Marge Simon, Executive Editor

CATEGORIES
Articles/Essays, Industry Reports, Interviews, Market Listings, Poetry, Reviews

*Star*Line* is the official letter of the the Science Fiction Poetry Association (SFPA), as well as a small literary magzine that publishes sf/fantasy poetry. Nonfiction in *Star*Line* includes articles, reviews, market reports and short interviews on topics related to sf/fantasy poetry. "We are receiving too many unusable submissions. Please read guidelines before submitting anything. Too many people send their work without having even seen a copy of the magazine."

The magazine also publishes nominees for the SFPA's Rhysling Award (see **Contest** section), which recognizes the best short/long poetry of the year. The winners are printed in the *Nebula Anthology*. *Star*Line* has published poetry by Jane Yolen, Joe Haldeman and Roger Zelazny.

HOW TO CONTACT: Query with SASE for guidelines before submitting. All correspondence other than submissions to Star*Line (including requests for writer's guidelines) should be sent to *SFPA Secretary/ Treasurer John Nichols, 6075 Bellevue Dr., North Olmsted OH 44070*. Send poetry and nonfiction articles to Marge Simon at the address below. Considers simultaneous submissions if so noted. No more than 5 poems/submission allowed. Preferred word length: 500-2,500 (for articles). Reports on manuscripts in 1 month. Sample copy available for $2. Subscription cost is $13 annually and includes mem-

TARGET THE MARKETS.

Order Form

☐ YES! Start my subscription to *Writer's Digest*, the magazine thousands of successful writers rely on to hit their target markets. I pay just $19.97 for 12 monthly issues...a savings of more than $15 off the newsstand price.

☐ I'm enclosing payment (or paying by credit card). Add an extra issue to my subscription FREE — 13 in all!

Charge my ☐ Visa ☐ MC

Exp. _____

Signature _____

☐ I prefer to be billed later for 12 issues.

NAME _____

ADDRESS _____

CITY _____ STATE _____ ZIP _____

Outside U.S. add $10 (includes GST in Canada) and remit in U.S. funds. Annual newsstand rate $35.88. Allow 4-6 weeks for first issue delivery.

SAVE MORE THAN $15!

YOUR MONTHLY GUIDE TO GETTING PUBLISHED

TTSF6

bership to the Science Fiction Poetry Association.

PAYMENT: Pays 5¢/line plus 1¢/word for poems; ¼¢/word for articles.

TERMS: Purchases first North American serial rights.

ADDRESS: 1412 N.E. 35th St., Ocala FL 34479

STARLOG: THE SCIENCE FICTION UNIVERSE

Established: 1976 • Published: Monthly • Size: 8 × 10¾ • Pages: 84

Contact: David McDonnell

CATEGORIES
Industry Reports, Interviews, Reviews, TV and Film Updates

Editor McDonnell says, "Our primary mission is to publish interviews with sf writers and artists and those involved with making sf/fantasy film and television series—past and present. For 20 years *Starlog* has explored the sf universe." *Starlog* does not accept fiction. They are looking for interviews with people involved in the sf field, book reviews and exciting articles on sf in general.

HOW TO CONTACT: Always query with a letter first, and always include SASE. "We love giving new writers their first chance to break into print in a national magazine." They respond in 5 weeks. Feature length articles should be 1,000-3,500 words. Single copies are $4.99. Annual subscriptions are $39.97 for the U.S., and Canadian and foreign subscriptions are $48.87 in U.S. funds only.

PAYMENT: Pays $125/article. Book reviews pay $15 each. *Starlog* buys all rights. They receive 20-30 manuscripts each month and publish 12 per issue. Articles are published 4-5 months after acceptance.

ADDRESS: %Starlog Group, 475 Park Ave. S., 8th Floor, New York NY 10016

TANGENT

Established: 1993 • Circulation: 800 • Frequency: Quarterly • Size: 8½ × 11 • Pages: 72

Contact: David A. Truesdale, Editor

CATEGORIES
Articles/Essays, Book Reviews, Interviews, Magazine Reviews

Tangent reviews every story in every issue of every professional sf magazine. They review 90% of semiprofessional sf magazines and others as they can fit them in. Editor Truesdale says: "We are currently the only short story sf/fantasy review magazine."

HOW TO CONTACT: *Tangent* is looking for reviewers, but query first. Editor Truesdale will also publish an occasional article on sf. Writers "must have a historical perspective of the field and be able to communicate such."

PAYMENT: Pays 3 contributor's copies. A single copy costs $5 U.S. add $1 foreign; $8 South Africa. Make checks payable to David Truesdale. A 1-year subscription costs $20 U.S.

ADDRESS: 5779 Norfleet, Raytown MO 64133

THYME: THE AUSTRALIAN SF NEWSZINE

Established: 1980 • Circulation: 300 • Frequency: Bimonthly • Size: 8½×11

Contact: Alan Stewart, Editor

CATEGORIES
Articles/Essays, Artwork, Book Reviews, Convention/Workshop Listings, Industry Reports, Interviews, Overseas Reports

Thyme is a collection of stapled sheets covered with articles and commentary on writing, extensive news and reviews. It lists nominees and winners of all the major awards and discusses conventions. *Thyme* also contains interviews with authors such as Robert Jordan and Kim Stanley Robinson.

HOW TO CONTACT: Editor Stewart is looking for writers of articles and interviews, but suggests reading the magazine first, then contacting him with your idea. He will accept simultaneous submissions and will report back in 2 weeks. A single copy costs $3 (Australian). A yearly subscription is $15 (Australian). Subscribers in U.S. can send payment in U.S. currency ($3 for 1 issue, $15 for 6 issues) to Janice Murray, P.O. Box 75684, Seattle WA 98125-0684.

PAYMENT: 3 contributor's copies.
ADDRESS: P.O. Box 222, Melbourne, Victoria 3005, Australia
E-MAIL: a.stewart@pgrad.unimelb.edu.au

WRITER'S DIGEST MAGAZINE

Established: 1921 • Circulation: 225,000 • Frequency: Monthly • Size: 8½ × 11

Contact: Thomas Clark, Editor

CATEGORIES
Articles/Essays, Industry Reports, Interviews, Market Listings

Writer's Digest is filled with instructional articles for writers, editors and self-publishers. It lists markets for fiction, including many slanted toward sf/fantasy. "We inspire the writer to write, instruct him or her on how to improve that work, and show how to direct it toward appropriate markets."

HOW TO CONTACT: Submission editor Amanda Boyd is interested in how-to articles, profiles and interviews. The magazine buys 90-100 manuscripts per year plus shorter pieces for the various departments. It is best to query first, but the editors reluctantly accept complete manuscripts with SASE. A single copy costs $2.99 ($3.50 postpaid), and an annual subscription costs $27.
ADDRESS: 1507 Dana Ave., Cincinnati OH 45207
PHONE: (513)531-2222

Glossary of Science Fiction and Fantasy Terms

In the following glossary we've included general publishing terms as well as specific science fiction/fantasy terms. The science fiction/fantasy terms are set in boldface type.

AAR—Association of Authors' Representatives. This is an organization for literary agents committed to maintaining excellence in literary representation.

Advance—Payment by a publisher to an author prior to the publication of a book, to be deducted from the author's future royalties.

All rights—The rights contracted to a publisher permitting a manuscript's use anywhere and in any form, including movie and book-club sales, without additional payment to the writer.

Alternate history—Fantasy, sometimes with science fiction elements, that changes the accepted account of actual historical events or people to suggest an alternate view of history.

Backlist—A publisher's books not published during the current season but still in print.

Bulletin Boards (electronic)—Free or low cost online information services available to computer users over a modem using telephone lines.

Chapbook—A booklet of 15 to 30 pages of fiction or poetry.

Commercial—Publishers whose concern is salability, profit and success with a large readership.

Contributor's copy—Copy of an issue of a magazine or published book sent to an author whose work is included.

Copyright— The legal right to exclusive publication, sale or distribution of a literary work.

Cover letter—A brief letter sent with a complete manuscript submitted to an editor.

Cyberpunk—Type of science fiction, usually concerned with computer networks and human-computer combinations, involving young, sophisticated protagonists.

Dark fantasy—Fantasy containing horror, mystery or Gothic elements and often dealing with some form of evil magic.

Fanzine—A noncommercial, small-circulation magazine usually dealing with fantasy, horror or science-fiction literature and art.

First North American serial rights—The right to publish material in a periodical before it appears in book form, for the first time, in the United States or Canada.

Galleys—The first typeset version of a manuscript that has not yet been divided into pages.

Gothic—A genre in which the central character is usually a beautiful young woman and the setting an old mansion or castle, involving a handsome hero and real danger, either natural or supernatural.

Graphic novel—An adaptation of a novel into a long comic strip or heavily illustrated story of 40 pages or more, produced in paperback.

Hard science fiction—Science fiction with an emphasis on science and technology.

High fantasy—Fantasy with a medieval setting and a heavy emphasis on chivalry and the quest.

Humorous science fiction—Science fiction with elements of humor. In fantasy, the related term is "funny fantasy."

Hypertext—Words or groups of words in an electronic document that are linked to other text, such as a definition or a related document.

International Reply Coupon (IRC)—A form purchased at a post office and enclosed with a letter or manuscript to an international publisher to cover return postage costs.

Juvenile—Fiction intended for children two to twelve.

Mass market paperback—Softcover book on a popular subject, usually around 4″×7″, directed to a general audience and sold in drugstores and groceries as well as in bookstores.

Military science fiction—Science fiction focusing on war and the military.

New Age—A term including categories such as astrology, psychic phenomena, spiritual healing, UFOs, mysticism, and other aspects of the occult.

Novel—Long, complete works of fiction, generally more than 40,000 words.

Novella—A work of fiction shorter than a novel, but longer than a novelette, usually from 20,000 to 40,000 words.

Novelette—A very long short story, usually between 8,000 and 20,000 words.

One-time rights—Permission to publish a story in periodical or book form one time only.

Outline—A summary of a book's contents, often in the form of chapter headings with a few sentences outlining the action of the story under each one; sometimes part of a book proposal.

Over the transom—Slang for the path of an unsolicited manuscript into the slush pile.

Payment on acceptance—Payment from the magazine or publishing house as soon as the decision to print a manuscript is made.

Payment on publication—Payment from the publisher after a manuscript is printed.

Proposal. An offer to write a specific work, usually consisting of an outline of the work and one or two completed chapters.

Pulp magazine—A periodical printed on inexpensive paper, usually containing lurid, sensational stories or articles.

Query—A letter written to an editor to elicit interest in a story the writer wants to submit.

Reporting time—The number of weeks or months it takes an editor to report back on an author's query or mansucript.

Reprint rights—Permission to print an already published work whose rights have been sold to another magazine or book publisher.

Romantic SF/Fantasy—Essentially, romance fiction set in a futuristic or fantasy setting, or incorporating those elements into the plot. While containing sf or fantasy elements, this type of fiction focuses mainly on the hero and heroine and their romance.

Royalties—A percentage of the retail price paid to an author for each copy of the book that is sold.

SASE—Self-addressed stamped envelope.

Second serial rights—Permission for the reprinting of a work in another periodical after its first publication in book or magazine form.

Sequel—A literary work that continues the narrative of a previous, related story or novel.

Serial rights—The rights given by an author to a publisher to print a piece in one or more periodicals.

SFWA—The Science Fiction and Fantasy Writers of America. Often pronounced "SIF-wuh," this organization is made up of published writers and other industry professionals dedicated to promoting the genres and subgenres of fantasy and science fiction.

Shared Universe/World—A novel in which more than one author shares in creating characters or situations based in the same science fiction universe. Usually one author creates the setting and invites other authors to participate in a novel by bringing their own interpretation and ideas to that setting.

Short short—A very short story, usually between 25 and 700 words.

Short story—A work of fiction, usually under 8,000 words.

SIG—A computer user's term for Special Interest Group, a special area of an online computer service devoted to specific interests. Users participate in discussions and post messages about a specific topic.

Simultaneous submission—The practice of sending copies of the same manuscript to several editors or publishers at the same time. Some people refuse to consider such submissions.

Slush pile—A stack of unsolicited manuscripts in the editorial offices of a publisher.

Small Press—Newer and/or lower budget publishers and magazines that are usually more open to beginning writers.

Sociological science fiction—Science fiction with an emphasis on society and culture.

Space Opera—Epic science fiction with an emphasis on good guys versus bad guys as in the western subgenre term "horse opera."

Speculative fiction (SpecFic)—The all-inclusive term for science fiction, fantasy and horror.

Splatterpunk—Science fiction (often cyberpunk) with excessively gory images and/ or horror themes.

Steampunk—A subgenre of alternate history science fiction set in Victorian England in which characters have access to 20th-century technology.

Subsidiary rights—All rights other than book publishing rights included in a book contract, such as paperback, book-club and movie rights.

Subsidy publisher—A book publisher who charges the author for the cost of typesetting, printing and promoting a book. Also vanity publisher.

Surrealism—Fiction which emphasizes the writer's imaginative expressions of the unconscious mind. Surrealistic fiction often has a dream-like quality.

Synopsis—A brief summary of a story, novel or play. As part of a book proposal, it is a comprehensive summary condensed in a page or page and a half.

Trade paperback—A softbound volume, usually around 5″ × 8″, published and designed for the general public, available mainly in bookstores.

Traditional fantasy—Fantasy with an emphasis on magic, using characters with the ability to do magic such as wizards, witches, dragons, elves and unicorns.
Unsolicited mansucript—A story or novel manuscript that an editor did not specifically ask to see.

Urban fantasy—Fantasy that takes magical characters such as elves, fairies, vampires or wizards and places them in modern-day settings, often in the inner city.

Webpage—(also called *home page* or *website*) An address on the World Wide Web which can be accessed by computer modem. Webpages are hypertext based, and often have text, graphics and sound.

WGA—Writers Guild of America. An organization of writers and agents promoting fair treatment of and support for writers.

Work-for-hire—Work that another party commissions you to do, generally for a flat fee. The creator does not own the copyright and therefore can not sell any rights.

Young adult—The general classification of books written for readers 12 to 18.

About the Contributors

The editor would like to thank the following writers for their help in updating this edition:

Donna Collingwood

Donna Collingwood is a freelance writer and editor living in Madison, Wisconsin. She interviewed Betsy Mitchell at Warner Aspect and Shelly Shapiro at Del Rey.

Dorothy Goepel

Dorothy Goepel works as a freelance writer for ad agencies, hospitals and businesses, and serves as a Public Affairs Specialist in the U.S. Air Force Reserve. Her articles have appeared in magazines and newspapers including *Capper's, Kentucky Living Magazine, Marketing News* and *Mature Living*. Two of her short stories were finalists in the 1993 and 1994 *Writer's Digest Magazine*'s Writing Competitions. She resides in Cincinnati. Dorothy interviewed Tom Dupree, senior editor at Bantam, and Shawna McCarthy at *Realms of Fantasy* for this edition.

Heather K. Hardy

Heather K. Hardy is a graduate of the College of Charleston with a degree in English. She lives in Cincinnati, Ohio, and works for Paragon Advertising Inc. She interviewed Gardner Dozois at *Asimov's* for this book.

Jack Heffron

Jack Heffron is an editor at Writer's Digest Books. He has published fiction and nonficiton in a number of magazines including the *Black Warrior Review, North American Review, Triquarterly Review* and the

Utne Reader. He met with Ginjer Buchanan, Gordon Van Gelder and John Silbersack during a trip to New York City.

H. Robert Perry

H. Robert Perry is a Cincinnati writer whose short fiction has appeared in *Tomorrow Speculative Fiction, Gaslight, Mean Lizard, The Stake* and *Tense Moments* magazines. Rob interviewed Jennifer Brehl at AvoNova, Scott Edelman at *Science Fiction Age*, Robert J. Killheffer at *Century* magazine and Charles Ryan at *Aboriginal* magazine.

Robert Schofield

Robert Schofield is a local Cincinnati writer who has had short fiction, computer programs, and articles published. His profile of Tor/Forge editor Camille Cline appeared in the *Mystery Writer's Sourcebook, 2nd Edition.* Robert also works at Procter & Gamble as a Systems Analyst. He interviewed Warren Lapine at *Absolute Magnitude* for this edition.

Patrick G. Souhan

Patrick G. Souhan is an assistant production editor in the trade book division of F&W Publications. He resides in Dayton, Ohio, also alleged home of Hangar 13 and the Roswell remains. Patrick, who served as production editor for this book before assuming his current duties, interviewed Edward McFadden at Pirate Writings Publishing and first novelist Ron Sarti.

Jennifer Stark

Jennifer Stark is a Cincinnati writer who has had articles and feature stories published in the local media. She is currently completing her first fantasy novel. She also works at Great American Life Insurance Company as a writer and marketing communications specialist. Jennifer interviewed John Douglas at HarperPrism for this edition.

EDITOR INDEX

Elfpunk: Downstate Story 131; Fantastic Worlds 136; Horse Lattitudes Press 289; Intermix 149; Samsara, The Magazine of Suffering 180; Space & Time 186; The Zone 215

Experimental Fiction: Aberrations 111; Ageless Press 276; Art: Mag 115; Blue Lady, The 117; Bones 118; Crazy Quilt 124; Dead Lines 129; Downstate Story 131; Dreams & Visions: New Frontiers in Christian Fiction 134; Fantastic Worlds 136; FC2 Black Ice Books 284; Fractal, The 138; Freezer Burn Magazine 139; Golden Isis 140; Grue Magazine 142; Hecate's Loom 144; Hollow Earth Publishing 289; Horse Lattitudes Press 289; I.E. Magazine 148; Intermix 149; Kopfgeburten 208; Lacunae 150; Literal Latté 153; Lost Worlds, The Science Fiction and Fantasy Forum 155; Lynx Eye 156; Medusa's Hairdo 157; Mind In Motion 159; Mobius: The Journal of Social Change 160; Nova Express 165; Psychotrope 213; Puck, The Unofficial Magazine of the Irrepresible 176; Ralph's Review 177; Riverside Quarterly 179; Samsara, The Magazine of Suffering 180; Serendipity Systems 299; Shadow Magazine 183; Silver Web, The 185; Space & Time 186; Speculative Fiction and Beyond 187; Square One, A Magazine of Dark Fiction 188; Tale Spinner 189; Talebones: Fiction on the Dark Edge 190; Terra Incognita 192; Thistledown Press Ltd. 300; Urbanite, The 199; Virgin Meat 201; White Wolf Pubilshing 303; World of H.P. Lovecraft 202; The Zone 215

Hard SF: Aberrations 111; Aboriginal Science Fiction 61; Absolute Magnitude 64; Ace Science Fiction and Fantasy 228; Alien Contact 208; Amelia 114; Analog Science Fiction and Fact 67; Asimov's Science Fiction 70; Aurealis, Australian Fantasy and Science Fiction 206; AvoNova Books 232; Baen Books 234; Bantam Spectra Books 239; Century 78; CRANK! 81; Dagger of the Mind, Beyond the Realms of Imagination 124; DAW Books, Inc. 243; Del Rey Books 248; Dell Publishing 282; Downstate Story 131; Dreams & Visions: New Frontiers in Christian Fiction 134; Dreams & Nightmares, The Magazine of Fantastic Poetry 133; ELF: Eclectic Literary Forum 135; Fantastic Worlds 136; Fractal, The 138; Freezer Burn Magazine 139; Gotta Write Network LitMag 141; Gryphon Publications 287; HarperPrism 252; Hobson's Choice 147; Hollow Earth Publishing 289; Horse Lattitudes Press 289; I.E. Magazine 148; Intermix 149; Interzone: Science Fiction and Fantasy 209; ISF—Integra Speculative Fiction 290; Kopfgeburten 208; Lacunae 150; The Leading Edge, Magazine of Science Fiction and Fantasy 151; Literal Latté 153; Lost Worlds, The Science Fiction and Fantasy Forum 155; Magazine of Fantasy & Science Fiction, The 84; Miraguano Ediciones 308; Mobius: The Journal of Social Change 160; NEL 310; Nocturnal Ecstasy Vampire Coven Journal 164; Obelesk Books 293; Omni 87; On Spec, The Canadian Magazine of Speculative Writing 166; Other Worlds, The Paperback Magazine of Science Fiction-Science Fantasy 167; Pablo Lennis, The Magazine of Science Fiction, Fantasy and Fact 169; Pan Macmillan Ltd 311; Permeable Press 295; Pirate Writings: Tales of Fantasy, Mystery & Science Fiction 92; PREMONITIONS 212; Puck, The Unofficial Magazine of the Irrepresible 176; Rising Tide Press 297; River-Bend Press 298; Riverside Quarterly 179; Robinson Publishing Ltd. 312; Roc Books 257; Samsara, The Magazine of Suffering 180; Science Fiction Age 100; Serendipity Systems 299; Severn House Publishers 313; Shadow Magazine 183; Sidetrekked 184; Silver Web, The 185; Space & Time 186; St. Martin's Press 261; Tale Spinner 189; Terra Incognita 192; The Cosmic Unicorn 123; Time Pilot 195; Tomorrow, Speculative Fiction 103; Tor Books 265; TSR 268; 2 AM Magazine 197; Ultimate Unknown, The 198; VB Tech Journal 200; Virtual Press, The 301; Voyager 315; Warner Aspect Books 272; Writer's Block Magazine 204; Ziesing Books, Mark V. 305; The Zone 215

High Fantasy: Aberrations 111; Ace Science Fiction and Fantasy 228; Adventures

state Story 131; Dragon® Magazine 132; Dragon Moon Press 281; Dreams & Nightmares, The Magazine of Fantastic Poetry 133; ELF: Eclectic Literary Forum 135; Fantastic Worlds 136; Fedogan & Bremer 285; For Dickheads Only 137; Freezer Burn Magazine 139; HarperPrism 252; Heliocentric Net Magazine 145; Hollow Earth Publishing 289; Horse Lattitudes Press 289; I.E. Magazine 148; Intermix 149; Interzone: Science Fiction and Fantasy 209; Lacunae 150; The Leading Edge, Magazine of Science Fiction and Fantasy 151; Literal Latté 153; Lynx Eye 156; Magazine of Fantasy & Science Fiction, The 84; Medusa's Hairdo 157; Millennium 309; Mind In Motion 159; Mobius: The Journal of Social Change 160; NEL 310; New Victoria Publishers 292; Next Phase 161; Nocturnal Ecstasy Vampire Coven Journal 164; Obelesk Books 293; Pablo Lennis, The Magazine of Science Fiction, Fantasy and Fact 169; Pan Macmillan Ltd 311; Paper Radio 170; Permeable Press 295; Pirate Writings: Tales of Fantasy, Mystery & Science Fiction 92; Plot Magazine 175; Puck, The Unofficial Magazine of the Irrepresible 176; Ralph's Review 177; Rising Tide Press 297; Samsara, The Magazine of Suffering 180; Science Fiction Age 100; Serendipity Systems 299; Serendipity's Circle 182; Shadow Magazine 183; Sidetrekked 184; Space & Time 186; Speculative Fiction and Beyond 187; St. Martin's Press 261; Tale Spinner 189; Talebones: Fiction on the Dark Edge 190; Terra Incognita 192; The Cosmic Unicorn 123; Thirteenth Moon Magazine 193; Thistledown Press Ltd. 300; Thresholds Quarterly, School of Metaphysics Associates Journal 195; Time Pilot 195; Tomorrow, Speculative Fiction 103; Tor Books 265; TSR 268; 2 AM Magazine 197; Ultimate Unknown, The 198; Urbanite, The 199; VB Tech Journal 200; Voyager 315; Works, A Magazine of Speculative & Imaginative Fiction 214; Writer's Block Magazine 204; The Zone 215

Interviews: Aberrations 111; Alien Contact 208; Art: Mag 115; Black Moon Magazine 116; Cabal Asylum 119; Cemetery Dance 120; Dagger of the Mind, Beyond the Realms of Imagination 124; Eldritch Tales 134; Fantastic Worlds 136; Fractal, The 138; Gotta Write Network LitMag 141; Intermix 149; Kopfgeburten 208; Lacunae 150; Minas Tirith Evening-Star: Journal of the American Tolkien Society 158; Next Phase 161; Nocturnal Ecstasy Vampire Coven Journal 164; Nova Express 165; Puck, The Unofficial Magazine of the Irrepresible 176; Riverside Quarterly 179; Shadow Magazine 183; Speculative Fiction and Beyond 187; Tale Spinner 189; Talebones: Fiction on the Dark Edge 190; Terra Incognita 192; Thresholds Quarterly, School of Metaphysics Associates Journal 195; Urbanite, The 199; World of H.P. Lovecraft 202; Writer's Block Magazine 204; The Zone 215

Magic Realism: Aberrations 111; Bluestar Productions 278; Bones 118; Century 78; Dead Lines 129; Downstate Story 131; Dragon Moon Press 281; Dreams & Visions: New Frontiers in Christian Fiction 134; Fantastic Worlds 136; Fedogan & Bremer 285; Fractal, The 138; Golden Isis 140; Hecate's Loom 144; Hollow Earth Publishing 289; Horse Lattitudes Press 289; I.E. Magazine 148; Intermix 149; Kopfgeburten 208; The Lamp-Post: of the Southern California C.S. Lewis Society 151; Literal Latté 153; Lynx Eye 156; Mobius: The Journal of Social Change 160; New Victoria Publishers 292; Plot Magazine 175; Puck, The Unofficial Magazine of the Irrepresible 176; Pulp: A Fiction Magazine 177; Rising Tide Press 297; Robinson Publishing Ltd. 312; Samsara, The Magazine of Suffering 180; Shadow Magazine 183; Space & Time 186; Speculative Fiction and Beyond 187; Square One, A Magazine of Dark Fiction 188; Talebones: Fiction on the Dark Edge 190; Thirteenth Moon Magazine 193; Thistledown Press Ltd. 300; Thresholds Quarterly, School of Metaphysics Associates Journal 195; Urbanite, The 199; VB Tech Journal 200; Virgin Meat 201; White Wolf Pubilshing 303; Write Way Publishing 304; Writer's Block Magazine 204; The Zone 215

Military: Aberrations 111; Aboriginal Science Fiction 61; Absolute Magnitude 64;

Ace Science Fiction and Fantasy 228; Amelia 114; Analog Science Fiction and Fact 67; Asimov's Science Fiction 70; Aurealis, Australian Fantasy and Science Fiction 206; AvoNova Books 232; Baen Books 234; Bantam Spectra Books 239; DAW Books, Inc. 243; Del Rey Books 248; Downstate Story 131; Fantastic Worlds 136; FASA Corporation 283; Fractal, The 138; HarperPrism 252; Horse Lattitudes Press 289; Intermix 149; Interzone: Science Fiction and Fantasy 209; The Leading Edge, Magazine of Science Fiction and Fantasy 151; Magazine of Fantasy & Science Fiction, The 84; Miraguano Ediciones 308; Obelesk Books 293; On Spec, The Canadian Magazine of Speculative Writing 166; Other Worlds, The Paperback Magazine of Science Fiction-Science Fantasy 167; Pirate Writings: Tales of Fantasy, Mystery & Science Fiction 92; PREMONITIONS 212; Rising Tide Press 297; RiverBend Press 298; Roc Books 257; Samsara, The Magazine of Suffering 180; Science Fiction Age 100; Shadow Magazine 183; Space & Time 186; Square One, A Magazine of Dark Fiction 188; Tale Spinner 189; The Cosmic Unicorn 123; Time Pilot 195; Tomorrow, Speculative Fiction 103; Tor Books 265; TSR 268; Ultimate Unknown, The 198; Warner Aspect Books 272; Works, A Magazine of Speculative & Imaginative Fiction 214; The Zone 215

Poetry: Amelia 114; Art: Mag 115; Blue Lady, The 117; Bones 118; Cabal Asylum 119; Chrysalis, Journal of the Swedenborg Foundation 121; Dark Regions 126; Dead Lines 129; Deathrealm The Land Where Horror Dwells 130; Downstate Story 131; Dreams & Nightmares, The Magazine of Fantastic Poetry 133; Eldritch Tales 134; Fantastic Worlds 136; Fractal, The 138; Freezer Burn Magazine 139; Golden Isis 140; Gotta Write Network LitMag 141; Grue Magazine 142; Horse Lattitudes Press 289; I.E. Magazine 148; Intermix 149; Kopfgeburten 208; Lacunae 150; The Lamp-Post: of the Southern California C.S. Lewis Society 151; Literal Latté 153; Lynx Eye 156; Magazine of Speculative Poetry 157; Medusa's Hairdo 157; Mind In Motion 159; Mobius: The Journal of Social Change 160; Next Phase 161; Night Songs 162; Nova Express 165; Pablo Lennis, The Magazine of Science Fiction, Fantasy and Fact 169; Pirate Writings: Tales of Fantasy, Mystery & Science Fiction 92; PREMONITIONS 212; Psychotrain 174; Puck, The Unofficial Magazine of the Irrepresible 176; Ralph's Review 177; Riverside Quarterly 179; Samsara, The Magazine of Suffering 180; Sensations Magazine 181; Silver Web, The 185; Space & Time 186; Tale Spinner 189; Talebones: Fiction on the Dark Edge 190; Terra Incognita 192; Thirteenth Moon Magazine 193; Thistledown Press Ltd. 300; Thresholds Quarterly, School of Metaphysics Associates Journal 195; Twisted 196; Ultimate Unknown, The 198; Urbanite, The 199; Virgin Meat 201; Works, A Magazine of Speculative & Imaginative Fiction 214; World of H.P. Lovecraft 202; Writer's Block Magazine 204; The Zone 215

Reviews: A Companion in Zeor 122; Aberrations 111; Adventures of Sword & Sorcery 113; Alien Contact 208; Amelia 114; Art: Mag 115; Black Moon Magazine 116; Cabal Asylum 119; Cemetery Dance 120; 121; Chrysalis, Journal of the Swedenborg Foundation 121; Daughters of Nyx, A Magazine of Goddess Stories, Mythmaking, and Fairy Tales 128; Fantastic Worlds 136; For Dickheads Only 137; Fractal, The 138; Golden Isis 140; Gotta Write Network LitMag 141; Hecate's Loom 144; Heliocentric Net Magazine 145; Intermix 149; Lacunae 150; The Lamp-Post: of the Southern California C.S. Lewis Society 151; Magazine of Speculative Poetry 157; Minas Tirith Evening-Star: Journal of the American Tolkien Society 158; Next Phase 161; Nocturnal Ecstasy Vampire Coven Journal 164; Puck, The Unofficial Magazine of the Irrepresible 176; Riverside Quarterly 179; Serendipity's Circle 182; Speculative Fiction and Beyond 187; Tale Spinner 189; Talebones: Fiction on the Dark Edge 190; Terra Incognita 192; Thirteenth Moon Magazine 193; Thresholds Quarterly, School of Metaphysics Associates Journal 195; Urbanite, The 199; Virgin

Meat 201; World of H.P. Lovecraft 202; Writer's Block Magazine 204; The Zone 215

Science Fantasy: Aberrations 111; Ageless Press 276; Alien Contact 208; Blue Lady, The 117; Bluestar Productions 278; Crazy Quilt 124; Dark Regions 126; Downstate Story 131; Dreams & Visions: New Frontiers in Christian Fiction 134; E.M. Press, Inc. 282; Fantastic Worlds 136; Freezer Burn Magazine 139; Gotta Write Network LitMag 141; Hollow Earth Publishing 289; Horse Lattitudes Press 289; I.E. Magazine 148; Intermix 149; Literal Latté 153; Lynx Eye 156; Magazine of Speculative Poetry 157; Mind In Motion 159; Miraguano Ediciones 308; Mobius: The Journal of Social Change 160; New Victoria Publishers 292; Other Worlds, The Paperback Magazine of Science Fiction-Science Fantasy 167; Pirate Writings: Tales of Fantasy, Mystery & Science Fiction 92; Plot Magazine 175; PREMONITIONS 212; Puck, The Unofficial Magazine of the Irrepresible 176; Pulp: A Fiction Magazine 177; Ralph's Review 177; Rising Tide Press 297; Riverside Quarterly 179; Robinson Publishing Ltd. 312; Samsara, The Magazine of Suffering 180; Sensations Magazine 181; Shadow Magazine 183; Space & Time 186; Speculative Fiction and Beyond 187; Square One, A Magazine of Dark Fiction 188; Terra Incognita 192; Thirteenth Moon Magazine 193; Thistledown Press Ltd. 300; Thresholds Quarterly, School of Metaphysics Associates Journal 195; Ultimate Unknown, The 198; VB Tech Journal 200; Virtual Press, The 301; White Wolf Publishing 303; Write Way Publishing 304; Writer's Block Magazine 204; The Zone 215

Sociological SF: Aberrations 111; Aboriginal Science Fiction 61; Absolute Magnitude 64; Ace Science Fiction and Fantasy 228; Alien Contact 208; Amelia 114; Analog Science Fiction and Fact 67; Asimov's Science Fiction 70; Aurealis, Australian Fantasy and Science Fiction 206; AvoNova Books 232; Baen Books 234; Bantam Spectra Books 239; Black Heron Press 277; Blue Lady, The 117; Century 78; CRANK! 81; Dagger of the Mind, Beyond the Realms of Imagination 124; DAW Books, Inc. 243; Dead Lines 129; Dead of Night™ 129; Del Rey Books 248; Dell Publishing 282; Downstate Story 131; Dreams & Nightmares, The Magazine of Fantastic Poetry 133; ELF: Eclectic Literary Forum 135; Fantastic Worlds 136; Fractal, The 138; Freezer Burn Magazine 139; HarperPrism 252; Heaven Bone 143; Hobson's Choice 147; Horse Lattitudes Press 289; I.E. Magazine 148; Intermix 149; Interzone: Science Fiction and Fantasy 209; Kopfgeburten 208; The Leading Edge, Magazine of Science Fiction and Fantasy 151; Literal Latté 153; Lost Worlds, The Science Fiction and Fantasy Forum 155; Lynx Eye 156; Magazine of Fantasy & Science Fiction, The 84; Medusa's Hairdo 157; Mind In Motion 159; Miraguano Ediciones 308; Mobius: The Journal of Social Change 160; New Victoria Publishers 292; Next Phase 161; Nocturnal Ecstasy Vampire Coven Journal 164; Nova Express 165; Obelesk Books 293; Omni 87; On Spec, The Canadian Magazine of Speculative Writing 166; Other Worlds, The Paperback Magazine of Science Fiction-Science Fantasy 167; Pan Macmillan Ltd 311; Paper Radio 170; Permeable Press 295; Pirate Writings: Tales of Fantasy, Mystery & Science Fiction 92; Plot Magazine 175; Prisoners of the Night, An Adult Anthology of Erotica, Fright, Allure and . . . Vampirism 172; Psychotrain 174; Puck, The Unofficial Magazine of the Irrepresible 176; Rising Tide Press 297; RiverBend Press 298; Riverside Quarterly 179; Robinson Publishing Ltd. 312; Roc Books 257; Samsara, The Magazine of Suffering 180; Science Fiction Age 100; Sensations Magazine 181; Shadow Magazine 183; Sidetrekked 184; Silver Web, The 185; Space & Time 186; Speculative Fiction and Beyond 187; Square One, A Magazine of Dark Fiction 188; St. Martin's Press 261; Talebones: Fiction on the Dark Edge 190; Terra Incognita 192; The Cosmic Unicorn 123; Thirteenth Moon Magazine 193; Time Pilot 195; Tomorrow, Speculative Fiction 103; Tor Books 265; TSR 268; 2 AM Magazine 197; Ultimate Unknown, The 198; Voyager 315; Warner

Aspect Books 272; White Wolf Pubilshing 303; Ziesing Books, Mark V. 305; The Zone 215

Space Opera: Aberrations 111; Aboriginal Science Fiction 61; Absolute Magnitude 64; Ace Science Fiction and Fantasy 228; Alien Contact 208; Analog Science Fiction and Fact 67; Asimov's Science Fiction 70; Aurealis, Australian Fantasy and Science Fiction 206; AvoNova Books 232; Baen Books 234; Bantam Spectra Books 239; Del Rey Books 248; Downstate Story 131; Dreams & Nightmares, The Magazine of Fantastic Poetry 133; Fantastic Worlds 136; Fractal, The 138; HarperPrism 252; Horse Lattitudes Press 289; Intermix 149; ISF—Integra Speculative Fiction 290; Kopfgeburten 208; The Leading Edge, Magazine of Science Fiction and Fantasy 152; Magazine of Fantasy & Science Fiction, The 84; Millennium 309; Miraguano Ediciones 308; NEL 310; Other Worlds, The Paperback Magazine of Science Fiction-Science Fantasy 167; Pan Macmillan Ltd 311; Pirate Writings: Tales of Fantasy, Mystery & Science Fiction 92; Plot Magazine 175; Prisoners of the Night, An Adult Anthology of Erotica, Fright, Allure and . . . Vampirism 172; RiverBend Press 298; Robinson Publishing Ltd. 312; Roc Books 257; Samsara, The Magazine of Suffering 180; Science Fiction Age 100; Space & Time 186; St. Martin's Press 261; Talebones: Fiction on the Dark Edge 190; The Cosmic Unicorn 123; Tomorrow, Speculative Fiction 103; Tor Books 265; TSR 268; 2 AM Magazine 197; Ultimate Unknown, The 198; Virtual Press, The 301; Voyager 315; Warner Aspect Books 272; Write Way Publishing 304; Writer's Block Magazine 204; The Zone 215

Splatterpunk: Aberrations 111; Blue Lady, The 117; Bones 118; Dark Tome 127; Downstate Story 131; Eldritch Tales 134; Fantastic Worlds 136; Fractal, The 138; Grue Magazine 142; Horse Lattitudes Press 289; Lacunae 150; Miraguano Ediciones 308; Nova Express 165; Pirate Writings: Tales of Fantasy, Mystery & Science Fiction 92; PREMONITIONS 212; Puck, The Unofficial Magazine of the Irrepresible 176; Pulp: A Fiction Magazine 177; Robinson Publishing Ltd. 312; Samsara, The Magazine of Suffering 180; Serendipity's Circle 182; Space & Time 186; Speculative Fiction and Beyond 187; Square One, A Magazine of Dark Fiction 188; White Wolf Pubilshing 303; The Zone 215

Steampunk: Aberrations 111; Blue Lady, The 117; Downstate Story 131; Fantastic Worlds 136; Four Walls Eight Windows 286; Fractal, The 138; Grue Magazine 142; Hollow Earth Publishing 289; Horse Lattitudes Press 289; Miraguano Ediciones 308; Nova Express 165; Pirate Writings: Tales of Fantasy, Mystery & Science Fiction 92; Puck, The Unofficial Magazine of the Irrepresible 176; Pulp: A Fiction Magazine 177; Rising Tide Press 297; Samsara, The Magazine of Suffering 180; Serendipity's Circle 182; Space & Time 186; Speculative Fiction and Beyond 187; Square One, A Magazine of Dark Fiction 188; The Zone 215

Traditional Fantasy: A Companion in Zeor 122; Aberrations 111; Ace Science Fiction and Fantasy 228; Adventures of Sword & Sorcery 113; Amelia 114; Art: Mag 115; Aurealis, Australian Fantasy and Science Fiction 206; AvoNova Books 232; Baen Books 234; Bantam Spectra Books 239; Bardic Runes 116; Black Moon Magazine 116; Bluestar Productions 278; Chrysalis, Journal of the Swedenborg Foundation 121; Dagger of the Mind, Beyond the Realms of Imagination 124; DAW Books, Inc. 243; Dead of Night™ 129; Del Rey Books 248; Downstate Story 131; Dragon® Magazine 132; Dragon Moon Press 281; Dreams & Nightmares, The Magazine of Fantastic Poetry 133; ELF: Eclectic Literary Forum 135; Fantastic Worlds 136; Fedogan & Bremer 285; Fractal, The 138; Freezer Burn Magazine 139; Gotta Write Network LitMag 141; HarperPrism 252; Heaven Bone 143; Hobson's Choice 147; Hollow Earth Publishing 289; Horse Lattitudes Press 289; I.E. Magazine 148; Intermix 149; Interzone: Science Fiction and Fantasy 209; ISF—Integra Speculative

The Robert 352; McGrath, Helen 352; Scovil Chichak Galen Literary Agency, Inc. 355; Smith Literary Agent, Valerie 356; Vicinanza Ltd., Ralph M. 358; Weiner Literary Agency, Cherry 359; Writers House 360

Splatterpunk: Circle of Confusion Ltd. 342

Steampunk: Circle of Confusion Ltd. 342; Jabberwocky Literary Agency 348

Traditional Fantasy: Agents Inc. For Medical and Mental Health Professionals 336; Allen, Literary Agent, James 336; Behar Literary Agency, The Josh 338; Blassingame Spectrum Corp. 338; Bova Literary Agency, The Barbara 339; Butler, Art and Literary Agent, Jane 340; Cantrell-Colas Inc., Literary Agency 341; Carvainis Agency, Inc., Maria 341; Circle of Confusion Ltd. 342; Curtis Associates, Inc., Richard 343; Doyen Literary Services, Inc. 344; Ellenberg Literary Agency, Ethan 345; Graham Literary Agency, Inc. 346; Herner, Rights Agency, Susan 347; Ievleva Literary Agency 347; Jabberwocky Literary Agency 348; Kidd, Virginia, Literary Agent 349; Larsen/Elizabeth Pomada, Literary Agents, Michael 350; Maass Literary Agency, Donald 351; Madsen Literary Agency, The Robert 352; McGrath, Helen 352; Protter Literary Agent. Susan Ann 354; Scovil Chichak Galen Literary Agency, Inc. 355; Smith Literary Agent, Valerie 356; Toad Hall, Inc. 357; Vicinanza Ltd., Ralph M. 358; Weiner Literary Agency, Cherry 359; Writers House 360;

GENERAL INDEX

More Great Books for Writers!

The Craft of Writing Science Fiction That Sells by Ben Bova—You'll discover how to fascinate audiences (and attract editors) with imaginative, well-told science fiction. Bova shows you how to market your ideas, submit your manuscripts and more! *#10395/$16.99/224 pages*

The Writer's Guide to Creating a Science Fiction Universe—An easy-to-read guide for writers to put the science back in science-fiction. You'll find contemporary science tailored to the needs of writers plus the "wrong science" you must avoid to be credible in this demanding market. *#10349/$18.95/336 pages*

How to Write Tales of Horror, Fantasy & Science Fiction—Explore the worlds of the weird, the fantastic and the unknown to create extraordinary speculative fiction! Masters of the craft give you their writing secrets in 27 succinct chapters. *#10245/$14.99/242 pages/paperback*

How To Write Science Fiction and Fantasy by Orson Scott Card—You'll discover how to break into this ever-expanding market as you share in vital marketing strategies that made this author a bestseller! *#10181/$14.99/176 pages*

The Writer's Ultimate Research Guide—Save research time and frustration with the help of this guide. Three hundred fifty-two information-packed pages will point you straight to the knowledge you need to create better, more accurate fiction and nonfiction. Hundreds of listings of books and databases reveal how current the information is, what the content and organization is like and much more! *#10447/$19.99/352 pages*

The Fiction Dictionary—The essential guide to the inside language of fiction. You'll discover genres you've never explored, writing devices you'll want to attempt, fresh characters to populate your stories. *The Fiction Dictionary* dusts off the traditional concept of "dictionary" by giving full, vivid descriptions, and by using lively examples from classic and contemporary fiction . . . turning an authoritative reference into a can't-put-it-down browser. *#48008/$18.99/336 pages*

Description—Discover how to use detailed description to awaken the reader's senses; advance the story using only relevant description; create original word depictions of people, animals, places, weather and much more! *#10451/$15.99/176 pages*

How to Write Like an Expert About Anything—Find out how to use new technology and traditional research methods to get the information you need, envision new markets and write proposals that sell, find and interview experts on any topic and much more! *#10449/$17.99/224 pages*

Voice & Style—Discover how to create character and story voices! You'll learn to write with a spellbinding narrative voice, create original character voices, write dialogue that conveys personality, control tone of voice to create mood and make the story's voices harmonize into a solid style. *#10452/$15.99/176 pages*

The Complete Guide to Writing Fiction—This concise guide will help you develop the skills you need to write and sell long and short fiction. You'll get a complete rundown on outlining, narrative writing details, description, pacing and action. *#10158/$18.95/312 pages*

Setting—Expert instruction on using sensual detail, vivid language and keen observation will help you create settings that provide the perfect backdrop to every story. *#10397/$14.99/176 pages*

Conflict, Action & Suspense—Discover how to grab your reader with an action-packed beginning, build the suspense throughout your story and bring it all to a fever pitch through powerful, gripping conflict. *#10396/$14.99/176 pages*

Creating Characters: How to Build Story People—Grab the empathy of your reader with characters so real they'll jump off the page. You'll discover how to make characters come alive with vibrant emotion, quirky personality traits, inspiring heroism, tragic weaknesses and other uniquely human qualities. *#10417/$14.99/192 pages/paperback*

Writing Mysteries—Sue Grafton weaves the experience of today's top mystery authors into a mystery writing "how-to." You'll learn how to create great mystery, including making stories more taut, more immediate and more fraught with tension. *#10286/$18.99/204 pages*

1996 Novel & Short Story Writer's Market—Get the information you need to get your short stories and novels published. You'll discover listings on fiction publishers, plus original articles on fiction writing techniques; detailed subject categories to help you target appropriate publishers; and interviews with writers, publishers and editors! *#10441/$22.99/624 pages*

Writing the Modern Mystery—If you're guilty of plot, character and construction murder, let this guide show you how to write tightly crafted, salable mysteries that will appeal to today's editors and readers. *#10290/$14.99/224 pages/paperback*

Fiction Writer's Workshop—In this interactive workshop, you'll explore each aspect of the art of fiction including point of view, description, revision, voice and more. At the end of each chapter you'll find more than a dozen writing exercises to help you put what you've learned into action. *#48003/$17.99/256 pages*

38 Most Common Fiction Writing Mistakes—Take steps to diagnose and correct the 38 most common fiction writing land mines that can turn dynamite story ideas into slush pile rejects. *#10284/$12.99/118 pages*

Writing the Blockbuster Novel—Let a top-flight agent show you how to weave the essential elements of a blockbuster into your own novels with memorable characters, exotic settings, clashing conflicts and more! *#10393/$18.99/224 pages*

The Writer's Complete Crime Reference Book—Now completely revised and updated! Incredible encyclopedia of hard-to-find facts about the ways of criminals and cops, prosecutors and defenders, victims and juries—everything the crime and mystery writer needs is at your fingertips. *#10371/$19.99/304 pages*

Write Tight—Discover how to say exactly what you want with grace and power, using the right word and the right number of words. Specific instructions and helpful exercises will help you make your writing compact, concise and precise. *#10360/$16.99/192 pages*

Handbook of Short Story Writing, Volume II—Orson Scott Card, Dwight V. Swain, Kit Reed and other noted authors bring you sound advice and timeless techniques for every aspect of the writing process. *#10239/$12.99/252 pages/paperback*

Freeing Your Creativity—Discover how to escape the traps that stifle your creativity. You'll tackle techniques for banishing fears and nourishing ideas so you can get your juices flowing again. *#10430/$14.99/176 pages/paperback*